For Lenore and Milton,
my only aunt and uncle,
with love from your nephew

THE PHILISTINES IN TRANSITION

STUDIES IN THE HISTORY AND CULTURE OF THE ANCIENT NEAR EAST

EDITED BY

B. HALPERN AND M.H.E. WEIPPERT

VOLUME X

TUTA SUB AEGIDE PALLAS

·1683·

THE PHILISTINES IN TRANSITION

A History from ca. 1000-730 B.C.E.

BY

CARL S. EHRLICH

E.J. BRILL
LEIDEN · NEW YORK · KÖLN
1996

The paper in this book meets the guidelines for permanence and durability of the Committee on Production Guidelines for Book Longevity of the Council on Library Resources.

Library of Congress Cataloging-in-Publication Data

Ehrlich, Carl S.
  The Philistines in transition : a history from ca. 1000-730 B.C.E.
/ by Carl S. Ehrlich.
      p. cm.—(Studies in the history and culture of the Ancient
Near East, ISSN 0169-9024; v. 10)
  Revision of the author's doctoral dissertation (Harvard
University, 1991).
  Includes bibliographical references and index.
  ISBN 9004104267 (alk. paper)
  1. Philistines—History.   2. Jews—History—953-586 B.C.
3. Bible. O.T.—History of Biblical events.   4. Palestine—History-
-To 70 A.D.   I. Title.   II. Series.
DS90.E37   1996
959.9'01—dc20
                                                                    96-39015
                                                                         CIP

ISSN   0169-9024
ISBN   90 04 10426 7

PRINTED IN THE NETHERLANDS

For

Michal

למיכל

רעיתי

CONTENTS

ACKNOWLEDGMENTS

The following is a revision of a doctoral dissertation presented to the Department of Near Eastern Languages and Civilizations at Harvard University in 1991.

I am grateful to my *Doktorvater*, Frank M. Cross, and to the other members of my doctoral committee, Peter Machinist, Lawrence E. Stager, and Piotr Steinkeller, for their advice and encouragement in the early stages of this work. The major impetus for returning to this topic and publishing it in book form has come from many of my colleagues in Heidelberg, Germany, where I spent the four years after receiving my doctorate as a *Wissenschaftlicher Mitarbeiter* at the *Hochschule für Jüdische Studien*. First and foremost among these colleagues has been Manfred Weippert, who prevailed upon me to publish this work, encouraged and advised me at every step of the way, and accepted this book into the series Studies in the History and Culture of the Ancient Near East. My debt of gratitude to Weippert's co-editor, Baruch Halpern, has recently extended to include his unintentionally generous vacating of his position at York University. Patricia Radder of E. J. Brill has patiently overseen my fumbling attempts at producing a camera ready copy of the manuscript.

In the spirit of enviromentalism, Lowell K. Handy has allowed me to recycle a chapter which I wrote for a volume which he is editing as the first chapter of this book.

The bulk of the revisions was completed during my stay as a guest professor at the *Kirchliche Hochschule* of Wuppertal, Germany, during the *Sommersemester* 1996. I am grateful to my colleagues, the library staff, and my research assistant, Vanessa Kluge, for their aid in the process of revision. Any omissions or mistakes are of course my personal responsibility.

I had hoped to make even more extensive revisions, in particular to the archaeological sections of this work and in the incorporation of more of the recent larger synthetic studies in the field. However, the exigencies of three intercontinental moves and three different jobs within the space of barely a year, combined both with the labor of producing a camera ready copy and with an ironclad publisher's deadline, have set limits to the extent of the revisions. Yet, to quote (and distort) Qohelet 12:12, "of making ( ) books there is no end." Every book is an incomplete work. If it weren't, there wouldn't be anything left to write. This book may be premature, but it is my baby.

My doctoral thesis was dedicated to my parents, Professor emeritus Leonard H. Ehrlich and Dr. Edith Ehrlich, née Schwarz. The sentiments which I expressed in the earlier introduction are still valid. However, I trust that my parents will understand my dedication of this revised version to my wife and mentor, Rabbi Michal Shekel, in honor of her "special" birthday. Over the last five years, she and our children, Yossi (Joseph Emanuel) and Shimi (Simeon David), have had to put up with a *pater et maritus absconditus*, while I pursued job opportunities far from home. Having recently received a position at York University in Toronto, Ontario, I can finally hope that in the near future we will be living not only on the same continent, but also in the same country and even, א״יה, in the same city and community.

Carl S. Ehrlich
Toronto, Ontario, Canada
Yāmîm Nôrā'îm 5757 (September 1996)

CHAPTER ONE

PHILISTIA AND THE PHILISTINES

By Way of an Introduction

The first quarter of the first millennium B.C.E. was a transitional period in Philistine history. After the Philistines' initial period of settlement and consolidation, their boundaries were set on the southwestern coast of Canaan. The distinctive Aegean-influenced material culture traditionally associated with them disappeared, and they developed new forms of material cultural expression. Their settlement pattern, which had included both coastal and inland centers, shifted toward the coastal regions. This situation prevailed until the time of the Assyrian conquest in the latter third of the eighth century. During the subsequent period of the *pax assyriaca* the inland Philistine centers enjoyed a revival and flourished as never before. Archaeological and textual evidence has been most helpful in investigating the earliest and the latest periods in Philistine history. The following study is the first to be devoted exclusively to the "dark ages" between their supposed defeat at the hands of David and their conquest by Tiglath-pileser III, both of whom can be regarded as the pegs upon which the transitions in Philistine studies can be hung.

Until recently, the post-Davidic history of the Philistines had - for the most part - been treated as incidental to the study of other better documented civilizations. Only in its earlier phases was Philistine history thought worthy of special interest. Thus, the vast majority of studies devoted to the Philistines and their civilization was concentrated on their period of settlement and consolidation in Iron Age I. On the one hand, von Rad[1] decried such an attitude: "So gross das Interesse war, das man seit

---

[1] 1933: 30.

jeher den Philisterkämpfen Israels zur Zeit Samuels, Sauls und Davids entgegenbrachte, so wenig Aufmerksamkeit pflegte man der Frage nach dem Verhältnis Israels zu den Philistern in der nachdavidischen Zeit zu schenken." On the other hand, Eissfeldt[2] epitomized this attitude by declaring: "Die Geschichte der Philister ... ist dagegen so eng mit der Geschichte Israels verzahnt, dass [diesem Volke] keine besondere Darstellung gewidmet zu werden braucht, sondern [seine] Geschichte mit der des Volkes Israel erzählt werden kann." Writing in the mid-sixties this may have been a reasonable point of view. However, our knowledge of Israel's neighbors has expanded considerably. Not only are there now more sources, particularly archaeological, at our disposal, but we also have a better understanding of the sources which bear on the later history of the Philistines.

The structure of the following investigation is quite simple. Following this introductory chapter, Chapter Two will attempt to determine the extent of David's subjugation of the Philistines and their place, if any, within the context of the united Israelite monarchy. Chapter Three will trace the fortunes of the Philistines from the time of the dissolution of the Israelite empire until the arrival of the Assyrian empire in the Levant. Chapter Four will discuss the first contacts of Philistia with Assyria.

The appendices will examine in minute detail the literary corpora which serve as the basis of historical reconstruction, in order to determine what information can be adduced and judged useful in the task at hand. Appendix A will be devoted to the biblical source materials, the choice of which is self-evident by the historical time frame of the thesis, although some prophetic texts which cannot be dated with any certainty to the period in question have been left out of consideration.[3] Appendix B will deal with relevant Assyrian texts from the reigns of Adad-nirari III and Tiglath-pileser III.

Intercalated in the bibliography are abbreviations of the titles of works cited in the main text. Unless otherwise noted, the dates employed for the Judean and Israelite kings are taken from Miller and Hayes 1986.

Owing to the relative paucity of the sources and their varied nature, a history of the Philistines in the later Iron Age cannot aspire to be more than a series of episodes. It is hoped, however, that the inquiry that follows will

---

[2] 1967: 135-36.

[3] E.g. Zech 9:5-7, which Tadmor (1961a: 269) has dated to 739/8 B.C.E. For an alternate treatment of the passage and a much later dating see Reventlow 1993: 89-94.

prove useful in advancing the study of an underinvestigated phase of the history of a people that has been undeservedly maligned for close to three thousand years.

Philistia and the Philistines

Philistia and the Philistines have been the object of an ever increasing amount of scholarly attention over the course of the past few decades. Although textual sources for Philistine history remain scarce,[4] the archaeologist's spade has uncovered a wealth of information relating to the material culture of the southern coastal plain of Canaan, in particular during the Iron Age I and IIC periods. The region of Philistia is bordered in the north by the Yarkon or Sorek Rivers (depending on the period), in the south by the Wadi el-Arish (the "Brook of Egypt"), on the east by the Judean Hills or Judah, and on the west by the Mediterranean Sea. Included within this geographical framework are the cities of the Philistine Pentapolis of biblical fame, i.e., Ashdod, Ashkelon, Gaza, Ekron (Tel Miqne[5]), and Gath (Tell es-Safi?[6]),[7] as well as a number of secondary settlements. The results of the excavations of Ashdod,[8] Ashkelon,[9] Tel Batash-Timnah,[10] Tel Miqne-Ekron,[11] and Tell Qasile,[12] as well as of a number of smaller sites and regional surveys (both in Philistia proper and at which evidence of Philistine material culture has been adduced) are still being analyzed and

---

[4] See the general surveys in T. Dothan 1982a: 1-24; Brug 1985: 5-50; Katzenstein 1992: 326-28; Noort 1994: 27-112. Somewhat more limited in their textual scope are Tadmor 1966 and the present study.

[5] This identification was established by Naveh (1958).

[6] On this identification, which is viewed as the most probable by the majority of contemporary scholars, see Rainey 1975; and Seger 1992. Following Stager, Stone (1995: 22) has tentatively proposed Tel Haror as the site of Gath.

[7] The first three cities on this list are situated along the coast from north to south, the latter two are inland sites. Their geographical location was a determining factor in their changing fortunes over the course of time.

[8] On this and the other sites see the relevant articles in the *NEAEHL*, in addition to the selection of publications in this and the following notes: *Ashdod I*; *Ashdod II-III*; *Ashdod IV*.

[9] Stager 1991; Johnson and Stager 1995.

[10] Kelm and A. Mazar 1995.

[11] T. Dothan 1995; Gitin 1993; 1995; 1989; Gitin and T. Dothan 1987.

[12] A. Mazar 1980; 1985.

debated.[13] The fact that a number of these projects are yet to be completed
or published does not simplify the analysis. However, a number of general
tendencies, directions, and controversies in the scholarly discussion have
become evident.

   Most of the attention devoted to the Philistines has focused on the period
of their settlement and on the distinctive material culture traditionally
associated with them in Iron Age I.[14] The material basic to all theories is the
distinctive bichrome ware of that period, which has been found at sites
traditionally associated with the Philistines, as well as at a number of other
sites throughout the land. It is mainly on T. Dothan's ground-breaking
synthesis of *The Philistines and Their Material Culture*[15] that all
subsequent work rests, irrespective of whether it is supportive or critical of
individual aspects of her reconstruction. Hence a presentation of her
synthesis may serve as the basis of discussion.[16]

Trude Dothan and the Material Culture of the Philistines

The association of the Philistines with the bichrome ware of the early Iron
Age is one which goes back to the turn of the century.[17] It is an assemblage
of white-slipped ware, which is decorated with red and black paint. The
decoration consists of various bands and oftentimes intricate geometric
forms, in addition to metopes with depictions of animals, in particular birds
looking backward. As Dothan points out, the identification as "Philistine"
pottery is based on its "typology, stratigraphy, and geographical

---

[13] See the listing of sites and their remains in T. Dothan 1982a: 25-93. Also useful in this regard is Brug
1985: 66-106, in which the discussion centers on the ceramic evidence.

[14] The major exception to this can be found in the work of Gitin, who in a series of studies has been
attempting to trace the development of the regional material culture of the southern coastal plain in Iron
Age II. See the works cited above n. 11.

[15] See above n. 4.

[16] In addition to the above mentioned work, she has presented a number of shorter and/or more popular
syntheses of her conclusions, many of them reached in conjunction with her husband, Moshe. See T. Dothan
1971; 1982b; 1992. See also Dothan and Dothan 1992.

[17] For a succint summary of the history of interpretation of this ware see T. Dothan 1982a: 94 n. 1.

distribution."[18] It is particularly in the area of typology that Dothan has made her greatest contribution.[19]

Dothan has distinguished five major typological groups within the Philistine ceramic repertoire. These consist of types derived from Mycenean prototypes (Group I, Types 1-8), those derived from Cypriote prototypes (Group II, Types 9-11), those evidencing Egyptian influence (Group III, Type 12), those continuing the ceramic tradition of Late Bronze Age Canaan (Group IV, Types 13-16), as well as a late group of forms derived from Group I (i.e., Group V, Types 17-18).

Group I forms derived from Mycenean prototypes include bell-shaped bowls (Type 1) and kraters (Type 2), stirrup jars (Type 3), pyxides and amphoriskoi (Type 4), three-handled jars (Type 5), strainer-spout or "beer" jugs[20] (Type 6), basket-handled jugs with spout (Type 7), and juglets with pinched-in girth (Type 8). Group II types derived from Cypriote prototypes include cylindrical bottles (Type 9), horn-shaped vessels (Type 10), and gourd-shaped jars (Type 11). Group III consists of one vessel, a jug with an elongated and oftentimes bulging neck, which evidences Egyptian influence in both shape and design (Type 12). Group IV consists of forms derived from local Canaanite traditions, yet decorated in the Philistine style. These include small bowls with bar handles (Type 13), jugs (Type 14), juglets (Type 15), and juglets with trefoil mouths (Type 16). Group V, which Dothan dates to the late eleventh and early tenth centuries B.C.E., includes forms derived from Group I, namely jugs with strainer spouts and basket handles (Type 17, derived from Types 6 and 7), and deep kraters (Type 18, derived from Type 2).

In her discussion of Philistine ceramics Dothan also made reference to a style of pottery found at Ashdod as of Stratum XIIIb, which appeared to be antecedent to the Philistine bichrome ware and in its later stages partially overlapped with the latter.[21] This she designated monochrome ware, on account of its monochrome dark brown painted designs. It has since been

---

[18] T. Dothan 1982a: 94.

[19] T. Dothan 1982a: 94-218. See also H. Weippert 1988: 373-82; and the critical discussions in Brug 1985: 53-144; and Noort 1994: 113-28.

[20] In reaction to Johnson and Stager's conclusion that wine and not beer was the Philistines' beverage of choice (Johnson and Stager 1995: 95), Dever has commended them for gentrifying the Philistines and for turning them from "loutish beer-guzzlers to genteel sippers of white wine - no doubt, properly chilled and accompanied by just the right brie" (Dever 1995: 116).

[21] T. Dothan 1982a: 96.

found in abundance at Ekron[22] and Ashkelon,[23] and appears to be a locally produced assemblage derived from the Myc(enean) IIIB import ware of the Late Bronze Age. Owing to its similarity to contemporaneous examples from Cyprus it has been given the name Myc IIIC:1b. Emphasizing the differences between the earlier monochrome Myc IIIC:1b and the later bichrome "Philistine" pottery, the Dothans have concluded that they are representative of two waves of immigration to Canaan in the twelfth century B.C.E.[24] Most other scholars, however, view the bichrome pottery as a direct outgrowth of the earlier monochrome. The latter thus posit an initial monochrome phase which lasted about one generation and is indicative of the initial Philistine settlement in Canaan. This was followed by a more eclectic assemblage, which developed from it ca. 1050 B.C.E. and reflected the diverse cultural influences acting on the southern coastal strip of Canaan.[25] Tied in with these analyses are fundamental questions concerning the origins and initial settlement of the Philistines.[26]

Philistine Origins

The question of Philistine origins is closely linked with the question of the transition from the Bronze Age to the Iron Age throughout the world of the eastern Mediterranean. The phenomenon of the seemingly simultaneous collapse of the great Bronze Age civilizations of the eastern Mediterranean world is still the subject of intense speculation. This also holds true for the possible relationship of the legends of the Trojan War and the subsequent wanderings of the Achaeans as related in the Homeric epics to that collapse.[27] There is a growing body of evidence which indicates that groups of Aegean/Mycenean background were on the move in the eastern

---

[22] Gunneweg, Perlman, Dothan, and Gitin 1986.

[23] Stager 1991a: 13.

[24] See M. Dothan 1989: esp. 65-68; and 1993, in which Dothan attempts to identify this presumed pre-Philistine Sea People population at Ashdod with the biblical Anakim. See also *Ashdod II-III*, 20; Dothan and Dothan 1992: 165-70, 258; T. Dothan 1982a: 294-95; 1989: esp. 1-7; and B. Mazar 1992: 14.

[25] Dever 1992: 18-19; A. Mazar 1990: 307-08, 327; Redford 1992: 291 (in which Redford argues against postulating two immigration waves on the basis of destruction levels); Stager 1991a: 13; H. Weippert 1988: 380-82.

[26] See the discussion in Stone 1995: 14-16, and esp. the comparative stratigraphic chart on p. 15 (Fig. 1).

[27] See e.g. Redford (1992: 254) and Stager (1991a: 15-18); both of whom deduce a direct relationship.

Mediterranean world during the period of transition between the Bronze and Iron Ages ca. 1200 B.C.E. The phenomenon of pirates of Aegean origin was well known in the Late Bronze Age.[28] At quite a number of sites remains of the so-called "Sea Peoples"[29] were found in levels following those related to the destruction of the Late Bronze. Yet the question arises, whether their presence was indicative of a cause or of a result of the collapse of the Bronze Age civilizations, or of an unrelated phenomenon.

Egyptian texts of the 19th and 20th Dynasties are central to the debate. In the account of Ramses II's campaign against the Hittites, which ended in a stalemate at the battle of Kadesh on the Orontes, mention is found of one of the Sea Peoples, namely the Sherden, among the Egyptian mercenary troops.[30] Merneptah listed five Sea Peoples as enemies of Egypt in an account of a war against the Lybians.[31] The Onomasticon of Amenope lists the coastal Philistine cities and three of the Sea Peoples, including the Philistines.[32] The account of the journey of Wen-Amon to Phoenicia in ca. 1100 B.C.E. refers to Dor on the Canaanite coast as a city of the Tjeker.[33]

However, the most important among the texts for understanding the putative settlement of the Sea Peoples in Canaan are those dated to the reign of Ramses III, among which the pride of place undoubtedly belongs to the Medinet Habu inscriptions and their associated reliefs.[34] They relate an egyptocentric account of Ramses III's battle against the Sea Peoples. In this account, dated to Ramses' eighth year (ca. 1175 B.C.E.), Egypt was threatened with a massive invasion by land and by sea by a large coalition

---

[28] See Redford 1992: 225, 243, 250; Noort 1994: 84-85 (regarding the Sherden).

[29] This is a general term for the peoples of a supposedly Aegean/Anatolian origin who were on the move in the transitional period between the Bronze and Iron Ages. On the genesis of the term "Sea Peoples" see Noort 1994: 54-55.

[30] *ANET* 255-56. The Sherden may also be mentioned in three letters from Byblos (Gubla) found among the Amarna correspondence (EA 81, 122, 123) and dating to the mid 14th century B.C.E. See Noort 1994: 85; Rohl 1995: 78-79; but see Moran 1992: 393. The Sherden are thought by some (e.g. Dothan and Dothan 1992: 214) to have given their name to the island of Sardinia. They have also been linked with the region of Sardis on the Ionian coast. See Redford 1992: 243 and n. 13.

[31] See Noort 1994: 84; Redford 1992: 247-49.

[32] See T. Dothan 1982a: 3-4; Redford 1992: 292-93.

[33] *ANET* 25-29. The Tjeker have been identified both with the Teukrians (Redford 1992: 252, 292) and with the Sikeloi or Sikilayu, the latter designation of which is known from Ugaritic texts (see Edel 1984; Stager 1991a: 19 n. 23; Stern 1994: 20, 85-101). Assuming that the second identification is indeed correct, they both settled in the region of Dor and gave their name to the island of Sicily.

[34] *ANET* 262-63.

of Sea Peoples including the Philistines,[35] the Tjeker, the Shekelesh, the
Denyen,[36] and the Weshesh, as well as the Teresh and the Sherden. The
Pharoah met them in Djahi[37] and at the mouth of the rivers[38] and inflicted
an annihilating defeat upon them. The associated reliefs depict both the land
and the sea battles, as well as details concerning the personal appearance
and family structure of the various defeated groups. The defeat of Egypt's
enemies is thorough. The Sea Peoples' fleet is surrounded, their sails
furled.[39] Also depicted are a number of Sea Peoples, both combatants and
civilians, including the Philistines, Denyen, and Tjeker with their distinctive
"feathered" headdresses.[40] Papyrus Harris I summarizes Ramses III's war
against the Sea Peoples.[41] The defeat of the Denyen, the Tjeker, the
Philistines, the Sherden, and the Weshesh is recapitulated, with the
additional information that the foes, who were slain, turned to ashes and
made non-existent, were brought in captivity to Egypt and settled in
fortresses.[42]

     Among the major indicators of the transition from the Bronze Age to the
Iron Age in Canaan are the lessening of Egyptian control and the
replacement at many sites of Egyptian material culture with the classic

---

[35] Egyptian *prst*. The name Palestine is their indirect legacy.

[36] In cuneiform inscriptions they are referred to as Danuna. Many scholars connect them with the Danaoi
of Greek fame. Yadin (1968) theorized that the Israelite tribe of Dan was descended from the Denyen, who
had settled on the coast between the Tjeker to the north and the Philistines to the south. There is, however,
no external evidence that the Denyen settled on the coast of Canaan. In addition, Niemann has adduced no
archaeological connection between the material culture of the region originally assigned to the tribe of Dan
in the biblical texts (Josh 19:40-48) and the remains from Tel Dan to which the tribe supposedly migrated
(Judg 17-18). He thus rejects Yadin's effort to link the Danites and the Denyen/ Danuna/ Danaoi, as well as
those of Cyrus H. Gordon and Michael C. Astour. See Niemann 1985: 273-91.

[37] This term refers in a general sense to the eastern Mediterranean coastal regions.

[38] The reference here is most likely to the Nile delta region.

[39] This is one of the pieces of evidence presumably adduced by Raban and Stieglitz (1991: 35-36) in their
argument that the Egyptians attacked the Sea Peoples by surprise.

[40] For discussions and interpretations of the reliefs see T. Dothan 1982a: 13; Noort 1994: 56-83.

[41] *ANET* 260-62. See also Wood 1991: 49.

[42] Whether the last two clauses are to be understood sequentially or as independent statements has
occasioned debate. In a sequential understanding, the captives were settled in Egypt, while the rest of the
Philistines or Sea Peoples carved out a territory for themselves in Canaan. See e.g. Wood 1991. To this
reconstruction Redford (1992: 289) adds the observation that if Ramses III claims to have allowed the
Philistines to settle as mercenaries in Canaan, it would have been "*post eventum.*" The paratactic nature of
the text also allows an interpretation as evidence that Ramses III settled captive Sea Peoples (mainly the
Philistines) as mercenaries in Canaan. See e.g. Singer 1985.

Philistine ware.[43] Since the first literary mention of the Philistines places them among the Sea Peoples in the texts dating to the eighth year of the reign of Ramses III, a connection has been sought between their arrival in Canaan and Ramses' war against the Sea Peoples. Among the various reconstructions of the historical sequence of events, one may identify both maximal and minimal positions, in addition to a myriad of variations on them.

"Maximalists" and "Minimalists"

A maximal position would hold that at the collapse of Mycenean civilization hordes of refugees invaded the eastern Mediterranean in search of a new land to settle. During the course of their long journey by land and by sea toward the fertile Nile Valley, they destroyed the Hittite empire and the coastal Phoenician/Canaanite city-states. Ramses III was able to prevent them from invading Egyptian soil and settled the Sea Peoples, among whom the Philistines played a leading role, as mercenaries on the southwestern coastal strip of Canaan. However, the weakened Egyptian New Kingdom, already in decline, never recovered from the exertion and eventually lost its holdings in Canaan to the Philistines.[44]

This reconstruction, with modifications including the question of the location of the two (-pronged) battle(s)[45] and of whether the Philistines were settled by the Egyptians as mercenaries[46] or seized the land for themselves,[47] has become the dominant model in the field. Although there

---

[43] Other characteristics adduced for the transition from the LB to the IA include the breakdown of international trade and the change in settlement patterns.

[44] For recent variations of such a reconstruction see Redford 1992: 241-56 (on pp. 253-54 he refers to a major coalition groups centered in Caria, who had fought in the Trojan war); Stager 1991a: 9-18; and Wood 1991: 44-52.

[45] In essence there have been three models of the relationship of the land and sea battles to each other: The first would place both in Syria or northern Palestine (see Singer 1985: 109 and n. 1); the second would place the land battle in Syria and the sea battle in the eastern delta region of Egypt (see Barnett 1975: 372); while the third model places both in the eastern Nile delta, thus postulating an attack on Egypt from Philistines/Sea Peoples already in Canaan as settlers or as sojourners (see Bietak 1993: 299-300).

[46] T. Dothan (1992: 329) has referred to the Egyptians' granting permission to the Philistines to settle in Canaan; while Itamar Singer (1988: 6) has referred to the Egyptians' "[s]ettling Philistines in Egyptian bases along the coast after Ramses III's eighth year." See also B. Mazar 1992: 28.

[47] Bietak 1993: 300; Wood 1991: 46-48.

is some discussion of whether the eighth year of Ramses III represents the first Philistine incursion into the Near East or not, a direct correlation is sought between the settlement of the Philistines and the bichrome pottery which made its appearance in the twelfth century B.C.E. Those who find a direct progression from the monochrome Myc IIIC:1b ware to the bichrome ware date the appearance of the former to Ramses' eighth year and the latter to ca. one generation later, i.e. ca. 1150 B.C.E.[48]

The position labeled minimalist takes a much more critical stance vis-à-vis the historical credibility of the Medinet Habu inscriptions and their association with the settlement of the Philistines in Canaan.[49] The texts are viewed as standardized literary texts which may contain a historical kernel. However, the reference to a grand coalition of "Sea Peoples" is interpreted in typological terms, and the engagement between them and Ramses is understood as the conflation of a gradual process of tension between Canaan and Egypt or as the reinterpretation of a local conflict in the Nile Delta as a battle of quasi mythic proportions in order to glorify the Pharaoh.[50] Butressing these interpretations are the literary structure of the inscriptions and the ideological ordering of the reliefs, in which two of the reported wars of Ramses III appear to have no basis in historical reality.[51]

The difficulty of associating pots with peoples or ethnic groups has often been commented on.[52] Nonetheless, the association of the Philistines with the Iron Age I bichrome pottery bearing their name is most often taken for granted. Although most scholars have backed off from postulating that every site with bichrome pottery was under Philistine control, the ethnic association remains. Wherever the distinctive early Iron Age bichrome ware is found, Philistine ethnic presence is assumed. Indeed, Singer has recently argued that the Myc IIIC:1b ware should be designated "Monochrome (or

---

[48] E.g. A. Mazar 1990: 307-08; Stager 1991a: 13.

[49] For sceptical attitudes towards Ramses III's claims in his Medinet Habu inscriptions see, in addition to those listed below, Bietak, 1993; Brug 1985: 27-28; and especially Cifola 1988.

[50] See Cifola 1988: 303; and Noort 1994: 54-55, 104-12, who follows Helck among others in this interpretation. In Noort's opinion, Ramses III's battle against the Sea Peoples was nothing more than a local revolt of Egyptian mercenaries against their overlord.

[51] These would be the campaigns against the Nubians and the Asiatics. See Noort 1994: 108, and literature there.

[52] See i.a. London 1989, and literature there.

early) Philistine pottery."[53] A cautionary note has, however, been sounded in particular by Brug, Bunimovitz, H. Weippert, and Noort, among others.[54]

In essence their theories rest on the fact that even among sites in the Philistine heartland, the supposed Philistine pottery does not represent the major portion of the finds.[55] Although Brug's statistical analysis of the proportion of bichrome pottery to other forms (mainly the continuation of LB Canaanite traditions) is flawed by his reliance on samples not gathered to be analyzed in this manner, the cumulative thrust of his argument is probably valid, namely that the bichrome ware represents a small proportion of the total assemblage from supposedly Philistine sites.[56] For example, at Tell Qasile, the only city thought to have been *founded* by the Philistines, the bichrome pottery represents just 20% of the total assemblage.[57] It is thus conjectured that the bichrome ware and its antecedent monochrome ware were the fine china or luxury ware of their time. The fact that both the monochrome and the bichrome wares were locally produced (along with pottery which continued the Bronze Age Canaanite traditions) after the cessation of trade contacts with Cyprus and the Aegean leads to the conclusion that, rather than being evidence of a massive foreign incursion into Canaan ca. 1175, these wares were local replacements for the now unavailable Late Bronze Age luxury import wares. While not denying Cypriote and/or Aegean/ Mycenean influence in the material cultural traditions of coastal Canaan in the early Iron Age, in addition to that of Egyptian and local Canaanite traditions, the above named "minimalist" scholars emphasize the continuities between the ages and not the differences. As H. Weippert has stated, "Könige kommen, Könige gehen,

---

[53] Singer 1985: 112.

[54] See Brug 1985: 53-144; Bunimovitz 1990: 212-13; Noort 1993: 373-79; 1994: 113-28; H. Weippert 1988: 380-82.

[55] See also M. Weippert 1971: 16-18.

[56] Brug himself is aware of the problems associated with his sample, yet he assumes that the results would more likely be skewed to overemphasize the presence of the decorated bichrome ware. See Brug 1985: 53-144. Stone (1995: 13) has attacked Brug's overly heavy reliance on statistical analysis. While he agrees that the Mycenean origin of isolated pieces of evidence could be questioned, the cumulative force of the evidence has to point in the direction of an invasion theory.

[57] A. Mazar 1990: 316. The one exception to this general trend would appear to be Tel Miqne-Ekron Stratum VII, in which Myc IIIC:1b ware accounts for over half of the pottery excavated. See T. Dothan 1995: 46; T. Dothan and Gitin 1993: 1053. The large amounts of Myc IIIC:1b pottery combined with the expansion of the city from 10 to 50 acres lead e.g. A. Mazar to see at Iron Age IA Ekron clear evidence of the settlement of a large group of Aegeans. See A. Mazar 1994: 250. See also Stone 1995: 18, who following Stager has claimed that the Myc IIIC:1b ware made up 30%-50% of the ceramic repertoire of the cities of the Philistine Pentapolis.

aber die Kochtöpfe bleiben."[58] In regard to the bichrome pottery she
follows Galling[59] and speculates that it was produced by a family or
families of Cypriote potters who followed their markets and immigrated into
Canaan once the preexisting trade connections had been severed. The find at
Tell Qasile of both bichrome and Canaanite types originating in the same
pottery workshop[60] would appear to indicate that the ethnic identification of
the potters is at best an open question. At any rate it cannot be facilely
assumed that all bichrome ware was produced by "ethnic" Philistines.[61]
Thus Bunimovitz's suggestion to refer to "Philistia pottery" rather than to
"Philistine" must be given serious consideration.[62]

What holds true for the pottery of Philistia also holds true for other
aspects of the regional material culture. Whereas Aegean cultural influence
cannot be denied, the continuity with the Late Bronze traditions in Philistia
has increasingly come to attention. A number of Iron Age I features which
were thought to be imported by the Philistines have been shown to have
Late Bronze Age antecedents.[63] It would hence appear that the Philistines of
foreign (or "Philistine") origin were the minority in Philistia.[64] Just as the
origins of Israel in Iron Age I are shrouded in mystery and we are unable to
pinpoint the changeover from a "Canaanite" consciousness to an "Israelite"
one on the basis of isolated cultural phenomena, so too in the case of the
contemporaneous inhabitants of the coastal regions of Canaan. Many

---

[58] H. Weippert 1988: 352.

[59] Galling 1970: 91-92.

[60] A. Mazar 1992: 271.

[61] A. Mazar 1990: 317.

[62] Bunimovitz 1990: 212-13. H. Weippert (1988: 382) has suggested the name "palästinische
submykenische Keramik" in order to draw attention both to the place of production of this style of pottery
and to its foreign antecedents.

[63] These features will be discussed in the following pages. It should be noted, however, that a number of
scholars are now proposing that certain material cultural features, thought to be native to Canaan, are in
reality Sea People imports. Thus Raban and Stieglitz (1991: 34-42, 92-93) have argued that among other
innovations the Sea Peoples introduced ashlar masonry, composite anchors, and collared rim jars to the
ancient Near East. Dever (1995: 115) also attributes the introduction of ashlar masonry to the Sea Peoples,
in addition to the dromos bench-tomb and possibly also some types of four-room houses.

[64] Thus Kelm and A. Mazar (1995: 93) have speculated that the Philistines were the "overlords and
aristocrats" at Tel Batash-Timnah, which was populated in the main by the "descendants of the earlier
Canaanite inhabitants." Mazar has also argued that Egyptian domination of cities in Canaan was replaced by
Philistine domination. Thus the local Canaanite population continued in existence as vassals to their new
overlords. See A. Mazar 1990: 313, 327.

cultural influences were at work in a variegated population[65] to which the name "Philistine" was given - similarly to Israel - *pars pro toto*, possibly by the late eleventh century B.C.E., ironically a time in which the distinctive material culture traditionally associated with the Philistines was waning.[66]

A Portrait of the Philistines

Drawing on the evidence of remains spanning a number of centuries, a picture of the culture and society of Philistia emerges.

The emergence of a new cultural tradition in Canaan is most evident in a distinct change of diet identified at some Philistine sites. Faunal remains at Tel Miqne-Ekron indicate that in the change from the Bronze Age to the Iron Age the diet changed from one in which mutton and goat were the meats most often consumed to one in which pork and beef were preferred.[67] The phenomenon of a shift in domesticated species, indicative of change both in consumption patterns and in the general pastoral economy, from sheep and goats to pigs and cattle as sources of meat in the diet, is also attested at Ashkelon.[68] The latter site has also presented evidence concerning the importance of fish in the diet in Iron Age II.[69]

---

[65] Noort (1994: 179, 183) refers to the Philistines as a mixture of *plst* and Canaanites. H. Weippert (1988: 392) has referred to an ethnic mixture consisting of Canaanites, Sea Peoples, Syrians, Phoenicians, and Cypriotes in various proportions at various sites. On the difficulties associated with the ethnic identification of the Philistines see Gitin 1989: 54 n. 22; Stone 1995: 16-17.

[66] As pointed out by Stone in his important article on "The Philistines and Acculturation" (1995), it has been traditional in the scholarly community to speak of the *assimilation* of Philistine culture to Canaanite models. This is due to the fact that most scholars have focused their attention solely on the earliest phases of Philistine history and, hence, viewed the disappearance of the bichrome ware and associated Aegean influence styles as evidence of this alleged assimilation. However, Stone argues persuasively that it is more proper to speak of the *acculturation* of the Philistines to life in the Levant, in which they were but a tiny minority (see Broshi and Finkelstein 1992: 53). As is only now coming to be appreciated, the region of Philistia retained an independent existence and a distinct material culture throughout the Iron Age II period.

[67] See in particular Hesse 1986); and also T. Dothan 1995: 46; Dothan and Dothan 1992: 248; Wapnish 1993: esp. 439.

[68] Stager 1991a: 9; 1993: 107. The emphasis on pork in the diet at these Philistine sites stands in contrast to the eating habits at presumably Israelite highland sites such as Ai and Raddana. Compare the dietary patterns at presumably Israelite Tel Kinneret in Iron Age II. Pork played a marginal role in the diet (2% of total meat consumption), in spite of the fact that it was native to Kinneret region. See Ziegler and Boessneck 1990. Hübner (1989) has argued that the Iron Age Israelite consumption of pork did not differ that greatly from the Bronze Age Canaanite habits. Pork always played a minor role in the Canaanite diet. Yet it is continuously attested.

[69] Stager 1993: 107.

The attempt has been made to identify at least the later large clay sarcophagoi found in Canaan with the Philistines.[70] However, a direct correlation has been shown to be doubtful.[71] The large anthropoid coffins are evidence of the presence of Egyptians and their mercenaries, some of whom may have been of Sea People descent. In essence, very little evidence can be adduced for Philistine burial practices and beliefs, other than to claim that they appear to have been eclectic.[72]

Philistine sanctuaries have been excavated at Ashdod, Tell Qasile, and Tel Miqne-Ekron. Although a number of the cultic implements, such as lion headed rhyta and kernoi, evidence Aegean connections, in these specific cases the claim can be made that these forms were already known and employed in Bronze Age Canaan and, hence, cannot be used as indicators of newly imported cultures.[73] The cult stands found at Ashdod[74] and Tell Qasile[75] would also be carryovers of the Late Bronze Canaanite traditions. In fact a large proportion of the cultic finds at Philistine sites would not be out of place in a Canaanite cultural context.[76]

Clearer Aegean or Cypriote influence may, however, be identified in a number of distinctive finds of a cultic nature in Philistia. Bovine scapulae, which were incised on their edges, have been found both at Philistine Tel Miqne-Ekron[77] and at Tel Dor,[78] the latter of which was inhabited by another of the Sea Peoples, namely the Tjeker. These scapulae, which may have been used as cultic instruments, have also been found in large numbers on Cyprus.

---

[70] T. Dothan 1982a: 252-88.

[71] Noort 1994: 128-33; H. Weippert 1988: 366-73.

[72] See Bunimovitz 1990: 216-17; A. Mazar 1990: 326-27.

[73] Bunimovitz 1990: 213-16; Noort 1994: 160; H. Weippert 1988: 389-90. On the rhyta see also A. Mazar 1985a: 126.

[74] On the "Musician Stand" from Ashdod see *Ashdod II-III*, 20-21, 125-35; M. Dothan 1970; Dothan and Dothan 1992: pl. 7.

[75] A. Mazar 1980: 87-96, pls. 32-33 (34); see also T. Dothan 1982a: 249-51. Some of the Qasile examples were topped by bird-shaped bowls in an Egyptian or Canaanite style (A. Mazar 1980: 99-100). Yet, it must be added that the bird motif played an important role in Philistine art. It is found as a frequent decoration on both monochrome and in particular on bichrome pottery. Both the prows and sterns of the Sea People's ships in the Medinet Habu reliefs are bird-shaped. See Dothan and Dothan 1992: 229.

[76] H. Weippert 1988: 386-92.

[77] T. Dothan 1989: 9; 1995: 48.

[78] Stern 1993: 330; 1994: 96, 99; 1995: 84.

That the Philistines at least initially worshipped a mother goddess in the Aegean mold may be indicated by the find of an almost complete figurine of a sitting woman at Ashdod and parts of similar figurines there as well as at Tell Qasile and Tel Miqne-Ekron.[79] In this figurine, nicknamed "Ashdoda,"[80] the woman merges with the chair. Thus the back of the chair is the woman's torso and the seat her lap. Parallels have been adduced in Mycenean figurines of seated goddesses, in which, however, the figure of the goddess is generally molded in the round and is more or less distinct from the chair upon which she sits. The Mycenean models also have arms and make a somewhat more naturalistic impression. The decoration of the Philistine models evidences Egyptian influence, particularly in the stylized lotus pattern on the torso. Later examples of the Ashdoda-type have lost their applied breasts and are interpreted as masculine deities.[81] This has been viewed as an example of the assimilation of the Philistine religion to the male-dominated pantheon of Canaan.

Philistine worship of a goddess at a later date is, however, indicated by a number of inscriptions found at Tel Miqne-Ekron from a 7th century context, in which the Canaanite-Phoenician-Israelite(?) goddess 'šrt is mentioned, as well as by the find of petal chalices which are associated with her worship.[82] On the basis of these and related finds Gitin observes that there were both centralized and individual Philistine cult places, the former of which were served by a priestly support system.[83] The presence of large numbers of limestone altars at Ekron, on the other hand, would bear witness to the influx of (northern) Israelites after the fall of Samaria in 720 B.C.E.[84]

Female figurines molded in the round also play a role in the case of the "mourning women" found at Ashdod, Azor, Tell Jemmeh, Tell Jerishe, and (probably) Tell 'Aitun (Tel Eton).[85] These latter figurines hold one or both of their hands to their head in a gesture of mourning. Although artistically in the Canaanite tradition, they were originally attached to the rim of a krater and, hence, reflect a local expression of a type of figurine known from the

---

[79] T. Dothan 1992: 330.

[80] Concerning the discovery and significance of "Ashdoda" see Dothan and Dothan 1992: 153-57.

[81] T. Dothan and Cohn 1994: 69.

[82] Gitin 1993: 253-54.

[83] Gitin 1993: 253.

[84] Gitin 1993: 250; see also his 1989a.

[85] T. Dothan 1982a: 237-49.

Aegean world and attached to vessels associated with the burial cult known as *lekanai*.

Among the additional artifacts found in cultic contexts at Philistine sites are bi-metallic knives with ivory handles (Tell Qasile, Tel Miqne-Ekron),[86] parts of a miniature bronze wheeled cult stand (Tel Miqne-Ekron),[87] and a gynamorphic vessel whose breasts served as spouts (Tell Qasile).[88]

In the public architecture of Philistine sites both Aegean and Canaanite architectural features have been identified. To the former belong the hearths found at Tels Qasile[89] and Miqne-Ekron.[90] To the latter belong e.g. the *bamot* found at the latter site. The hearth is an architectural feature known from sites in Cyprus and the Aegean. It played a central role in the life of the community. The hearths found at Tell Qasile and Tel Miqne-Ekron belong to the earliest Iron Age levels at these sites. At Tell Qasile the hearth was found in a public building built to the southeast of the temple precinct. In the hall of the building an elliptical raised mud-brick platform was found, in which a round plastered depression served as a hearth. It was founded in Stratum XII (second half of twelfth century B.C.E.) and probably continued in use through Stratum XI (first half of eleventh century). At Tel Miqne a round hearth set in the plastered floor and measuring 2.5 meters in diameter, and thus somewhat smaller than parallels from the Cypro-Mycenean world, was found as the central feature in the "hearth sanctuary" of Stratum VII (early twelfth century B.C.E.). It was subsequently incorporated into the large public building 351 of Statum VI, dating to the latter two thirds of twelfth century. By the turn of the century building 351 had been replaced by the monumental building 350, which spanned Strata V-IV. Here a hearth was still in evidence at less than half its original size and constructed of pebbles. By the final phase of Stratum IV (late eleventh-early tenth century) the hearth had ceased to exist. This has been understood as a graphic example of the loss of the Philistine's Aegean heritage and of their gradual

---

[86] T. Dothan 1995: 48; Dothan and Dothan 1992: 225.

[87] T. Dothan 1995: 49-50.

[88] A. Mazar 1980: 78-81, pl. 29. There are no clear parallels to this vessel, yet T. Dothan (per ex. in T. Dothan and Cohn 1994: 69) speculates that it may be a representation of the Mycenean "Mother" or "Great Goddess." For a short listing of other small cultic finds see A. Mazar 1990: 326.

[89] See A. Mazar 1993: 1207-08; and 1990: 317-19.

[90] Concerning the hearths at Tel Miqne-Ekron see T. Dothan 1995: 42-45; and T. Dothan and Gitin 1993: 1054-55; and Dothan and Dothan 1992: 242-45.

assimiliation to indigenous culture.[91] A parallel cultural development may be observed in the contemporaneous disappearance of the bichrome ware.

Northwest of the building with the hearth at Tell Qasile was a sacred precinct. Three superimposed and increasingly larger temples were found there dating to the twelfth through tenth centuries B.C.E. Although the temples' irregular plan and lack of uniformity in design from one level to the next led some to speculate that the Philistines brought with them an amorphous Aegean sacred building tradition, more recent work has indicated that the Tell Qasile temples stood in a Late Bronze and early Iron Age Canaanite architectural tradition.[92] Since some parallels to this type of architecture have been adduced in the Aegean and Cypriote world, the question of direction of influence has been raised. In this case Bunimovitz and A. Mazar agree that the influence would have had to have been from Canaan westward.[93]

Information has also been uncovered relating to the economy of Philistia in the Iron Age. Surprisingly enough, maritime trade does not appear to have played all that great a role in the Philistine economy.[94] Oded speculates that this was due to the Phoenicians' driving them out of that market.[95] However, this would not have applied to the period of Philistine settlement. Agriculture appears to have been a major focus of production at Philistine sites. Both Tell Qasile, which was founded in the mid-twelfth century B.C.E., and Tel Mor, the port of Ashdod, which became Philistine about a century later, bear witness to this phenomenon, in spite of the fact that they were both port cities. The importance of textiles to the Philistine

---

[91] See, however, Noort (1994: 147), who is willing to go no farther than to recognize an affinity between the Ekronite and Cypriote (not Aegean!) hearths.

[92] A. Mazar (1992a) has classified the Qasile temples as among those "with indirect entrances and irregular plans" (p. 177). Other Canaanite examples include the Lachish Fosse Temples, the temple at Tel Mevorakh, and the temples of Bet Shean Strata IX and V (as well as those of VII-VI). Mazar also includes two buildings whose function as temples is unclear: Tell Abu Hawam Building 30 and the "Lion Temple" at Jaffa. In spite of the fact that they form a diverse group, the features they have in common are: "their size; in several cases they are not freestanding buildings; they have a corner or indirect entrance which does not allow the holy-of-holies to be seen from the doorway; benches are built along the walls; the ceiling is supported by columns; the holy-of-holies is in the form of a raised platform; and the temples contain back rooms which served as treasure rooms or storerooms for offerings" (pp. 181-82). See also Bunimovitz 1990: 213-16.

[93] Bunimovitz 1990: 214; A. Mazar 1992a: 182. However, Mazar does speculate (p. 182 n. 78) that the clustering of temples at Qasile XI-X may be evidence of Aegean influence.

[94] Dothan and Dothan 1992: 125.

[95] Oded 1979: 236.

economy had already been deduced from Assyrian inscriptions.[96] The discovery of biconical loomweights at both Ashkelon[97] and Tel Miqne-Ekron[98] from twelfth century levels substantiates this deduction. Under Assyrian rule, seventh century Tel Miqne-Ekron together with its satellite Tel Batash-Timnah[99] became the major olive oil producing center in the entire ancient Near East.[100] However, oil production was limited to only four months of the year. The industrial zones could not be allowed to lie fallow and the workers employed there could not be allowed to remain inactive for the rest of the year. Thus evidence was uncovered that the industrial complexes which were employed in the production of olive oil for one third of the year were converted into textile production facilities for the remainder of the year. Textile dyeing seems to have been a facet of Tell Qasile's economy.[101] Finds at Ashdod indicate that it was a major hub for international trade. Concurrent with the expansion and specialization of the olive oil trade at Tels Miqne and Batash during the seventh century *pax assyriaca*, Ashdod served as a major producer of pottery, as is indicated by a potters' quarter found in Stratum VII.[102] Evidence has been found at Ashkelon of a flourishing wine industry in the destruction layer of 604 B.C.E.[103] In later periods the production of wine was a major factor in the city's economic life. Working backwards on the basis of archaeological finds and the regional ecology, Johnson and Stager have concluded that wine making was a major industry at Ashkelon throughout its history.

The picture that has emerged of Philistine city planning is one of carefully conceived and executed settlements, with well defined zones: public, private, industrial, and cultic.[104] Tell Qasile Stratum X (late eleventh

---

[96] Oded 1979: 236; Tadmor 1966: 93.

[97] Stager 1991a: 14-15; 1993: 107. This style of unbaked cylinder had not previously been identified in Canaan. Its identification as a loomweight is dependent on parallels in Cyprus and in the Mycenean world, as well as on the high concentration of textile fibers which was found in the surrounding fill and was isolated by water sieving. The typical Canaanite loomweight is pyramidal and has a perforation at the upper end.

[98] T. Dothan 1995: 46-47.

[99] Kelm and A. Mazar 1995: 150-64; A. Mazar 1994: 260-63.

[100] Gitin 1989: 48-50; 1990: 36-39; 1995: 63-69. See the latter article in its entirety for an exemplary discussion of the place of Ekron within the context of Assyrian imperial economic policy.

[101] T. Dothan and Cohn 1994: 67.

[102] M. Dothan 1993a: 100; Oded 1979: 237.

[103] Johnson and Stager 1995: esp. 92.

[104] T. Dothan and Cohn 1994: 66.

to early tenth century B.C.E.) was carefully laid out in an orthogonal pattern. The rarity of this concept in Canaan has led the excavator, A. Mazar, to conclude that this may be another indication of the relationship between the settlers of Qasile and the island of Cyprus, specifically Enkomi.[105]

Stratum VII at Tel Miqne-Ekron (first third of twelfth century), which followed upon the last level of the Late Bronze Age city, was a well planned urban area, which was protected by a mud-brick wall and which had a distinct industrial area in which a number of kilns were found.[106] In Stratum VI (last two thirds of the twelfth century) the city, which had been restricted to the 10 acre acropolis of the tell during the Late Bronze Age, expanded into the area of the lower city and grew to the size of 50 acres.[107] It was in the elite area of the lower city, which spanned Strata VI-IV (12th to early 10th centuries), that the "hearth sanctuary" was found. The high point of the early Iron Age city was reached in Stratum IV, during which the distinctive material culture associated with the Philistines waned.

A destruction level associated with the end of the Late Bronze Age at Ashkelon has not yet been identified throughout the site.[108] The last Bronze Age levels were followed in Iron Age I by an enormous fortified port city which expanded to a size of 150 acres. The excavation of the site is ongoing.

The story of Ashdod in Iron Age I is one of continual expansion.[109] Founded on the widespread destruction layer of the Late Bronze Age city, the first phase of the Iron Age city (Stratum XIII), which was characterized by the presence of Myc IIIC:1b pottery, was poorly inhabited. Parts of the Late Bronze "stronghold palace" were reused as an industrial area, including a pottery making workshop. Throughout the following strata the city continued expanding until it reached its greatest extension in Stratum X (late eleventh or early tenth century[110]), when it expanded outside of the

---

[105] A. Mazar 1980: 76-77.

[106] Concerning the Iron Age I city see T. Dothan 1989; 1995 (pl. 4 on p. 59 following the article has the most recent stratigraphic and chronological chart of Tel Miqne); Dothan and Gitin 1993: 1053-56.

[107] This part of the tell had been abandoned since the close of the Middle Bronze Age. See T. Dothan 1995: 42.

[108] Stager 1993: 107.

[109] See the reports in *Ashdod I, II-III, IV*; and the relevant articles in *NEAEHL* and *ABD*.

[110] See A. Mazar 1994: 254, who sees a direct correlation between the decline of Ekron and the expansion of Ashdod in the early tenth century.

acropolis into the lower city. A major feature of the fortification of the lower city was a massive two (i.e. four) chambered gate.[111]

A Philistine town has been identified at Tel Batash-Timnah (Stratum V).[112] It followed upon a Late Bronze Age Canaanite city which had been in decline for some time.[113] The early "Philistine" inhabitants in part reused some of the remaining Late Bronze walls. Yet, two *tabuns* were constructed over some of the Late Bronze walls. The city appears to have been well planned and densely settled. Although evidencing some classic Philistine characteristics in material culture, i.e. bichrome pottery as luxury ware and a pyramidal limestone seal depicting a lyre player,[114] the continuity with Late Bronze Age traditions in most aspects of the material culture leads to the aforementioned theory that the Philistines were overlords of a mainly Canaanite population.[115]

A. Mazar views Beth-Shemesh, east of Tel Batash-Timnah along the Sorek Brook, as a problem.[116] In essence, Beth-Shemesh's material culture in Iron Age I is indistinguishable from that of Tel Batash-Timnah. However, the Bible claims that it was an Israelite town during the period of the Judges, in contrast to Philistine Timnah. On the one hand this underlines the difficulty of relying on the witness of the biblical text. On the other hand this tension also evidences the problems associated with the ethnic identification of pots and other isolated aspects of material culture.[117]

---

[111] In the first phases of the Iron Age, defensive issues seemed not to play as major an issue as during the latter part of Iron Age I, since a number of extra-mural buildings have been discovered at Philistine sites dating to these earlier phases. See T. Dothan and Cohn 1994: 65. See also Dothan and Dothan (1992: 173) who attribute the need for protective fortifications to the burgeoning conflict with Israel in the latter half of the eleventh century B.C.E.

[112] The latest treatment is in Kelm and A. Mazar 1995: 91-104.

[113] The excavators are undecided whether there was an occupation gap between the LB and IA levels. Kelm and A. Mazar 1995: 92.

[114] Thus Kelm and A. Mazar 1995: 98. However, in his study of the group of seals to which the example from Tel Batash-Timnah belongs, O. Keel (1994) has concluded that the group as a whole developed Late Bronze Age Canaanite traditions, although some may be of Egyptian origin. It is only the seal from Tel Batash which, in his opinion, evidences a *decoration* which can be considered new, i.e. Philistine.

[115] Kelm and A. Mazar 1995: 93. This tempers their claim on the previous page that the expulsion of the Canaanite population of Timnah was "almost inevitable."

[116] A. Mazar 1992: 273. See also his 1994: 251-53, in which Mazar speculates that the Samson stories in Judges 13-16 may reflect tensions between two groups of Sea Peoples.

[117] See e.g. Brug 1985: 135-44; Noort 1994: 113-28.

Although there are many other sites with "Philistine" remains,[118] the question of their identification as Philistine is at best an open issue.[119]

Summation

The picture that emerges of Philistia at the turn of the tenth century B.C.E. is that of a flourishing urban culture. It stands in marked contrast to the highland culture of central Canaan in the same period. In her thorough survey of the archaeology of ancient Palestine, H. Weippert distinguishes not between "Israelite" and "Philistine" culture, but between the *Dorfkultur* in the inland regions and the *Stadtkultur* of the Canaanite coast.[120] As she has noted, the successors to the urban culture of Late Bronze Age Canaan were to be found in the coastal plain, specifically in Philistia.[121] While retaining and developing many aspects of Canaanite culture, the coastal plain was, owing to its mixture of cultural influences, a creative cauldron during the early Iron Age. However, the tenth century brought with it a change in the material culture and settlement patterns of Philistia.

The disappearance of the bichrome ware, hearths, and other "Aegean" aspects of Philistine culture has been alluded to above. A number of Philistine sites evidence a development from the bichrome ware to a red-slipped ware which was to take its place in the regional assemblage.[122] However, the regional culture of Philistia was never again to have as wide a distribution as it had until the end of the eleventh century B.C.E. Thus, the tenth century, which is the subject of the following chapter, was a transitional period in Philistine history and culture.

---

[118] T. Dothan 1982a: 25-91.

[119] See Bunimovitz (1990: 217-19), who views Philistine culture as a subgroup of the regional culture of the coastal plain.

[120] H. Weippert 1988: 383 ff., 393 ff.

[121] H. Weippert 1988: 353. The city-state system of government was also retained in Phoenicia, in distinction to the system of national states which arose throughout the rest of Palestine.

[122] On Tel Miqne-Ekron see T. Dothan 1989: 12; on Ashdod and its "Ashdod Ware" see Dothan and Dothan 1992: 178, 252; A. Mazar 1990: 533.

CHAPTER TWO

LOSS OF SUPREMACY

The Stage Is Set

At the turn of the first millennium B.C.E. the Philistines appeared to have established themselves as the leading commercial and political power in Canaan. Their defeat of Saul, king of a temporarily united Israel, at the battle of Gilboa (1 Sam 31) provided ample support for such a view. Since settling on the southwestern coast of Palestine subsequent to their failed attempt to colonize the delta region of Egypt some two hundred years before, this conglomeration of miscellaneous peoples of a generally Aegean origin had imposed themselves on the indigenous population of the southern Canaanite coastal strip and expanded their influence steadily inland. Dominated by five city-states, Ashdod, Ashkelon, Ekron, Gath, and Gaza, the Philistines' political and commercial influence extended from Gaza and the Brook of Egypt in the south, northwards to the Jezreel Valley, eastwards into the Jordan Valley, and possibly also into Transjordan.[1]

Through their subjugation of the fertile valleys of Canaan, the Philistines were able to provide for their own subsistance needs through an agrarian economy, supplemented by their favorable position at the crossroads of international overland trade routes leading from Egypt and the Arabian peninsula northwards through Canaan and beyond.[2] In addition, the port cities of Ashdod (at Tel Mor), Ashkelon and Gaza were most probably important stops on the sea trade routes in the eastern Mediterranean.

For a period of about two centuries the Philistine city-states were able to flourish and enrich themselves. This was partly due to a power vacuum in the

---

[1] See Har-El 1977.

[2] See Oded 1979: 223.

ancient Near East. At the end of the Late Bronze Age the Egyptian New Kingdom, which had dominated Canaan, began to collapse, gradually losing control and influence over its extended holdings in Palestine. Meanwhile the indigenous peoples of the region were badly fragmented into mutually unsupportive factions, clearing the way for domination by a power with a set agenda. The Philistines were able to establish their regional dominance, while inexorably assimilating to the culture of their new homeland.[3]

A major threat to Philistine hegemony arose when Saul was able to unite the fractious tribes of Israel into one military and political unit to challenge Philistine expansion into the hill country of central Palestine. Although Saul had some initial success against the Philistines, the latter were able to take advantage of a split in the Israelite ranks between Saul and his rival David. In return for their protection, David entered into a vassal relationship with Achish, king of Gath, and received the fiefdom of Ziklag in the northwestern Negeb, at the southeastern border of Philistine settlement. Although the remoteness of the outpost did allow David some measure of freedom to engage in activities which may not have been in the best interest of his overlord, there can be little doubt that David served a useful function in Philistine geopolitics by securing a buffer zone region.[4]

The defeat and death of Saul and three of his sons appeared to settle the issue between Philistia and Israel. The Philistines had warded off the first organized threat to the expansion of their political and economic spheres of influence. Israel was in disarray. The northern tribes loyal to the house of Saul were dominated by Abner and his puppet scion of Saul, Ishbaal (2 Sam 2:8-10), who, moreover, had had to remove themselves from their former haunts and withdraw across the Jordan River to Mahanaim. Meanwhile, the southern tribes, Judah and its allies, had turned to the condottiere David for leadership (2 Sam 2:4, 10b-11). There can be little doubt that David had used his position at Ziklag to curry favor with the leaders of his ancestral Judah, and the death of Saul led to the rejection of his house's claims over the southern tribe.

Within a short time after Saul's death, David became king over Judah at the ancient city of Hebron. Even if they were powerless to stop this development, there can be little doubt that the Philistines looked upon David's assumption of rule over Judah with favor.[5] Although the central highlands had not been

---

[3] See Kassis 1965: 264-67; T. Dothan 1982a: 1, 296. See Stone 1995, regarding the more proper use of the term "acculturating."

[4] On this latter point see Herrmann 1981: 152.

[5] See e.g. McCarter 1986: 124.

conquered, the Philistines had managed to extend their influence through a combination of military and diplomatic means. Israel's attempt to halt Philistine expansion had been thwarted. Israel itself was divided into two warring factions, one of which was beholden as a vassal to the king of Gath.[6] Northern Israel was divided from southern Judah by a wedge consisting of at least two cities which were still ruled by the vestiges of ancient Canaanite civilization, namely Gezer and Jerusalem.[7] At least the former, and possibly the latter of these was also under Philistine hegemony. Yet within a few years, the former Philistine vassal David had become supreme ruler of a short lived empire which dominated the region between the Euphrates River in the north to Philistia itself in the south.[8]

The stages in the formation of the Davidic empire have been ably analyzed by Malamat.[9] However, before David could expand his small national state outside of the central highlands, he had to neutralize or defeat the Philistines. How that took place, when it took place, what relationship it bore to his assumption of rule over a united Israel, the nature of his subjugation of the Philistines, and their status vis-à-vis the Davidic empire have been a subject of much discussion, inversely proportional to the amount of evidence there is for any firm conclusions.

Biblical historians have been reluctant to engage in literary-critical analyses of the passages which they call into evidence in the task of bringing the

---

[6] Noth 1960: 183; Aharoni 1979: 292; Herrmann 1981: 152-53; Soggin 1984: 51. There has been some debate in the literature regarding the character and status of Achish, the king of Gath. The most common assumption regarding Achish is that he was a Philistine, one of the *sĕrānîm* "tyrants" who ruled the Philistine pentapolis. The name Achish is commonly given an Aegean/West Anatolian origin, the equivalent of the name Anchises, known from the *Aeneid* as the name of the father that Aeneas carried on his back from burning Troy (see McCarter 1980: 356). The fact that Achish is referred to as a king in the Bible rather than as a tyrant, along with his singular position among the Philistine rulers in 1 Sam 29 has led some to view his status as unique. B. Mazar (1986: 55, 67; which are reprints of articles that originally appeared in 1969 and 1964 respectively) viewed Gath as the center of Philistine rule under Achish during the days of the united Israelite monarchy. Achish was thus possibly a transitional figure between the days of the coordinated *sĕrānîm* and the independent kings who ruled the Philistine city-states during the coming centuries. Following Mazar, Rainey (1975: 71*) considered Achish to be the *primus inter pares*, the chief king of the Philistines. Among the more unusual views concerning Achish the following two may be cited: First, using the same evidence as the above, Kassis (1965: 267-69) and Wright (1966: 81-81) concluded that Achish was a Canaanite client king of the Philistines. They referred to the liberation of Gath by Achish's friend David, once the latter had assumed rule over all Israel. Second, basing himself on the supposed Davidic conquest of Gath and the presence at Ekron of the name Ikausu at the time of Esarhaddon and Ashurbanipal, Bork (1939-41: 226) has theorized that the family of Achish was thrown out of Gath at the time of David, only to settle in Ekron and rule there. Unfortunately he did not explain how the move to a city closer to the Israelite heartland would relieve the pressure on Achish and his house.

[7] Alt 1968: 276; about the latter see Yeivin 1964: 151; Delcor 1966: 1266; Bright 1981: 198.

[8] *Contra* Garbini 1988: 21-32.

[9] Malamat 1982: 192-95; 1983: 11-16.

past to life. Literary critics, on the other hand, have often stopped short of applying their conclusions toward the larger task of determining "*wie es eigentlich gewesen*" (L. von Ranke). In the pages that follow, the possible reconstructions of the history of the Philistines as can be gleaned from the mainly literary biblical sources will be analyzed, bearing in mind the individual discussions of the sources in the first part of this study.

David's Philistine Wars

Any analysis of David's defeat of the Philistines revolves around two main passages: 2 Sam 5:17-25 = 1 Chr 14:8-16/17 (two battles in the Rephaim Valley) and 2 Sam 8:1 = 1 Chr 18:1 (a summation of Davidic victory[10]). In addition, evidence from the collections of hero tales (2 Sam 21:15-22 = 1 Chr 20:4-8; 2 Sam 23:9-17 = 1 Chr 11:12-19) has in varying degrees been brought to bear on the subject.

As indicated above, it has become axiomatic to refer to David's assumption of rule over Judah at Hebron as an act with which the Philistines were in full accord.[11] Startling differences of opinion arise, however, once a discussion of the break between the Philistines and David commences.

Although various literary-critical arguments have been adduced in support of dating the inception of an adversarial relationship to the period immediately following David's assumption of rule over a reunited Israel, there is no agreement in the secondary literature regarding this concatenation of events.

There are many[12] who have followed the order of events in the Bible and viewed the capture of Jerusalem as the stroke which provided the Philistines with the realization that their putative vassal had overstepped his bounds and was now a threat to their hegemony.

Although B. Mazar[13] dated the capture of Jerusalem to the very beginning of David's reign (first year), he also viewed David's assumption of rule over a united Israel as being the trigger for hostilities between Israel and Philistia (third year). This position was taken up by Garsiel,[14] who followed Mazar in the

---

[10] See Noth 1960: 194.

[11] See Aharoni 1979: 292; Bright 1981: 196; McCarter 1986: 124; Miller and Hayes 1986: 169; Noth 1960: 183; Soggin 1984: 51.

[12] E.g. Aharoni 1979: 292; Eissfeldt 1936: 27; 1967: 146; Hauer 1970: 573-74; Oded 1979: 238 (implied); Yeivin 1964: 151-52.

[13] B. Mazar 1963: 241, 243; 1979: 78.

[14] Garsiel 1975: 41-43.

dating of the capture of Jerusalem, but dated the commencement of hostilities to David's seventh year, after he had assumed kingship over all Israel. In Garsiel's view, the Philistines sat around bemused for six years after David's conquest of Zion, while mistakenly assuming that he was fortifying it against the north.[15] Yeivin[16] viewed the capture of Jerusalem as a partial catalyst for Philistine aggression, the other cause of which he sought in an overtly rebellious act on the part of David, unfortunately undocumented, such as the withholding of tribute to Achish. Soggin[17] also followed Mazar's dating of the capture of Jerusalem. However, he speculated that the cause of David's falling out with the Philistines was a direct result of the initiation of an alliance with Tyre, which dealt an economic blow to the Philistines and served to awaken the Philistines to the enormous threat posed by David. This led then to a series of attacks on Jerusalem, with the result that any semblance of Philistine hegemony was lost.

If one assumes that Jerusalem was in David's hands before the initiation of conflict with the Philistines and the union of north and south, then it follows that David's capture of Jerusalem was not tied in with his desire to provide himself with a suitable capital in a central location; unless one is to assume either that David was preparing a beachhead against Israel (as did the Philistines according to Garsiel), or that he was anticipating his future union of north and south.

Although the order of events in the Hebrew Bible is supportive of the above reconstruction of events, literary-critical arguments would tend to support a historical sequence in which an altercation with the Philistines followed immediately upon David's assumption of the throne over a united Israel.[18] *Contra* Hauer,[19] who attributed an appalling lack of intelligence to the Philistine military, it can be assumed that the Philistines had knowledge of the negotiations and the resulting union of the two groups which they had been attempting to keep in an adversarial relationship with each other. The Bible is also quite explicit in its analysis of the catalyst which served to rouse the Philistines against their erstwhile vassal David, namely his anointing as king over all Israel (2 Sam 5:17).

The one thing that the Philistines wanted to avoid was a united Israel controlling the whole of the central highlands of Canaan. They thus turned to the offensive. It is impossible, however, to determine the extent of the forces used in

---

[15] See Segal 1965-66: 32 for an attack on this type of historical sequencing.

[16] Yeivin 1964: 151-52.

[17] Soggin 1984: 55-57.

[18] See Japhet 1993: 287.

[19] Hauer 1970: 574.

the Philistine incursions in 2 Sam 5:17-25, nor who among the Philistines participated, nor what the temporal relationship between the two campaigns was, if any. Putative solutions to these questions have, however, not been lacking.[20]

Rather than attacking David in his fortified citadel in Jerusalem, as some[21] would have it, the Philistines probably moved into the Rephaim Valley[22] in order to cut the two halves of David's kingdom off from each other. Gezer to the west and Jerusalem to the east were still not in Israelite hands. As indicated above, they were quite possibly under Philistine jurisdiction.[23] Jerusalem in particular was of immense strategic importance, for the major north-south artery between Israel and Judah went by that city.[24] By moving into the Rephaim Valley, the Philistines hoped to sever David's fledgling kingdom and to keep him from his new subjects in the north.

Although there are some[25] who theorize that the Philistines took Bethlehem in the context of their ultimately decisive campaign against David, it is likely that 2 Sam 23:14 should be regarded as a later gloss, and hence not to be relied upon in a reconstruction of the course of the campaign.[26]

In spite of Garsiel's somewhat too ingenious suggestion that Jerusalem's citadel was indeed a destination to which one could "go down,"[27] and in spite of others who would ignore that inconvenient verb of motion in 2 Sam 5:17, it still appears most likely that David "went down" from Hebron (his location

---

[20] To give some examples: Miller and Hayes (1986: 170) have referred to two minor skirmishes. Noth (1960: 187-89) referred to two attacks, the second one with full force. Tidwell (1979: 192-209) felt that the two accounts were unrelated, drawn together solely by their subject matter and genre as short battle reports. In his opinion also the first one was a minor action, while the second resulted in a major victory for David.

[21] E.g. Aharoni 1979: 293.

[22] A valley to the southwest of Jerusalem. It was cut on its eastern end by the Hinnom Valley. It was probably a branch of the Soreq Valley (thus Pritchard 1987: 78; implied in McCarter 1984: 153), whence the Philistines came up into the Judean hill country. The Rephaim Valley served as part of the traditional boundary between the tribal territories of Judah and Benjamin (Josh 15:8; 18:16). It has been identified with the Baqa' Valley within the confines of modern Jerusalem, near the train station (Barrois 1962: 36; McCarter 1984: 153).

[23] About the latter, see Yeivin 1964: 151.

[24] See Garsiel 1975: 41; Aharoni 1979: 57.

[25] E.g. Yeivin 1964: 152; Hauer 1970: 575; Garsiel 1975: 41; Bright 1981: 195 n. 26.

[26] See below Appendix A.

[27] Garsiel 1975: 43. His understanding of the verse is informed by geography. The ancient citadel of Zion was situated on the Ophel hill, of which the Temple Mount is its highest and northernmost extension. It is the lowest of the hills of Jerusalem, a fact which is alluded to in the well-known passage from Ps 125:2 which refers to the hills surrounding (biblical) Mount Zion. Nonetheless, Garsiel has no case, since the standard biblical image is invariably that of going up to Jerusalem.

according to 2 Sam 5:1-3) to his "hideaway" (to use Schunck's terminology) at Adullam.[28] Yeivin[29] has theorized that this was in order to have a base from which to observe the massing of the Philistine troops at the entrance to the Elah Valley and to observe their progress into the Judean hills. The verbs *n.t.š* and *p.š.t* have been taken to refer to the Philistines splitting up into smaller units, although whether to seek David (an unlikely activity for those who assume David was already ensconsed in Jerusalem) or to wreak havoc on the surrounding land or populace remains unclear.[30] The size also of the Philistine thrust into the Rephaim Valley is unknown, with some assuming that the first incursion was of limited size, and others assuming that the Philistines attacked with all their might.[31] It may have been that David lay in wait for a time when the Philistine forces had been dispersed in order to attack the main camp and then pick off the smaller units one by one.[32] At any rate, the first Philistine attack was repulsed at Baal-Perazim. Although it is quite possible that images of the Philistine gods accompanied them into battle, the account of David's spoliation of their idols may also be a literary device visiting the ignominy of the capture of the ark at the battle of Ebenezer on the Philistines.[33]

At some later point, whether immediately, a year later,[34] after the capture of Jerusalem, or with a larger force, the Philistines once again went on the offensive against David (2 Sam 5:22-25; 1 Chr 14:13-17). Since they followed the same line of march up into the Rephaim Valley, one can only assume that the Philistine objectives were similar, if not identical to those in the previous campaign. One can also assume, unless one would want to impute an alarming lack of intelligence to them, that the Philistines did not expose themselves to the kind of guerilla warfare that had been so successful against them in their

---

[28] See the discussion of interpretative possibilities in Kalimi 1995: 19-20 n. 4.

[29] 1964: 153.

[30] Eissfeldt (1967: 146-47), who supported the identification of Jerusalem as the "fortress" and dated the defeat of the Philistines after David's capture of Jerusalem, felt that the Philistine incursions into the Rephaim Valley were part of a strategy of spoliation, designed to incite the Jebusites to join the Philistines in their war against David (see also 1936: 28). A similar line of reasoning was followed by Tidwell (1979: 200), who argued that the aim of the raid was to destroy the enemy's crops in order to starve the Israelites out. Regarding the verbs *n.t.š* and *p.š.t*, Japhet (1993: 288) referred to the substitution by the Chronicler of a more common word for the rare term in Samuel. She has also drawn attention to a greater emphasis in Chronicles on the "raiding" aspect of the latter term.

[31] Yeivin (1964: 152) found support for this latter position in the use of *kol-pĕlištîm* "all the Philistines" in 2 Sam 5:17. See also Hauer 1970: 574.

[32] Yeivin 1964: 154.

[33] See McCarter 1984: 159.

[34] Yeivin 1964: 154.

previous venture. This necessitated a change of strategy on David's part, one which has come down to us owing to an account of it in oracular form (2 Sam 5:23-24; 1 Chr 14:14-15). In spite of the suggestion that has been made to read *běkā'îm* as a place name,[35] the traditional understanding of this word as a reference to a species of tree or shrub cannot be ruled out, and it appears as most likely in one specific interpretation of the course of battle. According to this analysis, the account of God's oracular response to David's inquiry masks the strategy that David himself employed in the course of this engagement.[36] Eschewing a frontal attack on the Philistines, David used the cover of night, presumably a time when the rustling of the wind in the trees would mask the sound of his advancing troops, to sneak up on the enemy camp.[37] Needless to say, this surprise attack threw a probably larger Philistine force into confusion. In the resulting pursuit and retreat, the Philistines were pushed northwards past Gibeon (or Geba[38]) and then to the west down to Gezer. The expression *'ad-bō'ăkā gāzer* "until the entrance of Gezer" combined with the notice in 1 Kgs 9:16 regarding Gezer make it unlikely that Gezer was captured at this time, unless one is to assume that Gezer changed hands more frequently than recorded in the Bible.

What then was the extent of the Philistine defeat recorded in 2 Sam 5:17-25? It is impossible to tell. On the one hand there are no other accounts of seemingly major encounters between the Philistines and David. On the other hand the summary statement in 2 Sam 8:1 and 1 Chr 18:1 has been taken both as a formula referring in general terms to the final defeat of the Philistines,[39] which may be summarized in the passages just discussed, or it may be a reference to an otherwise unknown decisive third encounter.[40] Arguments have been

---

[35] Eissfeldt (1936: 28 n. 4) advocated reading the place name Bechaim in place of Rephaim in 2 Sam 5:22. Tidwell (1979: 190, 202) also cast doubt on the setting of 2 Sam 5:22-25 at Rephaim. Grønbaek (1971: 252) viewed v 22, in which the setting of the second encounter at Rephaim is mentioned, as a later redactional insertion.

[36] See, however, Gelander 1991: 26-27, who follows medieval Jewish commentators in not viewing this oracle as evidence of the strategy that David employed. In his view this passage is a miracle story, in which God acts alone without recourse to human agents.

[37] See Yeivin 1964: 155; Garsiel 1975: 45; and above section 1.1.2.

[38] See A. Demsky, "Geba, Gibeah, and Gibeon - An Historico-Geographical Riddle," *BASOR* 212 (1973) 26-31.

[39] Alt 1936: 150.

[40] Macalister 1914: 53; Eissfeldt 1943: 117; B. Mazar 1979: 78. 7. For Eissfeldt (1943: 116-17) the two skirmishes of 2 Sam 5: 17-25 were insufficient to drive the Philistines out of Israelite territory. Therefore he postulated that the report of a third, decisive encounter must be hidden in the notice of 2 Sam 8:1; 1 Chr 18:1. In this he was followed by Kitchen (1973: 64). Believing the Philistines to be independent of Israel, Kitchen further postulated an additional campaign against Israel, notice of which is hidden in the hero stories of 2

adduced on both sides, upon which larger theories regarding the relative positions of the Philistines and David/Israel vis-à-vis one another have been based.

A major part of the difficulty of interpreting 2 Sam 8:1 and 1 Chr 18:1 lies in the variation of the conclusions of the two parallel statements. In the former David is to have seized "Metheg-Amma" from the Philistines, in the latter "Gath and its dependencies." Of these two variants, the latter is readily understood on a purely linguistic level. However, it is viewed by most as a secondary tradition.[41] It is, therefore, on the former variant that scholars have expended their energy, with no consensus yet reached regarding its meaning. The word *meteg* means "bridle," "bit," or "reins."[42] The consonantal *h'mh* can be read in a number of ways. As pointed in the MT, *'ammâ* can refer to a "fore-arm," a "cubit," or a "water-channel." Repointed as *'āmâ* it could refer to a "female servant," while repointed as *'ummâ* it would refer to a "nation." Although most Bible translations simply reproduce the expression as a place name,[43] scholars have have been reluctant to accept the term as a simple place name, partly on account of the incongruity of the notice of David's assumed major defeat of the Philistines being coupled with an unknown and, therefore, insignificant place. They have thus attempted to determine what "bridle/reins of the cubit" means. Unfortunately, the ancient versions are of no help in this endeavor.[44] The heterogeneous state of the evidence would lead to the conclusion that the ancients were as unsure of the meaning of the phrase as we are.

Among the various attempts to understand the expression the following may be cited:

Following earlier commentators, S. R. Driver[45] suggested that *meteg hā'ammâ* be translated as "bridle of the mother-city," taking *'ammâ* in the sense

---

Sam 21:15-22; 1 Chr 20:4-8, which he has placed at either Gob or Gath. Vigouroux (1908: 297) dated the supposed offensive battle of 1 Chr 18:1, in which Gath was captured, to a time seven years after the defensive battles of 2 Sam 5:17-25. Segal dated the capture of Jerusalem after the campaigns of 2 Sam 5:17-25, but before the capture of Gath in 2 Sam 8:1 and 2 Sam 21:20-21. On his theories regarding the ascription of bits of the texts of 2 Sam 5; 8; 21; and 23 to three postulated campaigns lasting two to three years, see Segal 1965-66: 33-34. Rainey (1975: 72*), to a certain extent following B. Mazar, understood the notice of a defeat of the Philistines in 2 Sam 8:1 as a reference to an isolated campaign of David toward the Mediterranean Sea to recapture Dan's ancestral lands.

[41] E.g. Williamson 1982: 138; Kalimi 1995: 104; but see A. B. Ehrlich 1910: 291.

[42] See Dahood (1967: 435), who in Ps 32:9; Isa 37:29 = 2 Kgs 19:18; and Prov 26:3 has advocated translating *meteg* as "muzzle".

[43] E.g. RSV, NJV. But see the *Einheitsübersetzung*: *Zügel der Herrschaft* "reins of dominion."

[44] See S. R. Driver 1912: 280. The variant versions are all conveniently listed in Ulrich 1978: 183.

[45] 1912: 279.

of '*m* as used occasionally in Phoenician and Syriac. The phrase would then refer to the authority or jurisdiction of the local metropolis, presumably Gath. He further interpreted 1 Chr 18:1 in this light,[46] presuming that the Chronicler read *mgt* "from Gath" instead of *mtg*, while understanding the jurisdiction of the "mother-city" to include its dependencies (*běnōtêhâ*).

H. P. Smith[47] was unwilling to commit himself to more than an admission that the object referred to was probably a "tangible possession," such as a piece of territory. He was troubled by the supposed use of an obscure poetic metaphor in the midst of a most prosaic passage to express the wresting of dominion from the enemy.

After quoting a lengthy passage from *Hastings Dictionary of the Bible* (1900), listing various previous attempts at understanding the passage, Tolkowsky[48] arrived at the conclusion that the phrase was to be understood in a literal manner as "iron rod (< bridle) of the cubit." Thus he speculated that what David captured was a tangible object, an iron measuring rod based on the Egyptian cubit, which was to serve as the standard in Israel as of that time.

G. R. Driver[49] expressed strong doubts about the translation of '*ammâ* as "mother-city," since it is otherwise unknown as such. He preferred to read as in 2 Sam 2:24 and as reflected in Aquila's translation of the passage under consideration *ton chalinon tou hydragōgiou* "bridle of the water-channel," perhaps referring to David's capture of a dam or an aqueduct from the Philistines. In spite of this, the younger Driver felt that in this context *meteg hā'ammâ* was probably a proper name.

Alt[50] felt that the phrase, whether to be understood in a figurative or a literal sense, referred to the new political relationship between Philistia and Israel as a consequence of David's ultimate defeat of the Philistines as recounted in 2 Sam 5:17-25.

Eissfeldt[51] felt that *Zaum der Elle* "a cubit-long bit" was figurative for the size of the yoke which had been put off by the Israelites.

Hertzberg[52] translated the phrase as "reins of the fore-arm," the latter being the appendage around which the reins were presumably wound. In his opinion

---

[46] S. R. Driver 1912: 280.

[47] 1899: 306-07.

[48] 1920-21.

[49] 1958: 17-18.

[50] 1936.

[51] 1943: 117-18.

[52] 1964: 288.

also this was presumed to be a metaphor for the passing of power in Palestine from the Philistines to David, who "took the leading reins." Since up to this point, the Philistines had been "in the saddle in Palestine," it made sense in his eyes for David to take the reins out of their hands. It is questionable, however, to what extent modern equestrian imagery would have found resonance among the ancient Israelites.

Mittmann[53] has argued that the phrase be translated as "bridle of the fore-arm" (*Trense des Unterarms*), which he understood as a *terminus technicus* for "handcuffs." Like Alt, Mittmann has thus interpreted the phrase metaphorically. In his reconstruction, David was able to remove the "handcuffs" with which the Philistines had subjugated the Israelites, without, however, exercising control over their heartland. This inability of David to turn the tables completely on the Philistines and to subjugate them in turn is attributed by Mittmann to the intervention of the Egyptians, whose capture of Gezer he has dated to David's reign.[54]

Since McCarter[55] was uncomfortable with the literal translation of the phrase, he suggested that an earlier *mgt h'mh/h'mth* "from Gath to Ammah"[56] may have lain behind the text of the MT. Albeit, he provisionally followed the G *tēn aphorismenēn*, reflecting Hebrew *hmgrš*,[57] and translated the phrase "the common land," which he defined as the "rural territory adjacent to the Israelite cities."[58]

Two additional possibilities, *hā'āmâ* and *hā'ummâ*, for understanding the text were mentioned above. It is highly unlikely that the text would be speaking about David's capture of an otherwise unknown "Metheg the maid-servant" from the Philistines. On the other hand, the reading *meteg hā'ummâ* "bridle/reins of the nation" would seem to fit the context and would appear at first glance to be comprehensible and to solve the crux of interpretation. In its few attestations in biblical Hebrew (Gen 25:16; Num 25:15; Ps 117:1 [*'ummîm*]), however, the word *'ummâ* is applied to non-Israelite tribes or

---

[53] 1983.

[54] Mittmann 1983: 333-36.

[55] 1984: 242-43.

[56] Ammah is known from 2 Sam 2:24 as the site of an encounter between Abner and Joab. However, the occurrence of the word in this latter passage has also been cited as the one definite mention of *'ammâ* with the meaning of "water-channel" in biblical Hebrew (see e.g. G. R. Driver 1958: 17-18).

[57] In retroverting in this manner, McCarter is following in the footsteps of Wellhausen (1871: 174), who retroverted the G as *mtgrš*, retaining the element *mtg* at the beginning of the word. Wellhausen, however, unlike McCarter supported the primacy of the MT reading in this passage.

[58] McCarter 1984: 247.

clans.[59] This makes difficult its usage in this sense in the passage in question. Whatever solution one advocates in regard to this passage must remain tentative, unless one is to conclude that the passage is hopelessly corrupt. It is seemly in this context, however, to mention Williamson's contention that the text of 1 Chr 18:1, while most probably representing a secondary tradition derived from 2 Sam 8:1, may be factually correct in its assertion of David's control over the Israelite/Philistine border area up to and including Gath.[60]

The Status of the Philistines vis-à-vis the United Monarchy

As the progression of this discussion will indicate, there have been many who are confused about the status of the Philistines within the context of the Davidic empire. Did they manage to retain their independence? Were they vassals? Were they independent vassals?[61] Did David conquer them? If not, why not?[62] Or were they simply restricted to their heartland, their power and hopes for an imperium broken?

At a minimum it can be assumed that the Philistines had to relinquish their inland holdings, as well as the territory that had been under their control north of Jaffa and the Yarkon River. An era of expansionism had ended for them. As of the time of David, the Philistines were confined to the southwestern coastal strip of the land to which they were destined to bequeath their name.[63] Any wars that they were to fight in the future were to be either of a defensive nature, or limited to minor border skirmishes. As a number of commentators have pointed out, the Philistines' political and commercial decline, both a direct result of their defeat by David, was a a major factor in the concomitant rise of Phoenicia as a leading power in international maritime trade.[64]

---

[59] See Malamat 1962: 144; 1989: 41-43; Mittmann 1983: 330. The word also appears eight times in the late Aramaic sections of the Bible (Dan 3:4, 7, 29, 31; 5:19; 6:26; 7:14; Ezra 4:10).

[60] See also Bright 1981: 199 n. 33. Kalimi (1995: 104, 336), on the other hand, views the Chronicles text as historically impossible. See also the criticism of Mittmann (1983: 327-28).

[61] As per Alt 1968: 287.

[62] Those who assume that David did not conquer Philistia proper generally ascribe this to one of two factors. Either David was not strong enough militarily (e.g. B. Mazar 1986: 75), or he feared encroaching upon territory traditionally claimed by Egypt (e.g. Bright 1976: 197).

[63] See Eissfeldt 1943: 118; Noth 1960: 192-94; B. Mazar 1986: 75.

[64] Peckham 1976: 231; B. Mazar 1979: 90; 1986: 76-77. Although Donner (1982: 51-52) discounted any contact between David and the Phoenician coast, the initiation of which he attributed to Solomon, Katzenstein (1973: 74-75) followed Albright in assuming that Israel and Tyre joined forces to break the Philistine economic monopoly on both land and sea. David broke the inland Philistine monopoly, while Tyre

Although one can reckon with general agreement on the minimal position taken above, once one attempts to go beyond that opinions vary quite considerably. Did David simply restrict the Philistines to the southern coastal strip,[65] or did he actually capture or annex part or all of Philistia?[66] A number of scholars assume that, in addition to Gath, Ekron, which belonged to the oftentimes disputed border region between Israel and Philistia, may have been absorbed into the Israelite empire at about this time.[67] In this context it is well to bear in mind that, unlike the accounts of David's other conquests, the account of David's defeat of the Philistines includes no mention of an occupation, nor the imposition of either tribute or a governing authority.[68]

The dearth of hard and fast information in our only written source (the Bible) for the epoch in question allows elaborate reconstructions to be hung on very slender threads. The account of the escape of Shimei's slaves to Gath and of their subsequent return to Jerusalem has been used, for example, as an indication of: (1) the *independence* of Gath during the course of the united Israelite monarchy,[69] as well as (2) the *dependence* of Gath during the course of the united Israelite monarchy.[70] On the other hand, Rehoboam's fortification of a town named Gath (2 Chr 11:8) has been viewed as evidence of Philistine Gath's capture by Israel under David,[71] or of its coming into Israel's possession with Gezer during the reign of Solomon.[72] Were Gath and Israel bound by a parity treaty or a vassal/suzerainty treaty?[73] Under the circumstances, it is impossible to determine.

---

took care of the maritime monopoly. As the Phoenicians usurped the Philistine sea routes, the Philistines developed their land routes via the Via Maris and the Negeb according to Oded (1979: 236). Needless to say, those who question the status of the Philistine city-states as maritime powers would not be in full agreement with this reconstruction (e.g. Brug 1985: 13). In Oded's opinion (1979: 223), during the days of the Israelite kings the Philistines were interested in the sea only as a source of fish.

[65] See e.g. Peckham 1976: 231.

[66] See e.g. Malamat 1963: 16; Bright 1976: 196, who represents a common position in assuming that at least Gath was conquered by David; T. Dothan 1982a: 16; Donner 1982: 46 n. 17, who views the Philistines as vassals of David, similar to the Moabites; Seger 1984: 52.

[67] E.g. Wright 1966: 84, basing himself on Josh 20:43.

[68] Delcor 1966: 1266; Japhet 1993: 345-46.

[69] See e.g. Macalister 1914: 60; Eissfeldt 1943: 123; Malamat 1963: 15; Delcor 1966: 1266.

[70] See e.g. Wright 1966: 82; Lance 1976: 40-41; Seger 1984: 52.

[71] Bright 1981: 199.

[72] Delcor 1966: 1267.

[73] Aharoni 1979: 297.

Gath and Israel

One theme which leaps out of the biblical narrative is that of the relationship between Israel and Gath. In the narratives of the united monarchy no other city of the Philistine pentapolis is mentioned with the importance or frequency of Gath. Although this has led some to assume that Achish's Gath was not a member of the Philistine pentapolis at this time,[74] others have seen Gath as the leading city[75] of a Philistia which was moving away from the concept of a pentapolis acting in concert, to one of five ethnically related, albeit independent city-states. Be that as it may, the relationship between Gath and the house of David is striking.

Besides the personal relations between Achish and David which predate David's assumption of rule over united Israel may be mentioned the important position accorded Obed-Edom the Gittite in the narrative of the ark's ascent to Jerusalem (2 Sam 6:10-12; 1 Chr 13:12-14; 15:25), the incorporation of a unit of Gittite warriors and their families under the leadership of Ittai into the ranks of the minority remaining loyal to David at the time of Absalom's rebellion (2 Sam 15:18-22; 18:2, 5, 12), and the open borders which allowed Israelite slaves to run away to Gath and then to be fetched from there (1 Kgs 2:39-41).

The designation of Obed-Edom as a Gittite has generally been taken to imply that he was a Philistine who entered into David's service while David was a servant of Achish of Gath.[76] Hertzberg[77] has suggested that Obed-Edom, as a

---

[74] Kassis (1965: 267-69) followed by Wright (1966: 81-82).

[75] Rainey 1975: 71.

[76] H. P. Smith 1899: 293; S. R. Driver 1912: 269; McCarter 1984: 170; see also the discussion of Ittai the Gittite 2 Sam 15:18-22; 18:2, 5, 12 below . The lodging of the ark at a non-Israelite's dwelling and the concurrent blessing bestowed upon him and his household began to be a source of concern at a very early age. Already in the book of Chronicles Obed-Edom was transformed into a cultic singer, gatekeeper, and Levite (1 Chr 15:18, 21, 24; 16:5, 38; 26:4, 8; Corney [1962b: 579-80] has assumed the existence of two to three different Obed-Edoms -- not including the Temple functionary of the days of Amaziah in 2 Chr 25:24). In Josephus (*Antiquities* VII. 83) Obed-Edom is referred to not as a Gittite, but as a Levite. Both Rashi and Kimhi also identify him on the basis of the Chronicles passages, the latter harmonizing the traditions by . assuming that Obed-Edom was called "the Gittite" because of a sojourn at Gath. More recently Ahituv (1971a: 15) has questioned Obed-Edom's Philistine origin on the basis of the indefinite nature of an identification as a Gittite, there being no way to determine which Gath was the source of his ethnicity. However, Ahituv's argument leaves out of account David's often attested connections with the region of Philistine Gath and the frequency of free intercourse between Jerusalem and Gath during the days of the united monarchy (about which see below). Thus while Ahituv has a theoretical basis for his argument, the weight of contextual evidence is against it. How did a Philistine in David's service metamorphose into a cultic functionary? In the words of R. H. Pfeiffer (1948: 623): "Obed-edom ... was adopted by a Levitical guild of gatekeepers as their eponym ... manifestly because the ark remained three months in his house. Obed-edom's connection with the ark would inevitably lead to his metamorphosis into a Levite." See also Kalimi 1995: 54.

[77] 1964: 279.

foreigner, must have been uncomfortable with the unwanted presence of the ark in his house. How much greater then the miracle when it brought him blessing![78] Whatever Obed-Edom's personal convictions were,[79] Hertzberg's assumption reads too much into the text. On the other hand, H. P. Smith[80] might be guilty of erring in the opposite direction by assuming that Obed-Edom was a loyal Yahwist. Obed-Edom was probably a Philistine mercenary who owed his primary loyalty to David. Religious loyalty was thus a function of one's political/ethnic affiliation; obviously a condition which could change over time. In addition a person could be a Yahwist and have a non-Yahwistic name. It is significant that of the eight names of his sons preserved in Obed-Edom's genealogy in 1 Chr 26:4-8 three are Yahwistic names, two are El-names, and the remaining three would not be out of place in Israel.[81]

As for the Gittite mercenaries in David's service, a major factor in David's successful rise to power had been his habit of engaging mercenaries owing loyalty to his person alone as the core of his troops. As of the time of the formation of his empire, we find among his forces Gittites, as well as the somewhat enigmatic Cherethites and Pelethites.[82] Since there are many who identify the Cherethites and the Pelethites with the Philistines,[83] it is appropriate to digress on this subject.[84]

Cherethites and Pelethites

The military unit called the Cherethites and the Pelethites is mentioned seven times in the Bible (2 Sam 8:18; 15:18; 20:7, 23 [Qere]; 1 Kgs 1:38, 44; 1 Chr 18:17), all in references to the reign of David as (putative) king over a (more or less) united Israel. In addition the Cherethites are mentioned thrice   by

---

[78] As commentators as of Rashi have indicated, the theme of blessing conferred upon Obed-Edom is taken up again in 1 Chr 26:5 (in the context of the genealogy of Obed-Edom in vv 4-8) כי ברכו אלהים "for God had blessed him."

[79] Hertzberg (1964: 279) has referred to him also as the worshipper of a "strange god," the first word of which I assume (and would hope!) is simply a contextually inappropriate translation of the German *fremd* "foreign, strange."

[80] (1899: 295.

[81] Regarding the possibility that the Chronicles text may reflect an earlier tradition, see Japhet 1993: 281.

[82] This has been regarded as a sign of David's superior position vis-à-vis the Philistines (e.g. Bright 1981: 199).

[83] E.g. Alt 1968: 287 and n. 27; Bright 1976: 196; Malamat 1982: 195.

[84] The following discussion is based in large part on my entries "Cherethites," "Pelethites," and "Carites" in the *Anchor Bible Dictionary.*

themselves, in contexts which would appear to refer to their ethnicity (1 Sam 30:14; Ezek 25:16; Zeph 2:5).

As part of David's personal guard distinct from the regular army, the Cherethites and the Pelethites were under the direct command of Benaiah (2 Sam 8:18; 20:23 [Qere]; 1 Chr 18:17[85]). Their allegiance was owed to David, and they showed him great loyalty at times of crisis.

The Cherethites and the Pelethites accompanied David on his flight from his son Absalom's attempt at usurpation (2 Sam 15:18); they took part in the pursuit of Sheba son of Bichri during his revolt against Davidic rule (2 Sam 20:7); and they provided valuable support in following Benaiah's lead in assuring that Solomon, rather than Adonijah, would succeed David on the throne. For his ruthless support of Solomon, Benaiah would eventually be appointed the realm's supreme military commander (1 Kgs 2:35). After Solomon's coronation, the Cherethites and the Pelethites disappeared from the historical record, probably to be accorded an important position and to be swallowed up in the new military structure headed by Benaiah. Although it has been theorized that the Carites, who were instrumental in the overthrow of the usurper Athaliah in the mid ninth century (2 Kgs 11:4, 19), were a direct descendent of the Cherethites,[86] the evidence for this is at best inconclusive.

The Cherethites by themselves are mentioned in several contexts from which their identity as an ethnic group can be deduced. In the story of the sick Egyptian slave who was abandoned by his Amalekite master, a region of the Negeb is referred to as the "Negeb of the Cherethites" (1 Sam 30:14), presumably a southern Philistine holding according to v 16.[87] After an appreciable hiatus, the Cherethites are mentioned again in poetic parallel with the Philistines in two late prophetic oracles (Ezek 25:16; Zeph 2:5). This juxtaposition would indicate that, at least in the mind of later tradition, there was an ethnic relationship between the Philistines and the Cherethites.

Research on both the Cherethites and the Pelethites has tended to concentrate on their ethnic affiliations. This is easier to do in the case of the former than the latter.

In spite of the fact the the island of Crete is referred to in the MT as *kaptōr* (Deut 2:23; Jer 47:4; etc; see also Akkadian *Kaptara* and Egyptian *Keftiu*), most

---

[85] See also de Vaux 1965: 123, 219-22.

[86] Greenfield 1962a: 557.

[87] See also Aharoni 1958: 28-30.

scholars would understand the term *kĕrētī* as meaning Cretan. They thus would search for the roots of the Cherethites on Crete.[88]

The exact relationship between the Cherethites and the Philistines remains unclear. Since, however, the biblical author attributed the origin of the Philistines to the island of Caphtor (Amos 9:7), it would appear that an ethnic relationship between the two was assumed in at least a part of the ancient world. The nature of that relationship cannot, however, be determined to any satisfactory degree. Were the Cherethites identical with the Philistines, a subgroup of the Philistines, or a separate ethnic group of Aegean origin which had been absorbed by and under the rubric of the Philistines?

The absence of the name of the Cherethites among the names of the various Sea Peoples listed in the Medinet Habu inscriptions of Ramses III[89] has given rise to differing theories regarding the period of their settlement. Albright viewed this as an indication that the Cherethites had arrived on the scene as Egyptian mercenaries well before the mass movements of Sea Peoples at the close of the Bronze Age and the beginning of the Iron Age.[90] Thus they were unrelated to the Philistines and hence able to enter David's employ, in which capacity they presumably fought against the Philistines. Delcor on the other hand surmised that the Cherethites were late arrivals, reaching Canaan concurrent with the rise of David, or shortly before.[91] They then either merged with or formed a subgroup of the Philistines.

Owing to their location in the northwestern Negeb, it appears likely that David first came into contact with the Cherethites and engaged their services while resident at Ziklag (1 Sam 27; 29[92]).

While certain claims regarding the Cherethites as an ethnic group with a circumscribed area of settlement and a possible place of origin can be presented with some degree of confidence, the same does not hold true for the Pelethites. The most common theory regarding the identity of the Pelethites is that which views them as identical to the Philistines.[93] According to this theory, the Hebrew *pĕlētī* "Pelethite" is derived by analogy to *kĕrētī* "Cherethite" from the

---

[88] See Albright 1920-21; Delcor 1978. 12. Virolleaud (1936: 8-10) and de Langhe (1939: 294-300) viewed the Cherethites as a Semitic people, who traced their roots back to the eponymous Ugaritic Keret. Their arguments have been decisively negated by Delcor (1978: 414-15).

[89] *ANET* 262-63.

[90] Albright 1920-21.

[91] Delcor 1978: 421.

[92] See also McCarter 1980: 435.

[93] E.g. Montgomery and Gehman 1951: 86; Mitchell 1967: 414 and n. 146.

word *pĕlištî* "Philistine." Evidence for this otherwise unattested assimilation of
sin and *taw* is sought in the G *pheleththei*, in which the doubled *theta* is
assumed to represent the supposed original form of the name.[94] The biblical
Cherethites and Pelethites are thus viewed as equivalent to Cretans and
Philistines.[95] Unfortunately, the evidence, based on an unattested linguistic
analogy, is at best circumstantial.

Other solutions to the problem have also been offered. Basing himself on an
alleged parallel with the Greek *peltē*, "light shield," Albright suggested
interpreting the biblical *kĕrētî ûpĕlētî* as a hendiadys, referring to "light-armed
Cretan" mercenaries.[96] Delcor, on the other hand, sought to find a connection
between the Pelethites and Peleth son of Jonathan who appears in the
Jerahmeelite genealogy (1 Chr 2:33).[97] Schult, however, pointed to a possible
parallel between the biblical *plty*, "Pelethite," and the identification in a Punic
inscription of a certain Hannibal son of Baalhanun as *hplty*, which term
presumably indicated his place of origin.[98]

Although the use of the term "Cherethites and Pelethites" in the Bible would
support Albright's contention that the phrase was understood as a hendiadys in
its seven biblical occurences, more cannot be claimed with any degree of
certainty. While clear indications exist supportive of understanding "Cherethite"
as an ethnic term on at least one level, the same cannot be claimed without
reservation for "Pelethite." A minimal position would be to view David's
Cherethites and Pelethites as a conglomeration of mercenaries from the
Philistine/Negebite borderland, part of the riffraff which David attracted so well.

It can be assumed that David was able to engage the services of at least some
of these mercenaries owing to his position as a Philistine vassal in Ziklag. In
addition to mercenaries from the region of Ziklag, David also managed to
engage a troop of Gittites. Whether this was a result of his defeat of the
Philistines, or just of Gath, or a function of his relationship with Achish, it is
significant that both of these non-Israelite military units were from territory that
was probably originally under the rule of Gath. One cannot escape the
conclusion that Gath and its dependencies stood in a special relationship with

---

[94] It is interesting to note that in some G passages (e.g. 2 Sam 8:18 in G^B) the linguistic influence goes in
the opposite direction. In these cases the Greek *phelettei* "Pelethites" has influenced the pronounciation of
cheleththei "Cherethites," the *lamda* of the former replacing the original *rho* of the latter.

[95] Macalister 1914: 61.

[96] Albright 1975: 512.

[97] Delcor 1978: 421.

[98] Schult 1965: 74-9.

the Davidic empire, a relationship unlike that of the coastal Philistine city-states. Unfortunately, the parameters of that relationship cannot be determined, other than to say that it was symbiotic, and that it carried over into the earlier part to Solomon's reign.

Shimei's Slaves[99]

The narrative of the escape of Shimei's slaves from Jerusalem to Gath as recorded in 1 Kings 2:39-41 relates how Shimei pursued his runaway slaves to Gath, and how he was able to bring them back to Jerusalem, only to meet his maker on their account. It is part of a larger unit comprising all of Chapter 2 of 1 Kings, in which it is related how "the kingdom was established in Solomon's hand" (v 46b) by means of the murders of Joab (vv 5-6, 28-34), Adonijah (vv 13-25), and Shimei (vv 8-9, 36-46), and the banishment of Abiathar to his ancestral home at Anathoth (vv 26-27). The interest of the narrator, and also presumably of King Solomon, was in ensuring Shimei's absence from Jerusalem in order to have a pretext for having him murdered. Leaving aside the implications of this passage for an understanding of Solomon's oftentimes brutal domestic policies, what is of interest here is the actual extradition of Shimei's slaves.

This passage detailing the slaves' extradition has on occasion been cited by scholars as a prooftext in discussions of the relationship between Israel and Gath. While no one would dispute that this incident implies the existence of a formal relationship between these two political entities, the definition of that relationship has been open to discussion. On the one hand are those who claim that the fact of extradition is evidence of Gath's vassal status vis-à-vis Israel. On the other are those who claim the exact opposite, namely that this extradition is proof of Gath's independence of Israel, any linkage between the two being one of equals, bound through the stipulations of a parity treaty. Thus, for example, Greenfield was able to claim in the *Encyclopedia Judaica* that "[t]he vassal status of Gath remained unchanged at the beginning of the reign of Solomon (c. 960), as can be seen by the ease with which Shimei son of Gera moved into and out of that city;"[100] whereas Noth referring to the same passage in 1 Kings 2 declared that Gath "still enjoyed political independence when Solomon came to

---

[99] This section is based on C. S. Ehrlich 1994.

[100] Greenfield 1972: 402; see also 1962.

the throne,"[101] and Malamat maintained that Gath "still retained its
independence in the third year of Solomon's reign, as is evident from the
incident of the flight of Shimei's slaves to Achish king of Gath."[102] Whichever
interpretation one follows has broad implications for the reconstruction of the
political history of the united monarchy, from the extent of David's conquests to
the configuration of Solomon's empire and the extent of Egyptian influence in
Canaan.

In consideration of this diversity of readings, the question can be posed, on
what basis do these scholars decide on their interpretation of these verses?
Unfortunately, in most works of biblical history, on none. With the exception of
Malamat, whose interpretation was guided by a reference to ancient Near
Eastern legal practices,[103] the vast majority of biblical scholars who have based
aspects of their historical reconstructions on this passage have not taken the time
to investigate the implications of the extradition of slaves within its biblical nor
within its ancient Near Eastern context. The following brief discussion proposes
to correct this oversight by discussing the passage in its broader context, in
order to see how it might best be employed in the task at hand. The corpora of
comparative evidence to which recourse will be made include ancient Near
Eastern so-called "law codes," better perhaps to be referred to as "collections of
laws"[104] (which are subsumed in A. K. Grayson's terminology under the rubric
of "royal decrees/inscriptions"[105]), treaty texts, and a few miscellaneous texts
from the practice of law. Rounding out the discussion will be references to
possible inner biblical parallels.

At the outset it can be stated that the extradition of slaves was a major
concern of the various law codes which have been preserved. Societal structure
and stability demanded that property, as slaves were viewed, not be stolen, nor
be allowed or helped to disappear. The different legal collections differ not in
the enunciation of this principle, but in the case specific emphasis and adduced
penalties for escaping and/or aiding in the flight of a fugitive slave.

The Laws of Urnammu[106] are a fragmentarily preserved collection of laws
dating to the reign of Urnammu, the founder of the Third Dynasty of Ur, or to

---

[101] Noth 1960: 238.

[102] Malamat 1963: 15.

[103] Albeit, Malamat did ultimately base his interpretation of the relationship of Gath and Israel not on his
evaluation of the extradition of Shimei's slaves, but on his overall historical scheme.

[104] On the problems of terminology see Boecker 1976: 45-47.

[105] Grayson 1992: 769-71.

[106] Translations of the Laws of Urnammu are to be found in *ANET* 523-25 and *TUAT* 1: 17-23. See also
Cardellini 1981: 15-19.

that of his successor Shulgi around the year 2100 B.C.E.[107] Among the few decipherable laws is one concerning the reward in silver shekels a person is to receive, who has found and returned to her owner a female slave who had passed beyond the boundary of her city. In this case the emphasis is on the reward for the return of lost property. Unfortunately nothing can be deduced regarding any punishments for either the slave nor for the one who may have aided her in her flight.

Approximately two hundred years later are the Laws of Lipit-Ishtar, the fifth king of the First Dynasty of Isin.[108] This collection is also very fragmentary. Among the extant laws are two dealing with fugitive slaves. Paragraph 12[109] deals with the case of either a male or a female slave who has fled into the city and taken service with another master. After confirmation of the situation, and if the term of service with the new master has lasted at least a month, the new owner is obligated either to replace the runaway slave with another one, or to give the original owner another slave in addition to the runaway. The exact meaning is still a source of debate.[110] If he does not own a slave, then Paragraph 13 stipulates that he shall pay the original owner a fine of fifteen[111] silver shekels. The concern of these laws is with the compensation that the original owner of a fugitive slave is to receive for the loss of his slave's services. The one month waiting period can be viewed either as a grace period during which the intent of the new master to keep and exploit or to return and restore the slave will become evident, or with the minimum amount of time lost for which compensation becomes obligatory.

Some of the lack of clarity in the interpretation of the Laws of Lipit-Ishtar can be elucidated with the help of the slightly later Laws of the city of Eshnunna.[112] This collection has four paragraphs dealing with slaves, the first two of which directly address the question of fugitives. Law 49 stipulates that an

---

[107] On the Laws of Urnammu as a whole see Klíma in Klíma, Petschow, Cardascia and Korošec 1957-71: 247-48. Concerning the possibility that the author of the Laws was actually Shulgi see Kramer 1983.

[108] Translations are to be found in *ANET* 159ff.; and *TUAT* 1: 23-31. See also the editions of Steele (1948); and Cardellini (1981: 34); as well as the discussion of Klíma in Klíma, Petschow, Cardascia and Korošec 1957-71: 248-50.

[109] Cardellini (1981: 34) numbers the respective paragraphs 17 and 18.

[110] See Steele 1948: 25; Klíma in Klíma, Petschow, Cardascia and Korošec 1957-71: 249; Cardellini 1981: 34 n. 19.

[111] 25 according to Cardellini 1981: 34.

[112] Translations: *ANET* 161-63 and *TUAT* 1: 32-38. See the editions of Goetze (1956) and Yaron (1969), as well as the discussions of David (1949), Klíma (in Klíma, Petschow, Cardascia and Korošec 1957-71: 252-55), Cardellini (1981: 41-56), and Eckardt Otto (1989).

awīlum, a "citizen," caught with a stolen slave is to compensate the owner of the slave with an additional slave of the same gender. Thus an *awīlum* harboring a slave is not only to return the slave to his or her owner, but to pay a penalty of an equivalent slave. According to Law 50 an official who has seized and held a fugitive slave, a stray ox or a stray donkey belonging to the palace or to a *muškēnum*[113] for a period of time exceeding a month will be charged with theft. Once again the import of the law is slightly unclear. Yaron maintains that the reference to the palace or to a *muškēnum* indicates that the harboring of any fugitive slave will be punished as theft if the harboring has exceeded one month in time.[114] On the other hand Otto has understood Law 49 as implying that an *awīlum* or private citizen is obligated to return the runaway immediately and to pay a fine according to the principles of the *lex talionis*, i.e. returning the slave and compensating with an additional one, while Law 50 refers only to property of the palace and its functionaries. The one month would be a grace period allowed officials who had stolen property to make their intentions clear. In distinction to the *awīlum*, who had only to pay a fine for the harboring of the fugitive, the official would be liable for a charge of theft.[115] Although the punishment is not spelled out, from comparative data it can be assumed that the potential punishment would far exceed a simple fine. Eshnunna Laws 51-52, although not directly addressing the topic of fugitive slaves, do contain instructions for the marking of slaves of both citizens and (official?) visitors to Eshnunna. The guards at the city gate are to watch for the telltale markings and ensure that those thus marked do not leave the city without their owner's permission. Hence we see in these laws a concern that fugitive slaves be returned to their rightful owners, that the harboring of a fugitive is likened to theft and can be punished accordingly, and that the society take measures that work to ensure that slaves can be clearly identified and restricted in their movement.

The most famous legal collection of the ancient Near East, the Code of Hammurapi, dating to the first half of the eighteenth century B.C.E., contains a number of stipulations of interest in the current discussion.[116] Following after Law 14, which deals with the kidnapping or theft of a child, come six laws

---

[113] For a discussion of the problems of interpretation associated with the terms *awīlum* and *muškēnum* see Yaron 1969: 132-54. On *muškēnum* see Cardellini 1981: 91-92.

[114] Yaron 1969: 5-6.

[115] Eckart Otto 1989: 164-65.

[116] Translations: *ANET* 163-64, 166-77, and *TUAT* 1: 39-79. Text, transliteration and notes are to be found in Borger 1979: 2-50, 286-314. See also G. R. Driver and Miles 1952; Petschow in Klíma, Petschow, Cardascia and Korošec 1957-71: 255-69; Cardellini 1981: 57-90.

dealing with fugitive slaves. According to Law 15 an *awīlum* who has taken a slave of either gender belonging to the palace or to a *muškēnum* out of the gate shall be put to death. Although it is generally assumed that the gate in question out of which a slave must be led in order for the delict to be realized is the city gate, G. R. Driver and Miles have advocated understanding KÁ.GAL=*abullum* as referring to the gate of the palace in this case.[117] Whichever way one interprets it, the consequences are clear. It should be pointed out in this regard that the punishment here is an example of the emphasis on capital punishment for crimes against property which Greenberg has identified as one of the basic characteristics of Mesopotamian criminal law that distinguish it from biblical formulations.[118] Law 16 stipulates that an *awīlum* who has harbored a fugitive slave belonging to the palace or to a *muškēnum* and has not produced him or her at the herald's call shall be put to death. In both of these cases, guilt is assumed on the basis of action taken, whether it was in taking the slave out of the gate or in not producing the slave when ordered. Law 17 sets a reward of two silver shekels for the one who captures and returns a slave to his or her owner. In the case that the fugitive slave refuses to reveal who his or her owner is, Law 18 provides a legal procedure under the auspices of the palace to determine the slave's provenance and to return the slave to the owner. Taking up the theme of property delicts once again, Law 19 implies that even after the passage of some time, if a runaway slave is found in an *awīlum*'s house, the houseowner shall be put to death. Finally Law 20 establishes a procedure whereby one who has found a fugitive slave, who, however, has once again escaped, can swear to the veracity of the occurrence before a god in the presence of the slave's owner and go free. This implies not only that the one who has found a slave is obligated not to keep the slave for his personal use, but also that he is responsible for ensuring that the slave is returned to his or her owner.

The controversial Laws 280-81 deal with the purchase of slaves in foreign lands and brought back to Babylon. If it should turn out that they were originally in the possession of a Babylonian and presumably had fled or been abducted to foreign soil, then they are to be restored to their original owners. In the case of a native Babylonian slave, he or she is to be given outright to the original owner.[119] The purchaser, presumably being held responsible for indentifying the

---

[117] G. R. Driver and Miles 1952: 106-07.

[118] See Greenberg 1976; 1986.

[119] The text reads: ba-lum KÙ.BABBAR-ma an-du-ra-ar-šu-nu iš-ša-ak-ka-an, which can be translated literally as "without silver/money their freedom shall be established." Although this could be understood as implying that the slaves are to be released, this is most unlikely in context. The word *andurāru* in this case

slave as Babylonian, would have lost his money in the transaction. In the case of a foreign slave, however, the purchaser cannot have been expected to surmise that the slave belonged to a Babylonian. Therefore the original owner would have had to repay the cost of the purchase in order to regain his slave.[120] Once again the emphasis is on the ordering of society and its property, rather than on any moral principle connected with the redemption of one's fellow, as some would have it in this case.[121]

The Hittite Laws in their original form stem from ca. 1600 B.C.E. and were found in the Hittite capital of Hattusa, modern Boghazkoy.[122] The older laws in the collection preserve distinctions between the rights accorded to and the obligations expected of inhabitants of different parts of the later realm.[123] Thus a Hittite who has stolen the slave of a Hittite from Luwiya, the later Arzawa in south-western Anatolia, is liable for a fine of twelve silver shekels in addition to having to return the slave (Law 20). If, however, he had stolen the slave of a Luwian and brought him or her to Hatti, he would be liable only for the return of the slave, and no penalty would be assessed (Law 21). Laws 22-23 deal with the various rewards that the one who finds and returns a fugitive slave is to receive, including the receipt of the slave if the slave is brought back from an inimical land. In distinction to the Laws of Hammurapi, if a runaway slave is found by his or her owner in the home of another, the one in whose home the slave has been found is liable only for the rental of the slave at a fixed monthly rent of twelve shekels for males and six shekels for females (Law 24). Although also concerned with the structuring of society, the Hittite Laws do not view the theft of property as deserving of corporeal or even of capital punishment.

These examples from the various legal collections have hopefully served to establish the importance of the return of fugitive slaves to their owners in ancient Near Eastern society. To what extent these texts can be used in reconstructing ancient legal practices is a much debated issue. As has often been observed, there has yet to be found one ancient legal decision which quotes the

---

must refer to the slaves' being "freed" > "released" > "handed over" to their rightful owner. Thus the "freedom" that this text speaks about is that of the slave-owner's "freedom" from financial obligation in receiving his lost property. See *AHW* 50b-51a, s.v. *andurāru* + *šakānu* = "Abgabenbefreiung durchführen."

[120] Contrast with the situation at Alalakh. See Mendelsohn 1955: 68.

[121] See Mendelsohn 1949: 75-78; G. R. Driver & Miles 1952: 482-90; Petschow in Klíma, Petschow, Cardascia and Korošec 1957-71: 268.

[122] Translations: *ANET* 188ff., *TUAT* 1: 96ff. See also Korošec in Klíma, Petschow, Cardascia and Korošec 1957-71: 288-97; Friedrich 1959; Haase 1968; Cardellini 1981: 121-57.

[123] On the geographical divisions of the Hittite realm see Korošec in Klíma, Petschow, Cardascia and Korošec 1957-71: 292; and Houwink ten Cate 1992: 219, 224-25 (bibliography.).

precedent of the Laws of Hammurapi. The evidence presented so far has also been limited to the late third and early second millennium B.C.E. That the return of fugitive slaves was indeed a major societal issue is indicated too by a plethora of documents from the actual practice of law from a wide range of periods and cultures. Indeed many documents refer to the issue,[124] as well as to the concern of providing surety in anticipation of the potential flight of rented or bought slaves.[125] Space constraints, however, do not allow a deeper discussion of this corpus of evidence in this context.[126]

Of direct import for an understanding of Shimei's extradition of his slaves from Gath to Jerusalem is the testimony to be gleaned from ancient Near Eastern treaty texts. Having established the centrality of the return of fugitive slaves to their owners, at least in theory, any evidence from international treaties would be able to elucidate whether this principle was observed in the relations between states, and in which contexts.

Two of the earliest treaties mentioning the extradition of fugitive slaves come from fifteenth century B.C.E. Alalakh.[127] Both were treaties concluded between Syrian vassals of the Hittite king. The earlier one, AT 3, was concluded between Idrimi of Alalakh and Pilliya, "possibly of Kizzuwatna."[128] The whole purpose of this diplomatic document was to spell out an extradition agreement between the two cities and kings, each pledging to return fugitive slaves to the other. The reward for the one who finds and returns the fugitives is set at five hundred copper shekels for a male and one thousand shekels for a female.[129] If the fugitive is not seized by anyone, then the owner has the right to enter the territory of the other king's jurisdiction and to retrieve his runaway slave by himself. In this case, naturally, no reward is paid. What is striking in this case are the reciprocal nature of the extradition of fugitives and the right of the owner to cross borders in order to seek what is rightfully his. The parallels to the case of Shimei are evident.[130] The second treaty from Alalakh, AT 2, concluded

---

[124] See i.a. Mendelsohn 1949: 58-64; 1955: 69-70 (re: Alalakh Text [= AT] 101); Yaron 1969: 37 (re: Driver Letter 3); Bakir 1952: 78-79.

[125] See *TUAT* 1: 201 (from Nippur), 213-15 (from Ugarit).

[126] See Cardellini 1981: 25, 105, 108, 160-62, 165-67, 183, 222. For an incantation "to recapture a runaway slave," see Foster 1993: 897.

[127] *Editio princeps*: Wiseman 1953: 26-32, pls. I-IV. Translations: *ANET* 531-32.

[128] Wiseman 1953: 31.

[129] The financial discrepancy between males and females has led Wiseman (1953: 32) to postulate that -- at least in the case of the women under discussion -- the reference is probably to temple functionaries or to another important class of women.

[130] See Mendelsohn 1955: 70.

between Idrimi's younger son Niqmepa and Ir-^{d}IM of Tunip, is much more comprehensive in its composition. Among other provisions are some regarding the extradition of political refugees and of fugitive slaves. Once again the right of the owner not only to seek but to demand the return of his slave is guaranteed, the local officials being bound under threat of bodily punishment and fine to aid in the matter. Another fragmentary provision seems to protect against the theft and exploitation of one another's slaves.

In the form-critical study of ancient Near Eastern treaties a central role has been played by those from the Hittite empire of the mid second millennium B.C.E.[131] Indeed it is to these treaties that some look for the origin of the genre as a whole.[132] In some of these treaties, the clauses concerning the extradition of fugitives have been preserved. From the reign of Suppiluliuma in the mid fourteenth century come two vassal treaties which deal with this subject. The first was concluded with Niqmaddu II of Ugarit,[133] the second with Aziras of Amurru.[134] In the former, Suppiluliuma granted Niqmaddu the right not to return fugitives from outside of their mutual jurisdiction; whereas in the latter he emphasized the return of Hittite fugitives, both captives and slaves. From the middle of the thirteenth century comes a parity treaty between Ramses II of Egypt and Hattusili III of Hatti. This treaty has been preserved in both an Akkadian and in an abbreviated Egyptian version.[135] Paragraphs 11-20 deal with the mutual extradition of fugitives of all classes and ranks, a process to which both treaty partners feel themselves obligated. Of particular interest is the general amnesty for returned fugitives to which both Ramses and Hattusili pledge themselves (paras. 17-18). The fact that extradition of fugitives plays such a central role in this parity treaty needs to be emphasized.

From the middle of the eighth century B.C.E. come the Aramaic Sefire inscriptions.[136] These three stelae record the text of a treaty between Bar-Ga'yah of the as yet not conclusively identified KTK and Mati'il of Arpad. Although the suzerain reiterates his right to return of his fugitives, he does indicate that if fugitives are returned to him, he will also reciprocate. Once again emphasis is placed upon the reciprocal extradition of fugitives. Thus we can see

---

[131] See McCarthy 1978 *passim*.

[132] E.g. Tadmor 1982a. See also Barré 1992: esp. 654.

[133] Nougayrol 1956: 48ff., pls. xlviii-xlix (= RS 17.340); *TUAT* 1: 131-34.

[134] *ANET* 529-30.

[135] Weidner 1923: 112-23 (Akkadian version); *ANET* 201ff.; *TUAT* 1: 135-53.

[136] Fitzmyer 1967; Donner and Röllig 1969-73, texts 222-24, pls. xv-xxiii; *ANET* 659-61; *TUAT* 1: 178-89.

that the extradition of fugitives continued to play a major role in international relations into the first millennium B.C.E.

Having briefly surveyed some of the ancient Near Eastern literature which has bearing on the problem of the extradition of fugitives, and in particular fugitive slaves, it remains to mention a small number of biblical passages which may have bearing on the subject. That runaway slaves were a phenomenon at home in the milieu of the biblical authors is indicated possibly by the story of the flight of Hagar from her mistress Sarah in Genesis 21, but definitely by two accounts in 1 Samuel. The first reference, Nabal's insulting answer to the servants of David: "Who is David? Who is the son of Jesse? Nowadays there are many slaves who escape from their masters" (1 Sam 25:10), indicates at least a familiarity with the phenomenon. The second reference, the story of the Egyptian servant of an Amalekite, who begs David not to kill him or to send him back to his master (1 Sam 30:11-16), indicates a familiarity with the accepted ancient Near Eastern practice of the return of slaves to their owners, even across ethnic or national boundaries. Although not referring to a runaway slave, but to a fugitive prophet, the editorial aside in Jer 26:20-23 does bear on the issue. It concerns the flight of a certain Uriah son of Shemaiah, who prophesied against Judah and Jerusalem during the reign of Jehoiakim (609-597 B.C.E.). In response to his prophecies, Jehoiakim and his retainers wanted to silence Uriah. Fearing for his life, the prophet fled to Egypt. Jehoiakim, however, was able to send a retainer to Egypt, obtain custody of Uriah, bring him to Judah, and have him executed. From this we must conclude that a reciprocal treaty of extradition, whether formal or informal, existed between Jehoiakim and Pharaoh Necho II, whose vassal he was.

Problematic, in that it would seem to contradict what is otherwise known of biblical and ancient Near Eastern practice, is the passage Deut 23:16, in which it is written "You shall not extradite a slave, who seeks refuge with you from his master, to his master."[137] If one views the Deuteronomic law as a utopian humanitarian expression that was never realized in actual case law, since the consequence would have been societal anarchy, then the problem disappears. In the context of the law as an expression of the covenant between God and Israel, one could argue that the release from the obligation to return fugitive slaves is a provision which could be granted by the suzerain (in this case God) to his vassal (Israel), as was the case in the treaty between Suppiluliuma and Niqmaddu.

---

[137] See e.g. Cardellini 1981: 276-79, who follows Weinfeld in viewing the origin of this stipulation in the wisdom tradition.

It is evident that the return or extradition of fugitive slaves became an integral part of ancient Near Eastern societal structure. The beginnings of this process are to be sought in the late third millennium B.C.E. As Assyriological studies have shown, fugitives and their treatment became a major legal concern during the Old Babylonian Period, in the early second millennium.[138] Legal documents and treaty texts from Mesopotamia, Anatolia, Syria, Canaan and Egypt all attest to this fact throughout ancient times. Evidence from treaties indicates that the extradition of fugitives was an issue which concerned both parties to an agreement. In other words, although the suzerain could demand the extradition of his fugitives from his vassals, he could also grant the vassal the privilege of reciprocity.

Thus, the fact of extradition does not necessarily indicate that the one extraditing, in our example Achish of Gath, would necessarily be a vassal of the one to whom the fugitives are extradited, in our case Shimei, putative subject of Solomon, king of Israel. Those who argue that Gath must have been subject to Israel on the basis of the extradition of Shimei's slaves simply have no argument, leaving aside the question of how they would explain the extradition of Uriah from Egypt, the suzerain, to Judah, the vassal. On the other hand, the fact that the reciprocal extradition of slaves is an integral part of both vassal *and* parity treaties would also mitigate against being able to claim on the basis of 1 Kings 2:39-41 that Gath and Israel were *independent* of each other, bound by a parity treaty. Thus, it must be concluded that, although the story of Shimei's slaves can be used to argue that there were formal diplomatic relations between Gath and Israel, the evidence is too ambiguous to enable one to use this passage in defining the quality and nature of that relationship.

It was probably Gath's position as the nearest non-Israelite city which induced Shimei's slaves to hope for sanctuary there (unless the whole incident was simply contrived to assure Shimei's absence from Jerusalem, whether on the part of the redactor or of Solomon). The episode indicates that Gath had managed to retain a measure of autonomy, maybe even of independence, and that Achish, or a member of his house, still held sway there. The situation probably changed as a result of an incident which is narrated parenthetically in 1 Kgs 9:15-19, namely the capture of Gezer by a ruler of Egypt, and the city's subsequent transference to Solomon.

---

[138] See e.g. Renger 1972: 167-82.

Philistia During the Waning Days of the United Monarchy

Although the historicity of the motif of Solomon's marriage to a daughter of Pharaoh, most commonly identified as Siamun,[139] has been challenged by some in recent years,[140] the plausibility of an Egyptian incursion into Palestine following the death of David has been amply demonstrated.[141] City gates similar in plan have often been taken as evidence of a unified building plan during Solomon's reign at Gezer, Hazor, and Megiddo, possibly against a putative Egyptian threat.[142] Although not specifically mentioned in the sparse biblical notation of the event, it must be deduced that the march of the Egyptian army up

---

[139] Over the years there have been three main contenders for the identity of the Pharaoh who conquered Gezer and subsequently transferred it to Solomon. Chronological considerations have fairly well eliminated Shoshenq from the list. Working backward from a supposed synchronism between Rehoboam and Shoshenq (1 Kgs 14:25-26; Gardiner 1961: 329), it would appear that Shoshenq's reign (940-919 B.C.E. according to Hallo and Simpson 1971: 301) commenced much too late to be a viable candidate for an event which is assumed to have taken place in the early part of Solomon's reign (definitely before his eleventh year, probably within the first four; see Gray 1970: 119; Kitchen 1986: 280; Lance 1976: 210-212; Green 1978: 354-59; see also Malamat's arguments [1963: 11] for an Egyptian attack shortly after the death of David). Siamun and Psusennes II, the last two kings of the twenty-first dynasty are the two leading candidates for synchronism with the early part of Solomon's reign (Redford 1973: 5 and n. 21; Lance 1976: 210-12). The former, who reigned from 978-959 B.C.E. (Kitchen 1986: 280; Soggin 1984: 80-81), is the most frequently cited candidate, assuming that Solomon's first decade was in the range of 970-960 or 962-952 B.C.E. (see Green 1978: 354-55, 360-63). There have also been two pieces of circumstantial evidence used to support the identification of Siamun as the conqueror of Gezer. First is a fragmentary relief from Tanis of Siamun in the act of smiting an enemy (Montet 1941: 195-96 and fig. 58; 1959: 39-40 and fig. 5). On the basis of the depiction of an object which Montet identified as an Aegean double-ax being held in the hand of the vanquished enemy, Montet conjectured that the enemy depicted was a Philistine and that, hence, the venue of the scene was of Siamun's campaign to Philistia, during the course of which he captured Gezer. Although Montet originally ascribed the handing over of Gezer to the same pharaoh, he later attributed that act to Siamun's successor Psusennes II (1959: 42). Although the latter attribution did not take hold in the scholarly world, the first part of Montet's argument, namely that the Tanis relief was a depiction of Siamun's campaign to Philistia subsequent to the death of David, did (see e.g. Malamat 1963: 12; Gray 1970: 119; Kitchen 1986: 280-81). In recent years some doubt has been voiced over Montet's identification of the object held in Siamun's vanquished enemy's hand as an Aegean double-ax (Redford 1973: 4; Lance 1976: 212-17 and figs. 5a and 5b, who identifies it as a dipylon shield; but see Green 1978: 363-66). A scarab of Siamun, found at Tell el-Farah (South), has also been brought in as evidence of Siamun's involvement in a Philistine campaign (Malamat 1963: 12). However, the isolated presence of a seal is insufficient evidence upon which to hang such a theory, since there is no way of knowing how the seal came to the site (whether by trade or invasion), nor when (see Giveon 1972: 143 n. 4). Thus chronological criteria would favor an identification of Siamun as the pharaoh who conquered Gezer, while leaving open the possibility that it may have been Psusennes II (see Malamat 1964: 43; Redford 1973: 5; Soggin 1984: 80-81). As possible evidence of the result of an Egyptian expedition to Philistia, Redford (1973: 4) cites the mention of "Palestinian" slaves, possibly prisoners of war, in a mid-tenth century mortuary endowment text from Abydos.

[140] Miller and Hayes 1986: 216; Garbini 1988: 27-29.

[141] E.g. Malamat 1963: 11; 1982: 198-99.

[142] Lance 1967: 39-40; Dever 1967: 60-61; Gray 1970: 246; Milsom 1986: 92; but see Finkelstein 1990: 109-114; Ussishkin 1990: 74-77; Wightman 1990: 15-17, 19-20.

to the border of Israel must have had direct implications for the political situation of the Philistine states.

As Malamat has so eloquently argued, the Egyptian motive for the campaign to Palestine was to reassert its historical hegemony over at least the southwestern corner of Canaan, lands which Egypt had controlled until the two previous centuries. The death of the powerful David opened a supposed window of opportunity for the Egyptians. As has happened so often in recorded history, the Egyptians hoped that the death of the powerful ruler would usher in a period of weakness in Israel, which they would be able to exploit in order to reassert their political and economic influence. Egypt at that time was divided in two, with the northern part (lower Egypt) controlled by the twenty-first dynasty ruling from Tanis. Since the trade routes south were blocked by the theocratic rulers of Thebes, the only hope for expansion of rule and economic opportunity lay to the northeast, in Canaan.[143]

If the report of the capture of Gezer in 1 Kgs 9 is indeed historical, then it stands to reason that the Egyptian army transversed all of Philistia and brought it back under Egyptian hegemony. For the scope of this study it is irrelevant whether the ultimate Egyptian aim was to engage Israel in battle or not.[144] The consequence of the pharaonic adventure was to extend the limit of Egyptian influence to the very border between Philistia and Israel. Philistia was now

---

[143] See Malamat 1983: 21, 25.

[144] Malamat (1963: 13, 17; 1982: 199-200; 1983: 22-24) and those who follow him (e.g. Bright 1981: 212) argue that the actual aim of the pharaonic campaign in which Gezer was captured was the conquest of Israel itself. According to this reconstruction of events, the Egyptians were not content simply to reclaim land lost two centuries before. The object of the Egyptians was to conquer Israel itself following the death of David. After securing Gezer, however, the Egyptian advance was stymied by an Israelite force of far greater power and proportions than had been anticipated. Ceding Gezer to Solomon and giving him an Egyptian princess as a wife were face-saving measures imposed by the circumstances, which may have included a defeat of the Egyptian army (see also Peckham 1976: 232). In a milder version of this theory, Eissfeldt (1967: 154-55) viewed the pharaonic expedition to Gezer as an attempt to establish the Egyptian sphere of influence vis-à-vis Israel. Others, however, do not view the Egyptians and the Israelites as adversaries. Redford (1973: 3-5), for instance, viewed Egypt and Israel as allies united against a common foe, the Philistines (and the Shasu of Transjordan), in a case of "the enemy of my enemy is my friend." Egypt was anxious to recover its economic influence in Canaan through the subjugation of Philistia, and the cultivation of good relations with Israel, which had good relations with the Phoenicians that Egypt also wanted to cultivate. According to this scheme, the marriage of Pharaoh's daughter with Solomon was an attempt to secure an alliance through marriage. The gift of Gezer was a simple act of the transferral of the princess' landed property with her to her husband. In Kitchen's opinion (1986: 281-83), Siamun's motives were commercial. He wanted to eliminate Philistine competition from the lucrative trade with Phoenicia. By ceding Gezer to Solomon, Siamun relieved himself of an unimportant border town and won a valuable political and economic ally. Thus the campaign was basically a punitive raid against the Philistines. With more distant peoples, such as the Israelites, the Edomites, and the Phoenicians, the Egyptians were interested in forming economic alliances.

subsumed under Egypt's sphere of influence, which surely was a major, if not the major aim of the campaign.[145]

Archaeological Evidence Bearing on Philistine History in the Tenth Century B.C.E.

Has the archaeological record been able to lend support to the endeavor of historical reconstruction of this general period? The answer is a very tentative and vague "maybe."

A number of sites in Philistia show evidence of either destruction, abandonment, or cultural change which has been dated to the first part of the tenth century B.C.E. Unfortunately, there also exists a lively debate in the archaeological community regarding the exact dating and, hence, ascription to historical events and characters of the various strata. There are generally three candidates to whom the major upheavals at sites in Philistia during this period are ascribed: David, Siamun, and Shoshenq (biblical Shishak).

Among the major Philistine sites, Tel Batash-Timnah V ended without destruction around 1000 B.C.E. Since it lay between Philistine Tel Miqne-Ekron and possibly Israelite Beth-Shemesh,[146] it has been theorized that the site was abandoned by the Philistines as a consequence of the hostilities between Philistia and Israel during David's reign.[147] After a short uninhabited period, Tel Batash IV was in existence until destroyed near the end of the tenth century, probably by Shoshenq. Although the gate at Tel Batash IV has its closest parallel in the gate at Ashdod X, the pottery assemblage and other material culture remains find their closest parallels in the assemblages from sites in the Judean hills, the Shephelah, and the central coastal plains. Thus it is deduced that Tel Batash became an Israelite holding during the tenth century, i.e. the period of the united monarchy.[148]

Tel Miqne-Ekron Stratum IV-A suffered a violent destruction in the first part of the tenth century, which has been attributed either to David or to Siamun.[149] Subsequently the city was in decline for over two and a half centuries, until it experienced a dramatic economic revival under Assyrian hegemony. During this

---

[145] See Aharoni 1979: 307.

[146] See Dever 1982: 278-80.

[147] Kelm and A. Mazar 1995: 105-14.

[148] But see Ussishkin 1990: 82-88.

[149] T. Dothan 1987: 205; 1989: 9.

time of decline Ekron was restricted to the ten acre northeast acropolis. It was in the latter part of the tenth century or early ninth that a mud-brick tower faced with ashlar masonry in a header-stretcher pattern was constructed. It was part of a fortification system that included a mud-brick wall. Gitin speculates that this was the wall depicted in the reliefs of Sargon II at Khorsabad.[150] Since Tel Miqne lay on the border with Judah, tensions between the city-state of Ekron and the national state of Judah were probably the cause of Tel Miqne's 270 year long period of decline, during which it became a political and economic backwater. When the restoration came following Hezekiah's failed revolt against Assyria, the upswing in Ekron's economic situation was dramatic. Tel Miqne grew to such an extent that for the first time in its history it burst the bounds of the 50 acre Middle Bronze Age fortifications and grew to its greatest extent, namely 85 acres.[151]

Tel Mor (Ashdod-Yam, i.e. the port of Ashdod) Stratum III was also destroyed in the early tenth century, once again, it is felt, either by David or by Siamun.[152]

At Ashdod itself, Stratum X was destroyed about a third of the way into the tenth century.[153] Since this is the period to which Siamun's supposed capture of Gezer is dated, the excavators of Ashdod have attributed this destruction to him.[154] It would follow that this would also influence the dating of Tel Mor III to the same time.[155] Some[156] theorize that Solomon conquered or at least controlled Ashdod on the basis of the "Solomonic" or three (i.e. six) chambered gate found there. However, the date of the gate and its conceptual provenance are yet to be determined, although it would appear to be a development from the earlier two chambered one.[157] On the basis of recent work, it would appear that a Solomonic ascription of the gate and all that it would imply are at best questionable.

Three tenth century destruction layers have been identified at Tell Qasile. The excavator A. Mazar attributes the destruction of Stratum X to David in

---

[150] Gitin 1989: 25-26.

[151] See Gitin 1995: 62.

[152] M. Dothan 1977: 890; T. Dothan 1982a: 43.

[153] Since Dever (1982: 289-90) dates Stratum IX at Ashdod to the eleventh century, it follows that he would not agree with a dating of Stratum X in the tenth.

[154] *Ashdod IV* 54.

[155] Malamat 1963: 12; see also Ussishkin 1990: 77-82.

[156] E.g. Malamat 1982: 203 and n. 45.

[157] *Ashdod IV* 54-55; Ussishkin 1990: 77-82.

about 980 B.C.E.[158] The destruction of Statum VIII and possibly of Stratum IX is attributed to Shoshenq in the second half of the century.[159] At any rate, as of the early tenth century Tell Qasile belonged to a different sphere of influence.[160] The northern border of Philistia was now more likely to be determined by the Sorek Brook than by the Yarkon River.

The site of Gezer traditionally has been used as a type site in identifying architecture of the Solomonic period, thus providing researchers with, among other chronological hooks, a *terminus ad quem* for the pre-Israelite habitation of the city.[161] Recently, however, many of the assumptions used in dating the various layers of the site have been called into question.[162] Unless one is able to link a fortification with a definite historical moment, a most unlikely proposition in most cases, it is impossible to claim that the supposed tenth century fortifications at Gezer were directed solely against the Philistines,[163] rather than against the Egyptians.

To a great extent, an archaeologist's dating of a stratum to either David or Siamun is dependent on his or her interpretation of the biblical text. Those who assume that Philistia was conquered by David are more likely to date a site's destruction to that monarch, while those who assume that Siamun conquered Philistia are more likely to date the destruction levels at Philistine sites to the latter monarch.

Summation

If one were to follow B. Mazar's dating of the Danite tribal lists in Josh 19:40-46 to the period of the united monarchy,[164] then it would follow that broad regions of Philistia fell under Israelite control, or more properly were conquered by David and/or Solomon. On the other hand, the reticence of the Bible would

---

[158] A. Mazar 1980: 10-11.

[159] See also Dever 1982: 278-80.

[160] In spite of this, there is evidence that the "Philistine" sanctuary was rebuilt and continued in use through Strata IX-VIII (first and second half of the tenth century B.C.E.). See A. Mazar 1980: 50-57; as well as Dothan and Dothan 1992: 229-28.

[161] E.g. Kenyon 1971: 53-70.

[162] See Finkelstein 1990: 109-114; Ussishkin 1990: 74-77; Wightman 1990: 15-17; for counter arguments, see Dever 1990a.

[163] As do Miller and Hayes 1986: 214.

[164] B. Mazar 1986: 107-08; Aharoni 1979: 299; Oded 1979: 239; Kelm and A. Mazar 1982: 3; 1989: 41-42; *Gezer* I: 5 and n. 18; see also the discussion in Na'aman 1986a.

appear to make it unlikely that David pushed into the Philistine heartland, with the possible exception of the region of Gath. It is, however, likely that David was the one responsible for the cultural upheavals at border sites such as Tel Batash in the east and Tell Qasile in the north of Philistia. The destructions in the Philistine heartland in the first half of the tenth century should -- if one must find a circumstantial link between material remains and the written record -- be attributed to an Egyptian effort to reassert its hegemony over Philistia following the death of David.

From a position of power at the beginning of the first millennium B.C.E., a time at which it seemed that Philistia would be the legitimate heir to the ancient Egyptian empire in Canaan, the Philistines had fallen to the level of an object to be possessed, and the status as Egypt's heir passed temporarily to Israel.[165] First Achish's one-time vassal had declared his independence and established an empire, driving the Philistines out of the central and northern portions of Canaan and restricting them to their narrow coastal strip in southwestern Canaan. Then Egypt began to reassert its claim on the land. Over the next few centuries any niche that the Philistine cities would be able to carve out for themselves would be dependent on their situation within the international economic structures. Ekron, caught between Philistia and Israel/Judah entered a 270 year decline. Presumably so did Gath, which was eventually to disappear from the textual record. On the other hand, the cities of the coast flourished and became important conduits for international trade. The flourishing of sites along the Besor Brook, far removed from Israel and Judah, during the tenth century may also be indicative of the political situation.[166] The leading Philistine cities until the time of the Assyrian conquest were to be the coastal sites, which served as vital outlets for both land based and maritime international trade.[167] However, they were never to reestablish any grandiose plans of expansion, let alone empire. The battles that they were to fight in the future would be of a defensive nature, or relegated to minor border conflicts. Evidence for this claim will be adduced in the following chapter.

---

[165] See Alt 1968: 287; Malamat 1982: 194; McCarter 1986: 126-27.

[166] A. Mazar 1990: 533.

[167] For a mainly text-based discussion of the relationship between the Philistines and the united monarchy of Israel in the tenth century B.C.E. see the following chapter; as well as C. S. Ehrlich 1994.

CHAPTER THREE

DARK AGES?

Pre- and post-Davidic Philistines

Documentary sources for the history of the Philistines during the course of the following two centuries, until after the rise of the Neo-Assyrian empire in the west, are extremely limited. However, as recent excavations in Philistia have shown, there is very little justification for Macalister's statement that "[t]he contrast between the pre-Davidic and the post-Davidic Philistines is one of the most extraordinary in human history."[1] On the contrary, the Philistine states managed to retain their individuality[2] and to flourish economically under extraordinary pressure. Their period of expansion may have ended, but their regional role was still essential.

It was argued in the previous chapter that the cities of the Philistine pentapolis, with the possible exception of Gath, managed to retain their autonomy during the reign of David, only to fall under the nominal hegemony of Egypt subsequent to the campaign of Siamun to Canaan during Solomon's reign. That, together with the general loosening of Israelite control over its dependencies as outlined in 1 Kgs 11, would make it unlikely that Israel exerted any control over Philistia during the last days of the united monarchy. The division of the Israelite state following the death of Solomon sounded the

---

[1] Macalister 1914: 61.

[2] While the distinctive bichrome pottery tradition associated with the Philistines disappeared in the mid tenth century B.C.E., other regional traditions arose to take its place (see M. Dothan 1967: 183-84; 1975: 114-15; A. Mazar 1990: 533). Recently Stager (1991: 31-35) has argued that the traditional Philistine pottery actually represents the second phase of Philistine occupation, the first being represented by the locally made Mycenaean IIIC:1 monochrome ware. Presumably he will argue in the forthcoming conclusion to 1991 that at least the coastal Philistine cities were heavily influenced by Phoenician culture during the tenth to eighth centuries B.C.E. See Gitin 1990: 54 n. 22 for a brief discussion of the challenges yet remaining in determining the parameters of the Philistines' ethnicity.

death-knell of any Israelite hopes for empire. It also temporarily freed the Philistines from Israelite claims on their territory, once again with the possible exception of Gath, which is included in the list of cities fortified by Rehoboam in 2 Chr 11:5-10.

Gath and the List of Rehoboam's Fortifications

Many scholars have assumed that the document 2 Chr 11:5-10 has been assigned its correct historical place within the context of Rehoboam's reign.[3] However, a number of attacks have been mounted on this traditional position.

Expanding on a view first expressed by Junge, Alt argued that the list as a whole was to be assigned to the reign of Josiah (639-606 B.C.E.).[4] His reasoning, however, was circular. Alt was the first to recognize that the list of levitical cities in Josh 21 and 1 Chr 6 and the list of cities of Judah fortified by Rehoboam would appear to complement each other in the territory of Judah. The only exceptions to this are Aijalon and Hebron which appear in both lists. Since Alt dated the list of levitical cities to the time of Josiah, it followed that the list of Rehoboam's cities would have to be dated to the same time. If, however, one rejects Alt's dating of the former,[5] his main argument concerning the date of the latter is dealt a serious blow.

Alt's theory lay dormant until it was revived by Fritz in 1981. Although Fritz cautioned against facilely assuming a connection between the list of Rehoboam's fortresses and the list of levitical cities,[6] he did attempt to provide additional arguments in favor of dating the former list to Josiah's time. Drawing on Beyer's influential 1931 study of the topography of Rehoboam's system of fortifications, which sought to show that the cities were chosen in a logical order in order to protect the access routes to Jerusalem from the west and south, and on the results of archaeological excavations and surveys among the sites identified with the cities of 2 Chr

---

[3] E.g. Beyer 1931: 132-34; Noth 1938: 294; Welten 1973: 13, 192, 195; Miller and Hayes 1986: 238.

[4] Alt 1953: 2. 306-53.

[5] Most scholars, following Albright, date the list to the period of the united monarchy (e.g. Aharoni 1979: 301-02; Miller 1987: 279). On the other hand, Na'aman (1986b: 8) has categorically rejected any and all claims of historical validity for the levitical list.

[6] Fritz 1981: 46*.

11:6-10a,[7] Fritz sought to show that the archaeological record and the internal logic of the system would best fit the late seventh century B.C.E. However, Fritz himself had to concede that the archaeological evidence was not conclusive.[8] First, only a few of the sites have been excavated, and second, of these some had not been returned to since early in this century. Fritz's argument that the evidence from Lachish, Beth-Zur, and Gath does not admit of a date in the tenth century is specious. Whether one identifies the Gath of 2 Chr 11:8 as the Philistine city or as Moresheth-Gath, arguments could be adduced in favor of its inclusion in Rehoboam's list. Lachish definitely was settled during the latter half of the tenth century, whether one attributes Palace A of Level V or the fortifications of Level IV to the time of Rehoboam.[9] Although the paucity of evidence for a settlement at Beth-Zur between 1000 and 650 B.C.E.[10] would appear to lend support to Fritz's line of argument, scattered tenth century shards were found there, indicating that it may be too early to argue from hitherto negative evidence, always a risky procedure. Fritz's only positive argument is that the cities listed in 2 Chr 11:6-10a cover roughly the territory conquered by Sennacherib in 701 B.C.E. He thus deduces that Josiah, the next king who may have faced an acute Assyrian threat, must have fortified those cities on the basis of what he knew about Sennacherib's tactics. The evidence for this is at best circumstantial and admits of no compelling reason to change the traditional assessment of the place of the list.[11]

A more serious challenge has recently been mounted by the oftentimes iconoclastic Na'aman.[12] Starting from the presupposition that within the list is reflected the Judahite area conquered by Sennacherib, Na'aman has taken that argument to its logical conclusion, namely that the list itself dates from Hezekiah's time and represents the defensive measures undertaken by Hezekiah in the face of the Assyrian advance. Support for this is found in the

---

[7] With the exception of Gath, there is not much controversy regarding the identification of the cities mentioned in 2 Chr 11:6-10a. See the lists in Fritz 1981: 47*; Miller 1987: 276.

[8] Fritz 1981: 47*. See also Herrmann's (1989: 72*-73*) discussion of the inconclusive archaeological evidence.

[9] The former is preferable; see Ussishkin 1978: 93.

[10] See Funk 1975. Na'aman (1986b: 6) would move the latter date back into the latter half of the eighth century.

[11] While Herrmann (1989) would not concur with the latter phrase, his critical analysis of Fritz's reconstruction would support the first phrase of this sentence.

[12] 1986b: 5-14; 1988.

presence of *lmlk* seal impressions at all of the sites mentioned in the list which have been excavated (Beth-Zur, Gath, Mareshah, Lachish, Azekah), as well as at two sites which have only been surveyed (Bethlehem and Soco). The absence of *lmlk* seal impressions at the other sites is explained by the cursory nature of the surveys, which may not have revealed a representative sample of shards, and by the largely unpublished and therefore unknown results of the excavations at Hebron.[13]

Once again, however, the circumstantial and coincidental nature of the evidence does not offer any compelling reason to veer from the traditional dating of the list. As Timm has pointed out with reference to Ashdod, the mere presence of *lmlk* seals at a site does not automatically make it Judean.[14] In addition Na'aman's need to theorize that the Chronicler had to severely truncate the original document in front of him by lopping off the fortifications north of Jerusalem in order to get it to fit with the facts of Rehoboam's reign raises new literary-critical problems which admit no easy solution.[15]

After disposing of Fritz's attempt to provide a historical framework for the list, Herrmann[16] has sought to argue that the list of fortifications is an idealized construct of a system which never existed as a complete entity. Thus, the issue of dating becomes moot. Nonetheless, Herrmann procedes to date the "prototype" of the list to the time of Solomon, during which there was no threat from the north. The Chronicler then mistakenly attributed the list to his son, Rehoboam, who inherited the idea of a fortification system from his father, but never managed to make it a reality. In this manner Herrmann has his cake and eats it too. The system of fortifications never existed as an archaeologically recoverable reality, but it did have a long history as a literary and ideological construct. Herrmann[17] himself has admitted the hypothetical and unproveable nature of his theory.

The fact remains, when all is said and done, that there are no compelling reasons to redate the list of 2 Chr 11:5-10a to any time other than that of Rehoboam.[18] Indeed, the list fits quite comfortably into what is known about Rehoboam's reign. The small amount of territory covered is easily explained

---

[13] Na'aman 1986b: 11 and n. 9.

[14] Timm 1980: 30.

[15] See also the criticism of Na'aman's position in Garfinkel 1988.

[16] 1989.

[17] 1989: 76*.

[18] See Japhet 1993: 665-66.

by recourse to the historical situation. 1 Kgs 11 recounts how Aram and Edom had already moved out of the Israelite sphere of influence in the latter part of the reign of Solomon. The secession of Israel recounted in 1 Kgs 12 accounts for the loss of the territory of the northern tribes, while the biblical account of the campaign of Shoshenq I (called Shishak in 1 Kgs 14:25-26 and 2 Chr 12:2-12) in conjunction with the geographical information concerning Shoshenq's incursions into the Negeb listed in the Karnak inscription[19] would explain the loss of territory to the south of the Judahite heartland. As for the lack of mention of cities to the north, the border between Israel and Judah ran somewhere between Bethel and Jerusalem, the latter of which was presumably sufficient to demarcate the northern limits of Rehoboam's truncated holdings.[20]

A major advance in the understanding of the function of the cities in Rehoboam's list was hinted at by Miller and Hayes[21] and developed more fully by Miller.[22] According to this theory, the purpose of the cities "fortified", more properly perhaps stocked and manned[23] by Rehoboam was not to guard against external enemies (thus making the question of the list's dating to before or after Shoshenq's campaign in Rehoboam's fifth year a moot issue). Rather the distribution of garrisons and supplies in cities among the borders and the interior of the country would have served to secure the little land remaining under the dominion of a most unpopular ruler. The levitical cities and Jerusalem are not included since they would have formed the core of the areas loyal to the house of David, if not to Rehoboam himself. It was the remaining land that needed to be secured. The editorial comment in v 12b, "Judah and Benjamin were his," may thus be an accurate summary of the function of the list,[24] rather than the introduction to the following pericope.[25]

Once a decision has been made to date the list of cities to the period to which it has been ascribed in the biblical text, our focus can shift to our actual object of interest, namely to the city of Gath and its identity.

---

[19] See Noth 1938: 294-95; Aharoni 1979: 327-29; Kitchen 1986: 296.

[20] See also Kallai 1960: 56.

[21] 1986: 238.

[22] 1987.

[23] See e.g. Na'aman 1986b: 6; Rainey 1975: 73*.

[24] See Welten 1973: 12-13, 15.

[25] Thus Williamson 1982: 243 following Ackroyd.

There are many[26] who include the mention of Gath in 2 Chr 11:8 as another in a series of texts (often including 1 Kgs 2:39-41) which indicate that Gath belonged to Israel/Judah as of the time of the united monarchy up until Hazael's incursion in the late ninth century B.C.E. (2 Kgs 12:18-19--Eng 12:17-18).[27] According to this understanding, the fortification of Gath was to guard one of the western approaches to Jerusalem, although whether against the Philistines or the Egyptians is unclear.

In recent years, however, the followers of Aharoni's school of historical geography have gained the upper hand in the interpretation of the mention of Gath in 2 Chr 11:8. As first formulated by Aharoni,[28] this theory holds that Gath, which Israeli scholarship has predominantly come to locate at Tell es-Safi,[29] lay too far to the west to have logically been included within the western line of Judahite defenses, let alone within Judah at the time of Rehoboam. It is much more reasonable according to this view to include Tel Goded (Tell el-Judeideh; map reference 141115), which lies between Mareshah (Tell Sandahannah; map reference 140111) to the south and Azekah (Khirbet Tell Zakariyeh; map reference 144124) to the north, in Rehoboam's line of fortified cities. In light of the fact that Tel Goded has most frequently been identified as Moresheth-Gath, Aharoni and those who follow him have conjectured that the graphic and auditory similarity between Mareshah and the name which, it is conjectured, precedes it, Moresheth-Gath, in v 11 led to the dropping out of the element Moresheth in the biblical text, resulting in the reading which has come down to us.[30] The line of fortifications thus demarcated the extent of Judahite rule and did not include any of the Philistine territory. It is, therefore, to be concluded that the cities which were fortified by Rehoboam, whether they were meant to guard against an internal or an external enemy, served to secure the rump state which was

---

[26] E.g. Beyer 1931: 130; Eissfeldt 1943: 123-24; Noth 1960: 238; Delcor 1966: 1267; Bright 1981: 231-32.

[27] While Na'aman (1986b: 7) accepts the notion of Israel's domination of Gath during the reign of Solomon, in light of Shoshenq's campaign he rejects the notion that Rehoboam could have ruled over the city. He has thus accepted the equation of Philistine Gath with the Gath of 2 Chr 11:8, but rejected the historical context of the list within the traditional canon.

[28] See Aharoni 1979: 330-32.

[29] Concerning the identification of Tell es-Safi with Gath see Rainey 1975 and literature there. See Rainey 1975: 75*-76* n. 109 concerning B. Mazar's retreat from a theory of two Gaths, one northern identical with Gittaim and one southern identified as Philistine Gath, which he had originally proposed in 1954.

[30] See also Gichon 1964: 416, 418; Rainey 1975: 72*; Miller 1987: 276 Table 8.

all that was left to him following the division of the Israelite state, the withdrawal of dependencies from the empire, and the campaign of Pharaoh Shoshenq to Palestine.

The Campaign of Shoshenq I to Canaan

There are not many historical incidents which are recorded in the Bible and can be corroborated in Egyptian sources. The campaign of Shoshenq (Shishak)[31] to Canaan in the fifth year of Rehoboam, c. 925-920 B.C.E., is one. It is mentioned in 1 Kgs 14:25-26, in a context in which the author's concern is more with the Temple implements given as tribute to Shoshenq than with the historical event itself, as well as in the Karnak temple list of cities visited during the course of Shoshenq's campaign.[32] A fragment of an Egyptian victory stele dating to this campaign was unearthed during the course of the excavations at Megiddo. Indeed a number of destruction levels at sites in Israel, Judah, and the Negeb have been taken as tangible evidence of Shoshenq's activities.[33]

Shoshenq I was the founder of the twenty-second so-called Lybian or Bubastide dynasty.[34] Redford has attributed the need to prove and assert himself as one of foreign origin vis-à-vis the Theban theocracy as the personal motivation for his campaign against Canaan.[35] Some minor border disturbance with some Semitic tribe possibly provided Shoshenq with the justification he needed to move against Canaan.[36]

Entry 11 on the Karnak list mentions a city whose name is restored as Gaza, while the following entry 12 mentions either Gezer[37] or Makkedah.[38]

---

[31] On Shoshenq's name see Kitchen 1986: 73 n. 356.

[32] For translations of the list see Breasted 1906: 348-54; *ANET* 263-64; see also the drawing and transcription in Ahituv 1979: 91-96. Although the enumeration of towns and cities in the Karnak list has been taken as an indication of Shoshenq's conquests (e.g. Otto 1953: 223), Redford (1973: 11 n. 74) is probably correct in his interpretation of the list as an itinerary (see Miller and Hayes 1986: 245-46), although its exact interpretation is still a much debated topic (see Aharoni 1979: 323-30; Kitchen 1986: 432-47).

[33] See Wright 1967: 65*-66*; A. Mazar 1990: 395-98.

[34] See Otto 1953: 218-21; Kitchen 1986: 286-302

[35] Redford 1973: 6-11.

[36] Redford 1973: 10; Kitchen 1986: 294.

[37] Ahituv 1979: 91, 97; 1984: 98 and n. 197, 102 and n. 220.

Whichever is preferable, it seems probable that, except for a stop at Gaza, Shoshenq passed unimpeded through Philistia and moved on into the hill country, the northern coastal plain, and the Negeb. It may even be that Gaza served as the home base of Egyptian operations at the time.[39]

While Shoshenq's campaign had no lasting effect on the political structure of the region in terms of Egyptian interference in local affairs, in its treatment of Philistia it hearkened back to earlier days. Gaza once again served as the springboard for an action in Canaan.[40] The nominal Philistine dependence on Egypt was reasserted, at least temporarily, just as it had been a generation before during the days of Siamun.[41]

It can be assumed that at least part of the motivation for Shoshenq's campaign lay in the commercial sphere.[42] His receipt of tribute from Judah was recorded in the Bible, and it can be expected that he received the same from Israel. His movement into the Negeb quite possibly resulted in the cutting off of Judah from the lucrative trade routes with Edom and the Arabian peninsula.[43] Contact with the Philistines and various beduin tribes could only enhance Egypt's attempt to profit from the region's trade, even if with hindsight we realize that this attempt was to be futile.[44]

It is also to this time that a renewal of Egypt's close commercial ties with the Phoenician coast are traced.[45] This could only be of benefit to both partners, since Phoenicia, in particular Tyre, was at this time expanding into a major maritime commercial power.[46] It would appear that a major emphasis

---

[38] Kitchen 1986: 298 and n. 7, 435.

[39] Various theories of interpretation of the progress of Shoshenq's Palestinian campaign are conveniently collected in Kitchen 1986: 442-46, followed by the author's own interpetation (1986: 446-47).

[40] See Oded 1979: 237.

[41] See B. Mazar 1956: 61; Aharoni 1979: 325; Oded 1979: 239.

[42] See e.g. De Meulenaere 1967: 227-28.

[43] Aharoni 1979: 229-30; Miller and Hayes 1986: 246.

[44] On the basis of the lack of any lasting consequences from Shoshenq's incursion into Canaan, Noth (1938: 301) concluded that his campaign did not form a part of any larger strategy. This is fallacious reasoning, since the inability of a ruler or nation to take advantage of a political situation cannot be used in retrospect to cast doubt on the primary motivation of an action. On the other hand, Redford (1973: 11) has pointed out that Shoshenq made no attempt to secure his conquests in Canaan. In his opinion, Shoshenq's campaign was no more than a "large-scale razzia." In spite of this he did not deny that Shoshenq must have harbored dreams of reviving the lost Egyptian empire of the New Kingdom, dreams which neither he nor his successors were able to realize (1973: 13).

[45] Kitchen 1986: 292.

[46] See Katzenstein 1973: 122.

of Shoshenq's economic strategy was to expand Egypt's economic ties with the states of the eastern Mediterranean littoral, as far north as southern Anatolia, in addition to exerting influence over the land routes from the east.[47] An Egyptian presence in Philistia was thus a pivotal portion of Egypt's international economic posturing.[48]

Tangible proof of at least a trade relationship between Philistia and Egypt subsequent to Shoshenq's incursion may be found in an inscription on a statuette now in the Walters Art Gallery in Baltimore.[49] Although the statuette itself is a relic of the Middle Kingdom, the secondary inscription on its back pillar has most often been dated to the period of the twenty-second dynasty,[50] although a date in the twenty-sixth Saitic dynasty cannot be categorically ruled out.[51]

The secondary inscription mentions the funerary offering of a certain Pedeeset, the son of Api, "envoy/commissioner/messenger of/for Canaan and/of Philistia." It is unclear whether Pedeeset was a Canaanite or a Philistine serving in Egypt,[52] in which case he had an Egyptian name, or an Egyptian who had served in Canaan and/or Philistia,[53] in which case he had a Canaanite patronymic. Also unclear is whether the reference is to both Canaan and Philistia,[54] or to a city or a region within Philistia bearing the name of Canaan,[55] or to the Philistine region of Canaan.[56] What seems reasonably certain is that Egypt, in spite of its military weakness and isolationism for the two centuries following Shoshenq, did retain at least a weak economic link with Philistia.[57]

---

[47] Redford 1973: 14-15.

[48] See Aharoni 1979: 329-30.

[49] Steindorff 1939.

[50] Steindorff 1939: 33; Tadmor 1961b: 148 n. 24; De Meulenaere in Porten 1981: 43; Ahituv 1984: 85, 155 and n. 439.

[51] Albright in Tadmor 1961b: 150; Porten 1981: 43; Ahituv 1984: 85, 155.

[52] Steindorff 1939: 33; Alt 1952: 164.

[53] Albright in Tadmor 1961b: 150; Tadmor 1961b: 148 n. 34; Ahituv 1984: 85, 155.

[54] Tadmor 1961b: 148 n. 34; Ahituv 1984: 85, 155.

[55] Alt 1952: 164.

[56] Albright in Tadmor 1961b: 150.

[57] Ahituv (1984: 155) has claimed that the Pedeeset inscription is the only occurrence of *plst* as a geographical name referring to the land of Philistia in Egyptian documents, negating the putative references to Philistia from the time of Ramses III (1984: 155 n. 438; *contra* Steindorff 1939: 32). On the

Battles with Israel at Gibbethon

Until the rise of the Neo-Assyrian empire and its conquest of Canaan, which resulted in a flowering of the economic importance of Ekron[58] and its surrounding region[59] at the turn of the seventh century B.C.E., the inland areas of Philistia were the most hard-pressed and bore the brunt of the occasional rivalry between the states of Canaan.[60] The city of Gibbethon, which lay between Gezer and Ekron,[61] was at least twice besieged by Israel (1 Kgs 15:27; 16:15-17), while Gath was to prove an object of Judean desire (2 Chr 26:6).

Although Macalister could not understand why Gibbethon would have been an object of two Israelite campaigns within the space of a generation,[62] its situation at Tel Malot, presumably near the *Dreiländereck* between Israel, Judah, and Philistia, must have determined its desirability.[63] Located three miles west of Israelite Gezer (1 Kgs 9:15-17), Tel Malot lies five miles north of Ekron, which, although in a state of decline at this time, presumably ruled Gibbethon.[64] Thus Gibbethon would have defined the border between Israel and Philistia (Ekron) at the close of the tenth century B.C.E. It may have been either to forge an access to Jaffa and the Mediterranean and the trade routes that passed by there, or to provide a buffer zone west of Gezer, or to control

---

economic influence of Egypt in the post-Shoshenq period in general, including the adoption of hieratic numerals by the Israelites, see Redford 1973: 15.

[58] Gitin 1987: 207-12.

[59] Kelm and Mazar 1989: 46.

[60] See Oded 1979: 237.

[61] Following von Rad (1933: 38) Gibbethon is usually identified with Tel Malot (Tell Melat; grid reference 137140), in spite of the fact that von Rad was working on some now outdated assumptions including the putative location of Ekron. Kallai (1960: 62) viewed the identification of Gibbethon as possible, but not likely. However, Na'aman's argument (1986: 107-08 n. 49) that Tel Malot is too small for a city of such obvious importance as Gibbethon, which he would prefer to find at Ras Abu Hamid, is specious. Much stronger is his attempt to locate the city near a stream on the basis of Sargon's relief of his capture of the site (on the relief see el-Amin 1953: 36-37).

[62] Macalister 1914: 62.

[63] See Eissfeldt 1943: 122-23; Delcor 1966: 1267.

[64] So von Rad 1933: 39, who, however, misidentified Ekron; and Oded 1979: 237.

access from the coast to Gezer and the heartland of the hill country that Israel waged war on Gibbethon.[65]

Although it has been argued that the sieges of Gibbethon were existential issues for the survival of Israel that involved all of the army and/or people, and hence led to the deposition of the ruling monarch owing to his failure in the battle for the site,[66] it would appear most likely that either personal ambition or general dissatisfaction with the ruler's administration led in each case to his assassination. This is not to deny the importance of the siege for the personal prestige of the ruler involved. After all, it has become quasi-traditional in human history to engage in a war in order to divert the attention of the masses from the situation at home. Thus in theory, a military adventure could serve to bolster the position of the ruling regime.

In the first battle at Gibbethon in c. 903-902 B.C.E.,[67] Nadab the son of Jeroboam I was killed by a certain Baasha of unknown position while actually participating in the siege of the city (1 Kgs 15:27). During the course of the second siege in c. 885, two changes of ruler took place in Israel, both far removed from the site of the battle. First Zimri, one of the commanders of the realm's chariotry, assassinated Elah son of Baasha, while the latter was engaged in a drunken debauchery in his palace at Tirzah (1 Kgs 16:8-14). Zimri's reign, however, was to be short-lived. Within a week Omri, who had been laying siege to Gibbethon, removed his troops from there and besieged

---

[65] In Noth's opinion (1960: 239), the battles at Gibbethon were battles of conquest for the control of either Ekron or Gezer. Von Rad (1933: 40-41) saw in the battles an attempt on Israel's part to secure Gezer from a military threat from ⬚Ekron. Operating under the assumption that the region of Ekron had fallen under the control of the united monarchy, Oded (1979: 239) saw in the attacks on Gibbethon an attempt on the part of Israel to win back a region which it had lost as a result of the split of the kingdom, the invasion of Shoshenq, or the assertion of Philistine independence with the decline of Egypt. Timm (1980: 38, 40) saw in the attacks on Gibbethon an attempt by Israel to cut off the region of Jaffa, which was guarded by the much mightier fortress of Aphek from the south. His reconstruction is made possible by his assumption that the list of Danite towns in Josh 19 does not reflect the extent of the united monarchy's conquests to the west, but rather is a later artificial construct laying claim to territory in Philistine hands subsequent to the events related in 2 Chr 28:18 (see also von Rad 1933: 36-37). Donner (1977: 398) speculated that the impetus for Nadab's siege of Gibbethon (1 Kgs 15:27) was a need to prove his military prowess. See also Herrmann 1981: 201-02.

[66] Thus von Rad 1933: 31, 41; Timm 1980: 27.

[67] If one were to follow Redford's chronology of the reign of Shoshenq, according to which Shoshenq's campaign to Canaan fell in the early part of his reign and Shoshenq died in c. 906 B.C.E. (1973: 10, 13), then the first attack on Gibbethon could be assumed to be in part an attempt by Nadab to encroach upon territory which had at least nominally been under the protection of the recently deceased ruler. Most, however, date Shoshenq's death in the year following his campaign to Canaan (see e.g. Kitchen 1986: 110-11, 287-302), which would then preclude any relationship between the death of Shoshenq and Nadab's strategy.

Tirzah. Seeing himself abandoned, Zimri died in a self-set conflagration (1 Kgs 16:15-20). Before he could become ruler in Zimri's stead, however, Omri still had to overcome the opposition to his assumption of rule by Tibni son of Ginath and his followers (1 Kgs 16:21-22), thus proving that "all Israel" could not possibly have participated in either the battle at Gibbethon or in the election of Omri to the throne. Subsequently Omri was to found a relatively long-lived dynasty in Israel.

In both cases the siege of Gibbethon was abandoned, and hence the Philistine cause must be viewed as victorious. However, the victory was not attributable solely to the perseverance of the city under siege. Internal unrest in Israel worked in favor of Gibbethon, just as it had worked in favor of the Philistines and the peoples subjugated to a greater or a lesser extent by Israel at the time of the split of the united monarchy. The victory, if one may term it such, appears to have been Pyrrhic.[68] It is quite possible that military pressure, of which the sieges of Gibbethon would be examples, from Israel contributed to the well-attested decline of Ekron from the tenth to the eighth centuries B.C.E.[69] Timnah (Tel Batash), which lay in the border region between Ekron and Judah and had most recently been incorporated into the united monarchy, remained unsettled for an extended period of time.[70] On the other hand, concurrent with the decline of the region of Ekron, which faced both Israel and Judah, was the enormous increase in area and importance of Ashdod,[71] a process which one may assume was also operative at Ashkelon and Gaza.

A tension may then be observed in Philistia between the prosperous cities of the coastal plain (Ashdod, Ashkelon, Gaza), which exercised control over the international trade routes, and those of the Shephelah (Ekron, Gath), which were in a state of decline, attributable in part to their situation in an oftentimes hostile border region. The *pax assyriaca* was to help correct the

---

[68] Although formulated from the standpoint of Israel's history, Eissfeldt (1943: 127-28) reached a similar conclusion regarding the outcome of the battles at Gibbethon. In his opinion, the failure of Israel in its endeavor to conquer Gibbethon must also be attributed to the continued relative military might of the Philistine states, a picture not immediately evident in a cursory reading of the biblical text. Kallai (1960: 62) even emphasized the strength of the Philistines in the area of Ekron as shown in the accounts of the battles at Gibbethon. Subsequent excavation at Tel Miqne, however, has shown that any strength the Philistines may have had in this region until the coming of the Assyrians must have been military, since the economic center of Philistine activity had shifted to the coastal cities.

[69] Gitin 1987: 206; 1989: 25.

[70] Kelm 1984-85: 58; Kelm and Mazar 1984: 58, 78; 1989: 41; A. Mazar 1985: 321.

[71] See M. Dothan 1971: 23; 1975: 112; A. Mazar 1990: 532-33.

imbalance, at least for Ekron and its dependencies. It was to come too late for Gath.

Relations with Judah in the Mid-Ninth Century B.C.E.

It is difficult to determine the quality of the relationship between the Philistines and Judah in the period following the dissolution of the united monarchy. It is, however, safe to assume that it took Judah a while to recover from the truncation of its kingdom owing to revolt and Egyptian subjugation, even if the latter was only partial and ephemeral. Judah's weakness, combined with the lingering and undeserved reputation of Egypt under the Bubastides[72] were probably sufficient to guard Philistine territory, with the possible exception of the region bordering on the Judean Shephelah, from any threat from Judah.

The only hint in the biblical text that Judah had an interest in exploiting the Philistines comes in 2 Chr 17:10-11, in which "good" king Jehoshaphat is alleged to have received tribute from some of the Philistines and from the Arabs. If this passage does indeed stem from a historically reliable tradition,[73] then it is not unreasonable to assume that the Philistine tribute received was from one or more of the cities situated on the Philistine-Judean border. It has been suggested that the tribute came from Gath,[74] since it lay on the border and was often a point of conflict between the two nations. However, there is no evidence either to substantiate or to deny this suggestion.

If Judah was indeed able to exercise some form of hegemony over a part of Philistia during the reign of Jehoshaphat, then this was a short-lived exercise. Although a comparison of the accounts of the reigns of Jehoshaphat and his son Jehoram reveals a careful literary structure in which all that was positive in the former's days is negated in the latter's,[75] there may be some kernel of truth to the tradition that the Philistines and the Arabs threw off the Judean yoke during Jehoram's reign. At the least, credence must be given to

---

[72] See Redford 1973: 13-14.

[73] See Williamson 1982: 283; Japhet 1993: 751.

[74] Eissfeldt 1943: 124 n. 2.

[75] See Dillard 1987: 164, 169.

the tradition concerning the revolts of Libnah and Edom. It may be more than coincidence that the revolts of Libnah and Edom are paralleled by those of the Philistines and the Arabs. Once again, it cannot be determined which Philistines revolted. The mention of Libnah, which lay on the Philistine-Judean border, however, makes it appear likely that altercations once again took place in the Shephelah. Libnah, which traditionally belonged to the territory of Judah (Josh 15:42) and was one of the levitical cities (Josh 21:13), may have acted in concert with, have allied itself with, or become a vassal of one of the Philistine states. Oded viewed Libnah as a Philistine city under Judahite rule, in spite of its inclusion in the list of thirty-one Canaanite cities conquered by the Israelites (Josh 12:15).[76] It was, at any rate, an extraordinary occurrence that one of the Israelite cities should bolt from the covenantal community. This has quite rightly been taken as an indication of Judah's extreme weakness at the time.[77] Conversely, it can be taken as an indication of the relative might of Philistia. It seems reasonable to assume that the protection of one of the Philistine cities, possibly Gath,[78] was extended to Libnah, and that that was sufficient to preclude Judah's reclaiming what was historically hers.

Peace between Philistia and Israel

If peace can be defined as the absence of war, then it may be possible to speak of peace between Philistia and Israel in the latter half of the ninth century B.C.E. Although the dearth of information in the text of the Bible may be misleading in this regard, there appear no references to battles between Israel and the Philistines following Omri's abandonment of the siege of Gibbethon in 885 B.C.E. (1 Kgs 16:17). Indeed there are two passages which could lead to the conclusion that Israel and Philistia had come to an accommodation.

Although the account of the sojourn of the Shunammite woman in Philistia during a period of drought in Israel (2 Kgs 8:2-3) could be dismissed as an

---

[76] Oded 1979: 240.

[77] Eissfeldt 1967: 173.

[78] If relatively insignificant Libnah revolted against Judah and freed itself from the latter's rule, it is impossible to conceive of Judah's ruling over Gath, which was the city of the Philistine pentapolis closest to Libnah.

incidental detail of a folk-tale, when taken together with the notice of Ahaziah's inquiry at an Ekronite oracle (2 Kgs 1:2) it assumes new importance. It is, however, the latter reference which is pivotal to this conjecture.

The Philistine assimilation to various aspects of indigenous culture has been well documented.[79] So too in the area of religion the Philistines seem to have adopted the pantheon of Canaan.[80] Although the continued presence of the type of the Ashdoda figurine at Ashdod would indicate the survival of worship of a goddess based on the Mycenean Great Mother,[81] most indicators point to a cult based on Canaanite models.

With the exception of the temple of Ashtaroth (1 Sam 31:10; but see 1 Chr 10:10), presumably at Beth-Shean and, hence, possibly not strictly-speaking Philistine, the biblical textual evidence points to worship of specific male deities in Iron Age II Philistia (Baal and Dagon).[82] It is of interest to note that during this period the archaeological evidence from sites such as Ashdod[83] and Ekron[84] has emphasized the female aspects of the Philistine cult.

It is not surprising that a member of the royal house of Israel, heavily under the influence of the Tyrian Baal cult as transmitted by his (step?) mother Jezebel, would turn to an oracle of Baal. What is unexpected is that Ahaziah, who reigned from c. 851 to 849 B.C.E., would turn to an oracle in Philistine Ekron. This may have been due to a number of factors, including the reputation of the otherwise unknown oracle, as well as its proximity to Israel, thus allowing a speedy response.

This leads to the conjecture that Philistia, like Israel, was under Phoenician influence at this time. It appears, at any rate, that free movement between Philistia and Israel was possible. To a certain extent this may have been due to the mutual threat to the Levant which had been countered just a few short years before, namely the first great Assyrian thrust into the area

---

[79] See e.g. T. Dothan 1982: 1, 296; Brug 1985: 201-05.

[80] T. Dothan 1982: 20-21; Brug 1985: 182-88.

[81] *Ashdod II/III*: 21; M. Dothan 1971: 22; 1975: 109; T. Dothan 1982: 234-37; but see Brug 1985: 185-86.

[82] There are later literary traditions which bear witness to the existence of sanctuaries of both male and female deities among the Philistines. See e.g. 1 Macc 10:83; 11:4; Herodotus I.105; Lucian, *De Dea Syria* 14. M. Dothan found both male and female figurines, including so-called Astarte molds, at Iron II Ashdod (M. Dothan 1967: 184; 1971: 23).

[83] Fragmentary "Ashdoda" figurines; M. Dothan 1967: 184; 1971: 22.

[84] Dedicatory inscriptions to Asherah; see *Biblical Archaeologist* 53 (1990) 232.

under Shalmaneser III. In 853 B.C.E., a coalition of Levantine states had repulsed an attack of Shalmaneser's at Qarqar in Syria. Among the leaders of the coalition was Ahaziah's father, Ahab. Lists of the twelve coalition partners are to be found in Assyrian inscriptions.[85] Although the number of partners may be stylized, there appears to have been very little participation in the coalition by the southern Canaanite states. Egypt sent only a small contingent to the battle,[86] possibly to protect its trading interests with Tyre and the Phoenician coast,[87] while Judah, Moab, Edom, and the Philistine cities are conspicuous by their absence. In the case of Judah and Moab, it has been conjectured that their representation was subsumed under that of Israel, to which they may have stood in a subordinate position at the time.[88] An analogous conjecture has not been made with regard to the Philistine states, although it is not impossible that they also sought to protect their interests with a token show of support for the coalition, either on behalf of Phoenicia or Israel. On the other hand, their lack of interest in events so far to the north cannot be completely ruled out.

Aramean Interlude

After the failure of Shalmaneser to extend his reach into Canaan in a series of campaigns,[89] a new conqueror arose who was, for a time, able to banish worries about far-away Assyria, albeit not to the relief of the Canaanite states.

The Aramean usurper Hazael was to bring the city-state of Damascus to the pinnacle of its power in the latter half of the ninth century B.C.E.[90] During the course of his lengthy reign, he was able to subjugate most of the

---

[85] For translations of Shalmaneser's inscriptions see *ANET* 277-81; *ARAB* 1.200-52; *DOTT* 46-50; *TUAT* 1/4: 360-67.

[86] Redford (1973: 14) has drawn attention to Egypt's duplicitous policy in regard to Assyria and Shalmaneser. Osorkon II sent both a small contingent in support of the coalition and a gift to Shalmaneser.

[87] See Tadmor 1961b; Hallo 1964: 156-62.

[88] Miller and Hayes 1986: 270; Pitard 1987: 131.

[89] See Hallo 1964: 156-62; Hallo and Simpson 1971: 127-29.

[90] On the reign of Hazael see Jepsen 1942: 159-60, 167-68; B. Mazar 1962: 114-15; Pitard 1987: 145-60.

Canaanite states to his south and west, and to stand up against Shalmaneser of Assyria in 841 B.C.E.

Hazael's major thrust to the south came in the latter part of his reign. In 2 Kgs 12:18-19--Eng 12:17-18 it is related how Hazael seized Gath, marched on Jerusalem, and received a heavy tribute from Joash of Judah. In 2 Kgs 13:22-25 allusion is made to Hazael's oppression of Israel throughout the days of Jehoahaz. The G^L plus at 13:22 makes reference to Hazael's capture of the Philistine coast from Aphek to the Mediterranean.[91]

It is generally assumed that the campaign against Gath and Jerusalem and the one in which Hazael captured the northern Philistine coast fall in the same general time frame, if they are not indeed one and the same.[92]

An approximate date for the campaign is arrived at on the basis of a) the synchronism between Hazael, Joash, and Jehoahaz, and b) a presumed date after Joash's twenty-third year, on account of the placement of the passages in the biblical text (see 2 Kgs 12:7--Eng 12:6). Thus a date within the decade c. 815-805 B.C.E. would appear most reasonable.[93] There are some who would advocate a date nearer the beginning of this period, assuming that Hazael took advantage of the change of ruler in Israel, from Jehu to Jehoahaz, to make a play for regional hegemony.[94]

Hazael seems to have moved down the coast, taking the northern coastal plain out of Israelite hands (2 Kgs 13:22 G^L plus), capturing Gath, and proceding inland toward Jerusalem (2 Kgs 12:18-19). While it appears that the first action was detrimental to Israel, and the last was certainly not to Judah's benefit, it is difficult to assess the significance of the attack on Gath.

First the question arises, which Gath is meant. As Kassis has pointed out,[95] Philistine Gath served at various times as a gateway to the Judean hill country and thence to Jerusalem. On the other hand, the reference to the

[91] See above/below p. XXX.

[92] (See e.g. Jepsen 1942: 168.

[93] See e.g. Bright 1981: 255; but see Donner 1977: 413.

[94] On the synchronism of Joash's twenty-third year and Jehoahaz's first see 2 Kgs 13:1; Jepsen 1942: 159; Thiele 1965: 72, 74. For an alternate view see Hayes and Hooker 1988: 44-45. See also Hallo and Simpson 1971: 129. Pitard (1987: 151) has assumed that Israel was "virtually, if not in actuality, a vassal to Aram" following the death of Jehu and the accession of Jehoahaz. In his view, the same could probably be claimed for Judah (1987: 152). See also Jepsen 1942: 167.

[95] Kassis 1965: 261.

northern Philistine coastal plain in the region of Aphek could be used as an indication that northern Gath/Gittaim was the object of Hazael's campaign.[96]

Second, if one assumes that Philistine Gath is the referent, then the question arises, under whose dominion did Gath lie at the time. This is an issue which has been raised practically every time that Gath is mentioned in the post-Davidic period. Did Hazael subjugate the Philistines on his way to threaten Jerusalem?[97] Or did Hazael act as an ally of the Philistines in reclaiming Gath from Judahite control?[98] Whichever scenario one chooses to endorse, the outcome is clear. At least a part of Philistia was subordinate to Aram-Damascus in the late ninth century B.C.E.[99]

Pitard's certainty in including all of Philistia within the borders of a Damascene empire exaggerates the extent of the evidence available for such a conclusion.[100] It is probably safest to concur with Soggin's assessment of the situation,[101] namely that it is most difficult to know just how to evaluate the evidence concerning Gath (and Philistia) in 2 Kgs 12:18-19.

Judah Finds an Outlet to the Sea

Although the date of Hazael's demise is unknown, it probably occurred toward the end of the century. Shortly after his death, his empire fell apart, aided in great part by the appearance of Adad-nirari III,[102] who in the culmination of a series of western campaigns defeated Damascus in 796 B.C.E.[103] Among the tributaries of Adad-nirari after his defeat of Damascus

---

[96] Thus B. Mazar 1954: 230-31; but see Kassis's arguments against this in 1965: 261-64; also Rainey 1975: 73*.

[97] Miller and Hayes 1986: 293.

[98] Eissfeldt 1943: 124; Noth 1960: 238-39; 249; Donner 1977: 394; 1986: 254, 281; Bright 1981: 255 n. 66.

[99] Jepsen (1942: 162 n. 30) assumed that as of the time of Hazael's capture of Gath, Gath was removed from the Philistine pentapolis, which was henceforth to be a loosely constructed league of four cities. Kallai (1960: 67) conjectured that Hazael's raid enabled the Philistines to reassert themselves and to encroach upon territory in Israel which had not previously belonged to them, at any rate, not since the days preceding the united monarchy.

[100] Pitard 1987: 156-58.

[101] Soggin 1984: 214.

[102] See Pitard 1987: 160.

[103] About which see the next chapter and Pitard 1987: 164-67.

are listed the Philistines, along with most of the other peoples of Palestine. This has led to the conjecture that the tributaries were representative of the peoples who had once been subject to Damascus, and who now were paying their respects to their new overlord.[104] The tribute to Adad-nirari can also be viewed as the attempt of the peoples of Palestine, who had been threatened by the regional power of Damascus, to support the anti-Aramean aims of distant Assyria.[105] That Assyria was eventually to become the greatest threat, which they had encountered until then, to the collective autonomies of the petty states of Canaan was to become clear only two generations later.

The second quarter of the eighth century B.C.E. was dominated in Canaan by two long-lived rulers, Jeroboam II of Israel and Uzziah (Azariah) of Judah. Although the question of which one of the two was the dominant personality has not been settled to everyone's satisfaction,[106] it would appear from the evidence of 2 Chr 26 that Uzziah attempted to make himself at least master of southern Palestine.

If the historical kernel behind the deeds that are ascribed to him in Chronicles is to be believed,[107] then it would appear that Uzziah managed to bring many of the Levantine trade routes under his control. He seems to have regained access to the port of Elath and the Red Sea (2 Chr 26:2), thereby gaining access to the southern maritime markets and bisecting the Negeb trade routes from which Judah had at times been excluded. His exercise of control over the Meunites, a beduin people inhabiting the Negeb (2 Chr 26:7-8),[108] would have been a stage in establishing his control over this trade.[109]

Gath once again became an object of contention between Philistia and Judah (2 Chr 26:6).[110] However, this time the Judean push into Philistia did not end with the capture of Gath. Uzziah's aim seems to have been to push on

[104] B. Mazar 1962: 114-15; Katzenstein 1973: 190 n. 115; but see Hallo 1964: 166.

[105] See Jepsen 1942: 169.

[106] Since the collapse of Tadmor's theory of Uzziah as the leader of an anti-Assyrian coalition (1961a), it has most often been argued that Jeroboam was the stronger of the two monarchs.

[107] Miller and Hayes (1986: 311) have speculated that the Chronicler erroneously and deliberately assigned a triumph over Ashdod, Gath, and Jabneh to Uzziah in order to magnify his glory (2 Chr 26:6). In their opinion the deed is more likely to have taken place under Joash or Jeroboam of Israel.

[108] See Tadmor 1972.

[109] On Uzziah's economic policies see Aharoni 1979: 345; and vis-à-vis the Philistines in particular see Delcor 1966: 1268.

[110] *Contra* Tadmor (1961a: 233 n. 3), Kallai (1960: 66-67), and Rinaldi (1963: 227), who were following B. Mazar (1954: 231), there is no reason to doubt the fact that the Gath being referred to in 2 Chr 26:6 is indeed Philistine Gath. See Rainey 1975: 73*.

to the sea, by capturing Ashdod and coastal Jabneh. Judah now had control of the coastal trade route and access to the sea. Rinaldi has proposed that a major aim of Uzziah's Philistine policy was also to gain access to the rich and fertile Philistine coastal plain,[111] thus assuring himself of a venue for his agricultural proclivities (2 Chr 26:10).

The notice in 2 Chr 26:6a about Uzziah's breaching of the walls of Gath, Ashdod, and Jabneh has been taken to indicate that these cities were destroyed.[112] Macalister felt that Hazael's capture of Gath weakened the walls so that Uzziah was able to knock them down with ease.[113] It is, however, patently absurd to assume that the allegedly weakened walls of Gath, or those of any other city for that matter, were left in a state of disrepair for a space of decades. The Bible does not speak of the total destruction of the cities in question, but makes reference solely to the breaching of their walls (presumably as the result of a siege). Thus any attempt to understand Amos 6:2 as a reference to the total destruction of Gath at this time can be considered an example of eisegesis.[114]

At Ashdod, Stratum IX ended with the partial destruction of the fortifications of the lower city in Area M.[115] Additional evidence of destruction in the lower city was also found in Area D, including the small sanctuary of the late ninth and eighth centuries.[116] Since the general date of this destruction is the mid-eighth century B.C.E., it is felt by the excavators that this destruction is to be attributed to Uzziah.[117] Miller and Hayes would presumably attribute it to either Joash or Jeroboam.[118]

Although arguments have been adduced questioning the historical reliability of 2 Chr 26:6b,[119] in which building activity in Philistia is attributed

---

[111] Rinaldi 1963: 227-29. Compare the story of the Shunammite woman who went to escape a famine in Israel by going to Philistia in 2 Kgs 8:2-3.

[112] E.g. Katzenstein 1973: 197 n. 24. See, however, Kalimi (1995: 280-81) who views this notice as a theological construct, which by reversing the breaching of the walls of Jerusalem in the days of Uzziah's father, Amaziah, emphasizes the rewards which accrue to the one who follows God's commandments (at any rate, for as long as he follows them).

[113] Macalister 1914: 62-63.

[114] See also Eissfeldt 1943: 125 n. 4; Delcor 1966: 1268; but see Oded 1979: 240.

[115] Dothan and Porath 1982: 55-56.

[116] *Ashdod II/III* 21; M. Dothan 1967: 184; 1971: 22.

[117] See also A. Mazar 1990: 532.

[118] See above n. 103.

[119] See Appendix A regarding attacks on the use of this passage as a whole as a historical source.

to Uzziah, the search for evidence of such activity has been pursued. Any building activity in northern Philistia dating to the mid-eighth century B.C.E. is thought to be evidence of Uzziah's activity.[120] The evidence is, however, circumstantial at best, particularly in light of our lack of certainty concerning whether and when Uzziah's campaign took place.

It is worthy of note that once again Judah was primarily interested in Gath, which served in this case as the gateway to Ashdod and the coast. It is conceivable that Gath was at this time under the hegemony of Ashdod.[121] Ekron, which like Gath lay in the borderland between Judah and coastal Philistia, seems to have been bypassed and left as an enclave.[122] It appears to have been isolated from the other Philistine states and to have been relatively passive in its relations with Israel and Judah until the arrival of the Assyrians, who were to usher in a new period in the history of the Philistine states, the inception of which is the theme of the following chapter.

---

[120] See Tadmor 1961a: 233 n. 4 and M. Dothan 1977: 890 regarding the Stratum 2 fortress at Tel Mor ascribed to Uzziah; Kelm and Mazar 1982: 33; 1984: 78; ; 1989: 44; Kelm 1984-85: 59; A. Mazar 1985: 321 regarding Uzziah's alleged construction of Stratum III at Tel Batash; and also Gichon 1964: 422.

[121] See Eissfeldt 1943: 124-25 and n. 1; Oded 1979: 237.

[122] See Timm 1980: 33; but see Gitin 1987: 214; 1989: 41, 43.

CHAPTER FOUR

FIRST CONTACTS WITH ASSYRIA

Adad-nirari III

The first known contact between Philistia and Assyria dates to the time of Adad-nirari III.[1]

Turning back about half a century, it is worth noting that none of the Philistine city-states are mentioned as participating in any of the Syro-Palestinian coalitions opposing Shalmaneser III, most significantly at Qarqar in 853 B.C.E. The southern Palestinian states seem not to have been involved in meeting this early Assyrian threat, whether on account of political weakness or disinterest in events taking place so far to the north cannot be determined.[2]

Although Adad-nirari did not campaign in Palestine -- there is no evidence that he ever participated in any activity farther south than Aram-Damascus, he claimed that he caused all of Hatti, Amurru, Tyre and Sidon, Israel, Edom, and Philistia to bow down at his feet and imposed the payment of tribute upon them. It is, however, safe to assume that his scribes were guilty of recording royal hyperbole. Although Adad-nirari claimed that the tribute which he imposed upon these peoples was *madattu*, it is highly unlikely that this was the case, or if it was, its alleged imposition was of extremely short duration. Since *ma(n)dattu* was more correctly a *terminus technicus* for the annual tribute rendered by a vassal to his lord,[3] it is much more likely that the tribute

---

[1] Nimrud Slab inscription lines 13-14, see below pp. XXX.

[2] Tadmor (1961b) has suggested that an Egyptian contingent participated in the battle of Qarqar in reaction to a perceived a threat to its trade relationship with Byblos. See also Elat 1975a: 32.

[3] Postgate 1974: 111-30. According to Postgate, "*madattu* ... is applied strictly only to compulsory payments," yet "the tribute was paid by cities and countries which had been subdued by the Assyrians in war, or had peacefully tendered their submission" (p. 119). I believe that the latter holds true in this case.

rendered by these Levantine states belonged to the category of *biltu*, a general term denoting tribute including one-time payments.[4] The terms *biltu* and *madattu* often appear together as a hendiadys. However, it is likely that in this case there was no sense of a vassal relationship. Since Adad-nirari had broken the power of Aram-Damascus, the dominant state in Syria and Palestine in the latter half of the ninth century B.C.E.,[5] the bringing of tribute to him was probably an attempt by the petty kinglets to the south to curry his favor and buy him off (as some of them had Shalmaneser III[6]), rather than an entering into an enforced relationship with the Assyrian state.[7] Assyria, which was still in its pre-imperialistic[8] pre-Tiglath-pileser III days of campaigning mainly to fill the royal coffers, was probably still too distant to be conceived of as an immediate threat to the interests of the region. The

---

Elat (1977: 15) expands on the discussion of types of tribute. *biltu* and *ma(n/d)dattu*, either alone or paired, referred to tribute of two types: first, to the one time payment at the time of submission to Assyria, and second, to an annual tax imposed on a vassal by Ashur. The verbs used in conjunction with the report of the tribute help to distinguish between the two. In the former case, the king of Assyria "received" (forms of *maḫāru*) the tribute. In the latter case, the king "imposed" or "set" (forms of *kânu*, *emēdu*, *šakānu*) the tribute. Although the verb used in connection with the receipt of tribute in the case under consideration is *ukīn*, it is best to view its usage as braggadocio. As Grayson (1981: 45-46) has written in reference to scribal practice in the Assyrian royal inscriptions: "Any token of friendship and goodwill sent by a neighbouring power is recorded as tribute sent by way of submission as a vassal to the Assyrian king." There is nothing in the literature to indicate any long-term imposition of tribute at this time. The tribute probably represented a one time "protection" payment. After all, even the defeated Mari's tribute was "received" (*amḫur* line 21) by Adad-nirari (see the Saba'a and Tell el-Rimah stelae).

[4] Martin 1936: 13-19. Martin (1936: 16-17) understood the expression *biltu madattu* to be a hendiadys. *CAD* M/1 consistently translates the expression as "tax (and) tribute."

[5] Tadmor 1961a: 241-43.

[6] Elat (1975a: 31-35) attributes the bringing of tribute to Shalmaneser after his eighteenth year to the consequences of the dissolution of the Aramean-Israelite alliance, which led a number of the states south of Aram-Damascus to ally themselves with the power from Mesopotamia against their neighbor.

[7] Shea 1978: 110; Page 1968: 150; Donner 1970: 58 (who points out that fear was the motivating force behind the giving of the tribute, which he classifies as a one time *tāmartu* "Begrüssungsgeschenk" more than as regular tribute); Millard and Tadmor 1973: 64 (who refer to the tribute as free-will gifts in recognition of the overlordship of Adad-nirari); Wiseman in *DOTT* 50 (who refers to the tribute as "gifts and homage to him in recognition of his new power and of his aid against Damascus"); M. Weippert 1992: 59 (who views the tribute as a token of appreciation for Adad-nirari's lessening of the Aramean threat). According to Elat (1977: 16), *tāmartu* was on occasion used interchangeably with *mandattu* during the Sargonid period. Albeit in the period under discussion, *tāmartu* referred to the exceptional one time payment of tribute, while *mandattu* referred to the more moderate yearly payments (Tadmor 1975: 37). Donner (1970: 58) views its use as euphemistic. Lamprichs (1995: 104) has referred to the tribute tendered as an "*Interaktionsmerkmal*." He leaves the question open whether there was any real interaction subsequent to the payment.

[8] Concerning the Neo-Assyrian empire and the development of its imperialistic policies, see Lamprichs 1995.

defeat of Damascus and the placating of Assyria seemed to leave the way open for the local reassertion of power and authority in Palestine.[9]

The Date of Philistine Tribute

The exact dating of this campaign, at the conclusion of which the states of southern Palestine including the region of Philistia payed some sort of tribute, remains problematic, as indeed does the question of the number of campaigns that Adad-nirari waged in Syria. This is due to a number of factors. First, the inscriptions that Adad-nirari left are not annalistic, they are summary inscriptions.[10] Thus, possible telescoping of events and chronology must be reckoned with. Second, our major source for a chronology of the period of Adad-nirari, the Eponym Canon C^b 1, does not seem to mention any campaign against Damascus during his reign.[11] Third, the attempt is made to harmonize the data from the cuneiform sources with the presumed chronology of Jehoash, who is mentioned as a tribute bearer in the Rimah stela.[12]

The key to a solution, although it has given rise to a number of opposed "solutions", is the Eponym Canon. In lines 12-15 are recorded the geographical aims of the campaigns of the years 805-802 B.C.E: Arpad in 805, Hazazu in 804, the enigmatic Ba'li in 803, and the sea in 802. In addition the entry for 796 records Mansuate as the aim (line 21). Arpad and Hazazu are easily located in Syria. Ba'li has not yet been positively identified, although the name is a West-Semitic one. The sea of 802 can be one of three. And Mansuate's identification is still debated. Although Donner feels that a definitive resolution of the issues is unlikely, he certainly does not close the door on speculation.[13]

---

[9] Some feel that the *môsia'* of 2 Kgs 13:5, who saved Israel from the oppression of Aram, was none other than Adad-nirari (e.g. B. Mazar 1962: 115; refer also to his whole discussion of the period on pp. 114-16; see also Cogan and Tadmor 1988: 143 in reference to the various theories which have been advanced concerning the identity of the *môsia'*.

[10] See Lamprichs 1995: 98-100.

[11] Ungnad 1938: 429; Millard 1994: 33-38, 57-58. In Millard's classification Eponym Canon C^b 1 becomes B1, which is subsumed under the heading of "Eponym Chronicles" (Class B) in distinction to the "Eponym Lists" (Class A). See Millard 1994: 4-21, esp. 4-5, 19.

[12] Line 8; Page 1968: 148-49.

[13] Donner 1970: 54-57.

Shea would date the conquest of Damascus and the supposed submission of the states of Syria and Palestine to 805.[14] He arrives at this conclusion through a combining of evidence from six inscriptional sources which have bearing on the reign of Adad-nirari: the Eponym Canon, the Sheikh Hammad stela, a fragment of a stela of similar content first published by Scheil,[15] the Saba'a stela, the Rimah stela, and the Nimrud slab. In essence, what Shea does is to take the reference to a campaign against Arpad in 805, combine that with the accounts of battle against that city and its king, Atarshumki, in the Sheikh Hammad and Scheil inscriptions, assume that these texts are all referring to the same event, and include the information from the Saba'a, Rimah and Nimrud stelae as parts of the same campaign. In this manner, Adad-nirari's claim to have conquered all of Hatti in one year[16] would have been realized in 805. As a consequence of this dating, the traditional range of dates for the first year of Jehoash, from 802 to 798,[17] would have to be raised to 805.

Shea's argument, while very neat and compact, doesn't take a few pieces of information into account. First, if Adad-nirari had already conquered all of Syria in 805,[18] what was the impetus for his subsequent campaigns to the region? If it was to quell insurrection, one would expect graphic accounts of the vengeance wreaked by the Assyrian forces. Second, Shea treats the inscriptions as annals. He doesn't take into account the conflating and telescoping that is usually the hallmark of the summary inscription.[19] Third, his radical redating of the reign of Jehoash, which is plausible only if one were willing to accept the first part of his argument, but loses conviction if one is unwilling to accept his premises regarding Adad-nirari's dates.

Lipinski dates the submission of Damascus to 803, the year of the campaign against Ba'li.[20] First, he identifies Ba'li with the promontory of

---

[14] Shea 1978: 101-13.

[15] The original publication was in *Revue d'assyriologie* 14 (1917) 159-60. A reproduction of Scheil's copy is published in Millard and Tadmor 1973: 60 fig. 1. The ten line fragment is discussed there on pp. 60-61.

[16] Sheikh Hammad line 8, Rimah lines 4-5.

[17] 802: Bright 1981: 256 n. 68 (if one can speak of a recent revision of a tradition of 801 on the basis of the Rimah stela as a new tradition); 798: Thiele 1965: 75, 86, 205; see also M. Weippert 1992: 57.

[18] M. Weippert (1992: 56) views the claim that Adad-nirari conquered all of the western reaches in one year as hyperbole.

[19] Shea (1978: 111) somewhat cavalierly dismisses this as a counter argument.

[20] Lipinski 1971: 88-90.

Rosh Haniqra on the modern-day Israeli-Lebanese border.[21] Then he eliminates the campaign of 802 as a candidate for the final stop of Adad-nirari's "western express." The notation for 802, *ana muḫḫi tâmtim* "to the sea," could refer either to the Mediterranean, in which case it would be the final stop of Adad-nirari's western swing, or to the Persian Gulf, or, following a suggestion of Brinkman's, to the Sealand of Babylon, in which case it would represent a campaign against the Chaldaean tribes.[22] Lipinski clearly favors the latter possibility, which leaves the way open for Adad-nirari to have reached the Mediterranean at Baʻli in 803. Lipinski discounts the possiblity of any later campaign achieving as much as this third consecutive one of Adad-nirari against Syria in 803.

Although his reconstruction is possible, it hinges on two tenuous identifications: first of Baʻli,[23] and then of the Sea.[24] He also discounts the possiblity of the campaign of 796 to Mansuate as a rival for the defeat of Damascus and the receiving of tribute from the kings of Palestine.[25] Finally, in order to allow Baʻli to refer to a geographical feature, Lipinski must claim that the URU determinative which precedes the name of Baʻli is interchangeable with the KUR determinative in the neo-Assyrian period.[26] However, according to Tadmor,[27] this interchange is attested only when KUR stands for *mātu*, not when it stands for *šadû*.

Scholars who want to do as little damage as possible to the accepted date of the accession of Jehoash of Israel tend to date the campaign against Damascus to 802. Thus scholars such as Bright,[28] Jepsen[29] and Soggin[30] use their understanding of the biblical evidence to settle a question of Assyrian

---

[21] Lipinski 1971: 84-85.

[22] Brinkman 1968: 216-17 and n. 1359; Lipinski 1971: 89 and n. 32.

[23] Other suggestions for the location of Baʻli include Baʻalbek, Abila, and Baʻali-sapuna. See Millard and Tadmor 1973: 59 and nn. 12, 13; Pitard 1987: 163 and n. 37; M. Weippert 1992: 50, 56. Lamprichs (1995: 102) has raised the possibility that it lay on the northern border of Israel.

[24] See M. Weippert 1992: 47, 50, who regards the Mediterranean as the only realistic candidate, since he views the campaigns of 805-802 as conjoined, with the aim of reaching the Mediterranean Sea realized at the end (p. 56).

[25] Lipinski 1971: 89-90.

[26] Lipinski 1971: 90.

[27] In Millard and Tadmor 1973: 63 n. 23.

[28] 1981: 256 n. 68.

[29] 1970: 359-61.

[30] 1970: 368.

chronology.[31] The campaign of 802 must have been to the Mediterranean Sea since that conclusion necessitates the least fiddling with the accepted dates of Jehoash. It is possible, but the argument is not conclusive.

Poebel reached a similar conclusion by defining *ana muḫḫi tâmtim* as referring to Tyre, Sidon, Israel, Edom and Philistia, the mainly coastal states as listed in the Nimrud slab inscription.[32] Adad-nirari is then supposed to have forced the submission of Damascus on his way back from Philistia. Obviously then, Poebel's reconstruction depends on an interpretation of the Saba'a stela which has been proven faulty.[33] As shown above, there was no campaign against Philistia, and there is no evidence that Adad-nirari ever advanced farther south than Aram-Damascus.

None of these authors, however, offers an explanation for the absence of Damascus from the Eponym Canon. An absence which is surprising in light of the prominence given to its submission in the Nimrud, Saba'a, and Rimah stelae.

Millard and Tadmor offer a solution to this crux and to the other problems of the text in the following manner:

First, they assume that the campaigns of 805-803 were aimed at the states of northern Syria.[34] Second, they explain the absence of Damascus from the Eponym Canon by assuming that the geographical notations listed there represented neither the aim of the campaign, nor the major foe defeated, but rather represented the location of the Assyrian camp at the turn of the year, when a status report would be sent back to Ashur for inclusion in the yearly eponym entry.[35] Thus they must, third, decide which of the Eponym Canon geographical entries lies closest to Damascus, which was then defeated shortly after the turn of the year. In their opinion, the closest geographical entry in the Canon is Mansuate, which, following Honigman and Hoelscher, they identify with the valley of Massyas or Marsyas, known from Polybius

---

[31] For this dating, see most recently Lemaire 1993: 149*.

[32] Poebel 1943: 83.

[33] Whether or not von Soden would date the campaign to the same year, although it seems likely, he clearly follows Poebel's historical reconstruction in having Adad-nirari campaign in Palestine (his translation of Palastu?), "das er bis zum Süden durchzog" (1954: 90).

[34] Millard and Tadmor 1973: 60. This leaves open the question of the identity of the sea in 802, which could also be tied in with this series of campaigns, if it were indeed the Mediterranean (p. 62), and of the identity of Ba'li, which they assume lies in northern Syria.

[35] Millard and Tadmor 1973: 62.

and Strabo, and presumably located in the Beqaʿ Valley of Lebanon.[36] They thus date the campaign in which Damascus was defeated, and in which the other kings of southern Syria and Palestine, including the Philistines, brought Adad-nirari tribute, to 796.

Although this reconstruction also has its share of "ifs", it is ultimately the most satisfying.[37] First, it has an answer for the supposed discrepancy between the information of the Eponym Canon and the inscriptions of Adad-nirari. Second, the nature of an isolated campaign against Aram-Damascus, in the course of which quite a number of the kings of Hatti accorded honor and tribute to Assyria, fits quite neatly with the notice about a campaign waged *ina ištēt šatti* "during one year"[38] in which these events took place. And third, a date of 796 B.C.E. for the receipt of tribute by Adad-nirari from rulers including the Israelite Jehoash does not necessitate any difficult change in the biblical chronology. We thus can conclude that we have our first fairly certain neo-Assyrian date in Philistine history.[39]

Assyria's relative weakness and lack of expansionist policies during the nearly forty years following Adad-nirari III[40] left the Philistine states subject to the shifting fortunes of their immediate neighbors. As detailed in the last chapter, this was a situation which had prevailed since the mid-tenth century. It was to change quite radically and permanently with the conquests of Tiglath-pileser III.

Tiglath-pileser III and the Methods of Assyrian Imperialism

---

[36] Millard and Tadmor 1973: 63 and n. 21. They leave open the question of whether Mansuate was a city or a region. It appears without a determinative in the Eponym Canon. However in its other occurences in the literature, it appears preceded by URU, except for the one time that it is preceded by KUR. In one other occurence there is a lacuna at the beginning of the name (*Reallexikon der Assyriologie* 2. 427). See also Parpola 1970: 238; and M. Weippert, 1992: 51 pl. 1, who tries to locate the region of Mansuate on a map.

[37] See M. Weippert, 1992: 49-53, who follows Millard and Tadmor and brings additional arguments in favor of such a reconstruction.

[38] Rimah stela line 4; Sheikh Hammad line 8.

[39] On the historical background of Adad-nirari's campaign against Damascus, see M. Weippert 1992: 56-60; Lamprichs 1995: 100-05.

[40] Labat 1967: 44-51; Hallo and Simpson 1971: 130-32; Saggs 1984: 79-84.

Commencing during the latter part of the reign of Adad-nirari III and continuing for the following half century comprising the reigns of his sons Shalmaneser IV, Ashur-dan, and Ashur-nirari, Assyria was forced to postpone its dreams of an ever expanding empire and to assume a defensive posture. The rival kingdom of Urartu,[41] internal revolt, and recurring plague pushed the Assyrian kings out of the west and directed their energies toward keeping that which they felt was indisputably theirs. Freed from the threat from the east, the states of the Mediterranean littoral were able to devote their resources to the localized conflicts and power struggles which had dominated their history up to this point.

All was to change, however, with the accession of Tiglath-pileser III (745-727 B.C.E.) to the throne of Assyria. His advent was to mark a turning point in history not only for Assyria, but for the whole of the ancient Near East.

Attendant upon the disturbances in Calah which marked the end of the reign of Ashur-nirari, Tiglath-pileser, possibly the fourth son of Adad-nirari to sit upon the throne, possibly a usurper, possibly both,[42] assumed power at a time when the fortunes of Assyria were at a nadir. During the course of his reign he laid the groundwork, both military and administrative, as well as economic, that enabled Assyria to become an empire and to rise to its zenith under the Sargonids.

This final point needs to be emphasized. Tiglath-pileser was more than the dreaded conquerer who turned the Assyrian army into the most feared military machine in the ancient Near East.[43] Tiglath-pileser was an able administrator who reorganized the Assyrian bureaucracy, at one and the same time consolidating power in the hands of the king,[44] while using that power to delegate authority to those loyal to the throne in smaller administrative units than had existed previously, when much power had been concentrated in the hands of provincial governors.[45] As shall be seen below in the context of a discussion of Tiglath-pileser's policies vis-à-vis the states of the eastern Mediterranean coast, he also set in place a system whereby the conquered

---

[41] Labat 1967: 44-51; Saggs 1984: 79-82.

[42] See Anspacher 1912: 10, 15; Hallo and Simpson 1971: 132-33; von Soden 1954: 90-91; Tadmor 1981: 26-27.

[43] See Machinist 1983, who argues that fear of Assyria was based not only on acquired experience, but also on information disseminated by Assyrian propagandists intent on weakening the resolve of actual and potential enemies to resist Assyrian expansion.

[44] See Pečírková 1987: 173, 175.

[45] Labat 1967: 56-57; Saggs 1984: 85; von Soden 1954: 91.

territories immediately began contributing to the imperial coffers, thus ensuring the economic viability of the ever expanding empire.[46]

In the formation of his empire, Tiglath-pileser availed himself of two important administrative innovations. The first was to standardize the process whereby conquered states became vassals and provinces. The second was to institute deportation as a method of establishing control over a foreign territory by breaking down local loyalties and thereby weakening the impulse to rebel.[47]

The fledgling Assyrian empire before Tiglath-pileser had at times sought to extend its sphere of influence and put various states into a condition of vassalage. It was left to Tiglath-pileser, however, to formalize the steps leading to the gradual assimilation of vassal states into the Assyrian empire as provinces and to their absorption into the Assyrian body politic as a major method of Assyrian imperialism. Tiglath-pileser was the first Assyrian ruler to incoporate independent territories west of the Euphrates into Assyria proper.[48] Three stages in this process have been identified by Donner:[49]

1. The vassal status as had existed before the time of Tiglath-pileser. The vassal's obligations included payment of an annual tribute and the furnishing of troops to Assyria.

2. At the first sign of defection or disloyalty to Assyria, the tributary obligations of the vassal state were raised. The ruler was deposed and replaced by one of greater supposed fidelity to Assyria. There took place a limited deportation of the upper classes, coupled with a truncation of the vassal's territory.

3. After an anti-Assyrian revolt, the independence of the state would be put to an end, and it would be annexed as an Assyrian province with the attendant foreign administration. Mass deportations from and importations into the new province would work to eliminate its national character and integrate it into the multi-ethnic Assyrian empire.[50]

---

[46] Pečírková (1987: 164) has cautioned against simplistically assuming that economic needs were the sole driving force behind the creation of the Assyrian empire. While they were important both as a motivator and as a sustainer of the imperium, Pečírková seeks additional causes for the formation of the empire in the intersection of political, structural (both external and internal), and geographic factors.

[47] See Lamprichs 1995: 127-29.

[48] See Lamprichs 1995: 117-18, who feels that the ideological groundwork for the imperial expansion under Tiglath-pileser was laid during the reigns of Salmaneser III and Shamshi-adad V.

[49] 1977: 419; 1986: 297-98.

[50] Donner (1977: 42; 1986: 299-300) allows for exceptions to this three stage system, one of the prime examples of which is the Assyrian policies vis-à-vis the Philistine city-states. Pečírková (1987: 164-75)

Indeed, deportation accomplished a number of aims. First, it robbed a conquered people of its leadership, or at any rate reduced the population, usually already decimated by war, rendering it more docile and compliant with Assyrian administration. Second, by deporting people in family units mainly to Assyria, Tiglath-pileser was able to put into place a system from which new generations would arise to repopulate the Assyrian heartland, impoverished by the constant conscription of its population to serve at the forefront of the expanding empire. Third, the newly deported would be dependent for their welfare on the crown and would, therefore, be a source of support and stability for the existing order. Fourth, deportation and mixture of ethnically unrelated peoples gave the Assyrian empire the character of a uniform heterogeneity.[51] As has been pointed out by Garelli,[52] Tiglath-pileser still attempted to integrate deported populations into the Assyrian body politic, in contrast to the later Sargonids. Relying on older traditions Tiglath-pileser and his immediate successors "reckoned/counted [the deportees] as Assyrians."

Tiglath-pileser III and the West

One of Tiglath-pileser's major policy aims was to contain the expansionism of Urartu and to break its monopoly over the lucrative trade routes from Syria and the Mediterranean. To accomplish this aim he spent a goodly portion of his reign campaigning in the west. In the course of a series of campaigns during the years 743-740 and 738 B.C.E., he extended Assyrian control over northern Syria and the Phoenician coast,[53] turning Arpad, Unqi, Simirra, Kullani, and Hatarikka into provinces[54] and exercising control over the trade of Tyre and Sidon. In addition he received the tribute of a number of south

---

prefers to deal with only two administrative distinctions: the vassal and the province. Assyrian policy toward each was determined on an individual basis taking into account the nature and importance of the governed state.

[51] Labat 1967: 57-58; Pečírková 1987: 168-69; von Soden 1954: 91.

[52] 1991: 50.

[53] Hallo and Simpson 1971: 133-36; Labat 1967: 52; Saggs 1984: 87-89; M. Weippert 1973; Oded 1974: 42-45.

[54] Forrer 1919: 49.

Syrian and north Palestinian rulers including Rezin of Damascus and Menahem of Israel.[55]

Unrest fomented by Sarduri of Urartu kept Tiglath-pileser otherwise occupied during the years 737-735.[56] However, the Assyrian administration which he had left in place continued to function in his personal absence. From ND 2715 we learn about a tax revolt in Tyre and Sidon, which the local Assyrian *qēpu* official,[57] Qurdi-Ashur-lamur, had to suppress with force.[58] In that letter he stated (perhaps restated) an Assyrian policy which did not allow the Phoenicians to sell their lumber to either the Philistines or the Egyptians. It would appear unlikely that the primary motive for this prohibition was to express hostile intentions toward the Philistines and the Egyptians, as Saggs[59] has speculated. Far more likely would be reading with Tadmor[60] that the Assyrians simply desired to control and profit from the lucrative southern trade in Phoenicia's most important export. It was this desire to control the valuable trade with Egypt and Arabia that led Tiglath-pileser to invade Philistia as soon as he could in 734 B.C.E.[61]

The Syro-Ephraimite War[62]

Any discussion of Tiglath-pileser's campaigns of 734-732 against Philistia and Damascus is, however, inextricably tied in with discussions of the biblical Syro-Ephraimite war. In its narrow sense, the term "Syro-Ephraimite war" refers to the battle waged by Rezin of Damascus (= Syria) and Pekah of Israel (= Ephraim) against the state of Judah and its king, Ahaz. A number of claims has been made concerning the international importance -- or lack of same -- of the war.

---

[55] See M. Weippert 1973 and 2 Kgs 15:19-20.

[56] Saggs (1955: 146) speculates that this is all that kept Tiglath-pileser from further action in Philistia at this time.

[57] See Na'aman 1979a: 84.

[58] But see Oded's redating of the letter to post-734 in 1974: 48.

[59] 1955: 150 n. 1.

[60] 1966: 88.

[61] See Elat 1978: 28.

[62] The following discussion is based on C. S. Ehrlich 1991.

If it were not for the recovery of the various fragmentary texts from the reign of Tiglath-pileser discussed below[63] over the course of the last century and a quarter, our knowledge of Philistine involvement in the events centering on the years 734-732 B.C.E. would be based solely on 2 Chronicles 28:18, in which we are informed that, during the reign of Ahaz, the Philistines encroached upon Judahite territory in the Shephelah and the Negeb, capturing the towns of Beth-Shemesh, Aijalon, Gederoth, Soco, Timnah, and Gimzo.[64] Although no destruction level at any of these sites has been or can be dated to this period, the excavations of Tel Batash-Timnah have indicated that the material culture of the site in the latter part of the eighth century B.C.E., ending with Sennacherib's destruction of Stratum III in 701, does not reflect Judean patterns. It belongs, rather, to the coastal culture. Hence, A. Mazar[65] has concluded that Timnah was a Philistine city in the latter part of the eighth century.

The Eponym Canon C[b] 1 provides the chronological framework for the period, a campaign *ana māt Pilista* "against Philistia" being recorded for the year 734, and campaigns *ana māt Dimašqa* "against Damascus" being recorded for the two following years. Into this framework must then be put the information which can be gleaned from Tiglath-pileser's extremely fragmentary and only partly preserved inscriptional remains, as well as whatever information can be gleaned from the biblical record.

In the process of determining the relationship of the Philistines to the Syro-Ephraimite war a number of questions must be confronted. First, when was the war fought, by whom, and for what purpose? Second, what was the motivation of Tiglath-pileser's campaign to Gaza in 734 B.C.E.? And third, what relationship did that campaign have to the following two campaigns *ana māt Dimašqa* "against [the land] Damascus"?

The classic reconstruction of the circumstances and events of the Syro-Ephraimite war was published by Begrich in 1929. According to Begrich, a

---

[63] See Appendix B.

[64] For discussions of those biblical texts which definitely do and those which may or may not belong to the period of the Syro-Ephraimite war see Cazelles 1978: 72*; Machinist 1983: 721 n. 5; Thompson 1982: 13-21. Among studies making claims for and against specific texts see Alt 1953: 2. 163-87; Good 1966; Roberts 1985; Schütte 1987; Shaw 1987. See Kallai 1960: 68 for a discussion of the Philistine expansion of 2 Chr 28:18. Regarding the lack of archaeological evidence for a conquest of Timnah (Tel Batash) in the mid eighth century B.C.E., see Kelm and Mazar 1982: 34; 1989: 44. Following Welten (1973: 174-75), Na'aman (1988: 74) has dated the list as a whole to the post-exilic period, partly because in his opinion Ayalon and Gimzo could not have belonged to Ahaz's territory.

[65] 1994: 257-58.

massive anti-Assyrian coalition formed in Palestine and Syria during 737-735 B.C.E., while Tiglath-pileser was occupied in Urartu and Media. This coalition, which also included the Philistine cities, the Arabian tribes under the leadership of Samsi, and Egypt, was headed by Rezin of Damascus. In this situation Ahaz of Judah stood out by virtue of his alignment with Assyria. Thus Rezin of Damascus and Pekah the Israelite usurper attempted to force Judah to join the coalition by violent means, through an attack on Jerusalem and the placing of a puppet, Ben-Tabeel, on the throne. The Philistines and the Edomites would then have been party to the military pressure that the Syro-Ephraimite league put on Judah, since both gained territory at Judah's expense. The Philistines gained the aforementioned cities in the Shephelah and Negeb, the Edomites regained the port of Elath. Begrich thus viewed the campaigns of 734-732 as one entity. In responding to Ahaz's call to him for help, Tiglath-pileser saw an opportunity to bring the western Levant under his control. Also, owing to Ahaz's submission to Tiglath-pileser and his consequent vassal status, an attack on him would have been tantamount to an attack on Assyria itself. The aim of Tiglath-pileser's campaign of 734 "against Philistia" was to isolate Rezin and Pekah from their Egyptian allies. Hanunu's flight to Egypt is adduced as proof of Egypt's passive -- if not active -- involvement in the anti-Assyrian coalition. Once the threat of Egypt had been neutralized, Tiglath-pileser was free to turn his attention to Damascus and Israel, which he attacked from his Philistine base. When Tiglath-pileser was unable to capture Damascus at once, Mitinti of Ashkelon took heart and revolted against Assyrian hegemony in 733, however without success. The inevitable defeat of the coalition came the following year, comprising the obliteration of Damascus, the death of Rezin, the truncating of Israel, and the usurpation of the throne in Samaria by Hoshea, with full Assyrian support.[66]

Opposition to Begrich's reconstruction was first formulated within a year of the appearance of his article by Budde (1930). More recently Oded (1972) has been the most forceful critic of Begrich's classic reconstruction. In essence their argument is that the biblical Syro-Ephraimite war and Tiglath-

---

[66] See Irvine (1990) for a contemporary restatement and reworking of Begrich's theory. On pp. 70-71 Irvine presents his view of Philistine involvement in the Syro-Ephraimite coalition. On pp. 95-109 can be found his discussion of the models of Begrich, Donner, and Oded, as well as a critique of the latter, and his own reconstruction of the events surrounding the Syro-Ephraimite coalition. Irvine's reconstruction of the events depends to a great extent on Hayes' and Hooker's (1988) dating of the reigns of the Judean and Israelite kings (see pp. 73-74), and takes into account neither the previous course of Damascene history nor the implications of his dating on military history (about which see below).

pileser's campaigns of 734-732 have only the coincidence of contemporaneity in common. According to this theory, the causes of the Syro-Ephraimite war are to be found in purely local considerations: a) in the political reassertion of the Levantine states which had suffered on account of Judah's expansionism under Azariah/Uzziah (2 Chr 26:6-7), and b) in the attempt by Rezin to reestablish a Damascene *Grossreich*.[67] The aims of the Syro-Ephraimite league were stymied by the unrelated expansion of Tiglath-pileser's Assyrian empire. The Philistines, along with the Edomites, opportunistically took advantage of Ahaz's problems with the Syro-Ephraimite league to reclaim territory which Uzziah had seized from them (2 Chr 28:17-18). They were never any part of a coalition, whether anti-Assyrian or anti-Judean, and were completely caught off their guard by Tiglath-pileser's sudden push southwards.

Begrich relied too heavily on a non-critical or literal reading of the biblical text, except in the case of 2 Kgs 15:37 which he cavalierly dismissed as evidence.[68] He also evidenced no appreciation of the importance of economics as a factor in determining political policy. As regards the former, major strides have taken place in our understanding of the Hebrew Bible as a most tendentious source for historical reconstruction, one which can only be employed with the utmost caution. No study exemplifies this better for the period of the Syro-Ephraimite war than Thompson's *Situation and Theology*,[69] in which a development in biblical thought regarding the theological significance of the war has been traced through the different sources found in the Bible: Isaiah, the Deuteronomist, the Chronicler, and possibly Hosea.[70]

Budde minimized the complex web of interrelating cause and effect in international politics. An action can have more than one cause, and more than one result. In addition, much of Oded's argument depends on the now questionable identification of Azriyau in Tiglath-pileser's inscriptions and

---

[67] Na'aman (1995) has argued that Rezin's efforts never managed to lead to the establishment of a "Greater Syria" such as had existed under Hazael.

[68] Begrich 1929: 214; followed by Bickert 1987: 361 n. 1 and Ben-Zvi 1990, the latter of whom views 2 Kgs 15:37 as a prophetic and not as an archival text.

[69] = Thompson 1982.

[70] For a detailed critique of Begrich see Budde 1930 and Oded 1972: 153-54. Oded's views are critiqued in Thompson 1982: 107-09. Bickert (1987: 361-66) has also discussed and criticized all of the above. In his reexamination of the evidence for a Syro-Ephraimite war, Bickert has come to the conclusion that there never was a war such as this (1987: 367-84).

Azariah, king of Judah,[71] and on a speculative reconstruction of the status and political importance of Ben-Tabeel.[72]

Many modern scholars would not attribute Tiglath-pileser's *primary* military intervention in southern Palestine to Ahaz's request for aid.[73] Whether or not Tiglath-pileser had a master plan for exercising eventual control over the whole of the fertile crescent up to and including Egypt,[74] he did continuously expand the boundaries of Assyrian control. A war machine such as the Assyrian needed the sustenance that could be obtained only through international trade, and what better way to ensure a steady flow of money into the imperial coffers than by actually controlling that trade. To this end Tiglath-pileser had brought the major trading centers of the Syrian and Lebanese coast under Assyrian control by the year 738. Over the next three years, the unrest fomented in part by Sarduri kept him otherwise occupied; but once that had been brought under control, Tiglath-pileser acted decisively to subjugate the southern half of the eastern Mediterranean littoral.[75] That he had previous designs on the control of the area's trade is indicated by the letter of Qurdi-Ashur-lamur (ND 2715) in which the export of timber from Tyre to the Philistines and Egypt was prohibited. Thus, even during the years when he was occupied in Urartu and Media, Tiglath-pileser tried to isolate

---

[71] For the most persuasively presented argument for the identification of Azariah with Azriyau see Tadmor 1961a. However, Na'aman (1974) has shown that K 6205 = III R 9 #2, which mentions a certain ...yau of Yaudi, does not belong to the time of Tiglath-pileser III and, hence, cannot be identified with the Azriyau known from Tiglath-pileser's annals (Rost line 131). For current speculation regarding the identity of Azriyau and relevant literature see Cogan and Tadmor 1988: 165-66; Tadmor (with Cogan) 1994: 273-274. For a reconstruction of a campaign against a coalition led by Azriyau in 738 B.C.E., see Lamprichs: 1995: 116.

[72] On Ben-Tabeel and the various theories regarding his identification, from prince of Judah to rival king to scion of the royal house of Tyre see Albright 1955; B. Mazar 1957: 236-38; Hallo 1964: 173; Miller and Hayes 1986: 329, 343; Pitard 1987: 184-85 n. 104; Irvine 1990: 299. It should be noted that the standard transciption of Ben-Tabeel's name does not include the Canaanite shift. On the name itself see B. Mazar 1957: 236 and n. 75.

[73] See e.g. Noth 1960: 260; Tadmor 1966: 88; Thompson 1982: 10, 111; and by implication Eph'al 1982: 84; but see Cazelles 1978: 73*; Hallo 1964: 173; Saggs 1984: 85; Irvine 1990: 107-08; Lamprichs 1995: 121. While Na'aman leaves open the number of reasons for Tiglath-pileser's intervention in southern Palestine, he does view the attack on Ahaz, which he dates preceding the campaign of 734, as the immediate cause of the Assyrian advance. The campaign of 734 would then have been to rescue the Assyrians' loyal vassal, since an attack on Ahaz was tantamount to an attack on Assyria itself. See Na'aman 1991: 91-94, 97-98.

[74] As conjectured, for instance, by Anspacher (1912: 47), Noth (1960: 257, 260), and Saggs (1955: 150 and n. 1); but see Tadmor 1966: 87. Irvine (1990: 26) speaks of "Assyria's ongoing effort to control the Eastern Mediterranean Seaboard."

[75] See Oded 1974: 45-47.

the Philistines and Egypt economically from Tyre, their major trading partner to the north.[76]

Gaza and Hanunu

The prominence given to Gaza in the inscriptions of Tiglath-pileser relating the events of 734 B.C.E.[77] suggests that it was the aim of his campaign "against Philistia." The account of the campaign in the inscriptions seems to indicate active resistance to the Assyrian advance north of Philistia,[78] but its silence about the Philistine cities argues that there was no active resistance from them at this time.[79] The inscriptions do not mention any of the Philistine cities until relating the capture of Gaza, abandoned by its ruler Hanunu, who had fled to Egypt.

Gaza, as the southernmost city of the Philistine pentapolis, occupied a special place in the economic structure of the day. It was both the gateway to Egypt for overland trade and the major conduit to the west for the valuable

---

[76] But see Oded 1974: 48.

[77] Irvine (1990: 109) dates the formation of a putative Syro-Ephraimite coalition to the fall of 734 and the reaction of Tiglath-pileser, i.e. his Philistine campaign, to early 733. However, that would appear to mean that the Assyrian army was on the march during the rainy season, a highly unlikely event.

[78] Lines 10-13 of ND 400, which immediately precede the account of the capture of Gaza in lines 14-18, tell of a major battle. Unfortunately, as is so often the case, the names of the site of the engagement and of the Assyrian adversary are missing. This has given rise to rife speculation concerning the identity of the two, particularly of Assyria's foe. Wiseman (1951: 22) sought to place the battle on the northern border of Israel and speculated that line 13 might refer to tribute received from Tyre, Sidon, and Ashkelon. Alt (1953: 2. 155-57) sought the location of the battle, which he also assumed was fought against Israel, near the coast on the way to Philistia, in the Sharon Plain or in the region of Akko (but see Cogan 1974: 98-99 n. 9, who conjectured that Hiram of Tyre may have been a participant in this battle). In 1964 (264) Tadmor placed the battle in the region of Simirra. Thirty years later he speculated that the action was against either Tyre or Israel (Tadmor 1994: 156). However, Tadmor dated the events lines 10-13 to a time subsequent (733-732 B.C.E.) to the campaign against Gaza (734). Katzenstein (1973: 216) assumed that the battle was with either Damascus or Israel, although he rejected Wiseman's suggested interpretation of line 13, proposing instead that the tribute must have come from the defeated country, i.e. either Damascus or Israel.

[79] Although it is always dangerous to argue *e silentio*, the geographical order in the summary inscriptions of Tiglath-pileser III, particularly in the case of ND 400, does not leave much room for additional action in Philistia north of Gaza in 734 B.C.E. (see Alt 1953: 2. 157-59), that is if it is correct to assume that all the events recounted above the dividing line belong to the same campaign. On the other hand, neither the defeat of Mitinti nor the capture of Gezer is known from the summary inscriptions.

spice trade from the Arabian peninsula.[80] By capturing Gaza, Tiglath-pileser had managed to isolate Egypt and control her trade, and to control the Arabian trade routes as well. In a broader light, the capture of the whole eastern Mediterranean coast meant that Tiglath-pileser and Assyria now also controlled the international coastal sea trade.[81]

Hanunu's flight to Egypt in the face of Tiglath-pileser's attack has been interpreted as a sign of Egyptian involvement in an anti-Assyrian coalition.[82] However, this need not necessarily be understood in this manner. First, a call to Egypt for military assistance could have been effected just as well by a diplomatic mission, the sending of an envoy. Second is the fact of Hanunu's submission to Tiglath-pileser and return to Gaza. It would appear that Hanunu's primary reason to flee to Egypt in the face of the Assyrian attack was personal, to "save his skin." If he thought that he could agitate for Egyptian military help in driving the Assyrians out of Gaza, whether or not Gaza and Egypt stood in a formal relationship with each other, he must have been very quickly disabused of that notion. Indeed, we must reckon with a period during which Hanunu negotiated with Tiglath-pileser for his return to Gaza. His reinstatement as ruler of Gaza is an almost unique occurrence,[83] which must have been possible on two counts: First, there must have been some understanding among the Assyrians of Hanunu's position as that of a victim of Assyrian expansionism, not as that of an anti-Assyrian agitator, and thus not a direct enemy to the Assyrian cause (although he later did try to throw off the Assyrian yoke during the reign of Sargon II).[84] Second, and probably more important, the continuity of administration, now subject to

---

[80] On the spice trade and Gaza's importance in it see Van Beek 1960: 76; Groom 1981: 204-13. Concerning the pivotal importance of the Philistine cities to the Assyrian economy as conduits of trade from Egypt, see Elat 1978: 28-34. See also Na'aman 1979a: 85; Eph'al 1982: 87 n. 267. See Eph'al 1982: 15-16 for a discussion of the classical sources that comprise our source of information for the inferred spice trade in the first half of the first millennium B.C.E.

[81] See Otzen 1977-78: 101-02.

[82] E.g. Begrich 1929: 218; Cazelles 1978: 78*; Na'aman 1991: 92-93; Lamprichs 1995: 120-21.

[83] W. T. Pitard has indicated to me in a personal communication that there is no evidence that Adad-nirari III deposed Bir-Hadad, the ruler of Damascus, in 796 B.C.E. (see Pitard 1987: 160-67). There may, therefore, have been a difference in Assyrian policy toward enemies who had not previously been subjugated and were, if convenient, left on the throne and toward those who were rebellious vassals, and who were treated with the infamous Assyrian brutality. See Pečírková 1987: 166 about the consequences of the breaking of the vassal oath as sacrilege.

[84] Thus I would not accept Irvine's (1990: 52) argument that Hannunu was a party to the anti-Assyrian Syro-Ephraimite coalition. Irvine views this supposed agitatory activity as the reason for Tiglath-pileser's harsh treatment of Gaza.

Assyria, allowed for the highest immediate return on the Assyrian "investment".

In the absence of Hanunu, Tiglath-pileser plundered Gaza. Whether or not there was a military encounter there, Tiglath-pileser treated Gaza as a city taken by conquest, despoiling it of gold, silver, property of various types including divine images, and members of the royal family -- perhaps as hostages to ensure Hanunu's good faith, perhaps in order to train his heirs in Assyrian ways in order to ensure a pro-Assyrian ruling house in Gaza after Hanunu -- and erecting there Assyrian royal and divine images.[85] In addition, Tiglath-pileser erected at Gaza an Assyrian *bīt kāri* "custom-house," which indicates a direct Assyrian financial and economic interest in Gaza, and is a direct support for the theory of an economic reason for Tiglath-pileser's campaign of 734.[86]

The implications of these measures have been a source of debate. Although Cogan[87] has claimed not to have included the information in Tiglath-pileser's summary inscriptions about the spoliation of Gaza in his study of the religious and political impositions of the Assyrians, Spieckermann[88] has accorded these passages great import. In accord with Spieckermann, it is possible to apply much of what Cogan has written in general to Gaza's situation.

According to Cogan the spoliation of the divine images of a conquered entity by the Assyrians was to dramatise the abandonment of a country by its gods. The gods were taken away to ensure the acknowledgement of Assyrian suzerainty.[89] Cogan[90] has tentatively suggested taking the erection of Assyrian images, both divine and royal, at Gaza in place of the native images

---

[85] On the spoliation of Gaza's gods and the erection there of Assyrian royal and divine images see Spieckermann 1982: 327-29. Although Cogan (1974: 55 n. 79) does not include the evidence from Tiglath-pileser's campaign to Gaza, his work is essential for understanding the implications of Assyrian religious policy toward conquered nations (see especially pp. 1-60 and Table 1 on pp. 119-21; for a critique of Cogan's conclusions regarding the supposed Assyrian imposition of their cult see Spieckermann 1982: 307-72).

[86] On the institution of the *bīt-kāri* see Elat 1978: 26-28; Irvine 1990: 61; Lewy 1956: 35-51 (including a discussion of *kāru* as an element in town names); Tadmor 1975: 38; Wiseman 1956: 129. Dalley (1985: 46) has speculated that a major reason for both Tiglath-pileser III's and Sargon II's concern with *bīt-kāri*'s in trading contexts with Egypt was to have them serve as the conduits for the acquisition of Nubian horses for their chariotry.

[87] 1974: 55 n. 79.

[88] 1982: 327-29.

[89] Cogan 1974: 40-41.

[90] 1974: 57 n. 79.

as a sign of Gaza's annexation as a province by Tiglath-pileser. In this he
follows a suggested interpretation of ND 400 line 18 by Wiseman.[91] Cogan
would restore the parallel line in III R 10 #2 (*ITP* Summ. 4) to [*itti nišē māt*]
Aššur amnu "I reckoned them as Assyrians."[92] As, however, the treatment of
the text below[93] demonstrates, there are strong arguments for restoring the
text on the basis of ND 400 and ND 4301+ as [^{al}*Hazzutu ana bīt kāri ša māt*]
Aššur amnu "I reckoned [Gaza as an] Assyrian [custom-house]." Thus it is
highly unlikely that Gaza was turned into a province at this time.[94] Indeed
there is no evidence that any Philistine city, with the exception of Ashdod
briefly under Sargon II,[95] became an Assyrian province.[96] It is, however,
worth noting that according to Cogan[97] the erection of Assyrian images did
not imply Assyrian religious imperialism.[98] It was rather a sign of Assyrian
hegemony, with the image of the king serving not as an object of worship, but
as a visible symbol of the new overlord paying homage to the gods who
enabled him to conquer the new territory.[99]

The reason that Spieckermann[100] adduces for Tiglath-pileser's harsh
treatment of Gaza, a treatment more in keeping with that accorded a new
province, is that Gaza was to serve as an example for and a warning to Egypt
to avoid involving herself in the Assyrian affairs in Palestine. Although this
follows from his conclusion that the neutralization of Egypt was the major

---

[91] 1951: 22.

[92] The translation of this passage is not provided by Cogan, whose restoration of the text follows
Tadmor's 1964 (: 264) translation. Tadmor, however, emphasized that Gaza was not annexed as an
Assyrian province.

[93] See Appendix B, pp. XXX.

[94] See e.g. Spieckermann 1982: 328.

[95] See Alt 1953: 2. 158; Oded 1979: 244.

[96] In retaining their nominal independence for a prolonged period under Assyrian domination in spite of
repeated insurrections, the Philistine and the Phoenician city-states occupied a pivotal and unique place in
the economic and politic structure of the Assyrian empire. See Pečírková (1987: 165), followed by King
(1989: [8-]10). Also see Elat 1978: 29; Eph'al 1982: 87 and n. 267 (including a discussion of Tiglath-
pileser's exceptional policies regarding the Arab tribes living in border regions); Katzenstein 1973: 212;
Miller and Hayes 1986: 321-22.

[97] 1974: 58-61, 111-12.

[98] See also Thompson 1982: 85; *contra* Spieckermann 1982: 329.

[99] *Contra* Tadmor 1964: 264. On the unusual nature of the erection of an image of the Assyrian king in
addition to those of the gods in a conquered city, see Tadmor 1994: 177.

[100] 1982: 327-29.

aim of Tiglath-pileser's campaign of 734,[101] a conclusion which is implicitly rejected here, there may be some truth in his claim. Certainly the treatment of Gaza could not have failed to make an impression on both Hanunu and the Egyptians to whom he fled, nor could the subsequent advance to the Brook of Egypt.[102] Otzen[103] has proposed that, in addition to the obvious economic advantages that Assyria was accorded with the conquest of Philistia, the Philistine states were to act as a buffer zone between the Assyrian empire and Egypt. In this he has sought a parallel in David's policy vis-à-vis the Philistine cities, namely that David, like the Assyrian kings, did not annex Philistia, but dominated it as a buffer against Egypt.

The Revolt of Mitinti of Ashkelon

It is in the changeover from 734 to 733 B.C.E. that we have our most direct evidence for the formation of a specifically anti-Assyrian coalition. As a consequence of the Assyrian campaign to Philistia, the states of southern Palestine, including at least Moab, Edom, Ammon, Judah, Ashkelon, and Gaza had rendered tribute[104] and had thus entered into the first stage of vassaldom to Assyria. However, by the time of Tiglath-pileser's campaigns of 733 and 732 against Damascus, Ashkelon was allied with Damascus, Israel, Tyre, and the Arabs under Samsi in a battle against Assyria.

What would allow Mitinti of Ashkelon to undertake such a venture and revolt against his new Assyrian overlord? We might assume that after establishing Assyrian military and economic control over Gaza, including the surrounding desert approaches up to the Brook of Egypt, Tiglath-pileser withdrew the main contingent of his forces to the northern Syrian provinces, perhaps already with the aim of subjugating southern Syrian and north-central Palestine.[105] At the latest at this time, Rezin and Pekah, the leaders of the

---

[101] See also Wiseman 1951: 21; Soggin 1984: 226 about Tiglath-pileser's continuing to the Brook of Egypt.

[102] See Alt 1953: 2. 160-61.

[103] 1977-78: 102-04.

[104] K 3751 = II R 67 lines 10'-12'. The broken name at the end of line 11' ᵐmu-še-x[...] may have been that of the ruler of either Ekron or Ashdod. See Tadmor 1966: 89 and n. 13 (in which read Ashdod for Ashkelon).

[105] Concerning Tiglath-pileser's policies vis-à-vis the Arab tribes on the border between Philistia and Egypt in southwestern Palestine and northeastern Sinai and their importance to Assyrian economic policy,

Syro-Ephraimite league, would have been cognizant of the direct Assyrian threat to their independent existence. Thus, what may have originally been an anti-Judean coalition with the major aim of restoring a lost Aramean hegemony would now have assumed greater urgency as an anti-Assyrian coalition.

It is doubtful whether Tiglath-pileser needed the apparent legal sanction that a putative appeal from his vassal Ahaz (2 Kgs 16:7-9; 2 Chr 28:16, 21) would have given him in order to move against the coalition.[106] More probably it was a combination of factors, including the very fact of such a coalition being formed, probably accompanied by an overt anti-Assyrian action such as the withholding of tribute -- Israel and Damascus who had rendered tribute in 738 are not listed among the tributaries of 734, a desire to rid his flank of the pesky Rezin's delusions of grandeur, and his now realizable dreams of a unified Assyrian empire extending to the very borders with Egypt that led Tiglath-pileser to destroy Damascus and subjugate Palestine.

It would appear that Tiglath-pileser acted decisively against the anti-Assyrian coalition in 733 and 732. First he neutralized the two main coalition partners, Rezin and Pekah, in their capital cities of Damascus and Samaria, and ravaged their lands. He then turned his attention to the minor coalition partners, including Mitinti of Ashkelon, who -- according to the Assyrian records -- had broken his treaty (*ina adêya iḫṭīma*) with Tiglath-pileser and revolted against him.[107] It may have been during the course of this campaign that Gezer was captured. Owing to its inland position, it lay on the route that Tiglath-pileser's army may have traversed from Israel on the way to Ashkelon on the coast.[108] However the possiblity of its capture in the course of the campaign to Gaza cannot be completely ruled out.[109]

---

see Elat 1978: 28-30; Eph'al 1982: 75-100; Na'aman 1979a: 68-70; Tadmor 1972. The Brook of Egypt is generally identified with the Wadi el-Arish (e.g. Alt 1953: 2. 160). In recent years Na'aman (1979a: 74-86) has advocated identifying it with Nahal Besor (Wadi Ghazzeh), which is just south of Gaza (see also Miller and Hayes 1986: 330). Rainey (1982: 131-32) has sought to refute Na'aman's identification of the Brook of Egypt and to offer support once again for an identification with the Wadi el-Arish.

[106] See Tadmor 1966: 88.

[107] Irvine, who views the Philistines as participants in a pre-734 Syro-Ephraimite league, theorizes that Mitinti had *rejoined* the coalition in 733. See Irvine 1990: 71, 299. About the *adê* "oath" and its violations see Cogan 1974: 42-49, Table 2 on pp. 122-25; Tadmor 1975: 42-43; 1982a: 141-52 (who finds that the Assyrians borrowed the whole concept of the *adê* from the west); McCarthy 1978: 106-21; Watanabe 1987: 6-25; Parpola and Watanabe 1988: xv-xxv.

[108] Tadmor 1964: 267 and figure 44; 1966 89 n. 15.

[109] Aharoni 1979: 373 Map 30; Cazelles 1978: 78*.

The Assyrian advance against Mitinti came after a defeat of Rezin, presumably his initial defeat in 733. In the face of this advance, we are told that something happened to Mitinti. Unfortunately, exactly what happened to him is left unclear owing to an inconvenient break in the text after the words *ina miqit* "in an attack of ..." (Rost line 236). Essentially, there have been two restorations proposed for this phrase. The first would read that Mitinti died *ina miqit išāti* "in a conflagration."[110] The second and preferable restoration would restore the phrase to *ina miqit ṭēmi*, translated either as "in desperation" or as "in insanity."[111] What exactly Mitinti did "in desperation" or "in insanity" is open to question. It is usually assumed that he died at this time.[112] However the phrase restored to *ḫatti rāmāni[šu imqussu]* "he feared for his life" in the following line in Lay 72b + 73a "line-endings" (= *ITP* Annal 24) would appear to presuppose the continued existence of Mitinti, at least for a short while.

The Accession of Rukibtu over Ashkelon

After another break, we are informed that a certain Rukibtu became ruler of Ashkelon. Although the text reads that Rukibtu sat himself on the throne (*ūšib*), Luckenbill[113] and Tadmor[114] have both translated the text as "I set," presumably emending the word *ūšib* from the G form to the Š *ušēšib*. In this they would appear to be followed by Kitchen,[115] according to whom Tiglath-pileser enthroned Rukibtu after the subjugation of Ashkelon and deposition of Mitinti.

There is, however, no need to assume scribal error in this instance. In the event of a coup-d'etat, it would make sense for the usurper to seize and to sit on the throne by himself. He then would act quickly to bring the affairs of

---

[110] *ARAB* 1 para. 779; *CAD* M/2 105a. See also Tadmor 1994: 83.

[111] See *AHW* 657b; *ANET* 283; Rost 1893: line 239; Tadmor 1964: 268; 1994: 83; *TUAT* 1/4 373; also see Appendix B.

[112] Eph'al 1982: 24; Macalister 1914: 63; Miller and Hayes 1986: 330; Oded 1979: 242; Oppenheim in *ANET* 283; Tadmor 1964: 268. Tadmor (1994: 83) views both translations as indicative of suicide.

[113] *ARAB* 1 para. 779: "I set."

[114] 1964: 268 הושבתי. But see now Tadmor 1994: 83, who translates "sat."

[115] 1973: 66.

state in order, which in this case consisted of paying tribute to Assyria, presumably the subject of the following lines of text.

An underlying assumption of practically all translators of this text as of the time of G. Smith is that Rukibtu replaced his *father* on the throne.[116] However, there is no direct textual evidence for this assumption.[117] The name of Rukibtu's father is conveniently missing from the text. As in Israel, and unlike Judah, the dynastic principle may not have been universally operative in Philistia. There is, therefore, no need to assume that a son of the deposed king (whether he died, was removed [i.e. killed], or just went crazy[118]) was his successor.

There exist four possibilities for restoring the break after DUMU "son of" in the text. The first, and in essence universally accepted one, is to assume that Rukibtu was the son of Mitinti, thus restoring the text to read either "the son of Mitinti" or "his son." The second would be to assume that Mitinti was followed by his nephew. The third would be to assume that an unknown person, whose name would then be lost in the break, was Rukibtu's father. The fourth, and the one that is proposed here, would be to restore the passage as follows: *Rukibtu mār [lā mammāna] ina* ^{giš}*kussêšu ūšib* "Rukibtu the son of [a nobody] seized (lit. sat upon) his (Mitinti's) throne."[119]

Although Tadmor has pointed out[120] that it would be unprecedented for the Assyrians to have placed the "son of a nobody" on the throne, the basic assumption behind the reconstruction proposed here is that it was *Rukibtu* who seized the throne for himself.[121] He then secured it through the prompt payment of tribute and through the expected obeisance to his new overlord.

---

[116] G. Smith 1876: 284. Smith restored the phrase *Rukibtu mār* [...] in line 237 of Tiglath-pileser's annals to *Rukibtu mār[šu]*. In this he is followed by Borger in *TUAT* 1/4 373. Others have restored the break as *Rukibtu mār* [^{m}*Mitinti*] (*ANET* 283; *ARAB* para. 779; Rost 1893: 1. 38; Tadmor 1964: 268; Irvine 1990: 32-33, 36). Tadmor (1994: 83) has now suggested the possibility that Rukibtu was a *nephew* of Mitinti (i.e. the son of Mitinti's brother).

[117] See the discussion in Appendix B.

[118] Irvine (1990: 36) raises the possibility that Mitinti fled the approach of the Assyrian army. Yet, he admits that that is unlikely in this context.

[119] The phrase *mār lā mammāna* appears in two additional instances in the inscriptions of Tiglath-pileser: in ND 4301+ line 28', and in K 3751 = II R 67 line 15'. For additional attestations of the idiom in Assyrian texts, see *AHW* 601a and *CAD* M/1 200b.

[120] In an oral communication.

[121] Irvine (1990: 36, 299) suspects that the citizens of Ashkelon themselves deposed and executed Mitinti, on account of his disastrous anti-Assyrian policies, and then placed his son on the throne with the purpose of doing obeisance to Tiglath-pileser.

Thus he in effect aided Tiglath-pileser in the latter's effort to subdue the coastal reaches of Palestine leading to the Egyptian border. With his southwestern flank secured, Tiglath-pileser was then free to turn his attention to the rebels in Israel and Damascus, whence he was called away by the outbreak of revolts in Babylon in 732 B.C.E.[122]

Looking ahead one generation, we find that at the time of Sennacherib in 701 B.C.E. the son of Rukibtu was waiting in the wings during the reign of Sidqa, hoping to be installed as representative of the pro-Assyrian party by Sennacherib.[123] Mitinti and Sidqa were anti-Assyrian and were deposed. Rukibtu was the leader of the pro-Assyrian party in Ashkelon, who by seizing the throne, whether in a violent or a peaceful coup, was able to avert a military conquest of his city through subjugation to Assyria. Significantly he gave his son an Assyrian name in honor of his overlord, Sharru-lu-dari, "may the king (live) forever." Yet by the time of Sennacherib, someone else, of unknown parentage, bearing a West-Semitic name was seated on Ashkelon's throne. It was left to Sennacherib to reinstall a member of the family loyal to him as a ruler.[124]

It would be very tempting to find a contemporaneous parallel to this supposed pro-Assyrian coup-d'etat in Ashkelon in the assassination of Pekah of Israel by Hoshea ben Elah (2 Kgs 15:30).[125] In both cases we would have a non-legitimate change of ruler in the face of a grave Assyrian threat. In both cases the deposition of the ruling monarch would signal a change in policy which would ensure the continued existence of at least the capital city of the kingdom, albeit at a very high price in tribute and, in the case of Samaria, in territory.

However, there arises a chronological problem with such a strict historical parallelism. As Borger and Tadmor have shown, Hoshea rendered tribute to Tiglath-pileser in the Babylonian city of Sarrabanu.[126] This would date the tribute to the year 731/730, a year after the fall of Damascus, when Tiglath-

---

[122] See Brinkman 1984: 42-43. Following the suppression of the Babylonian revolts, Tiglath-pileser became the first neo-Assyrian ruler to assume a dual kingship over both Assyria and Babylonia.

[123] See Luckenbill 1924: 30-31 = col. ii lines 65-68.

[124] As Marcus (1977) has shown, it is likely that Sharru-lu-dari was not just installed as king by Sennacherib, but reinstalled.

[125] See Ephal 1982: 26; Tadmor (with Cogan) 1994: 277-78, 281.

[126] Borger and Tadmor 1982: 244-49.

pileser was already involved in his second series of Babylonian campaigns.[127] Hence, the two events were unrelated to each other.

Are we then to assume that Hoshea's coup took place after the Assyrian threat had terminated? What then was the reason for his coup? Unfortunately these questions cannot be answered. On the one hand, it is possible that Tiglath-pileser left a contingent in Palestine for mopping up the last pockets of resistance after the fall of Damascus, while he himself, along with the core of his army, hurried to Babylon. On the other hand, the texts which we know from the ancient world provide only a small window into that world. There may have existed reasons for the deposition of Pekah of which we have no evidence, such as ambition on the part of Hoshea, as well as general dissatisfaction with Pekah's administration.[128]

Summation

It appears, therefore, that there is very little evidence for Philistine participation in the Syro-Ephraimite campaign against Judah.[129] The witness of the Chronicler points to another in an ongoing series of border disputes between Philistia and Judah. The Assyrian texts do not give reason to assume that the Assyrian advance against Gaza and Philistia in 734 B.C.E. was in response to any threat to their interests. It was only in the following year that one of the Philistine cities, namely Ashkelon, made a failed attempt to join a

---

[127] See also Na'aman 1986: 71-74.

[128] See Tadmor (with Cogan) 1994: 278, for additional speculation, and pp. 279-282 for an attempt at reconstructing the sequence of events based on the sources.

[129] The dating of the Syro-Ephraimite war depends upon one's reconstruction of the events leading up to it and its causes. Those who would see in the war an attempt by Rezin of Damascus to extend his hegemony by the placing of a puppet ruler, Ben-Tabeel, on the throne of Judah are more inclined to date the war to the period before 734. Those who would see in the war an attempt to force Ahaz of Judah to join an anti-Assyrian coalition are divided between those who would for various reasons date the war to the period before Tiglath-pileser's campaign to Philistia in 734 and those who would date the coalition's constitution to the period immediately following Tiglath-pileser's campaign to Gaza and subsequent withdrawal to the north. For the former date (pre 734) see Bright 1981: 274; Cazelles 1978: 74*; Hallo and Simpson 1971: 136; Pitard 1987: 186-87; Saggs 1984: 89; Thompson 1982: 111; Na'aman 1991: 93. For the latter date (734/33) see Begrich 1929: 216 (who did not reckon with a withdrawal of Assyrian forces to the north); Donner 1977: 425; Eph'al 1982: 84; Noth 1960: 259; Otzen 1977-78: 101-02; Rost 1893: 1. xxxii; Tadmor 1961a: 264-65; Tadmor and Cogan 1979: 505. The present writer, seeing a development in the so-called Syro-Ephraimite coalition from an originally anti-Judean (pro-Damascene) one into an anti-Assyrian one subsequent to the coming of Tiglath-pileser III into Palestine, would date the coalition's emergence to the years preceding 734.

doomed anti-Assyrian coalition. The result was a foregone conclusion. The Philistine city-states had entered into a vassal relationship with Assyria from which they were unable to extricate themselves until the fall of Assyria, only to fall immediately under the next conquering power. Although in a perpetual state of vassalage as of the time of Tiglath-pileser III,[130] the Philistines were able to retain their semi-independence as a bridge between Asia, Arabia, and Egypt, and to survive economically as long as they managed to ally themselves with the correct power. Their successes and failures in the following centuries are worthy of a study in their own right.

---

[130] Lamprichs (1995: 124-26) speaks of Tiglath-pileser's differentiated policies vis-à-vis the various Philistine city-states, without, however, specifying the quality of the relationship with each independent unit.

APPENDIX A

BIBLICAL SOURCES

Since the area of settlement of the ancient Israelites bordered directly on the Philistine coastal plain, it comes as no surprise that a major source of our knowledge of Philistine history, indeed our only written source for the earliest phases of the period covered here, is the Hebrew Bible. In the following treatment of biblical passages dealing with the Philistines as of the time of their defeat by David, the Masoretic Text (MT) has served as the basis for discussion, with evidence from the ancient versions and the arguments of later commentators drawn in as needed.

Abner Predicts David's Victory over the Philistines: 2 Sam 3:17-18

(17) Abner[1] had taken counsel with[2] the elders of Israel, saying, "You have previously requested[3] David as king[4] over you. (18) Now act!

---

[1] Basing himself on the plene spelling of the name in 1 Sam 14:50, אבינר, McCarter has consistently vocalized the name as Abiner (see McCarter 1980: 254 and *passim* in 1980 and 1984).

[2] On the translation of this phrase as a pluperfect, referring as it does to an action which supposedly took place before that of the immediately preceding verses, see S. R. Driver 1912: 249. This understanding of the temporal context of the passage had been anticipated by Rashi in his comment to the verse. See also H. P. Smith 1899: 277-78. McCarter (1984: 108) has pointed out that among the G traditions only the Lucianic can be construed as reflecting the syntax of a *Vorlage* identical to the MT. His retroversion of G[ABMN] results in a Hebrew *wy'mr 'bnr 'l* "And Abiner said to ..." instead of a literal translation of the MT as "And the word of Abiner was with ..." However, in this case there is no need to assume a *Vorlage* other than the one known from the MT. G[ABMN] may have simply been translating an awkward and unusual Hebrew phrase with a smoother and more common idiom, both in Hebrew and in Greek. The principle of *lectio difficilior* would support the originality of the MT and Lucianic reading.

[3] S. R. Driver (1912: 249) translated the phrase הייתם מבקשים as "have been (continuously) seeking" with reference to his own study on Hebrew tenses (1892: para. 135.5) and to GKC para. 116 r. Regarding the

> For YHWH has spoken concerning David,[5] 'Through David my servant will I redeem[6] my people Israel[7] from the Philistines and from all their enemies.'"

At first glance this passage would seem to be an indicator of the quality of the relationship between the Philistines and the Israelites upon the death of Saul. Abner's reference to a prior oracle regarding David's ability to save Israel from the Philistine threat presupposes continued Philistine pressure upon Israel during the period of David's sole reign over Judah. While this cannot

---

occasional omission of the strong dagesh in the middle radical of the Pi'el and Pu'al conjugations when a shewa appears under it, see GKC para. 52 d.

[4] MT: *lĕmelek*. G βασιλευειν would support a vocalization of *limlōk* "to rule/be king." See also the targumic למהוי מלכא.

[5] MT אל-דוד: For the translation "concerning David" rather than the more literal "to David" see Rashi, KJV, NJV, McCarter 1984: 104. Supportive of viewing the preposition in this phrase as the result of the frequently attested auditory interchange of אל and על is the G περι. Opposed to this understanding would be RSV and H. P. Smith 1899: 278.

[6] Most commentators on the phrase "Through David my servant will I redeem" have corrected the MT ביד דוד עבדי הושיע from the third person singular הושיע to the first person אושיע, taking YHWH as the subject of the verb (see Wellhausen 1871: 159; H. P. Smith 1899: 278; S. R. Driver 1912: 249; Bergsträsser 1929: para. 12 k [note]; McCarter 1984: 108). This reconstruction bases itself on a number of variant Hebrew manuscripts and on the G σωσω. See also the targumic אפרוק. The late twelfth and early thirteenth century exegete David Kimhi (Radak) had already noticed the syntactic problem in the verse, in which the subject is in the first person and the verb in the third, and he speculated that the verb was to be understood as a first person form in parallel with הוציא in Ezek 11:7. Other attempts to understand the verse include A. B. Ehrlich's 1900 (: 189) suggestion that an *'aleph* had been dropped mistakenly from הושיע, thus forming a first person אהושיע in analogy with the third person יהושיע in 1 Sam 17:47 and Ps 116:6 (see GKC para. 53 q). By 1910 (: 279-80), however, Ehrlich had arrived at a different interpretation of the passage. By removing ביד from the text as a dittography and by changing הושיע to יהושיע on the basis of the two aforementioned attestations, he made David the subject of YHWH's oracle of salvation, a parallel to an anointed human instrument of salvation being sought in the person of Saul in 1 Sam 9:16. Hertzberg (1964: 255) has mentioned this possibility as one of two options open to the exegete in understanding this passage, which, following Caspari, he takes to be a conflate text. On the basis of the alleged orthographic similarity between ביד and דוד, he would restore the passage to either ביד עבדי אושיע "by the hand of my servant I will save" or דוד עבדי הושיע "David my servant has saved/is destined to save." Schmidt's more recent attempt (1970) to argue along similar lines has been negated by McCarter (1984: 108). Indeed, there is no need to engage in convoluted rearrangements of the text of this passage. The change of one letter, having as it does versional support, is all that is necessary to understand the verse. McCarter (1984: 108) has transposed the words דוד and עבדי on the basis of the accumulated G evidence. The fact that only Origen follows the order of the MT does give weight to McCarter's argument. Since either word could come first in an appositional relationship (see Mandelkern 1977: 811 b-c), more caution should probably be employed before categorically stating that one of the choices would definitely represent the *Hebraica veritas*, especially in the case of a minor variant such as this.

[7] "my people Israel": Thus MT and G[L]. McCarter has followed the *lectio brevior* as found in G[ABMN] and deleted "my people" from the text.

be categorically gainsaid, Hertzberg[8] has speculated that upon the defeat of Saul and his house at the battle of Gilboa (1 Sam 31; 1 Chr 10), the elders of Israel wished to have David crowned king in his place, only to be thwarted by Saul's relative and chief army commander Abner,[9] who managed to have a puppet, Ishbaal, installed on the throne of Israel. When Abner saw that Ishbaal's cause was lost, he attempted to switch his allegiance to David. As his trump card, he also attempted to bring the northern tribes, represented by the elders and the Benjaminites, into David's camp. His strategy based itself on their supposed original loyalty to David (2 Sam 3:17-19).

It is, however, on this latter point that this theory encounters a crux. The passage 2 Sam 3:17-19 is inserted into a larger unit 2 Sam 3:6-39 whose major aim is to absolve David of any involvement in the murder of Abner.[10] The anticipation, however, in Abner's speech of both David's future conquests of the Philistines and other miscellaneous enemies, as well as[11] the supposed desire of Benjamin, the tribe of Saul, Abner, and Ishbaal, for David to rule over them smacks of the worst sort of *ex post facto* apologetics. This has led most commentators, quite rightly, to view some[12] if not all of the passage as a later Deuteronomistic expansion/insertion.[13] Although the Philistines may very well have been viewed as a major threat to northern Israel's existence at this time,[14] this passage is a thin thread upon which to hang a theory of the Philistines' foreign policy during the years immediately following their victory over Israel at Gilboa.

---

[8] 1964: 260.

[9] Whether Abner was Saul's uncle or cousin is unclear, although the latter would appear to be more likely. See McCarter 1980: 256.

[10] It could be argued that the larger literary unit also includes 2 Sam 4, which strives to absolve David of the subsequent murder of Ishbaal, and 2 Sam 2, which serves as a prelude to the account of David's ascendancy over the house of Saul and rise to the throne over all Israel. According to Gunn's analysis (1982: 63-84), the account of David and Ishbaal, comprising the tale of David's rise to rule over united Israel at the expense of the house of Saul, is to be found in 2 Sam 2:8 (or 12) to 5:3 and includes the Michal narrative in chapter 6.

[11] *Pace* W. Safire *in re* the double emphasis, somewhat reluctantly, in *The New York Times Magazine*, Feb. 11, 1990, p. 20.

[12] According to McCarter (1984: 116) at least v 18b.

[13] H. P. Smith 1899: 278; Gunn 1982: 71-75, who draws a parallel in structure with 2 Sam 5:1-3.

[14] *Contra* Peckham (1976: 230-31), Miller and Hayes (1986: 148).

APPENDIX A

David's Dual Defeat of the Philistines[15]

2 Sam 5:17-25

(17) When the Philistines heard that they had anointed David[16] king[17] over Israel, all the Philistines[18] went up to seek[19] David; but David heard (about it) and went down to the fortress.[20] (18) Then the

---

[15] On the possible allusion to these defeats in Isa 28:21, see Kalimi 1995: 122-124, 173.

[16] "that they had annointed David": On the basis of the G οτι κεχρισται Δαυειδ and the parallel נמשׁח כי דויד in 1 Chr 14:8, McCarter (1984: 151) as well as the RSV and the NJV would all translate the phrase passively (on account of the passive voice in Greek and the supposedly indefinite verb in the Hebrew) as "that David had been anointed." Of course, McCarter is the only one of these who spells out his restoration of the Niph'al in 2 Sam 5:17. The phrasing in the RSV and the NJV could reflect no more than translational technique. While this phrase is arguably less awkward, the phrasing of the MT may be original. Other than the fact that the MT active may, in this case, be considered the *lectio difficilior*, editorial technique in the Book of Samuel would argue for its originality. As many commentators have argued, this account of David's Philistine wars was originally attached to 2 Sam 5:3, the conclusion of the account of David's rise to power over all Israel (see H. P. Smith 1899: 290; 286-87, 290; S. R. Driver 1912: 263; McCarter 1984: 157-58). Subsequently, an account of David's capture of Jerusalem (2 Sam 5:6-16) intruded on the original narrative, preceded by an editorial gloss concerning the length of David's reign (vv 4-5). This rearrangement of the historical order of events has resulted in some faulty juxtapositions which will be treated below. Evidence of the editor's hand is also to be found in the use of a *Wiederaufnahme* in 2 Sam 5:17. In 2 Sam 5:3 it is said that ויבאו כל-זקני ישראל ... וימשחו את-דוד "All the elders of Israel came ... and they anointed David." This act, actively performed by the elders of Israel, is alluded to in the *Wiederaufnahme* in v 17, when "they had anointed David," not when "David was anointed."

[17] As in 2 Sam 3:17 the consonantal text (למלך) may be understood as either a verbal or a nominal form. See Syr, T, G^h.

[18] MT כל-פלשתים. See also G^AB, etc. G^L omits παντες.

[19] As A. B. Ehrlich (1910: 285) has pointed out following Kimhi, the verb "to seek" is not neutral in this case, it implies hostile intent.

[20] The placement of this unit following the unit concerning the capture of Jerusalem would seem to imply that the fortress in question must be "the fortress of Zion" (2 Sam 5:7, 9; OL *ascendit in pontem Sionem*; see also Eissfeldt 1967: 146-47; Garsiel 1975: 43; Kempinski 1981: 63). That this is unlikely was already noticed by Kimhi, who had David go down from Jerusalem to the fortress. Kimhi's observation that one does not "go down" to Jerusalem has found resounding echo among modern commentators (Wellhausen 1871: 165; H. P. Smith 1899: 290; Curtis and Madsen 1910: 209; S. R. Driver 1912: 263; Hertzberg 1964: 273; Grønbaek 1971: 253; McCarter 1984: 153, 158; Kalimi 1995: 19-20 n. 4; but see B. Mazar 1963: 242 n. 12; Aharoni 1979: 293; Kempinski 1981: 63). Thus, assuming that this account belongs chronologically to the time before David's capture of Jerusalem, the common identification of the fortress is that of David's fortress at Adullam (1 Sam 22:1, 4), which is identified with Tell esh-Sheikh Madhkur (map reference 150117; McCarter 1984: 153; Miller and Hayes 1986: 164; Aharoni 1979: 429, who however does not accept the identification in the passage in question; Pritchard 1987: 210). If this identification of the fortress in v 17 is correct, it would make sense for David to go down (from Hebron?) to the fortress at Adullam, and thence to go up to meet the Philistines in the Valley of Rephaim (see S. R.

Philistines came[21] and spread out[22] in the Valley of Rephaim. (19) David inquired of YHWH, saying "Should I go up[23] against the Philistines? Will you give them into my hand?" YHWH answered David, "Go up, for I will surely give the Philistines into your hand."[24] (20) So David came to Baal-Perazim,[25] and David defeated them there.

Driver 1912: 263). Additional weight is given to the identification of the fortress in this verse with the one at Adullam by 2 Sam 23:13-14, in which an incident, probably relating to this campaign, is recounted (see below). Schunck (1983) has sought to argue that the meaning of מצודה in its occurrences in the Saulide and Davidic narratives is not "fortress" (*Festung*), but "hideaway/hideout" (*Schlupfwinkel/Versteck*; see also Grønbaek 1971: 254).

[21] S. R. Driver (1912: 263) advocated a translation in the pluperfect "had come."

[22] As McCarter (1984: 153), following Tidwell (1979: 195-97), has pointed out, the use of the verb וינטשו implies "a dispersal of troops for some purpose," which in this case would be to find David. The use of this verb would argue against a Philistine siege of Jerusalem, or their desire for a major military encounter (as may, however, be implied in the use of ויפשטו in 1 Chr 14:9, 13; see Wellhausen 1871: 165). For a similar use of the verb, see Judg 15:9, in which the Philistines "spread out" to capture Samson. It may be possible to translate the verb as "deployed."

[23] As H. P. Smith (1899: 290) has pointed out, the use of the imagery of going up from the fortress confirms the conclusion reached about the fortress in v 17. McCarter (1984: 153-54) draws attention to the fact that questions posed to oracles could be couched only in terms which would admit either a simple affirmative or a simple negative response.

[24] "my hand ... your hand": Both appear in the singular in the MT, although the NJV translates both occurrences in the plural. With minor exception, the G evidence points to an understanding in the plural.

[25] MT בבעל-פרצים. G reads εκ των επανω διακοπων, which when retroverted to Hebrew would appear to base itself on a consonantal text ממעל-פרצים "above Perazim/the breaches" (see also the OL). Although the MT is followed by all scholars consulted (e.g. Wellhausen 1871: 165; S. R. Driver 1912: 263-64; McCarter 1984: 151), until recently no one had proposed a mechanism to explain the G version. It is possible that, with all the verbs of motion up and down in this passage, a pair of *bet*'s were misread as *mem*'s, possible in light of their alleged similarity in some varieties of the Aramaic hand (see Tov 1981: 198; *contra* F. M. Cross, personal communication). Although it has been traditional to understand the play of words in this verse leading to the etiology of Baal-Perazim as referring to God's overwhelming the Philistines as waters burst forth out of a dam (e.g., KJV: The LORD hath broken forth upon mine enemies before me, as the breach of waters; RSV: The LORD has broken through my enemies before me, like a bursting flood; NJV: The LORD has broken through my enemies before me as waters break through [a dam]; [on this last translation see also Myers 1965: 104]), Hertzberg (1964: 273-74) is undoubtedly correct in his surmise that the reference is to the power of flash floods in the hill country, breaking through and sweeping away all in their path (see also McCarter 1984: 154). Thus the translation given here is obviously poetic, and not literal. It is an attempt to render the imagery as understood by Hertzberg. It is of interest to note that S. R. Driver (1912: 263-64), while probably correct in his understanding of Baal-Perazim as a reference to a local manifestation of Baal (see also Aharoni 1979: 108), conjectured that the actual etymology of the name was derived from a "fountain [which] burst[ ] forth out of the hillside." Albeit, as he also makes clear, by the time of this story, the name Baal-Perazim had been appropriated by the YHWH cult, and the reference to Baal became associated with a story about YHWH, from which the place was then supposed to have derived its name. McCarter (1984: 154), on the other hand, views the name as that of a sanctuary associated with Mount Perazim (Isa 28:21; and with YHWH?). He views the etiology in the verse as secondary and late, translating the "playful etiology" as "Yahweh has burst through (*pāraṣ*) my enemies before me like an outburst (*pereṣ*) of water."

He said,[26] "YHWH has swept away my foes before me like a watery torrent" (lit. "breach"). Therefore he named that place Baal-Perazim (Lord of the Torrents). (21) They (the Philistines) abandoned their idols[27] there; so David and his men carried them away.[28] (22) Once again the Philistines went up and spread out in the Valley of Rephaim. (23) David inquired of YHWH,[29] and he (YHWH) said,[30] "Do not go

---

[26] MT ויאמר שם דוד ויכם. G reads here και εκοπσεν ... εκει και ειπεν Δαυειδ, which would indicate a metathesis of "David" and "he said" in either the MT or the G. McCarter (1984: 151) solves the problem by dropping the name David altogether from the middle of the verse. The eclectic version of 1 Chr 14:11, however, preserves David's name in both positions.

[27] On the basis of the G τους θεους αυτων "their gods," it has become standard to emend the MT עצביהם to אלוהיהם as in the parallel in 1 Chr 14:12 (Wellhausen 1871: 166; H. P. Smith 1899: 290-91; S. R. Driver 1912: 264; McCarter 1984: 151; Tov 1992: 270; Kalimi 1995: 292 n. 53). The fact that this would be the only time in G that θεος would translate Hebrew עצב* strengthens the argument that the G translator had a text in front of him that read אלוהיהם. The change of the text would have been occasioned by the religious sensibilities of the redactor, who could not accept the thought of David making off with foreign gods. The theological implications of אלוהיהם would have been softened through the use of עצביהם. See also Tidwell's remote conjecture (1979: 210-11) that in עצביהם we have a reference not to cultic objects, but to vessels used to carry off spoil.

[28] The thought that David could carry away images of pagan deities has troubled later redactors and traditional commentators. In the parallel in 1 Chr 14:12 (about which see below), David burns the gods; while the Greek manuscripts Mabegiovwzc₂e₂ (largely Lucianic) add the phrase και ειπεν κατακαυσαι αυτους εν πυρι "and he said, 'burn them in fire'" to the end of the verse in 2 Sam 5:21. The Targum also has David order the burning of the idols, an interpretation of the 2 Sam text which is also followed by Rashi and Kimhi. Albeit, the latter attempted to harmonize the traditions by assuming that David was burning the idols until Ittai the Gittite came along and asked him to stop. Thus David was to have both burned the idols and taken them along. Among the moderns, A. B. Ehrlich's conjecture (1900: 196-97) that וישאם implies that David took them to worship them is probably exaggerated. This conjecture on Ehrlich's part led him further to speculate that the second account of a Philistine defeat (2 Sam 5:22-25) was occasioned by God's wish to exhibit his power in single-handedly defeating the Philistines, thus showing David who the true God was. Much more to the point is McCarter's description (1984: 154) of David's capture of the enemy's gods -- which had been brought into battle to ensure victory -- as analogous to the Philistines' capture of the ark of the covenant which the Israelites had brought with them into battle at Ebenezer (1 Sam 4). On the related motif of Assyrian policy vis-à-vis the capture and spoliation of foreign gods, see Cogan 1974: 9-41, 119-21. Cogan (1974: 116-17) further discusses 2 Sam 5:21 as one of the two instances of spoliation of divine images by the Israelites, the other being 2 Chr 25:14-16.

[29] A number of G manuscripts (Magijnv) followed by the Sahidic and Armenian versions add the phrase λεγων ει αναβω προς τους αλλοφυλους και παραδωσεις αυτους εις τας χειρας μου "saying, 'Should I go up against the Philistines and will you give them into my hands" as in v 19. The terse nature of this verse in the MT has been commented upon, both in support of leaving the text as is (A. B. Ehrlich 1910: 285) and in support of restoring missing words to the MT (e.g. Hertzberg 1964: 272).

[30] G^L (boc₂e₂) add αυτω "to him" (= Hebrew לו). The G evidence in general points to the specificity of the subject of the verb, namely κυριος, Hebrew יהוה. If one includes as evidence the parallel phrase from 1 Chr 14:14 ויאמר לו האלהים לא, it is possible to assume a haplography owing to homoiarkton or homophony in the text of Samuel, the scribe's eye or ear jumping from the first לו to the second לא.

up.[31] Circle around[32] behind them[33] and approach them across from the baka-trees.[34] (24) [35] When you hear[36] the sound of rustling[37] in the tops of the baka-trees,[38] then pay attention![39] For then YHWH will be

---

Hertzberg (1964: 272) has conjectured that the haplography was greater, going from the putative first occurrence of the root אמר (לאמר) to the second (ויאמר), thus restoring the text as in v 19.

[31] G adds εις συναντησιν αυτων "to meet them," which has been retroverted to Hebrew לקראתם (see Wellhausen 1871: 166; S. R. Driver 1912: 264). In the juxtaposition of restored לקראתם and the following אל-אחריהם, Wellhausen (1871: 166) saw a justification of the originality of the latter reading in the MT as against G and 1 Chr 14:14 (but see McCarter 1984: 152). Although Wellhausen and S. R. Driver advocated restoring לקראתם to the Hebrew text of Samuel, A. B. Ehrlich (1910: 285) felt that the brevity of the verse made such a restoration unnecessary.

[32] As S. R. Driver (1912: 264) has indicated, the occurrence of the root סבב in the Hiph'il is anomolous. Therefore he proposed dropping the *he* as a dittography of the preceding word's last letter. In this he was followed by H. P. Smith (1899: 291), who added that it may be better to read the word as a Niph'al. Others (e.g. McCarter 1984: 152) leave the word as is.

[33] MT אל-אחריהם. Reading with the G and some Hebrew manuscripts, McCarter (1984: 152) restores the text to מאחריהם (but see Wellhausen 1871: 166).

[34] This last word has been an interpretative crux for centuries. The G κλαυθμωνος "place of weeping" indicates that the Greek translator derived the word from the Hebrew root בכי. Possibly G tried to draw a connection between בכאים and the place name Bochim, known only from Judg 2:1-5 (McCarter 1984: 156). The problem with this theory is that whereas the MT arguably is understanding בכאים as a place name, in the G the addition of the article would indicate that a concrete object is being understood. The Targum, followed by traditional Jewish commentators, understood the reference as being to a type of tree (probably on the basis of the following verse). This understanding is the one that is most often reflected in later translations and in modern scholarship, albeit the exact type of tree has been a subject of intense debate. E.g., KJV: mulberry trees; RSV: balsam trees (see also BDB 113a); Hertzberg (1964: 274): mastic terebinths; more cautiously the NJV and *HALAT* (124a) hedge the issue (pun intended) by translating "*baca*'-trees" and "Baka-Sträucher" respectively. See further McCarter 1984: 155-56. As H. P. Smith (1899: 291) indicated, the word בכאים as stands in the MT is treated as a proper noun. This led S. R. Driver (1912: 264) to propose adding the definite article to the word (בכאים --> הבכאים) on the basis of the G and 1 Chr 14:14. B. Mazar (1963: 242) and McCarter (1984: 155-56) have proposed reading the word as the name of a place, Bechaim or Bachaim.

[35] The unexpected occurrence of the jussive form of the verb ויהי at the beginning of the verse has previously been commented on, both as regards its implausibility (GKC para. 112 z), and as regards its plausibility (S. R. Driver 1892: 121 obs. 3; 1912: 264).

[36] בשמעך: Thus the Kethib. The Qere reads כשמעך.

[37] את-קול צעדה [ה]צעדה MT את-קול צעדה. Most commentators correct the text on the basis of the את particle and 1 Chr 14:15 (Wellhausen 1871: 166; H. P. Smith 1899: 291; S. R. Driver 1912: 264). However, A. B. Ehrlich (1910: 285) proposed reading את-קול צעדי "the sound of my (YHWH's) marching." While McCarter (1984: 152) also restores a *he* at the beginning of the word (citing in addition some Hebrew manuscript traditions), he is unsure about whether to read with the MT, or whether to follow G^MNL (του συνσεισμου) in reading הסערה "the wind." Although he ultimately does decide for the latter, he makes clear that his choice is based on subjective criteria, either reading making sense in context. See also Tov 1981: 203.

[38] את- קול [ה]צעדה בראשי הבכאים. This phrase is normally taken to be a reference to the sound of the wind rustling in the tops of the baka-trees (see e.g. Yeivin 1964: 155), which has been interpreted by the biblical author as that of YHWH and/or the heavenly hosts. However, McCarter has recently proposed a

going forth before you to smite the Philistine camp."[40] (25) Thus David did, just as YHWH instructed him. He defeated the Philistines from Geba[41] until the entrance of Gezer.[42]

Although at first glance it might be assumed that vv 22-25 are a doublet of vv 17-21, McCarter[43] has effectively argued that the similarities in language and imagery in the two accounts are due to the set form of the genre of the battle account, to which they both belong. Indeed, most biblical histories treat the two accounts as seperate incidents in the war between Israel and Philistia.[44]

---

novel interpretation on the basis of the G αλσους/αλσων "groves." Since αλσος is the word usually employed in the G to translate the Hebrew אשרה and related forms, and since the plural form of the word אשרי is an anagram of the word ראשי, McCarter conjectures that the reference in this verse is to a sacred grove located at Bachaim, which was the site of this second Davidic-Philistine encounter. While McCarter marshalls very convincing circumstantial evidence for his conjecture (1984: 156-57), the matter must unfortunately remain that, a conjecture. Although it is quite possible that the redactor of Samuel would have wanted to submerge a reference to a sacred grove in connection with David (as a reference to David's carting away of foreign gods may have been submerged in v 21), the G and the MT are in agreement in understanding בכאים in this verse as a regular noun, and not as a proper noun. It is also of interest to note that this passage is not referred to in the Index of Passages (pp. 91-95) in Olyan's study (1988) of *Asherah and the Cult of Yahweh in Israel*, in spite of the reference to McCarter's aid and advice in Olyan's acknowledgements.

[39] Although תחרץ was translated as "to act with decision" in BDB 358b, since the time of H. P. Smith (1899: 291) it has become traditional to translate the word as a hapax legomenon "look sharp" (see also S. R. Driver 1912: 264; McCarter 1984: 152; *HALAT* 342b "pass auf").

[40] In place of "camp" the G reads εν τω πολεμω "in battle," a common confusion in G between Hebrew מחנה and מלחמה according to McCarter (1984: 152).

[41] In place of "from Geba" the G reads απο Γαβαων "from Gibeon," a reading that along with 1 Chr 14:16 (מגבעון) is preferred by most commentators (e.g. Wellhausen 1871: 166; Grønbaek 1971: 252 n. 107; McCarter 1984: 152-53), owing to Gibeon's location to the northwest of Jerusalem, in distinction to Geba's locations to the northeast. Even though both H. P. Smith (1899: 291) and S. R. Driver (1912: 265) preferred reading Gibeon in this context, they still worried that it lay too far to the north and east to fit comfortably into the geography of this passage as a whole, which led them to assume the existence of a hitherto unknown place named Geba (but see the map in Pritchard 1987: 78). Grønbaek (1971: 252) solved this problem by assuming that the mention of Rephaim in v 22 is the addition of a later redactor of the tradition, who was attempting to tie the two battle accounts together. McCarter (1984: 152-53) has revived a suggestion of Demsky's that Geba may have also been the original name of Gibeon, in which case the MT text of Samuel preserves a most ancient tradition. Segal (1965-66: 33 n. 15), on the other hand, proposed emending the text to מגב "from Gob," by assuming that the 'ayin of the MT מגבע was a dittography from the following word עד.

[42] G[AB] expansionistically read εως της γης Γαζηρα "until the land of Gezer." G[L], following MT, omits της γης.

[43] 1984: 154.

[44] Bright 1981: 198-99; Herrmann 1981: 154; Miller and Hayes 1986: 170; Noth 1960: 187-89; Soggin 1984: 57.

1 Chr 14:8-17

(8) When the Philistines heard that David had been anointed king over all[45] Israel, all the Philistines went up to seek David; but David heard (about it) and went out to face them.[46] (9) Then the Philistines came and made forays[47] in the Valley of Rephaim. (10) David inquired of God,[48] saying "Should I go up against the Philistines[49] and will you give give them into my hand?" YHWH answered him, "Go up, and I will give them into your hand."[50] (11) So he went up[51] to Baal-Perazim, and David defeated them there. David said, "God has swept[52] my foes into my hand like a watery torrent." Therefore he named[53] that place Baal-Perazim. (12) They (the Philistines) abandoned their gods

---

[45] The addition of the word כל "all" in this phrase in Chronicles is ideologically motivated (see Myers 1965a: 107). Showing that elements of all Israel were included in the Davidic covenant and in the Jerusalem cult as of their respective formation was a major historical concern of the Chronicler.

[46] The last phrase reads και εξηλθεν εις απαντησιν αυτοις in G, which has been retroverted as ויצא לקראתם "he went out to meet them" (Rudolph in *BHS ad loc.*). Whether the Greek indicates a different *Vorlage* or is simply an attempt to render the Hebrew text idiomatically, it would appear that this phrase in the Chronicler's tradition is representative of an attempt to understand the somewhat enigmatic וירד אל-המצודה in 2 Sam 5:17 (see above and Curtis and Madsen 1910: 208-09).

[47] ויפשטו: 2 Sam 5:18 reads וינטשו. The variation in Chronicles and Samuel may be due to synonymous parallels (to use Talmon's terminology), a misreading of a *Vorlage* (five of the six consonants in the two words are the same), or the replacement of an unusual expression by a more common one on the part of the Chronicler. Williamson (1982: 117) has raised the possibility that the use of ויפשטו in this verse is a conscious desire on the part of the Chronicler to indicate a reversal of the "stripping" (פשט in the Pi'el) of Saul in 1 Chr 10:8-9. It is worthy of note that the same verb is used of the Philistine encroachments on the Judean Shephelah and Negeb in 2 Chr 28:18.

[48] This is the first of a number of instances in this passage in which Chronicles has exhibited its preference for the generic name "God" over against the personal name "YHWH" (see also 1 Chr 14:11, 14, 15, 16). Kalimi (1995: 292-93) attributes this to a desire to heighten the contrast between the one true God (אלהים) of Israel and the effete gods (אלהיהם) of the Philistines.

[49] Qere: פלשתים. Kethib: פלשתיים.

[50] "my hand ... your hand": As in 2 Sam 5, where MT reads a singular "hand," G reads χειρας in the plural. Japhet (1993: 288) has drawn attention to the linguistic and stylistic characteristics of the Chronicler in this verse.

[51] Thus G singular ανεβη. MT plural ויעלו. See 2 Sam 5:20 ויבא, also in the singular (albeit a different verb). Williamson (1982: 118) finds in the use of "went up" rather than "came" an indication that the Chronicler envisioned Baal-Perazim as a mountain according to Isa 28:21. See also Kalimi 1995: 123. On the other hand, Japhet (1993: 288) has pointed to the use of the root עלה as a *Leitmotiv* in this passage and, hence, views its use in Chronicles as original.

[52] As Williamson (1982: 114) points out, the root פרץ has been made a keyword in 1 Chr 13-16.

[53] Thus G singular εκαλεσεν and 2 Sam 5:20. MT קראו in the plural. Curtis and Madsen (1910: 209) see in the latter part of this verse "a good illustration of abridgment by the Chronicler."

there; so David ordered that they be burned in fire.[54] (13) Once again the Philistines made forays[55] into the valley. (14) Once again[56] David inquired of God, and God said to him, "Do not go up after them. Circle around them[57] and approach them across from the baka-trees.[58] (15) When you hear[59] the sound of rustling in the tops of the baka-trees, then go forth in battle![60] For God will be going before you to smite the Philistine camp." (16) David[61] did just as God instructed him. He defeated[62] the Philistine camp from Gibeon[63] until Gezer. (17) David's

---

[54] Most commentators have remarked on this verse's attempt to make David's disposal of the Philistine gods accord with Deuteronomistic legislation (Deut 7:5, 12; 12:3; see Curtis and Madsen 1910: 209; Williamson 1982: 118-19). Lemke (1965: 351-52) has proposed on the basis of the G versions of the parallel in 2 Samuel that the reading in 1 Chronicles follows a different recension of Samuel "rather than distorting his sources." Whether or not one agrees with Williamson's counter-arguments (1982: 118-19), it is appropriate to conclude with him that the very fact of some such change being made to conform with the Deuteronomic legislation is of paramount importance to the historian of religion. Cogan (1974: 116 and n. 2) has ingeniously suggested that "the parallel account [to 2 Sam 5:21] in 1 Chr 14:12 exonerates David for non-compliance with the laws of *ḥerem* ... by midrashically parsing the verb *wayyiśśā'ēm*, 'carried off,' as 'set fire'" on the basis of the "noun, *maś'ēt*, 'signal-fire.'"

[55] See above v 9. Other than the change in this verb, Chronicles omits two words which appear in 2 Sam 5:22, לעלות "to go up" and רפאים "Rephaim." Williamson (1982: 119) speculates that this is due to the Chronicler's understanding of the passage in the light of Isa 28:21. In the G, εν τη κοιλαδι των γιγαντων appears as a translation of the full phrase בעמק רפאים.

[56] It has been speculated that the occurrence of עוד "once again" represents an emphasis on David's religiously correct action of inquiring of God (see Curtis and Madsen 1910: 209; Williamson 1982: 119). The propensity of this adverb to proliferate in this passage in Chronicles should be noted, as it appears one additional time in the previous verse in G[B].

[57] לא תעלה אחריהם הסב מעליהם. A possibly conflate text. Rudolph in *BHS* suggested restoring פניהם עלה על after תעלה, which he felt had been lost due to homoioteleuton. See also Curtis and Madsen 1910: 210.

[58] G[A] απιων "pear trees," probably also the original reading behind G[BS] αιτιων. Contrast this with the reading αλσους "groves" in 2 Sam 5:24

[59] כשמעך: As the Qere in 2 Samuel.

[60] אז תצא במלחמה: A weak paraphrase of 2 Sam 5:24 according to Curtis and Madsen 1910: 210.

[61] In the G the name only appears in bjmpqtze₂.

[62] Thus G singular επαταξεν and 2 Sam 5:25. MT plural ויכו.

[63] As the discussion of the parallel verse in 2 Samuel above indicated, most scholars prefer reading Gibeon to reading Geba. According to Williamson (1982: 119), however, the reading in 1 Chronicles is yet another instance of Isa 28:21 influencing the Chronicler's account of David's Philistine wars. In this case the Chronicler has misunderstood the reference to Gibeon in Isaiah, in which the reference should be to God's miraculous intervention in battle against the Canaanites in Josh 10, and not to the battle against the Philistines in 1 Chr 14 (see also Kaiser 1974: 255).

fame went forth among all the lands, and YHWH placed fear of him upon all the nations.[64]

The full import of these two parallel passages as a historical source has been discussed in Chapter Two. It is necessary here to make a few comments regarding the place of these passages in the contexts of their respective situations in the Hebrew Bible.

In 2 Samuel the question arises why the narratives about David's defeat of the Philistines have been placed out of historical sequence between the account of the capture of Jerusalem and related matters (2 Sam 5:6-16) and the bringing of the ark to that city (2 Sam 6:1-19). Although the editor of Samuel tried to tie the account of David's Philistine wars to the capture of Jerusalem by means of the word מצודה, it is obvious that the battle of Baal-Perazim at least must have taken place before the capture of Jerusalem, since the impetus for the Philistine attack was David's being crowned king over united Israel, an event which took place while David was still in Hebron (2 Sam 5:1-3).[65]

McCarter[66] has provided a most convincing resolution of the issue. First, following Alt, he views the two accounts of Philistine defeats as deliberate selections from an archive containing additional materials relating to the Philistine wars. The reason for their selection and placement by the Deuteronomistic editor is tied in with their fulfillment of Abner's (Deuteronomistic) prophecy of YHWH's defeat of the Philistines through David's agency (2 Sam 3:18). Therefore these accounts, fulfilling the aforementioned prophecy, were added to the conclusion of the account of David's rise to power. In addition,both of the accounts (vv 17-21 and 22-25) include mention of David's consultation of divine oracles, thus emphasizing the divine hand controlling the historical process. The capture of the Philistine gods would be an explicit reversal of the capture of the ark at the battle of Ebenezer, and the explusion of the Philistines from the Judean hills would

---

[64] This verse provides a summary to David's victories over the Philistines and is found only in Chronicles. It has the added effect of glorifying David's rule and YHWH's part in establishing it (see Curtis and Madsen 1910: 210; Myers 1965a: 107). Williamson (1982: 119) contrasts this summary with the one at the end of the disastrous events recorded in 1 Chr 10:13-14 and sees here another instance of the Chronicler's attempt to tie the two passages in with each other, the latter righting the wrongs of the former.

[65] See e.g. Kalimi 1995: 19-22.

[66] 1984: 157-60.

leave the way free for the transferral of the ark from Kiriath-Jearim to Jerusalem, which forms the subject of the following chapter.

Williamson,[67] following Mosis, has provided a succint explanation of the placement of the accounts in 1 Chronicles. In this book the accounts of David's Philistine wars have intruded upon the narrative of the transfer of the ark to Jerusalem (1 Chr 13-16).[68] After the failed attempt to bring the ark to Jerusalem in the previous chapter, 1 Chr 14 shows what good accrues to those who act in accordance with YHWH's will, specifically to David as the faithful executor of that will. Attention has been drawn above to the recurrence of words in the pericope. It remains only to mention Williamson's attempt to contrast the similar vocabulary of blessings associated with Davidic rule in this chapter with the "exilic" vocabulary of 1 Chr 10, which he accomplishes with varied success.[69]

Obed-Edom the Gittite

2 Sam 6:9-12

(9) David feared YHWH on that day, saying,[70] "How[71] can the ark of YHWH[72] come to me?"[73] (10) So David would not allow the ark of

---

[67] 1982: 113, 116-19. See also Japhet 1993: 283-285.

[68] Williamson (1982: 34) sketches the overall structure of the pericope as follows:

THE TRANSFER OF THE ARK TO JERUSALEM	[1 Chr] 13:1-16:43
The First Attempt to Move the Ark	13:1-14
David Under Blessing	14:1-17
The Successful Completion of the Transfer	15:1-16:43

[69] Instances in which I accept Williamson's arguments are incorporated into the discussion of the individual words. One instance in which I do not agree with Williamson is in his forced contention that the motif of David's taking of the Philistine gods is a literary construct reversing the Philistine's dedication of Saul's armor and head to their gods in 1 Chr 10:10 (1982: 118).

[70] Thus G (λεγων), 4QSam^a (לאמר), 1 Chr 13:12. MT: ויאמר. See also Ulrich 1978: 72, 84, 160, 196; McCarter 1984: 165.

[71] Behind the obvious practical question contained in David's utterance lies an expression of fear (see H. P. Smith 1899: 293, who negates the notion of any underlying practicality). NJV following Smith's interpretation has translated the question idiomatically as "How can I let the ark of the LORD come to me?"

[72] G^abovzc2^e2 η κιβωτος (του) θεου "the ark of God (the holy ark)." At the end of this verse, the Lucianic manuscripts boc₂e₂ also include an additional phrase και ηλθεν η κιβωτος του κυριου (θεου

YHWH[74] to be brought to him, to[75] the City of David.[76] But David had it diverted to the house[77] of Obed-Edom[78] the Gittite.[79] (11) The ark of YHWH remained in the house of Obed-Edom the Gittite for three months, and YHWH blessed Obed-Edom and his whole household.[80] (12) When it was recounted to King David as follows: "YHWH has blessed the house of Obed-Edom and all that is his on

---

oe₂) "and (when) the ark of the Lord (God) came (had come)." This could be construed either as the combination of variants, as a dittography of the foregoing phrase, or -- as is preferred by McCarter (1984: 165, and translation incorporating the plus on p. 161) -- as reflecting the original text, shortened in all other versions by haplography. McCarter (1984: 165) has retroverted the Lucianic tradition into Hebrew as האלהים ויבא ארון יהוה ויבא אלי ארון. The waw at the beginning of the phrase is, however, out of place. It would appear to belong more properly in the word ויבא, making ויבוא as is the orthographic practice in this section.

[73] By translating the text literally, the implication in David's question is "how can the ark be brought to my citadel in Jerusalem?" See Myers 1965a: 101. By translating אלי as "with me" rather than as "to me," McCarter (1984: 160) has put the emphasis on the journey, rather than on the destination.

[74] Thus MT. G την κιβωτον διαθηκης κυριου can be retroverted to את-ארון ברית יהוה "the ark of the covenant of YHWH" and is a frequent G expansion.

[75] MT על. This is an example of the frequently attested אל/על auditory interchange (see Kimhi; S. R. Driver 1912: 268).

[76] As has often been commented on, this refers specifically to the fortress or citadel of Jerusalem (e.g. H. P. Smith 1899: 293; McCarter 1984: 170).

[77] Since David's aim was to bring the ark to his citadel in Jerusalem, Obed-Edom's house could have been anywhere on the route from Kiriath-Jearim to Zion, although a location near or in Jerusalem would appear most likely in view of David's alleged sacrifice of animals every six steps upon the ark's leaving Obed-Edom's dwelling three months later (2 Sam 6:13; Miller and Roberts 1977: 96 n. 157; McCarter 1984: 170), if one views this as a historically accurate tradition. On the other hand, Ps 132:6 may indicate a location nearer Kiriath-Jearim.

[78] The focus of our interest in this passage. The pattern of the name, * 'abd "servant of" and a divine name is well attested in biblical Hebrew (e.g. Obadiah, Abdiel) and in other Semitic languages (H. P. Smith 1899: 293-95; S. R. Driver 1912: 268-69; Albright 1968: 140; McCarter 1984: 170). Although most have interpreted the name in this manner, until the publication of Albright's 1968 study other possibilities for understanding the second element of the name were not completely ruled out (see Wellhausen 1871: 169; S. R. Driver 1912: 268-69). Albright (1968: 140) identified the second element of the name as the name of a consort of the Canaanite god Resheph, Atum or Adum by name. The name appears in the Egyptian New Kingdom Leiden Magical Papyrus V, line 7, in the form 'A-tu-um. As a deity of the underworld, Atum/Adum had a name derived from the word for (red) earth.

[79] The Lucianic recension adds μηνας τρεις "three months" after "the Gittite." McCarter (1984: 165) has explained this as the remnant of a haplography in the recension. After the haplography had been corrected, the words μηνας τρεις were erroneously retained. The restored material is indicated as a Hexaplaric plus in e₂ at the beginning of v 11.

[80] Thus MT and G^A και ευλογησεν κυριος τον Αβεδδαρα και ολον τον οικον αυτου. G^B και ευλογησεν κυριος ολον τον οικον Αβεδδαρα και παντα τα αυτου "and the Lord blessed all the house of Obed-Edom and all which was his" is a phrase which appears in the following verse in MT. McCarter (1984: 165) has attributed this latter version to anticipation of the phrase in v 12.

account of the ark of God," [David said, "Let me return the blessing to my house."[81]] Then David went and had the ark of God[82] brought up from the house of Obed-Edom to the City of David with rejoicing.

1 Chr 13:12-14; 15:24-25

(12) David feared God on that day, saying, "How[83] will I bring myself[84] the ark of God?" (13) So David did not have the ark[85] brought to him, to the City of David, but had it diverted to the house of Obed-Edom the Gittite. (14) The ark of God remained with the household of Obed-Edom, in his house,[86] for three months, and YHWH[87] blessed the house of Obed-Edom and all that was his ... (15:24) Shebeniah, Joshaphat, Nethanel, Amasai, Zechariah, Benaiah, and Eliezer were the priests blowing[88] trumpets before the ark of God, and Obed-Edom and Jehiah[89] were the ark's gatekeepers.[90] (25) David

---

[81] This phrase has been restored on the basis of McCarter's retroversion (1984: 165) of G^L (bgozb₂e₂) και ειπεν δαυειδ επιστρεψω (G^b adds την κιβωτον του θεου και "the ark of God [= holy ark] and") την ευλογιαν εις τον οικον μου. This additional phrase is also preserved in the OL *et dixit David Revocabo benedictionem in domum meam* and is seemingly reflected in Josephus's version of the story (*Antiquities* VII.84; and see Ulrich 1978: 210). Following a suggestion of D. N. Freedman's, McCarter (1984: 165-66) has theorized that the phrase was lost in the MT owing to haplography, the scribe's eye jumping from ויאמר דוד to וילך דוד.

[82] Thus MT. G κυριου would reflect a reading as יהוה. However, the Targum, which McCarter (1984: 166) mentions in support of the latter reading, is of no use here since it consistently and solely employs the phrase ארונא דיי throughout chapter 6.

[83] MT היך. This form of the interrogative adverb appears one additional time in biblical Hebrew, in Dan 10:17. It is a form frequently attested in Aramaic (see Jastrow 1950: 345a).

[84] : G^{BShe}2 place προς εμαυτον at the end of the verse.

[85] "Ark" is omitted in G^S.

[86] The phrase "in his house" is not attested in G, except for G^b (εν τω οικω αυτου). Perhaps an original הגתי "the Gittite" stands behind this obvious corruption (as in 2 Sam 6:11). The redundancy of בביתו may have occasioned the addition of עם earlier in this verse (the change in meaning that this engendered is indicated in the above translation).

[87] Thus MT, G^{be}2 (otherwise ο θεος), and 2 Sam 6:11.

[88] Thus the Qere מחצרים as a Hiph'il participle. Kethib מחצצרים. On this form see GKC paras. 53 o and 55 e; Bergsträsser 1929: paras. 19h n. and 20a; Curtis and Madsen 1910: 217.

[89] MT ויחיה. Japhet (1993: 292, 305) views this as an error for ואחיו "and his brothers."

[90] "Obed-Edom ... gatekeepers": Curtis and Madsen (1910: 217) view this as a repetition and gloss from v 18 (where Jehiah = Jeiel). Conversely, Rudolph in *BHS*; Williamson 1982: 125.

and the elders of Israel and the captains of thousands[91] were the ones going[92] to bring the ark of YHWH's covenant[93] up from the house of Obed-Edom with rejoicing.

The importance of these passages in the present context is in the identification of Obed-Edom as a Gittite from Philistine Gath.[94] As indicated above, this is an acceptable identification, the full historical import of which was discussed above.

Although it has been argued that the longer account of David's transfer of the ark to Jerusalem, in the context of which the sojourn of the ark at the house of Obed-Edom is mentioned, forms the conclusion to -- or is drawn from the same source as -- the ark narrative of 1 Sam 4-6,[95] recent work has indicated that the account of David's transfer of the ark to Jerusalem belongs to the narrative of David's rise to power.[96] The similarities between the two traditions are to be explained by their similar emphasis on the ark, although in 1 Samuel the ark is the main emphasis, while in 2 Samuel it is secondary to the account of David and his rise.

In Chronicles the narrative about the coming of the ark to Jerusalem has been broken up in the middle of its sojourn with Obed-Edom by the account of the blessing that accrues on account of cultic fidelity. In addition much new material has been added, material which seeks to assign the origination of later Temple practice to the period of the ark's ascent to Jerusalem at the time of David.[97]

Summation of Philistine Defeat

[91] "David ... thousands": Another example of the Chronicler's concern to include all Israel in his account (see Williamson 1982: 126).

[92] MT ההלכים. The *he* at the beginning of the word is probably a dittography (Curtis and Madsen 1910: 219; Japhet 1993: 292).

[93] Thus MT and G^AN. G^BSc2 omit κυριου "YHWH." Curtis and Madsen (1910: 218) view the phrase "ark of the covenant of Yahweh" as a typical expression of the Chronicler.

[94] *Pace* Ahituv 1971a: 15.

[95] E.g. Hertzberg 1964: 277.

[96] Miller and Roberts 1977: 23-25; McCarter 1984: 182-84.

[97] See Williamson 1982: 113, 199-22.

2 Sam 8:1

Some time afterwards,[98] David defeated the Philistines and humbled them;[99] and David seized Metheg-Amma from the Philistines.

1 Chr 18:1

Some time afterwards, David defeated the Philistines and humbled them; and he seized Gath and its dependencies from the Philistines.[100]

This passage is of crucial importance in the context of this work both for what it does say, as well as for what is left unsaid. It is clear that David inflicted a defeat on the Philistines, which effectively ended their rivalry with Israel for the control of central Palestine. According to Wagner,[101] the theological import of this act is underlined by the biblical author's use of the root כנע to underline that defeat. However, the lack of mention in this context of Philistine servitude or tribute would serve to indicate a somewhat more autonomous position of the Philistines vis-à-vis the united monarchy and various other subjugated peoples.[102]

Depending upon one's interpretation of 2 Sam 8:1 and 1 Chr 18:1, this latter point may not hold for the region of Gath. It is clear from other passages that there was an unusually close relationship between the united

---

[98] As Hertzberg (1964: 290) has indicated, this introduction betrays the hand of the redactor, who sought to connect this chapter with the previous one. The question of whether this verse should function as the conclusion of the account of David's Philistine victories in 2 Sam 5:17-25 (Hertzberg 1964: 290) or is able to stand on its own as an independent battle tradition (Myers 1965a: 137; McCarter 1984: 247) has yet to be definitively answered.

[99] MT ויכניעם. This verb, meaning "to humble/subjugate" is used in the accounts of David's victories in 2 Sam 8 and 1 Chr 18 only in relation to the Philistines. In reference to David's other victories, we are informed that Moab (2 Sam 8:2; 1 Chr 18:2) and Aram (2 Sam 8:6; 1 Chr 18:6) rendered tribute to him and that they, as well as Edom (2 Sam 8:14; 1 Chr 18:13), became his servants. The lack of notice of the Philistines' entrance into vassaldom may be an indication of the Philistines' unique status vis-à-vis the Davidic empire (but see 2 Sam 8:11-12 and 1 Chr 18:11 in which spoils obtained from the Philistines are reckoned together with that of other conquests). For a discussion of the (theological) import of the root כנע in the Hebrew Bible, see Wagner 1984.

[100] The variation between 2 Sam 8:1 "Metheg-Amma" and 1 Chr 18:1 "Gath and its dependencies" is discussed in detail in Chapter Two.

[101] 1984: 218-19.

[102] See the discussion in Japhet 1993: 345-46.

Israelite monarchy and the city-state of Gath. Whether this was due to David's previous ties to Achish or to a conquest of the city is an issue that begs additional investigation.

David's Tribute From Conquered Peoples

2 Sam 8:11-12

(11) These[103] also King David[104] consecrated for YHWH, along with the silver and the gold which he had consecrated from all the peoples[105] he had defeated: (12) from Edom,[106] Moab,[107] the Ammonites, the Philistines, and Amalek; and from the booty of Hadadezer son of Rehob, king of Zobah.

1 Chr 18:11

(11) These also King David consecrated for YHWH, along with the silver and the gold which he had carried off from all the peoples: from Edom, Moab, the Ammonites, the Philistines, and Amalek.

This short passage is of some interest on account of its grouping of David's major conquests. Unfortunately, very little additional information can be gleaned from this passage. In the light of David's previously mentioned

---

[103] This refers to objects of silver, gold, and bronze brought as tribute to David by Joram son of Toi, king of Hamath (2 Sam 8:10; 1 Chr 18:10).

[104] McCarter (1984: 245), slavishly following G^B in this passage in which David's name is missing, has stricken "David" from this verse only to restore it in his translation in brackets!

[105] G πολεων "cities." A confusion in G probably arising from the graphic similarity between Hebrew הגוים and הערים. See Tov 1981: 200 regardingthe phenomenon of *resh/waw* interchange.

[106] Although printed Bibles read מארם "from Aram," a number of Hebrew manuscripts, the G, the Syriac, and 1 Chr 18:11 all read Edom. This is the reading favored by most modern scholars, especially in light of the frequently attested grouping of Edom, Moab, and Ammon in the biblical text (H. P. Smith 1899: 308; Curtis and Madsen 1910: 236; S. R. Driver 1912: 282; McCarter 1984: 245; *contra* Hertzberg 1964: 289).

[107] G^B expand the text to read εκ γης μωαβ "from the land of Moab."

defeats of the Philistines, it should come as no surprise that there ensued material benefit for the victor, although the present passage does not reveal whether this was in the form of tribute or booty. In addition, the information in this passage may be suspect owing to a redactor's possible expansion of an originally shorter list of place names.

As McCarter[108] has noted, part of the information in this passage contradicts the account of David's sole recorded campaign against the Amalekites in 1 Sam 30, in which David divided the spoil among the Judahites (vv 26-31) as a means of currying favor with them in the eventuality of Saul's imminent defeat at the hands of the Philistines. This would call into question the historical reliability of this passage, whose aim seems to be to whitewash David's treatment of captured booty by assigning a cultically correct course of action to David. Although McCarter[109] assumes that the booty "consecrated" in this passage eventually found its way into the temple treasury at the time of Solomon (1 Kgs 7:51), it may be safer to conclude with H. P. Smith[110] that this passage is a later pro-Davidic insertion into the text.

Ittai and the Gittites: 2 Sam 15:17-22; 18:2a

(17) The king and all of his courtiers[111] went out on foot and stopped at the "farthest house," (18)[112] while all of the people filed by; all the

---

[108] 1984: 251.

[109] 1984: 250.

[110] 1899: 308.

[111] "His courtiers" עבדיו has been transposed here with "people" העם in vv 17-18. In this we are following G[B] over against the MT. In the view of most commentators, it would make more sense for David to leave the city with his personal entourage, his עבדים, and then to take up station and review the passing of the masses following (see Wellhausen 1871: 196; A. B. Ehrlich 1910: 312; S. R. Driver 1912: 313; McCarter 1984: 364; *contra* H. P. Smith 1899: 343-44). A possible explanation for the MT transposition may be found in the graphic similarity of עבדיו and עבדים, which are now to be found in conjunction in v 18. Fokkelman (1981: 179) has remarked on the orderly nature of David's "flight" from Jerusalem in the face of Absalom's threat, from בית המרחק "the last house" of Jerusalem to the Kidron Valley to the Mount of Olives.

[112] The textual history of the G version of vv 17b-18 is quite convoluted. Wellhausen (1871: 195-96) was the first to recognize that G[B] contains the OG translation of the MT passage sandwiched between two later translations (see also S. R. Driver 1912: 312-13; McCarter 1984: 363; Pisano 1984: 130-36). The Lucianic traditions also evidence a conflate text -- albeit only a dual rather than a triple text -- exhibiting haplographic tendencies according to McCarter (1984: 364). Although most of the commentators mentioned above view the G traditions as of little help in restoring the *Hebraica veritas*, McCarter has gone beyond Wellhausen and others in assuming a haplography in the MT, which can be restored on the

Cherethites, all the Pelethites, all the Gittites, six hundred[113] in number who had come on foot[114] from Gath, filed by before the king. (19) Then the king asked Ittai[115] the Gittite, "Why are you also coming with us?[116] Go back and remain with the king, for you are a foreigner and you are also an exile[117] from your place.[118] (20) You have only arrived yesterday, and today I should have you roam[119] with us wherever I may be going? Return and take your brothers back with you. [May

---

basis of G. McCarter's reconstructed "primitive" Hebrew version reads as follows (1984: 363-64): *wyṣ' hmlk wkl 'bdyw brglyw wy'mdw byt hmrḥq wkl h'm 'brym 'l ydw wkl 'sr 'tw wkl hgdlym wkl hgbrym šš m'wt 'yš wyb'w 'l ydw wkl hkrty wkl hplty wkl hgtym 'šr b'w brlgyw mgt 'brym 'l pny hmlk*. It is interesting to observe the opposed treatments this passage received in the same year (1984) at the hands of McCarter and Pisano. McCarter in restoring a longer text went beyond Wellhausen's suggestion to read *haggibbōrîm* in place of *haggittîm* in v 18 and added it along with *haggĕdōlîm* to his text on the basis G^B, while retaining mention of the Gittites. Pisano on the other hand, while working with the shorter text of the OG as identified by Wellhausen, came to the conclusion that the translator of the OG employed common nouns in order to translate Hebrew proper names in this passage and, hence, saw no need to reconstruct any *Vorlage* other than that of the MT. See Wellhausen 1871: 195-97; McCarter 1984: 363-64, 370; Pisano 1984: 130-36. At least both McCarter and Pisano agree on the rejection of attempts to restore the name of Ittai in v 18 (on this restoration see Wellhausen 1871: 196; A. B. Ehrlich 1910: 312; S. R. Driver 1912: 313; Hertzberg 1964: 338). Among the attractive aspects of McCarter's work is his solution to the problem of a contingent of 600 Gittites (an unexpectedly high number in light of the fact that David's personal contingent did not surpass that number; see H. P. Smith 1899: 344 and McCarter 1984: 364, 370, the latter of whom speculates that the number may be in reference to the 600 men who were already following David *before* he became king [1 Sam 23:13; 25:13; 27:2; 30:9]).

[113] See McCarter (1984: 364, 370) for an alternate proposal for the correct placement of the mention of "600 men" in the verse.

[114] Reading ברגליו, following a number of manuscripts as against the MT singular ברגלו. This would bring the text into conformity with vv 16a and 17a (Fokkelman 1981: 454; see also A. B. Ehrlich 1900: 228; 1910: 312).

[115] A name of uncertain origin. Attempts have been made to draw parallels between the name Ittai and Hittite and Hurrian names containing the element *atta-* and *attai-* "father" respectively. Parallels have also been sought in names found in the Amarna correspondence (Itiya, Witiya), Nuzi and Ugarit. If it is a Semitic name, it would be derived from a hypocoristic name of the pattern *'itti/o* + DN "the god X is with me/him." See Delcor 1978: 411-13; McCarter 1984: 370.

[116] MT אתנו. A number of manuscripts read the synonym עמנו. The MT, however, is the preferable variant, since it preserves a play on words in David's questioning of Ittai (*'ittay*): why he is "with us" (*'ittānû*).

[117] MT גלה. McCarter (1984: 364) has proposed reading גלית "you have been exiled" on the basis of the equivalent verbal form in the G.

[118] MT למקומך. Many commentators (e.g. Wellhausen 1871: 197; S. R. Driver 1912: 313) have advocated following the G εκ του τοπου σου and correcting the text to ממקומך. Since, however, the preposition ל can have the meaning "from" in Hebrew, as it can have as well in Ugaritic (see Gordon 1965: 92), it is thus acceptable to leave the text as it is in the MT (see McCarter 1984: 364). Regarding the difficulty of retroverting Greek prepositions into Hebrew, see Tov 1981: 226-27.

[119] Thus the Qere אניעך. Kethib אנועך.

YHWH deal with you][120] mercifully and rightfully." (21) But Ittai answered the king by saying, "As YHWH lives, so may my lord the king live, surely[121] wherever my lord the king is, there shall be your servant, in death or in life!" (22) So the king responded to Ittai, "Go and pass by!" Thereupon Ittai the Gittite and all of his followers, as well as all of the children who were with him, filed by ... (2a) David divided the people into thirds:[122] one third under the command of Joab, one third under the command of Abishai son of Zeruriah, the brother of Joab, and one third under the command of Ittai the Gittite.

This passage provides a fascinating picture of David's relationship with those who chose to follow him. Mercenaries though they were, they evidenced great loyalty to their leader.

Two aspects of this passage in particular have struck commentators. First is David's unselfish concern for those serving him, whatever the fortunes of his personal situation. In the words of H. P. Smith,[123] "David's thoughtfulness for others shows itself in this incident, at a time when he might be excused for consulting his own interest." If this story is meant to serve as an example of David's leadership qualifications, then it succeeds admirably.

Second is the deep and abiding loyalty which David commanded from his followers, in this case ones who had not been in the fold very long.[124] In turn David rewarded Ittai's devotion in the manner that Hertzberg[125] has termed "the way in which a king expresses his thanks" by appointing him, along with

---

[120] This phrase has been restored as ויהוה יעשה עמך on the basis of the G και κυριος ποιησει μετα σου (Wellhausen 1871: 197; H. P. Smith 1899: 344; McCarter 1984: 365; Fokkelman 1981: 180, 454). Even though S. R. Driver (1912: 314) claimed that MT חסד ואמת could stand on its own as an adverbial accusative, he also preferred to follow the G, since the absence of the phrase in the MT is easily explicable as a haplography from one עמך to the next. A. B. Ehrlich's suggestion (1900: 228; 1910: 313) to read חסד ואמת as a valedictory formula, akin to German *auf Wiedersehen* or French *adieu*, has not found resonance.

[121] Thus the Qere כי. Kethib כי-אם. Most scholars follow the Qere since כי-אם in an oath would have a negative connotation (Wellhausen 1871: 197; H. P. Smith 1899: 344; S. R. Driver 1912: 314; McCarter 1984: 365; but see GKC para. 163 d where כי-אם after an oath is cited as an emphatic assurance).

[122] Following G^L και ετρισσευσε and a suggestion originally made by Klostermann (1887: 212; see also H. P. Smith 1899: 357; A. B. Ehrlich 1910: 317; S. R. Driver 1912: 327; Hertzberg 1964: 353; McCarter 1984: 399) we are reading the verb as וישלש rather than as the MT וישלח.

[123] 1899: 343.

[124] Fokkelman (1981: 179-80) has commented on the irony of foreigners, in particular the Gittites, evidencing greater loyalty to David than the Israelites in the Absalom pericope.

[125] 1964: 342.

Joab and Abishai, to the command of one third of his troops in the battle against Absalom.

As Gunn[126] has evaluated the dynamics of the situation: David's offer of freedom for Ittai was countered with Ittai's vow of total devotion; in contrast to David's reference to Absalom as king, for Ittai only David was king. Thus, although the Deuteronomist knows of only one king of Israel at this time, namely David, in his speech to Ittai, David addresses political reality and refers to the current ruler of Jerusalem, Absalom, as king. This places Ittai's great act of loyalty in clearer focus through his acknowledgement of only one king, David, second only to God in his estimation (v 21). Hence, David's selfless act of denial had as its consequence the elevation of the devotee into an instrument of the restoration through his position of command in David's army. For Fokkelman[127] one of the major motifs of this story is the empathy which David, himself a former exile, must have felt with Ittai.[128]

The People Call to Mind David's Defeat of the Philistines: 2 Sam 19:10-11-- Eng 19:9-10

(10) All the people were engaged in an argument[129] among all the tribes of Israel[130] as follows: "The king[131] saved us from the grasp of our enemies[132] and he rescued us from the grasp of the Philistines. But

---

[126] 1982: 101-02.

[127] 1981: 181-82.

[128] For a sensitive literary analysis of the David/Ittai episode, see Fokkelman 1981: 175-83.

[129] MT נדון. This is the only occurrence of the root דין in the Niphʻal. Its exact meaning in this context has been a source of controversy (see S. R. Driver 1912: 334; Conroy 1978: 149; Fokkelman 1981: 458). McCarter (1984: 415) has advocated following the G^LM γογγυζοντες and emending the Hebrew text to נלון "complaining."

[130] Thus the MT šibṭê yiśrā'ēl. McCarter (1984: 419-20), following a suggestion made by Reid in regard to 2 Sam 7:7, has suggested repointing the phrase as šōbṭê yiśrā'ēl and translating "the staff-bearers of Israel."

[131] G adds δαυειδ, a reading which is supported by 4QSamᵃ (Ulrich 1978: 86). It may, however, be simply an explanatory gloss.

[132] "from the grasp of our enemies": The G preserves here a conflate reading εκ χειρος απο παντων των εχθερων ημων which McCarter (1984: 415) uses as the basis for his conjecture that the OG read only απο παντων (= Hebrew מכל "from all") and thus reflects the original text.

now he has had to flee the land on account of Absalom.[133] (11) However, Absalom, whom we anointed over us, has died in battle. Why do you now hesitate to return the king?"[134]

This short passage, a "prelude to [David's] restoration" after Absalom's rebellion,[135] is of interest for two reasons. First, it provides an unfortunately vague *terminus ante quem* for David's defeat of the Philistines in the earlier part of his reign, before the onset of his familial difficulties. Second, it emphasizes the importance of the defeat of the Philistines both in the popular consciousness of Israel and vis-à-vis David's other conquests, which are lumped together in v 10.[136]

Four Philistine Champions Defeated in Individual Combat

2 Sam 21:15-22

(15) Once again there was a battle between the Philistines and Israel. David went down together with his followers and fought with the Philistines. But David grew weary, (16) and [Dodo son of Joash],[137]

---

[133] Thus the MT. G inserts the phrase και απο της βασιλειας αυτου "and from his kingdom" after "the land." This Greek phrase can be retroverted into Hebrew as וּמֵעַל מַמְלַכְתּוֹ. In McCarter's opinion (1984: 415), this represents the OG and original version of the verse, the later Greek versions retaining the original and conflating it with a newer translation of the incorrect Hebrew.

[134] In the G the phrase και το ρημα παντος ισραηλ ηλθεν προς τον βασιλεα appears at the end of this verse (marked with an obelus in c₂). The same phrase appears also at the end of the following verse (with the substitution of λογος for its synonym ρημα) where it translates Hebrew וּדְבַר כָּל־יִשְׂרָאֵל בָּא אֶל־ הַמֶּלֶךְ "the word of all Israel reached the king." It was realized early on (Wellhausen 1871: 204; but see A. B. Ehrlich 1910: 323-24) that the placement of the phrase at the end of v 11 (or between vv 11 and 12) is correct. It has not been indicated in the above translation since it forms the introduction to the following pericope. On the basis of column and line lengths, Ulrich has reconstructed the text of 4QSamᵃ in accordance with the G. See most extensively Pisano 1984: 57-61.

[135] Gunn 1982: 103.

[136] That is unless one is to assume that the "enemies" and the "Philistines" of v 11 stand in apposition to each other and not in opposition.

[137] "[Dodo son of Joash ... overcame him]": Although Pisano (1984: 153) has expressed reservations about employing the G plus of v 11 to correct the MT of v 16, McCarter (1984: 448) is probably correct in his lack of hesitation about so doing. The MT Kethib of the beginning of v 16 reads וַיִּשְׁבּוּ בְנֹב, while the Qere is בְּנֹב וְיִשְׁבִּי, neither of which has ever convincingly been shown to make sense. The Qere has given rise to the existence of a supposed adversary of David named Ishbi-Benob (KJV, RSV, NJV with the

one of the Raphaites, whose helmet[138] weighed three hundred shekels[139] of bronze and who was girded with a new [...],[140]

comment that the reading is uncertain; see also the various Bible dictionaries, including my article on Ishbi-Benob in the *ABD*). Most modern scholars, however, have seen fit to follow the Kethib and, with an emendation of the place name on the basis of vv 18 and 19, have vocalized the text *wayyēšēbû běgōb* "they dwelt at Gob" (see Segal 1965/66: 33 n. 12). Thus Wellhausen (1871: 210) proposed relocating the phrase from v 16 to v 15 following עמו "with him" and conjectured that in the phrase ויעף דוד "David grew weary" was hidden the name of David's adversary, as well as a verb such as ויקם "he arose. In this he was followed by S. R. Driver (1912: 353; but see Pisano 1984: 152). Wellhausen additionally proposed that an original "Gob" lay behind the "Nob" of the MT. Eissfeldt (1943: 120-22) amplified this suggestion, going so far as to identify the site with Gibbethon, a point of conflict between Israel and the Philistines in the late tenth and early ninth centuries B.C.E. (1 Kgs 15:27; 16:15; see also Malamat 1963: 15). Hertzberg (1964: 385) translated in a similar vein and added the phrase ואיש גבר "and there was a warrior" on the basis of the Syriac, which he conjectured fell out by haplography after the morphologically similar words וישבו בגב. H. P. Smith (1899: 378) raised the possibility that a proper name may be hidden in בנב אשר, consisting of the element בן plus a corrupt -- or at any rate misunderstood -- version of a proper name. A. B. Ehrlich (1910: 331) also sought a Philistine name in בנב, although he rejected the interpretation of וישבו as "they dwelt," since it makes no sense in reference to a military encampment. Instead he proposed reading וישבו as *wayyišběhû* "he (בנב) vanquished him (David)." This suggestion lay dormant until it was revived without ascription and, hence, independently by McCarter. However, rather than following Ehrlich's emendation of an additional *he* in the word, McCarter accepted the consonantal text of the MT וישבו and vocalized the word as *wayyišbēw* from *wayyissběhû*, following Cross and Freedman's work (1952: 50 and n. 28) in isolating short possessive forms in the colloquial language of biblical times. For the rest of his restoration of vv 15 and 16 McCarter has relied on the aforementioned Greek traditions, in particular a G plus in the vicinity of v 11. G^B reads at the end of v 11 και εξελυθησαν και κατελαβεν αυτους δαν υιος ιωα εκ των απογονων των γιγαντων, which together with the equivalent to Ishbi-Benob in G^L δαδου υιοσ ιωας has been retroverted by McCarter as indicated above (albeit without אשר; see also Bork 1939-41: 227-28). The corruption in the MT would have been occasioned by the loss of דד owing to homoioteleuton and the change of בן יואש to בנב אשר under the influence of בגוב in vv 18 and 19, for which some manuscripts read בנוב. Although McCarter (1984: 448) has referred to the G plus of v 11 as a marginal correction that has found its way into the text, Pisano (1984: 153-54) views it as the Old Greek version, itself possibly an interpretation, which has been displaced by the later καιγε translation.

[138] MT קינו. A hapax legomenon. Following G δορατος (<δορυ), S. R. Driver (1912: 354) advocated the translation "spear." In this he is followed by *HALAT* (1025b), in which a relationship to the Aramaic קנת is deduced. Others follow a suggestion to interpret the word as a mistake for קבעו "his helmet" (H. P. Smith 1899: 378; McCarter 1984: 448).

[139] Thus G (retroverting as שקל). MT משקל "weight." The error in the MT was occasioned by the presence of משקל earlier in the verse. See Wellhausen 1871: 210; H. P. Smith 1899: 378; S. R. Driver 1912: 354; McCarter 1984: 448.

[140] The word חדשה, here translated as "new," has remained an interpretative crux. Although it appears to be the feminine adjectival form of "new," there is no word in the text which it modifies. A. B. Ehrlich (1900: 250; 1910: 331) understood the word as an adverb, referring to the first time that the subject girded himself for war, which indicated his youth. S. R. Driver (1912: 354) conjectured that חדשה is a corruption of the name of a Philistine weapon. Although H. P. Smith (1899: 378) declared the text unintelligible without an object, McCarter (1984: 448) "fudged" and translated the word as the generic "armor." See Smith and McCarter for the plethora of attempts to translate the word in the versions. There is a small unpublished fragment of 2 Sam 21:15-17 from 4QSam^a (see Ulrich 1978: 271). According to a drawing of it which F. M. Cross was kind enough to send me, there does appear to be a four letter word in the same location as MT חדשה. However, the traces of letters that remain indicate a variant reading. Of the four letters, only the first three are legible. These spell [x]חור. In light of the illegible final letter, a reading as

[overcame him] and sought to kill David. (17) However, Abishai son of Zeruiah[141] came to his aid and struck the Philistine and killed him. Thereupon David's men swore [[142]], "No longer shall you go with us to battle, lest you extinguish the lamp of Israel."[143] (18) Afterwards there was another battle with the Philistines at Gob. At that time Sibbecai the Hushathite smote Saph, one of the Raphaites. (19) There was another battle with the Philistines at Gob; Elhanan son of Jair[144] the Bethlehemite smote Goliath the Gittite, the shaft of whose spear resembled a weaver's heddle rod. (20) There was another battle at Gath. A man of stature,[145] who had six fingers on his hands and six toes on his feet -- a total of twenty-four (digits), he too was a Raphaite -- (21) taunted Israel. Jonathan the son of Shimea,[146] David's brother, smote him. (22) These four[147] were Raphaites[148] in Gath and were felled by David and his followers.

חור "white garment" (Esth 1:6; 8:15) would appear to be ruled out. There are traces of two letters preceding the *ḥet*, however, the fragment is torn on the right side and much of the right-hand surface is missing. As in the MT, ויאמר follows the word under discussion (after which comes the left-hand margin of the column). Thus this 4QSamᵃ fragment ultimately fails to solve the critical problems of this verse.

[141] Gunn (1982: 40) has isolated a motif of "friction between David and the descendents of Zeruiah," vestiges of which he feels appear in this verse.

[142] The MT includes the declined preposition לו "to him." It is omitted by most commentators following the G (Wellhausen 1871: 210; H. P. Smith 1899: 378; McCarter 1984: 448).

[143] This phrase may refer to the king as a perpetual lamp, figurative of the prosperity of the land (S. R. Driver 1912: 354). The reference to David as the lamp of *Israel* may indicate that this incident is to be dated to the period following his assumption of rule over united Israel

[144] The MT אלחנן בן-יערי ארגים "Elhanan son of Woods of the Weavers" is incomprehensible. The element ארגים has obviously entered the text as a dittography from later in the verse. By reading יעיר, I am following the Qere of 1 Chr 20:5 (A. B. Ehrlich 1900: 250; H. P. Smith 1899: 378 who also mentions יעור as a possible reading; S. R. Driver 1912: 354), against McCarter's proposal (1984: 449-50) to read יערי as a gentilic "Jearite" (as in Kiriath-Jearim "City of the Jearites"). On the other hand, Boling (in Boling and Wright 1982: 369) has translated Kiriath Jearim as "Woodsville."

[145] Emending the text to מדה, as against MT Kethib מדין "Midian" and Qere מדון "strife." In this case it is probably best to follow the parallel in 1 Chr 20:6 and to translate the phrase in keeping with the impressive size of the vanquished opponents, "a man of stature," i.e. a giant. See Wellhausen 1871: 210; A. B. Ehrlich 1910: 331; H. P. Smith 1899: 378; S. R. Driver 1912: 355; McCarter 1984: 449. On the phenomenon of polydactylism in the literature of the Bible and the ancient Near East, see Barnett 1990.

[146] Thus the Qere שמעה. Kethib שמעי. See H. P. Smith 1899: 378; McCarter 1984: 449.

[147] In the MT "these four" is preceded with the direct object marker את. This is most likely in error since ארבעת אלה serves as the subject of the clause.

[148] Lit. "these four were born to the Raphah" להרפה. As indicated in GKC para. 35 n, this form is an exception to the rule regarding the elision of the definite articular *he* following the prefix ל. This is most likely occassioned in this instance by the understanding of the term להרפה in its entirety as a personal name, and hence indeclinable (S. R. Driver 1912: 355-56). Japhet (1993: 367) has also raised this

1 Chr 20:4-8

(4) Afterwards there was another battle[149] with the Philistines at Gezer.[150] At that time Sibbecai the Hushathite smote Sippai,[151] one of the Raphaites,[152] and they were humbled.[153] (5) There was another battle with the Philistines. Elhanan son of Jair[154] smote Lahmi the brother of Goliath[155] the Gittite, the shaft of whose spear resembled a

---

possibility and referred to Raphah/Haraphah as a matronym. Much later tradition also understood the word הרפה in its entirety as a personal name. I assume that this passage was Milton's source for the name of Samson's male Philistine nemesis in *Samson Agonistes*, i.e. Harapha. See (hear?) also Handel's magnificent oratorio *Samson*. On the understanding of the term ילידי הרפה/א as referring to devotees of a probably chthonian deity see McCarter 1984: 449-50. L'Heureux (1976) drew a comparison between these biblical Raphaites and those known from Ugarit, arguing that the Philistine Raphaites were devotees of a military order, whose existence possibly centered on the Rephaim Valley. In L'Heureux's opinion (1976: 85), the change from the expected *'aleph* to *he* at the end of the word in this passage may have been influenced by the biblical author's desire to denigrate the devotees of "the Hale One" by implying that they were devotees of "the one who became weak."

[149] Thus G και εγενετο ετι πολεμος and 2 Sam 21:18. MT ותעמד. See Curtis and Madsen 1910: 244.

[150] Thus MT בגזר. The parallel in 2 Sam 21:18 has the reading בגוב. Scholars are divided about which version has primacy in this context. Curtis and Madsen (1910: 244) and Williamson (1982: 141) view Gob as original, with the latter assuming that the Chronicler substituted the better known Gezer in the same general vicinity (see also H. P. Smith 1899: 377-78; Japhet 1993: 367). Myers (1965a: 141) and McCarter (1984: 448) on the other hand support the primacy of Gezer both here and in 2 Sam 21:18. Veering from the popular tendency to place up to three of the vignettes of battle between Israelite and Philistine champions at Gob (see e.g. Eissfeldt 1943: 120-22), McCarter accepts Gob as original only in the account of Elhanan's battle with Goliath (2 Sam 21:19). In placing the battle in 2 Sam 21:18 at Gezer, McCarter also relies in part on the Lucianic tradition which transcribes the name of the site of the battle as γαζε9. The MT Gob and the G^B Gath are explained as anticipatory of vv 19 and 20 respectively.

[151] On the name Sippai name see Bork 1939-41: 228.

[152] Following the singular as found in several manuscripts and in the parallel in 2 Sam 21:18, we are reading הרפא in place of the MT הרפאים.

[153] Thus the MT Niph'al *wayyikānē'û*. See Williamson 1982: 141. Others (*BHS*; Myers 1965a: 134) change it on the basis of the G και εταπεινωσεν αυτον to *wayyaknī'ô* "and he humbled him." The change is solely one of vocalization. Whichever form one chooses, the word is most probably an addition by the Chronicler, since it exhibits language typical of that author (Williamson 1982: 141-42).

[154] Thus the Qere. Kethib יעור.

[155] The apparent contradiction between 1 Sam 17, in which David killed Goliath, and 2 Sam 21, in which that deed is ascribed to Elhanan, is discussed below. It is easy to see how an original בית הלחמי את גלית was rearranged into את לחמי אחי גלית. Williamson (1982: 142), however, has cautioned against automatically assuming that the Chronicler deliberately changed his *Vorlage*. He raises the possibility that the Chronicler was simply attempting to make comprehensible a difficult source on the basis of his knowledge of 1 Sam 17. At any rate, the retention of the description of Goliath's spear makes clear of whom the account originally handled.

weaver's heddle rod. (6) There was another battle at Gath. A man of stature, whose (extremities) had six digits each -- (in total) twenty-four, he too was a Raphaite -- (7) taunted Israel. Jonathan son of Shimea, David's brother, smote him. (8) These[156] were[157] Raphaites in Gath and were felled by David and his followers.

As a series of anecdotes this passage is of minimal use in historical reconstruction. Some geographical information can be gleaned from this passage. Although there is a lively debate yet ongoing concerning the actual place names occurring in the pericope, commentators are in agreement that the action took place in the border region between Judah/Israel and Philistia. This would also mesh with the supposed historical context of these four episodes, namely in the period of David's Philistine wars (2 Sam 5:17-25; 1 Chr 14:8-16). These are to be dated in the earlier part of David's reign, after, however, his ascent to rule over all Israel.

It has been argued that the four episodes were lifted from a larger archive.[158] Hertzberg[159] even tried to pinpoint the excerpt as a "page from the honours list of Bethlehem" on account of the origin of all the heroes mentioned in the pericope from the same general area.

The placement of the text near the end of the account of David's reign may have been occasioned by a number of factors. First is the motif of David's weakness, which later tradition felt more comfortable ascribing to the latter part of his life. Second is its placement after the last account of a Davidic war in 2 Sam 20.[160] And third is the nature of the larger context in

---

[156] MT אל. On the short form of the demonstrative pronoun see GKC para. 34 b; *HALAT* 48b. It has become axiomatic to assume that the number of Philistine champions was omitted owing to the dropping of the first episode in Chronicles on account of the reluctance of the author of Chronicles to depict David in a weakened state or the eternal promise of a Davidic dynasty in doubt (Curtis and Madsen 1910: 243-44; Myers 1965a: 142; Kalimi 1995: 26-27, 90, who leaves open the reason for the missing passage). The G, however, preserves the words παντεσ ησαν τεσσαρες γιγαντες "all four of them were giants" after בגת "in Gath." Although it is possible that this is a reflection of an earlier state of this text, the syntax of the verse makes is more likely that this phrase was a marginal note referring back to the passage in 2 Samuel that crept into the text at this point.

[157] Lit. "were born to." MT *nûllĕdû.* This is probably a mixed-form, morphologically a Niph'al, but pointed as a Pu'al in order to bring it in line with the parallel in 2 Sam 21. See Bergsträsser 1912: para. 26m; GKC para. 69 t; *HALAT* 393b.

[158] See McCarter 1984: 451.

[159] 1964: 388.

[160] Hertzberg 1964: 386.

which it has been fit, namely into a collection of miscellaneous texts relating to the period of Davidic rule.[161]

Wellhausen was disturbed by the existence in the sources of an account of David's weakness in battle. Thus he felt compelled to exise the verb ויעף from the text. The spurious nature of this line of reasoning has compellingly been demonstrated by Pisano.[162] Although it has been argued that the reason for the placement of this pericope toward the end of David's history was the tradition's assumption that David could have been vanquished in battle only at an advanced age,[163] most commentators place these four episodes in the period of David's Philistine wars as recounted in 2 Sam 5:17-25; thus near the beginning of David's reign.[164] It may be of interest to note that the theme of the rescue of a newly crowned king occurs in Mallory's *Morte d'Arthur*, in which King Arthur is bested in battle at the very beginning of his reign and must be rescued by four of his knights.

The information contained in 2 Sam 21:19, namely that Elhanan slew Goliath the Gittite, openly contradicts the information contained in 1 Sam 17, in which the deed is ascribed to David. In spite of attempts which have been made to harmonize the accounts by assuming that Elhanan was the personal name and David the title of the same person,[165] or that Elhanan was the given name and David the throne name,[166] it appears most likely that 2 Sam 21:19 represents the earliest and most accurate layer of tradition and that Elhanan was indeed the slayer of Goliath. This argument is bolstered by the fact that the name of Goliath appears but two times (vv 4 and 23) in 1 Sam 17, each time in a context in which it appears to be secondary. At some early point, however, the killing of Goliath was also attributed to David and became an inseparable part of the legend of his defeat of a Philistine champion, without, however, displacing the earliest layer of tradition about Elhanan.[167] That the Goliath in both cases is the same person is indicated *inter alia* by the

---

[161] McCarter 1984: 451.

[162] 1984: 152.

[163] Hertzberg 1964: 386.

[164] E.g. McCarter 1984: 451.

[165] Von Pákozdy 1956: 257-59. A major component of his argument was his belief that behind יערי was hidden the name of David's father ישי "Jesse."

[166] Honeyman 1948: 23-24.

[167] See Japhet 1993: 368-69.

identical language used in the comparison of his spear to a weaver's heddle-rod.[168]

More Anecdotes

2 Sam 23:9-17

(9) After him[169] among the three champions[170] was Elazar son of Doday[171] the Ahohite.[172] [He was[173]] with David when [the Philistine] mocked them [at Ephes-dammim.][174] When the Philistines had

---

[168] About which see Yadin 1955: 58-69.

[169] Thus the Qere ואחריו. Kethib ואחרו. The literary unit actually begins in the previous verse with the introduction to the list of David's heroes.

[170] Thus the Qere הגברים. Kethib גברים. A *he* has been lost through haplography.

[171] Thus the Kethib דדי and 1 Chr 27:4 (see S. R. Driver 1912: 364-65, who derived the name from דדיה). Qere and 1 Chr 11:12, as well as G (υιος πατραδελφου αυτου) דדו (*dōdô*) "his uncle" (see also B. Mazar 1986: 97). In the G the patronymic "son of Dodo" has necessitated the change of Elazar to Elhanan as in 2 Sam 23:24 (Wellhausen 1871: 213).

[172] Reading האחחי as against MT בן-אחחי "son of Ahohi." This latter version is an obvious error attributable to a dittography of the בן of בן-דדי. See 2 Sam 23:28; 1 Chr 11:12, 29; 27:4; and Ahoah in the Benjaminite genealogy 1 Chr 8:4 (Wellhausen 1871: 213; S. R. Driver 1912: 365; McCarter 1984: 494).

[173] Read הוא היה with 1 Chr 11:13 and G^{c}2/^{MNZ}2 αυτος/ουτος ην (see also B. Mazar 1986: 97).

[174] McCarter (1984: 490) has undoubtedly solved a major crux in the text. It had been recognized that the verb בחרפם in the MT is plausible, at least until one arrives at the word שם, which requires an antecedent place name (see H. P. Smith 1899: 384). This necessitated the deletion of the temporal clause and verb from the MT of Samuel, and the substitution of the name Pas-dammim from 1 Chr 11 (Wellhausen 1871: 213; and others). Curtis and Madsen (1910: 188) felt that an original בעמק רפאים "in the Rephaim Valley" lay behind both versions. There existed, however, no mechanism to explain how the "correct" version in Chronicles could have metamorphosed into the Samuel reading. McCarter has solved the problem by including both readings in a conflate text from which it is possible to explain both versions (as well as the Lucianic version) as the results of haplographies. The restored text would then read: בחרפם הפלשתי באפס דמים והפלשתים. Pas-dammim has been assumed to be identical with Ephes-dammim between Azekah and Socoh in 1 Sam 17:1 (H. P. Smith 1899: 383; Hertzberg 1964: 402; Myers 1965a: 89; McCarter 1984: 494-95 [the latter tentatively identifies the site with modern Damun]; B. Mazar 1986: 91; Japhet 1993: 244). The reference to the mocking Philistine would also refer to the action of 1 Sam 17, in which a Philistine champion who mocks Israel is defeated in single combat by David. As indicated above in the discussion of Elhanan (2 Sam 21:19; 1 Chr 20:5), the association of Goliath with the champion defeated by David entered the tradition at a later stage. See also my entry on "Goliath" in the *ABD*.

gathered for battle and the Israelites had retreated, (10) he[175] stood firm and smote the Philistines until his arm grew weary and his hand stuck to the sword. Thus did YHWH grant great salvation[176] on that day. The people, however, followed after him only to strip (the slain[177]). (11) After him was Shamma[178] son of Agee the Hararite.[179] The Philistines had gathered at Lehi,[180] where there was a section of field full of lentils,[181] and the people fled before the Philistines. (12) He, however, positioned himself in the middle of the section and defended[182] it and smote the Philistines. Thus did YHWH grant great salvation. (13) Three[183] of the thirty went down at the beginning [of the harvest][184] and came to David at the fortress of Adullam, while a

---

[175] Reading והוא. MT הוא. A *waw* is restored on the basis of the syntax, as well as non-B G traditions and the Syriac (H. P. Smith 1899: 385; S. R. Driver 1912: 365).

[176] Heb. תשועה. In Hertzberg's opinion (1964: 405), the use of this word classifies this passage as one referring to Holy War.

[177] The Syriac, Targum, and Vulgate all make the object of the verb explicit.

[178] MT שמא. Some manuscripts read שמה.

[179] Reading ההררי in place of MT הררי. See 2 Sam 23:33 and 1 Chr 11:34 (S. R. Driver 1912: 365; McCarter 1984: 490). On B. Mazar's views linking Hararite with a number of orthographically more or less similar place names, all ultimately identified as Harod/Beth-harodo, see 1986: 91.

[180] Pointing the text as *leḥyâ* in place of the MT *laḥayyâ*, which has been influenced by the usage of the uncommon *ḥayyâ* "troop/clan" in v 13. As has often been commented on, a repointing of the Hebrew לחיה results in the place name Lehi, known from Judg 15:9-19 as the site of Samson's famous escapade with the jaw-bone of an ass (Wellhausen 1871: 213; A. B. Ehrlich 1900: 256; S. R. Driver 1912: 365; McCarter 1984: 490; but see B. Mazar 1986: 97 who translates "The Philistines had gathered in force").

[181] Thus MT עדשים.1 Chr 11:13 שערים "barley." The better variant is impossible to determine, since either one would fit the context, and the one is derivable from the other by a metathesis and the confusion of orthographically similar letters. The G follows the MT in both cases.

[182] On the translation of ויצילה as "defended" see H. P. Smith 1899: 384. A. B. Ehrlich (1900: 256) advocated translating it as "*und [er] säuberte es.*"

[183] Thus the Qere, 1 Chr 11:15, G, Syriac, Targum. Kethib: שלשים "thirty." See also Tov 1992: 62.

[184] In the MT ראש "beginning" stands alone, followed by ויבאו אל-קציר. It does not appear in the G. Various attempts have been made to incorporate the word into the syntax of the text, ranging from Ehrlich's suggestion (1910: 342) to read ראשנה "first" (referring to the "first threesome"), to S. R. Driver's very tentative הראשנים מהשלשים "from the first thirty" (1912: 366), to H. P. Smith's suggestion (1899: 385) to read ראש הצור with G^L (προς δαυειδ εις την πετραν "to David at the rock") and 1 Chr 11:15, to B. Mazar's tentative suggestion (1986: 97) to read מראש הצר "from the rock," to McCarter's suggestion (1984: 490) to omit ראש altogether. While most commentators change קציר to צור on the basis of the aforementioned Chronicles and G^L passages, McCarter is correct that קציר, the dry season when "kings become thirsty" (1984: 495), would not be out of place in this passage. Unlike in McCarter, however, ראש is preserved in the text above, and קציר has been repositioned. Although צור has not been included, it is possible that the original text included references to the orthographically similar קציר and צ(ו)ר, which gave rise to the confused versions which have come down to us.

Philistine contingent was encamped in the Valley of Rephaim. (14)[185] (David was then at the fortress, and the Philistines were then stationed at Bethlehem). (15) David felt a craving and asked, "Who will bring me water to drink from the well[186] of Bethlehem which is at the gate?" (16) Three of the champions hacked their way through the Philistine camp and drew water from the well of Bethlehem which is at the gate. They took (it) and brought (it) to David. David,[187] however, did not consent to drink it, but poured it out (as a libation) to YHWH, (17) saying, "May I be cursed by YHWH[188] if I do this! Should I drink the blood of the men who went forth, since they have brought it at the risk of their lives?"[189] Thus he did not consent to drink it. This is what the three champions did.

1 Chr 11:12-19

(12) After him was Elazar son of Dodo the Ahohite. He was among the three champions. (13)[190] He was with David at Pas-dammim. The Philistines were gathered there for battle ... and there was a section of field full of barley, and the people fled before the Philistines. (14) They[191] positioned themselves in the middle of the section and

---

[185] H. P. Smith (1899: 385-86) is very likely correct in his surmise that this verse is a gloss which has found its way into the main text.

[186] Thus the Kethib מבאר. Qere *mibbō'r* and 1 Chr 11:17 *mibbôr* "from the cistern." See also the following verse.

[187] Thus some Hebrew manuscripts and G[L]. The name is omitted in the MT.

[188] Reading מיהוה in place of MT יהוה with a number of Hebrew manuscripts, G[L], Syriac andTargum. McCarter (1984: 491) nonetheless sticks in this case with the MT and treats יהוה as a vocative.

[189] Although Wellhausen (1871: 214) doubted that it would be possible to restore this passage with any degree of certainty, a combination of the variants in Samuel (הדם האנשים ההלכים בנפשותם) and Chronicles (הדם האנשים ההלכים) yields a comprehensible text (הדם האנשים האלה אשתה בנפשותם כי בנפשפתם הביאום) (אשתה כי בנפשפתם הביאום). See McCarter 1984: 491. For a different reconstruction see B. Mazar 1986: 98.

[190] The problems of this verse have been discussed above in regard to 2 Sam 23:9-11. It remains only to note that there has taken place an extensive haplography in this verse in Chronicles, in which the eye of the scribe has skipped from נאספו-שם למלחמה to ויאספו פלשתים לחיה. This has resulted in the elimination of Shamma son of Agee from the text of Chronicles and the ascription of his deeds to Elazar.

[191] Another change occasioned by the haplography was the parsing of the first three verbs of this verse in the plural, since it appears that the antecedents would be both Elazar and David. See Curtis and Madsen 1910: 187-88; Myers 1965a: 86 n. d; Williamson 1982: 102.

defended it and smote the Philistines. Thus did YHWH grant[192] great salvation. (15) Three of the thirty went down at the beginning of the harvest[193] to David at the fortress of Adullam, while the Philistines were encamped[194] in the Valley of Rephaim. (16) (David was then at the fortress, and the Philistines were then stationed at Bethlehem). (17) David felt a craving[195] and asked, "Who will bring me water to drink from the cistern of Bethlehem which is at the gate?" (18) The three hacked their way through the Philistine camp and drew water from the cistern of Bethlehem which is at the gate. They took (it) and brought (it) to David. David, however, did not consent to drink it, but poured it out[196] (as a libation) to YHWH, (19) saying, "May I be cursed by my God if (I) do this![197] Should I drink the blood of these[198] men, since they have brought it at the risk of their lives?" Thus he did not consent to drink it. This is what the three champions did.

Once again a collection of biblical anecdotes adds but little to our understanding of the history of the Philistines. Although some information is contained in these verses regarding some sites of contention, the chronological information found here leaves the larger historical context vague.

It has been argued that the list of the thirty champions as a whole be assigned a *terminus ad quem* on the basis of the mention of Asahel, who was killed by Abner (2 Sam 2:18-23) during the period of contention between David, king of Judah at Hebron, and Ishbaal, king of Israel and successor of

---

[192] Reading ויעש with 2 Sam 23:10, 12, and G εποιησεν. MT וישע "he saved" was occasioned by a metathesis of the final two letters of ויעש. See Curtis and Madsen 1910: 188; Tov 1992: 250.

[193] MT ראש על-הצר. For the emendation see the discussion of 2 Sam 23:13 above. Likewise concerning the word "fortress," which has been imported from the parallel passage in 2 Sam 23.

[194] MT *ûmaḥănēh pĕlištîm ḥônâ*. This is one of only two times that מחנה "camp" is treated as a feminine (see the verb *ḥônâ*), the other being in Ps 27:3. The masoretes were probably influenced in their pointing by the feminine חיה in the parallel passage in 2 Samuel.

[195] Thus the Kethib ויתאו. Qere ויתיו. On the form of the apocopated imperfect Hithpaʿel see GKC para. 75 bb.

[196] This is the only occurrence of the verb נסך in the Piʿel, as against the common Hiphʿil as in the parallel in 2 Sam 23:16.

[197] Hebrew מאלהי מעשות. The change of יהוה to אלהי has caused the Chronicler to drop the possessive suffix from עשות. On the rest of this verse see the discussion of 2 Sam 23:17.

[198] On the change of 2 Sam 23:17 "went" to 1 Chr 11:19 "these," see Japhet 1993: 246.

Saul.[199] Elliger, upon whose 1935 investigation all later work depends, dated
the list in its primary form to the days of David's brigandage at Ziklag.[200] The
final form of the list was established a bit later, during David's days as king
over Judah in Hebron. In addition McCarter[201] has commented on the lack of
mention of Ittai, the Gittites, the Cherethites and the Pelethites in this list, all
of whom were integral to the military structure of the kingdom during the later
reign of David in Jerusalem.

As of the time of Wellhausen,[202] it has become traditional to view 2 Sam
23:13-17a as a separate tradition which has intruded on the text of the list of
the thirty Davidic heroes on the basis of its mention of three champions, who
have incorrectly been linked with the three at the top of the list. According to
this scenario, v 17b would be either the original conclusion to the account of
vv 8-12,[203] or would be an editor's attempt to link the two accounts of vv 8-
12 and vv 13-17a.[204]

The few chronological hints contained in the episodes in this pericope
would also indicate a time before David's assumption of power over both the
northern and the southern tribes, an act which -- as was argued above -- was
the catalyst for the resumption of hostilities between David and the
Philistines. The reference to the mocking Philistine at Pas/Ephes-dammim
could be an indication that Elazar's heroic stand took place around the time of
the events narrated in 1 Sam 17, namely during Saul's reign. Shamma's
defense of the field (whether barley or lentil) is undateable. The episode of
the three champions who brought David water at his thoughtless whim[205] has
been dated to the time of David's Philistine wars on the basis of the mention
of the Rephaim Valley (2 Sam 5:17-21[206]). The same evidence, in particular
the reference to David's hideaway at Adullam, has also been used to date the
episode to the time of David's flight from Saul, before he became a Philistine
vassal, or perhaps during the early part of his reign at Hebron.[207] In light of

---

[199] B. Mazar 1986: 100.

[200] See Elliger 1935: 64-75.

[201] 1984: 501.

[202] 1871: 214.

[203] Wellhausen 1871: 214; H. P. Smith 1899: 383; S. R. Driver 1912: 366.

[204] Hertzberg 1964: 405.

[205] See Hertzberg 1964: 405; McCarter 1984: 496.

[206] Hertzberg 1964: 405.

[207] Myers 1965a: 89; McCarter 1984: 495; Japhet 1993: 24-46.

the connection of the institution of the thirty with David's days as a mercenary/bandit, it may be best to regard these episodes as originating during his romantic days of youth, while leaving open the possibility that a later deed of heroic proportions was added to the basic list as illustrative of an individual's prowess.

Although the reference to both Adullam and Bethlehem in the same verse has been taken as an important piece of evidence in some reconstructions of David's strategy in his Philistine campaigns, arguments can be adduced for viewing the verse as a later gloss. Thus the information contained in this pericope most probably dates from a time before that which is within the scope of this thesis. Even if the possibility exists that a particular episode could be tied in with David's Philistine wars, the information contained in it is too vague to aid in the process of historical reconstruction.

Shimei's Slaves Escape to Gath: 1 Kgs 2:39-41

(39) At the end of three years, two of Shimei's slaves fled to Achish son of Maachah, king of Gath. Shimei was told, "Look, your slaves are in Gath." (40) Shimei arose, saddled his donkey and went to Gath, to Achish, to request his slaves. Shimei went[208] and brought his slaves (back) from Gath. (41) Solomon, however, was informed that Shimei had gone forth from Jerusalem to Gath and returned.[209]

Unfortunately, a literary analysis of the cold-blooded murder of the innocent Shimei is beyond the scope of this work. Suffice it to say that the above verses are exerpted from a longer account, which tries vainly to absolve Solomon of moral accountability for the murder of Shimei (1 Kgs 2:8-9, 36-46a). Indeed the whole of the chapter is an account of how "the kingdom was [made] secure in Solomon's hand" (v 46b) by means of the murders of Joab

---

[208] G[L] adds εξ ιερουσαλημ "from Jerusalem."

[209] Thus the MT *wayyāšob*. G reads the consonantal וישב as the Hiph'il *wayyāšēb*. G completes the sentence και απεστρεψεν (Ba₂e₂) τους δουλους αυτου "and he returned his slaves." This can be retroverted into Hebrew as *wayyāšēb 'et 'ăbādāyw*. Although the G version would make sense in this passage, there does not appear to be a mechanism to explain the absence of the final phrase in the MT. The slaves are integral to Shimei's absence from Jerusalem, but irrelevant to Solomon's need to find an excuse to murder Shimei. See Burney (1903: 26) who views the G conclusion to the verse as a gloss.

(vv 5-6, 28-34), Adonijah (vv 13-25) and Shimei, and the banishment of
Abiathar to his ancestral home at Anathoth (vv 26-17).[210]

Of interest to the present study are a) the relationship between Israel and
Gath, and b) the reference to Achish.

This passage is one of a number (see 2 Sam 6:10-12 = 1 Chr 13:12-14; 2
Sam 15:18-22) which indicate that there was a unique relationship between
Gath and Israel during the period of the united monarchy. This relationship
was probably based upon contacts David originally made during his time as a
Gittite vassal, and was expanded once the original political positions of the
actors were reversed. It has been conjectured that the return of Shimei's
slaves was expedited by a treaty of extradition which existed between Israel
and Gath, assuming that Gath was a vassal of Israel.[211]

As for Achish, it is of more than passing interest that he was on the throne
from the reign of Saul, through that of David and into that of Solomon, in
total over forty years. On the other hand, it has been called into question
whether the mention of his name in this passage is a later gloss,[212] and
Gray[213] has questioned whether the Achish of Solomon's time was the same
one under whom David served by assuming that the former was the latter's
son.

The Extent of Solomon's Rule

1 Kgs 5:1, 4--Eng 4:21, 24

(1) Solomon exercised control over all the kingdoms[214] from the
(Euphrates) River [unto[215]] the land of the Philistines[216] up to the

---

[210] On the larger political considerations behind the murder of Shimei, see Jones 1984: 117-18;
Würthwein 1977: 24-25.

[211] Montgomery and Gehman 1951: 96-97; de Vaux 1958: 33 n. a.

[212] Corney 1962b.

[213] 1970: 112.

[214] Thus MT הממלכות. G 2:46k τοις βασιλευσιν and 2 Chr 9:26 הממלכים "the kings" would agree in
gender and number with the following participles מגשים" and עבדים. On the comparative literary history of
the MT and the G in the larger unit from which this passage is exerpted, see Swete 1914: 237-38;
Montgomery and Gehman 1951: 126; DeVries 1985: lix-lxiv.

border of Egypt. They brought (him) tribute and served Solomon all the days of his life. ... (4) For he was sovereign over all trans-Euphrates,[217] from Tiphsah to Gaza, over all the kings of trans-Euphrates. He had peace on all sides[218] round about.

2 Chr 9:26[219]

(26) He exercised control over all the kings from the (Euphrates) River unto the land of the Philistines, and unto the border of Egypt.

Although at first glance this passage would seem to be a valuable source for the geopolitical situation of Philistia vis-à-vis Israel during the reign of Solomon, there are some hints in this passage, including the use of עבר הנהר in 1 Kgs 5:4, which would force the conclusion that this text is a late invention.[220]

The expression עבר הנהר is used in two ways in biblical Hebrew. First it can refer to the land on the east bank of the Jordan River (e.g. Josh 24:2, 14; 2 Sam 10:16; 1 Kgs 14:15). Second it can refer to the territory west of the

---

[215] Thus G 2:46k; 10:26a (και εως), Targum (מן נהר פרת עד ארע פלשתיא) "from the Euphrates River to the land of the Philistines"), and 2 Chr 9:26 (see also Gray 1970: 141, who views the phrase "up to the border of Egypt" as a gloss). It is missing in the MT. If one were to follow the defective text of the MT, two problems would arise. First one would have to identify an otherwise unknown "river of the land of the Philistines." Second the text, rather than giving cause to marvel at the extent of Solomon's empire, would give rise to derision at the tiny amount of territory controlled by that supposedly great king. Burney (1903: 48) arrived at a similar understanding of the text by assuming that the accusative "land of the Philistines" is "an accus[ative] of *motion towards*."

[216] The reference to the land of the Philistines was viewed by Würthwein (1977: 43) as a gloss.

[217] Hebrew עבר הנהר, about which see below.

[218] Hebrew עבריו. Some Hebrew manuscripts read here עבדיו "his servants/subjects." Some commentators (e.g. A. B. Ehrlich 1900: 278) have suggested following this latter reading, especially in light of the frequent confusion in Hebrew orthography between *dalet* and *resh* (see Tov 1981: 196-97). However, in light of the G 4:24 των μερων it appears best to follow the MT. In addition it would make more sense for Solomon to enjoy peaceful relations with all of the surrounding regions, rather than with all of his surrounding subjects. See also Burney 1903: 48. Although Hatch and Redpath (1897: 912a) decline to assign a formal equivalent to των μερων, it is obviously עבריו (see also Exod 32:15). In my opinion, there is no difficulty in accepting the two words as actual equivalents (see also DeVries 1985: 66). On the subjective nature of some of the listings of equivalents in Hatch and Redpath 1897, see Tov 1981: 144-46.

[219] On the "obscure" textual history of 2 Chr 9:25-28, see Williamson 1982: 235-36. Williamson does, however, provide a list of sources upon which the Chronicler drew in formulating the passage. See also Kalimi 1995: 43, 100-02.

[220] See also Würthwein 1977: 43, 47.

Euphrates River (Ezra 8:36; Neh 2:7, 9; 3:7). This is obviously the meaning which the phrase has in this passage. With this latter meaning, the phrase is derived from the Akkadian *eber nāri.*[221] The phrase, however, is first attested in neo-Assyrian texts, at the latest by the seventh century B.C.E. in the inscriptions of Ashurbanipal, and it achieved wide circulation during the Persian period in its Aramaic form עבר נהרא. Thus its use in this passage is anachronistic and serves to cast doubt on the historicity of the passage as a whole.[222]

The conclusion is inescapable that this is a text whose sole purpose is the glorification of Solomon by attributing to him an immense empire which existed only on paper and in the popular immagination.[223]

Gezer, Pharaoh, and Solomon: 1 Kgs 9:15-17a

(15) This is an account of the forced labor which King Solomon levied in order to build the temple of YHWH, his (own) palace, the Millo,[224] and the wall of Jerusalem, as well as Hazor, Megiddo, and Gezer. (16)[225] Pharaoh the king of Egypt had come up and conquered Gezer and burned it with fire.[226] He killed the Canaanites who were dwelling in the city and gave it as a dowry to his daughter, Solomon's wife. (17a) And Solomon rebuilt Gezer.

---

[221] *AHW* 181b; see also *HALAT* 738.

[222] So also the mention of Tiphsah, which is a name, according to the entry "Tiphsah" in the *Encyclopaedia Biblica* (Hebrew) 8: 922-23, that came into common use only in the Persian period. See also Burney 1903: 48; Montgomery and Gehman 1951: 128; de Vaux 1958: 41 n. c; Gray 1970: 143; Aharoni 1979: 78; DeVries 1985: 72.

[223] See Montgomery and Gehman 1951: 128; Herrmann 1981: 159.

[224] This word, whose meaning is "fill/filling" (<מלא), may refer to all or part of the system of rock filled terraces which hugged the steep eastern slope of biblical Jerusalem. In the light of the late Y. Shiloh's City of David excavations, it has been suggested that the reference was specifically to the massive stepped stone structure at the northern end of the city, south of the Temple Mount, whose function was most probably to support the citadel, or other important buildings there. See Kenyon 1974: 100-03; Dever 1990b: 114-15.

[225] The syntax of this verse differs from the MT to the G. The G begins the verse οτε (G^L: τοτε) ανεβη φαραω, which could be retroverted into Hebrew as אז עלה פרעה "Then Pharaoh went up." Würthwein (1977: 109, 111) viewed vv 16-17a as secondary insertions into the text.

[226] Thus MT followed by the Lucianic tradition. The reference to fire is missing in G^B.

These verses, although not mentioning the Philistines by name, contain much information of seemingly vital importance in determining borders and spheres of influence in tenth century Canaan. These issues have been discussed at their appropriate place in Chapter Two.

At this juncture a few literary critical remarks on the passage will suffice:

Once again the MT and the G diverge in their arrangement of the miscellaneous material relating to Solomon's reign. The crucial verses regarding the Egyptian conquest of Gezer are to be found in G in 4:32-33 (//9:16-17).[227]

According to Montgomery and Gehman's analysis,[228] v 15a originally served as the introduction to vv 20-23, a passage absolving Solomon of reducing the Israelites to corvee, and relating the enslavement of the remaining Canaanites.[229] Into this has been inserted a list of Solomon's major building projects (vv 15b-19). The mention of Gezer in this insertion has proved to be the catalyst for an additional insertion, an account of how Gezer came under Israelite rule (v 16). This final insertion concludes with a resumptive repetition (v 17a), which repeats the subject (שלמה), verb (בנה), and final object (גזר) of v 15b.

Rehoboam's Fortified Cities: 2 Chr 11:5-12

(5) While Rehoboam dwelt at Jerusalem, he built fortified towns throughout Judah. (6) He built Bethlehem, Etam, Tekoa, (7) Beth-zur, Soco, Adullam, (8) [Moresheth]-Gath,[230] Mareshah, Ziph, (9) Adoraim, Lachish, Azekah, (10) Zorah, Aijalon, and Hebron, which are in Judah and Benjamin, as fortified towns. (11) He strengthened the fortifications and assigned them commanders, and stores of food, oil,

---

[227] See also Montgomery and Gehman 1951: 214; DeVries 1985: lxii; and *BHS ad loc.*

[228] 1951: 205-06.

[229] See also Noth 1960: 211.

[230] Following a suggestion of Aharoni's (see 1979: 330), the element מרשת has been restored to this verse. Moreshet is absent from the verse owing to its auditory and graphic similarity to the following name, Mareshah. A fuller discussion of the restoration and its historical implications will be found in the historical synthesis in Chapter Three. With the exception of Broshi (1977: 694), all scholars consulted ascribe this suggested emendation to Aharoni. Broshi credits Yeivin with this proposal. Unfortunately, Broshi has provided no citation in support of his ascription.

and wine. (12) In each town there were shields and spears; he strengthened them to a great extent. Judah and Benjamin were his.

Although the major interest of this passage for this study lies in its putative mention of Gath, the information in this pericope delimiting Rehoboam's fortifications is of potential importance for the historical-geography of the borderland between Judah and Philistia in the late tenth century B.C.E.

Before that can be determined, however, the question of the pericope's place in the canon must be addressed.

Modern scholarship is for the most part in agreement that the list of cities in 2 Chr 11:6-10a must have been taken by the Chronicler from an ancient document which was not employed by the Deuteronomist.[231] Opinions diverge, however, when the question is raised whether the Chronicler inserted the list into its proper historical context. This issue, as well as the identification of the city of Gath mentioned in v 8 were discussed in Chapter Two.

Whatever position one takes on the subject, it is evident that the list of Rehoboam's building activities serves a supra-historical, ideological function in its placement in Chronicles. Contrary to the negative portrayal of Rehoboam's reign to be gleaned from 1 Kgs 12:1-24; 14:21-31, in Chronicles Rehoboam's reign is divided into an earlier positively and a later negatively evaluated period. The motif of building/fortification activity is subsumed in the Chronicler's reconstruction of history in the positive column as a sign of the fruits of faithfulness. Thus the list of cities in vv 5-12 is part of a longer section comprising vv 5-23 in which the themes of building (vv 5-12), the ingathering of the faithful from the apostate north (vv 13-17), and the blessing of family and descendents (vv 18-23) are presented as evidence of cultic fidelity and divine favor during the early part of Rehoboam's reign.[232]

The First Siege of Gibbethon: 1 Kgs 15:27

---

[231] E.g. Welten 1973: 13, 192, 195; Japhet 1993: 664.

[232] See Williamson 1982: 240-45.

(27) Baasha the son of Ahijah of the house of Issachar[233] conspired against him;[234] and Baasha struck him down[235] in Philistine Gibbethon,[236] while Nadab and all Israel[237] were besieging Gibbethon.

The mention of Gibbethon, incidental though it is, is important on two levels. First it helps determine the border between Israel and Philistia at the end of the tenth century. Second it is one of the few sources available to us in determining the relationship of Israel and Philistia, which in this case was an adversarial one. Since only the fact of a royal assassination has given the impetus for including this information in the biblical text, the information contained therein can be regarded as reliable. It can also be concluded, on the basis of this verse and 1 Kgs 16:15-17, that Gibbethon was a focus of conflict for a rather lengthy time.

The Second Siege of Gibbethon: 1 Kgs 16:15-17

(15) In the twenty-seventh year of Asa king of Judah,[238] Zimri reigned for seven days in Tirzah, while the people was encamped against

---

[233] Commentators have been disturbed by the expression "of the house of Issachar." Although there is nothing wrong with it syntactically, the identification by tribe, rather than by a place within the territory of the tribe, has given rise to speculation that the name of a town within Issachar has dropped out of the text at this point (see Gray 1970: 357 n. b). The G evidence would appear to point in this direction. G^B reads here επι τον οικον βελααν ο υιος αχεια "over/of the house of Belaan, the son of Ahijah," which appears to indicate that the place name in the MT may have fallen out by homoioarkton (בית "house" and a place name whose initial letter was *bet*). However, G^B is missing the name Issachar, in place of which it has a dittography of Ahijah's name. G^L, on the other hand, reads επι τον οικον βεδδαμα (βελλαμα b) του ισσαχαρ "over/of the house of (or: Beth-) Beddama/Bellama of/in Issachar," in which, one may surmise, is hidden the name of Baasha's ancestral home.

[234] This refers to Nadab, son of Jeroboam I, king of Israel from c. 903-902 B.C.E.

[235] Hebrew ויכהו. DeVries (1985: 192) has mistakenly referred to this form as a plural.

[236] Gibbethon is usually identified with Tel Malot (Tell el-Melat, grid reference 137140; see Aharoni 1979: 435; Pritchard 1987: 225), which lies about three miles west of Gezer and five miles north of Ekron (at Tel Miqne; see Naveh 1958), of which it was probably a satellite. Sargon II captured *Gabbutunu* together with Ekron in the year 720 B.C.E. (see el-Amin 1953: 36-40).

[237] As has been pointed out (e.g. Tadmor 1982: 244), it is highly unlikely that "all Israel" took part in the siege of Gibbethon.

[238] The date formula in v 15a through "king of Judah'" is missing in G^B. According to DeVries (1985: 198), this was probably occasioned by a differing overall chronological scheme in the G traditions. On the chronological confusion in this passage in G as a whole, including G^L, see Montgomery and Gehman 1950: 289; Shenkel 1968: 36.

Philistine Gibbethon. (16) The encamped people heard (about it) as
follows: "Zimri has conspired and even assassinated the king!"
Whereupon all Israel[239] made Omri,[240] the commander of the army,
king over Israel on that day in the camp. (17) Then Omri, and all Israel
with him, went up from Gibbethon and besieged Tirzah.

Once again the notice of the assassination of a king of Israel has resulted in
an important datum for Philistine history. Once again, perhaps still, the border
region north of Ekron was in dispute, this time in c. 885 B.C.E.

The Philistines Render Tribute to Judah: 2 Chr 17:10-11

(10) The fear of YHWH lay upon all the kingdoms of the countries[241]
which surrounded Judah, and they did not wage war with
Jehoshaphat.[242] (11) From among the Philistines they would bring
Jehoshaphat a gift and a load of silver;[243] even the Arabs[244] would
bring him flocks: 7700 rams and 7700 he-goats.

---

[239] Once again it is inconceivable that "all Israel" was present at the siege of Gibbethon (Montgomery and Gehman 1950: 290; Gray 1970: 364; Würthwein 1977: 197; Jones 1984: 294). At a minimum, both Zimri and Tibni, against the latter of whom Omri engaged in a protracted struggle for control of the land after the death of Zimri (1 Kgs 16:21-22), must have had their followers.

[240] G^B has consistently confused the names of Omri and Zimri in this passage, employing the latter's name for both. It should be noted that neither of the two has been provided with a genealogy in the biblical text.

[241] Thus the MT in the plural (see 2 Chr 12:8). G της γης in the singular.

[242] King of Judah c. 874-850 B.C.E.

[243] Thus the MT משא וכסף. G reads και αργυριον και δοματα "and silver and presents," which can be retroverted into Hebrew as ומשא וכסף.

[244] MT הערביאים with an extraneous *'aleph* and, hence, *yod*. The expected form הערבים does appear in a Hebrew manuscript. GKC para. 93 x attributes the MT form to a softening of the *yod* to *'aleph*. Bergsträsser (1918: para. 17 n) attributed the reduction of the *yod* into an *'aleph* to its intermediate position between a long and a short vowel. It has also been identified as a late Hebrew form (Curtis and Madsen 1910: 395). This has now been shown to be the case, as similar dissimulated forms from Qumran attest. Be that as it may, its occurrence here was most likely occasioned by the two instances of מביאים, with the combination of the letters יאי, in the verse, the latter of which immediately follows הערביאים (contrast the non-dissimulated forms in Neh 4:1; 2 Chr 21:16; 22:1; but see 2 Chr 26:7). Apropos an extraneous *'aleph*, the following poem by E. Geibel (1815-1884) helps put the endeavor of biblical criticism in (its proper?) perspective:

Es steht auf seinem Katheder
　　Es steht auf seinem Katheder

Jehoshaphat was one of the kings of Judah who received a fully positive evaluation. As such, the Chronicler has fleshed out the report of his reign, as presented in 1 Kgs 22:41-51, with the addition in part of material which adds to the luster of his reign and serves, by implication, to point up his cultic fidelity (2 Chr 17:1-21:1). Into such a section fall the verses under discussion.

V 10 serves to emphasize the rewards to which Jehoshaphat's faithfulness entitled him. The fear of YHWH, to which may be compared the Assyrian *puluḫtu* (*u*) *melammu*, which overwhelmed his enemies and made them docile, resulted in the divine blessing of peace during his reign. As Myers[245] has sketched the development in the Chronicler's account: Jehoshaphat's piety brought him strength, which led to tribute, which enabled him to engage in building projects.

In spite of the formulaic nature of much of this account, Williamson[246] has found four reasons to support his contention that the notice of the receipt of tribute from the Philistines and Arabs may be based on an authentic tradition:

1. Philistia is not treated as a whole. Rather, *some* of the Philistines rendered tribute.

Der Hofrat und doziert,
Der Meister, der mit Ruhme
Ebraica traktiert.
Rings lauschen die Studenten
Andächtig, wie er spricht;
Da stutzt er, und bedenklich
Umwölkt sich sein Gesicht.
"Hier steht ein Aleph", ruft er,
"Was will das Aleph hier?
Wo kommt es her? Vergebens
Den Kopf zerbrech' ich mir."
Mit neunundneunzig Gründen
Darauf beweist er scharf,
Dass hier bei Leib und Leben
Kein Aleph stehen darf.
"Und wer den Text verballhornt",
Beschliesst er indigniert,
"Hätt' besser Schafe gehütet
Als Habakuk ediert."
Er schlägt aufs Buch im Zorne,
Da springt das Aleph weg,
Was ihn so sehr verdrossen,
War nur ein Fliegendreck.

[245] 1965b: 100.

[246] 1982: 283.

2. The Arab tribes to the south and southwest of Judah had very possibly fallen under the Judean sphere of influence at the end of the reign of his predecessor Asa, as a result of his war against Zerah the Cushite (2 Chr 14:9-15[247]).
3. The tribute recorded in v 11 is localized.
4. The tribute is relatively modest, in spite of the numbers involved being "stylized."

Thus, following Williamson, it is valid to view this report as another important historical datum in our study of the course of Philistine history.

YHWH Stirs Up the Philistines: 2 Chr 21:16-17

(16) YHWH stirred up against Jehoram[248] the spirit[249] of the Philistines and the Arabs who bordered the Cushites.[250] (17) They invaded Judah, rent her and took away all the property found in the king's house, including his sons and his wives.[251] None of his sons remained other than Jehoahaz,[252] the youngest of his sons.

The account of Jehoram's reign in 2 Chr 21:2-20 is a well crafted story filled with irony.[253] As such, it goes to great length to contrast the reign of Jehoram

---

[247] See also Dillard 1987: 132.

[248] Son of Jehoshaphat, king of Judah c. 850-843. He was the first Davidid given a completely negative evaluation by the Chronicler (see Dillard 1987: 169).

[249] Not translated in G.

[250] G και τους ομορουσ των αιθιοπων "and those bordering the Ethiopians." The G translator has here made an error by failing to distinguish between the כושים who inhabited Ethiopia and those who belonged to a beduin tribe which settled in the area of Gerar (thus MT; G Gedor) in the Negeb (see 2 Chr 14:9-15--Eng 14:8-14; possibly also Num 12:1; Hab 3:7 Cushan). Since, according to the world-view of the G translator, the Arabs were located farther to the east and south than those mentioned in this verse who inhabited the Negeb, and the כושים dwelt south of the Egyptians, the MT relative clause modifying the Arabs has had to be changed into a mention of an otherwise unknown group living on the border of Ethiopia.

[251] G και τας θυγατερας αυτου "and his daughters," a somewhat free translation of ונשיו "and his wives," occasioned by the preceding mention of Jehoram's sons. See also v 14; Myers 1965b: 122; Dillard 1987: 163.

[252] The only other time that Judean Ahaziah is referred to in the MT by the biform of his name, i.e. Jehoahaz, is in 2 Chr 25:23, in which the form may have been influenced by the mention of Jehoahaz/Ahaziah of Israel two verses later. G^BA reflect the common form of his name.

[253] See Dillard 1987: 164, 169-70.

with the reigns of his father, Jehoshaphat, and grandfather, Asa. Whereas their political power and gift of progeny were a sign of divine favor, Jehoram's losses of territory (revolts of Edom and Libnah), battles (Philistines and Arabs), and progeny (contrast 2 Kgs 10:13-14) indicated divine wrath and retribution.[254] Whereas Jehoshaphat had received the tribute of the Philistines and the Arabs, Jehoram was attacked by them at YHWH's instigation.

Although Williamson[255] would find behind vv 16-17 an exaggerated report of an originally minor border incident,[256] the passage is historically problematic. According to v 17, the brothers of Ahaziah were deported by invaders before his accession. In 2 Kgs 10:13-14, on the other hand, his brothers were killed by Jehu subsequent to his own murder in 2 Kgs 9:27. In addition, the inclusion of Philistines in the party which invaded Judah does not square with 2 Chr 22:1, in which the brothers of Ahaziah were killed solely by Arabs who had overrun their camp. V 17, which mentions the incursion, does not provide a definite subject for the verbs of action. It is possible, therefore, that the Arabs, the immediate antecedent in v 16 of the verbs of v 17, should be regarded as the only actors in the latter verse.

There seems to be a symmetry in the accounts of the rebellions of Libnah and Edom (2 Chr 21:8-10), on the one hand, and of the incursions of the Philistines and the Arabs, on the other. Libnah, tentatively identified as Tel Burna,[257] lay to the southeast of Gath (at Tell es-Safi) and west of Moresheth-Gath (at Tel Goded/Tell el-Judeideh), and thus lay in the Shephelah borderland between Philistia and Judah. It is possible that it asserted its independence at this time, or even came under the control of Gath. Thus Libnah and the Philistines occupied the same general region vis-à-vis Judah, to the west. The region of Edomite and Arab control, on the other hand, lay to the south and east of Judah.[258]

---

[254] Dillard 1987: 166-68.

[255] 1982: 308.

[256] As has been pointed out (Curtis and Madsen 1910: 417; Williamson 1982: 308; Dillard 1987: 168), it is highly unlikely that בית-המלך would refer to the palace in Jerusalem. Rather, it was in an outlying encampment or fortress in which a number of his sons and wives were gathered, while Ahaziah was safely ensconced in Jerusalem.

[257] Tell Bornat, grid reference 138115; Aharoni 1979: 439; Pritchard 1987: 235.

[258] See Dillard 1987: 166-67, who, however, locates Libnah at Tell es-Safi.

Careful literary structure does not preclude the possibility that ancient documents were used by the Chronicler in his reconstruction of the reign of Jehoram, although it is difficult to determine the putative historical kernel.[259]

Ahaziah of Israel Inquires of a Philistine Oracle: 2 Kgs 1:2

(2) Ahaziah[260] fell through the lattice-work[261] in his upper chamber[262] which was in Samaria and injured himself. So he sent messengers and instructed them, "Go, inquire of Prince Baal,[263] the god of Ekron, whether I will recover from this injury."[264]

---

[259] See Williamson 1982: 308, who views the use of the form Jehoahaz as a possible indication of the antiquity of the source used by the Chronicler. Japhet (1993: 814-16) distinguishes between a short historical kernel, which related an account of raids against Judah, and a Chronistic expansion, which tries to interpret the raids theologically.

[260] Son and successor of Ahab, he reigned briefly over Israel c. 851-849 B.C.E.

[261] An architectural feature, presumably some sort of flimsy screen to keep out the sun and let in the cooling breezes, in the roof or balcony story of the royal palace at Samaria. The architectural concept as a whole has been related to the north Syrian *bīt-ḫilani* (see Montgomery and Gehman 1951: 349; Gray 1970: 462-63; Jones 1984: 377; Hobbs 1985: 8).

[262] The "upper chamber" at Samaria must have been considerably more elaborate than the one in which Elisha was sheltered in 2 Kgs 4:10-11.

[263] Reading בעל זבול as against MT בעל זבוב "Baal of the Flies." See also vv 3, 6, 16. Although classical parallels to the concept of gods in fly guises have been adduced (see Eissfeldt 1936: 36; Gray 1970: 463; Jones 1984: 377; Cogan and Tadmor 1988: 25; and in a lighter vein, Zeus in Act 2 of Jacques Offenbach's *Orpheus in the Underworld*), it appears most likely that the biblical text is attempting to denigrate a title of Baal known from the Ugaritic texts (see Gordon 1965: 393a, s.v. *zbl* I). The appellation זבל/zbl also appears as an element in the name of Ahaziah's presumed mother's name, Jezebel, wherein it has been repointed by the masoretes to refer to refuse, rather than to Prince Baal. Most of the G traditions and Josephus support the MT version of the name. However, Symmachus does read βεελζεβουλ (see G²), possibly under the influence of the earliest NT traditions (see the Chester Beatty papyri), wherein Beelzebub is termed Beelzebul (Matt 10:25; 12:24, 27; Mark 3:22; Luke 11:15, 18-19). For an attempt to explain the name as "Baal, the Flame," see Fensham 1967.

[264] Hebrew אם-אחיה מחלי זה. Compare Ben-Hadad's האחיה מחלי זה "Will I recover from this illness?" in 2 Kgs 8:8-9. In neither case, nor in that of Jeroboam seeking to know the chances of recovery of his son (1 Kgs 14: 1-3), is the divinity petitioned to provide healing (contrast the case of Naaman the leper in 2 Kgs 5; see also A. B. Ehrlich 1900: 330). Rather the aim is to elicit a positive or negative prognosis from an oracle regarding the ultimate chances of recovery. Regarding the MT phrase מחלי זה: The G, Syr, Vulg, and Targ evidence would support a reading מחליי זה "from this injury of mine." Gray (1970: 461 n. a) assumes a haplography of the final letter of מחליי in the MT. On the other hand, GKC (para. 126 y) cites this as an example of a non-articulated attribute with a substantive determined only by a suffix, assuming that חלי is a contracted form (see also 2 Kgs 8:8-9; Jer 10:19).

This passage is important to this study in what it reveals about Philistine religion and the possible intercourse between the petty states of Canaan in the late Iron Age. Although it would be tempting to see in the mention of "Baal of the Flies" a combination of the indigenous Canaanite name for the contemporaneous head of the pantheon with a holdover of a divine manifestation (gods in fly guises) from the Philistines' original Aegean homeland, it is much more likely that what we have here is evidence for the Philistines' assimilation to the cult of the land in which they settled.[265] This is all the more likely in view of the strength of the cult of Baal at the time, as reflected in the biblical texts, particularly in the Elijah and Elisha cycles. It would be expected that Ahaziah, the son of Ahab and the son or step-son of Jezebel, would turn to an oracle of Baal for answer to a question of such great personal concern. His subsequent reception by Elijah, if one can consider the biblical account of Elijah's denunciation as reflecting an actual event, was to be anticipated.

Shunammite Sojourn in Philistia: 2 Kgs 8:2-3

(2) The woman arose and did[266] as the man of God[267] had told her.[268] She went with her household and dwelt in[269] the land of the Philistines

---

[265] Gray (1970: 463) has made the piquant observation that the Philistines' assimilation to the local cult arose at an early stage of their settlement in response to a need to placate the local gods. An analogous case is provided in the need of the settlers in the territory of the former kingdom of Israel following the Assyrian conquest to placate YHWH and to include him in their worship (2 Kgs 17:24-41). At this point notice should be taken of Rofe's 1973 dating of 2 Kgs 1 to the same time as Zech 1-6; 1 Chr 21; Dan 7-12; Enoch, and Baruch, all of which he has identified as late prophetic/apocalyptic texts.

[266] Thus MT ותעש and G. Although the text of 6QKgs is quite damaged at this point, since it has a shorter text than MT it is inferred that 6QKgs read שתלך כדבר איש האלה[י]ם] אל ארץ [פלשתים] שבע שנים ותקם האשה] "The woman arose and went according to the word of the man of God to the land of the Philistines for seven years" in this verse (Baillet, Milik, and de Vaux 1962: 109, Gray 1970: 526; Cogan and Tadmor 1988: 87).

[267] Thus MT איש האלהים, G^L, and 6QKgs. G^BAN read "Elishah."

[268] "and did as the man of God had told her": Because this clause breaks the narrative flow of the passage, Jones (1984: 439) has assumed that this is an editorial addition. The placement of καθως ειπεν αυτη ο ανθρωπος του θεου "as the man of God had said to her," which presumably is the equivalent of the MT כדבר איש האלהים, at the end of the verse in G^L may indicate that this phrase was secondarily added to the verse, or crept into it as a marginal note.

[269] 6QKgs' shorter text, in which the antecedent of the preposition is the verb ותלך "she went," rather than the MT's ותגר "she dwelt," has necessitated a change in preposition from the MT's ב "in" to אל "to."

for seven years. (3) At the end of seven years[270] the woman returned from the land of the Philistines[271] and went forth[272] to plead her case[273] before the king concerning her house and her field.

These two verses are an exerpt from the second story (2 Kgs 8:1-6) about the nameless woman whose son Elisha had revived. In the first story about her in 2 Kgs 4:8-37, she is termed a Shunammite. In the later account, she is identified solely through her relationship with her son and Elisha. On the question of this account's relationship to the remainder of the Elisha cycle, see Jones[274] and Hobbs.[275]

It is difficult to come to any conclusions regarding freedom of movement between Philistia and Israel on the basis of this story. As a folk-tale, it is possible that borders which may have existed in actuality were able magically to disappear for the sake of the storyteller's convenience. What cannot, however, be gainsaid is the rich reputation which the fertile Philistine plain had among the Israelites. The fertility of the Philistine plain in this story is all the more ironic, since it was to escape a famine that the woman from Shunem, which if located correctly at Shunem (Solem) overlooked the supposedly fertile Jezreel Valley, went to sojourn for seven years in Philistia.

Hazael of Aram Captures Gath: 2 Kgs 12:18--Eng 12:17

(18) At that time Hazael[276] king of Aram went up and fought against Gath and captured it; whereupon he set his sights on going up against Jerusalem.

---

[270] The first phrase of v 3 is missing in 6Q Kgs by haplography (see Baillet, Milik, and de Vaux 1962: 109), the scribe's eye having jumped from שבע שנים at the end of v 2 to the same words in v 3a. G[L] adds the explicative του λιμου "of famine."

[271] G[Bju] add εις την πολιν "into the city." Baillet, Milik, and de Vaux (1962: 109-110), followed by Hobbs (1985: 95), have restored the equivalent Hebrew phrase אל העיר at the same point in 6QKgs. Cogan and Tadmor (1988: 87) read a badly damaged לצעק אל "to plead her cse before" following פלשתים.

[272] Thus MT and 6QKgs (ותצא), G[L] (εξηλθε), and OL. G[BA] ηλθεν does not necessarily reflect a *Vorlage* ותבא "she came" (*contra* Gray 1970: 526 n. f).

[273] Hebrew לצעק. On this word as a legal term see Jones 1984: 440; Cogan and Tadmor 1988: 79-80.

[274] 1984: 438-39.

[275] 1985: 96-98.

[276] King of Aram, c. 844/842-800 B.C.E. (Pitard 1986: 189).

If this verse refers to a conquest of Philistine Gath,[277] then it is of great significance for this study, whether or not one assumes that Gath was autonomous at the time. Hobbs[278] has remarked on the dispassionate archival style of writing in vv 18-19, thus assuming that this notice in 2 Kgs bases itself on an ancient tradition. For a full discussion, see the historical synthesis in Chapter Three, in addition to the next section.

Hazael Captures the North Philistine Coast: 2 Kgs 13:22 + G^{Lg}

(22) Hazael king of Aram[279] oppressed Israel throughout the reign of Jehoahaz,[280] (G^{Lg})[281] and he seized Philistia out of his hands from the Western Sea up to Aphek.

Although G^L is the best witness to G in 2 Kings, this half verse in G^L bristles with difficulties. First, what is meant by τον αλλοφυλον? Second, what is the "Western Sea." Third, which of the two cities named Aphek is being referred to?

Some[282] would assume that the reference must be to the Aphek that lay in northern Israel, which has tentatively been identified with En-Gev[283] on the southeastern side of the Sea of Galilee. In this case the Western Sea would refer to the Galilee.[284] The problem with this is that 1) the Sea of Galilee was never referred to as the "Western Sea," that name being reserved for the Mediterranean; and 2) this territory never belonged to the Philistines, at least

---

[277] As claimed e.g. by Würthwein 1984: 358.

[278] 1985: 151.

[279] "king of Aram": Missing in G^B.

[280] As with the king of Judah, a biform of the name Ahaziah. Jehoahaz was king of Israel c. 816-800 B.C.E.

[281] In G^L, represented by borc₂e₂, this addition appears at the beginning of v 24. This follows immediately upon the end of v 22, since in G^L v 23 is omitted here. G^g, which often preserves Lucianic readings, places the addition at the end of v 23.

[282] E.g. Gray 1970: 601.

[283] Khirbet el-Asheq, grid reference 210243; Aharoni 1979: 430; Pritchard 1987: 213.

[284] Gray (1970: 601 n. a) has argued that in τον αλλοφυλον, literally "the stranger," is hidden the Hebrew הגוי "the gentile," a misreading of הגליל "the Galilee."

subsequent to their being restricted to their heartland by David. Some have conjectured that the Western Sea must be a result of G^L's mistakenly reading ים המערב for ים הערבה "the Sea of the Plain," which we know as the Dead Sea, in its *Vorlage*.[285] An unstated assumption of such a view is that G^L's reading was present in a Hebrew *Vorlage*.

These two difficulties disappear if one assumes that the Aphek being referred to is Aphek-Antipatris (Ras el-Ain, grid reference 143168), at the source of the Yarkon River, which flows from Aphek in a westerly direction until it empties into the Western Sea, the Mediterranean. That Hazael campaigned in this area is demonstrated by 2 Kgs 12:18--Eng 12:17, in which a campaign against Gath and Jerusalem, which would have entailed movement through the coastal plain, is mentioned. However, even that area bounding the Yarkon River is presumed to be too far north for Philistine territory at the time.

The form αλλοφυλον[286] in the singular is unexpected, unless translating the gentilic פלשתי. When translating the term for the people as a whole (פלשתים) or the name of the region (פלשת), the plural αλλοφυλοι is normally employed. Although the formal equivalent of the first occurrence of פלשתים in 1 Sam 13:3 is τον αλλοφυλον, G^B has misunderstood the word נציב "commander" as a proper name and, hence, has translated the putative adjective modifying it as a singular. In this manner the MT "commander of the Philistines" has become in G "Nasib the Philistine." It is of interest to note that in 2 Kgs 8:28 Hazael is referred to as βασιλεως αλλοφυλων "king of the Philistines," instead of "king of Aram/Syria." However, that is an error which appears only in G^{BAN}, and not in G^L and, hence, cannot be used as evidence for a translational tendency in this passage in G^L.

Complicating the picture in this passage is the order of verses in the various versions of the biblical text. On the basis of their annalistic style and their content, it would appear that MT v 22 belongs most properly with either v 3, v 7,[287] or v 24.[288] In G^L, MT v 23 is placed following v 7. The variation between G^L and G^g in the placement of the plus has been noted above.

Whatever the original annalistic account of Jehoahaz's reign looked like, it has been edited by the Deuteronomist and interwoven with the Elisha

---

[285] See Montgomery and Gehman [following Rahlfs] 1951: 438; Gray 1970: 601.

[286] Translated above as "Philistia."

[287] In a note to v 7, the NJV (NJPS) suggests that the original place of v 7 was after v 3.

[288] See Gray 1970: 600; Jones 1984: 505.

tradition in order to demonstrate the power of the true prophetic word and to explain how Israel got out from under the grip of Aram. 2 Kgs 13:1-9 is an account of Jehoahaz's reign, including an account of God's intercession on his people's behalf (vv 4-5). Vv 10-13 present an annalistic account of the reign of Jehoash, son of Jehoahaz, while vv 14-21 complete the Elisha cycle with accounts of his last sign act predicting a victory over Aram (vv 14-19), of his death (v 20a), and of a miracle associated with his grave (vv 20b-21). Vv 22-25 recapitulate the history of Aramean oppression (v 22, possibly in the form of a resumptive repetition), God's intercession on Israel's behalf (v 23), and the deliverance of Israel and recovery of its territory (vv 24-25). Thus, while an argument can be made that the original document underlying the Deuteronomist's historical reconstruction was organized differently, the Deuteronomist has so skillfully constructed the material in 2 Kgs 13 that it is most difficult to disentangle the sources.

Uzziah of Judah Expands into Northern Philistia: 2 Chr 26:6-7

(6) He (Uzziah[289]) went out and fought against the Philistines, breaching the wall of Gath, the wall of Jabneh,[290] and the wall of Ashdod; he built towns/fortresses in Ashdod and among the Philistines.[291] (7) God[292] assisted him[293] against the Philistines, against the Arabs[294] who dwell in Gur, [and] against the Meunites.[295]

---

[289] King of Judah for 52 years in the mid-eighth century B.C.E. His exact dates have been a source of great debate among biblical chronologists, although a reign overlapping with those of his predecessor, Amaziah, and of his successors, Jotham and Ahaz, c. 785-734 B.C.E. appears most likely (see Tadmor 1961a: 252-66; Thiele 1965: 73-115; Hayes and Hooker 1988: 48-54).

[290] This is the only mention of this town in this form in the Hebrew Bible. It is generally identified with the Jabneel on the border of Judah in Josh 15:11 and with Hellenistic Jamnia (located at Yavne [Yebna], grid reference 126141; see Curtis and Madsen 1910: 449; Aharoni 1979: 437; Williamson 1982: 334-35).

[291] This last clause, beginning with a non-apocopated converted verbal form (ויבנה "he built") and ending with the unbalanced pair Ashdod and the Philistines, could be a result of a corrupting dittography of elements from the first part of the verse. Of the four elements in this clause, three of them have parallels in the first half of the verse: בפלשתים (v 6a) - ובפלשתים (v 6b), יבנה - ויבנה, אשדוד - באשדוד (see Williamson 1982: 335). On the other hand, Curtis and Madsen (1910: 451) have speculated that the original version of v 6b read ערים בפלשתים ויבנה "he built fortresses among the Philistines." Ashdod would have crept into the text as a dittography. They have also cited Winckler's theory (in Schrader 1903: 262-63) that v 6b arose because of a marginal note explaining the early citation of Jabneh, עיר באשדוד "a city in Ashdod," creeping into the text and giving rise to both citations of Ashdod in the verse. Rudolph in *BHS* has proposed reconstructing v 6b as ויבז הערים באשדוד ובפלשתים "he plundered the cities of Ashdod and Philistia." In this emendation of ויבנה he is followed by Japhet (1993: 875). Since, however, the motif

Most scholars have understood this passage as an important historical source.[296] If so, then it provides a significant perspective on the politico-economic situation of the Philistines toward the middle of the eighth century B.C.E.[297] On the other hand, Miller and Hayes[298] have questioned the ascription of the information in the context of Chronicles. In spite of her support for the general historicity of the passage, Japhet[299] has identified a tension between the weakness of Ahaz vis-à-vis the Philistines as recorded in this passage and his supposed strength, as gleaned from Isa 14:28-29. However, the strongest argument against the common acceptance of the essential historicity of the passage has been mounted by Kalimi.[300] In his opinion, the motif of the breaching of the wall in this passage (ויפרץ את-חומת

---

of building is one which indicated a reward for fidelity to the divine in Chronicles, the mention of building cities or fortresses may not be out of keeping with the character of the Chronicler. In this connection it should be noted that Welten (1973: 195-96, 197) has included v 6a among the passages in which the Chronicler has relied on a historically reliable pre-exilic source, while v 6b is viewed as a gloss, which he dates to the Maccabean period.

[292] Thus the MT. G κυριος, which is, strictly speaking, equivalent to יהוה.

[293] Hebrew ויעזרהו, a pun on the bi-form of Uzziah's name, Azariah (עזריה).

[294] Thus the MT Qere ערבים. The Kethib reads ערביים.

[295] Reading בגור ועל המעונים. MT בגור-בעל והמעונים "in Gur-Baal and the Meunites." The putative name Gur-Baal has yet to be understood to everyone's satisfaction in this context, although the form *gr* + DN is attested as a pattern of personal names in Canaanite/Phoenician (see Donner and Röllig 1969: 47). The G επι της πετρας και επι "upon the rock and over/against" would probably indicate an understanding of the Hebrew *Vorlage* as בצור ועל(see also the Vulgate). The Targum, on the other hand, reads the place name as גרר "Gerar," which reading is supported by Rudolph in *BHS* and Myers (1965b: 149), and which is raised as a possibility by Japhet (1993: 875). However, Rinaldi (1963: 229-31), following a suggestion first made by Alt (1953 [1959]: 3.396-408), has advocated identifying the biblical Gur with the region of Gari, mentioned in El-Amarna letter 256 and located in the Negeb to the east of Beersheba (see also Williamson 1982: 335; Dillard 1987: 206). As Tadmor (1972: 222-30) has shown on the basis of ND 400 (first published by Wiseman 1951: 21-24 and pl. xi), the reference to the Meunites is to a beduin tribe inhabiting the northeastern Sinai peninsula. Hence, this reference should not be emended to read העמונים "the Ammonites," as appears in a few Hebrew manuscripts (and as was advocated by A. B. Ehrlich [1900: 463]). As a matter of fact, the reference to "Ammonites" in MT v 8 should be corrected to read "Meunites" with G (see also *BHS*). This would then make understandable the reference to Uzziah's fame spreading up to the border of Egypt, since that was the Meunites' area of habitation.

[296] Williamson 1982: 333-34; Dillard 1987: 206-07; Japhet 1993: 877.

[297] On the structure of this passage and a discussion of how the Chronicler utilized the sources available in fitting the facts of Uzziah's reign to support his ideology, see Williamson 1982: 332-33.

[298] 1986: 311.

[299] 1993: 906.

[300] 1995: 280-81.

... גת) is a literary construct, reversing the punishment inflicted on Uzziah's father, Amaziah, in 2 Kgs 14:13 and 2 Chr 25:23 (ירושלם ויפרץ בחומת).

The Philistines Exploit Judah's Weakness: 2 Chr 28:18

(18) The Philistines encroached upon Judahite cities in the Shephelah and the Negeb, capturing Beth-Shemesh,[301] Aijalon, Gederoth, Soco and its satellites, Timnah and its satellites,[302] and Gimzo and its satellites;[303] and they settled there.

V 18 belongs to a longer unit comprising vv 16 (upon which v 18 is dependent) to 21. If one accepts that the Chronicler employed in part reliable ancient documents in the composition of this passage, then this is an invaluable source for the history of the Philistines preceding their conquest by Assyria.[304] Although v 18a refers to towns captured in both the Shephelah and the Negeb, the towns listed in this verse which can be identified with reasonable certainty lie solely in the Shephelah: Beth-Shemesh and Timnah in the Sorek Valley, Soco in the Valley of Elah, and Aijalon in the valley of the same name.[305] Most would identify Gimzo with modern Gimzo (Jimzu) in the Aijalon Valley.[306] However, Doermann[307] has recently, without convincing evidence, suggested locating it at Tell el-Hesi[308] in the Philistine coastal plain. If ancient Gimzo is indeed located correctly at modern Gimzo (Jimzu), then the question arises, at what time this site, which would appear to lie in Israel's territory, came under the jurisdiction of Judah. Timm[309] has

---

[301] G^B exacerbates the situation for Ahaz, king of Judah, by expanding the text through the addition of και τα εν οικω κυριου και τα εν οικω βασιλεως και των αρχοντων και εδωκαν τω βασιλει "and the things in the house of the Lord, and the things in the house of the king and of the princes and they gave the king."

[302] The reference to "Timnah and its satellites" is missing in G^B owing to a haplography.

[303] In place of MT ואת-גמזו ואת-בנותיה it is preferable to read ואת-גמזו ובנותיה.

[304] See Williamson 1982: 343-34, 347-48; Dillard 1987: 219-21, 223; Irvine 1990: 95.

[305] See Aharoni 1974: 92.

[306] Grid reference 145148; see Abel 1938: 2.338; Aharoni 1979: 435.

[307] 1987: 142, 144.

[308] Tell el-Hesi, grid reference 124106.

[309] 1980: 38-39.

conjectured that the Judean-Israelite border ran north of Gimzo and, hence, that Gimzo belonged to Judah. Gederoth was also located in the Shephelah, in the third administrative district of Judah according to Josh 15:41. Its site is unknown.

A Prophecy Against the Philistines: Amos 1:6-8

(6) Thus says YHWH: "On account of the three transgressions of Gaza, and on account of four, I will not rescind it! On account of their exiling a complete[310] exile in order to hand (them) over to Edom,[311] (7) I will send fire on the wall[s][312] of Gaza, and it shall consume its citadels. (8) I will uproot him who sits (enthroned)[313] from Ashdod and him who grasps the scepter from Ashkelon; I will turn my hand against Ekron, and (even) the remnant of the Philistines shall perish!" Says [ ] YHWH.[314]

---

[310] Thus the MT שלמה.G has misread the consonantal text as the name σαλωμων "Solomon." See Symmachus, Theodotian, and the Vulgate for the correct reading.

[311] The suggestion has been made to emend the text to read לארם "to Aram" instead of לאדום (e.g. Barton 1980: 31). In support of this emendation Barton cited not only the common epigraphic confusion between *dalet* and *resh*, but also the supposed lack of contact between Philistia and Edom. Thus he conjectured that the Philistines may have bought off Hazael with the handing over of prisoners of war when he threatened Gath in 2 Kgs 12:18. On the other hand, Barton (1980: 35) concluded that it is impossible to date or to localize the putative historical references in Amos's oracles against the nations. As, however, Andersen and Freedman (1989: 259) have indicated, the plene spelling of Edom and, more importantly, the unanimity of the ancient versions in this reading would weaken the argument in favor of the proposed emendation. In addition, contrary to Barton, there is evidence in the Bible which indicates that Edom and Philistia did have a common economic interest in keeping Judah out of the southern Negeb and from being able to act as a middleman controlling access to the trade routes from Arabia, through Edom to Gaza (see 2 Chr 11:5-10; 21: 10; 28:17-18). Ultimately, the arguments on either side do not admit a clear decision.

[312] Thus G επι τα τειχη and Targ בשורי. See also A. B. Ehrlich 1912: 229. MT בחומת pointed as singular *běhômat* "on the wall." See also vv 10, 14.

[313] MT יושב. This is translated as a metaphor for the ruler of the city. See also Exod 15:15; Cross 1973: 130 and n. 65; Andersen and Freedman 1989: 253-54 "sovereign." More traditionally, NJV translates the phrase as "every inhabitant," which misses the parallelism between יושב "who sits (enthroned)" and שבט תומך "who grasps the scepter."

[314] Thus G (except for G^C κυριος κυριος). See Mays 1969: 32. MT אמר אדני יהוה "says Lord YHWH." The latter reading is supported by the Targumic אמר יי אלהים and by the Scroll of the Twelve Minor Prophets from Wadi Murabba'at (Wolff 1977: 130), and by the frequent incidence of this phrase throughout the book of Amos, with the exception of the oracles against the nations in chapters 1-2 (3:7, 8, 11, 13; 4:2, 5; 5:3; 6:8; 7:1, 2, 4 [2X], 5, 6; 8:1, 3, 9, 11; 9:8).

The collection of eight oracles against the nations in Amos 1:3-2:16 has been a subject of intense speculation over the years.[315] The major areas of investigation have included the structure of the oracles,[316] the date of their composition, and their historical context. Needless to say, these investigations are often intertwined.

At a minimum, the oracles against Aram (Amos 1:3-5), Philistia (1:6-8),[317] Ammon (1:13-15), and Moab (2:1-3), as well as the one against Israel (2:6-16), are viewed as original to the composition. Recently, Andersen and Freedman[318] have argued that the form-critical arguments adduced for questioning the inclusion of the oracles against Tyre (1:9-10), Edom (1:11-12), and Judah (2:4-5) can just as easily be employed to affirm their integrality to the composition.[319] As a matter of fact, Andersen and Freedman go on to treat this collection as a unit, albeit a composite one.

Speculation regarding the date of these oracles (at least Aram, Philistia, Ammon, Moab, and Israel) has also ranged widely. Dates have been adduced ranging from the time of Amos c. 760 B.C.E.,[320] to the period following the destruction of Israel in 722,[321] to the Judean post-exilic period in the late sixth century B.C.E., contemporaneous with Ezek 25.[322]

Unfortunately, the historical allusions in this series of oracles do not provide any basis, firm or otherwise, for dating the oracles,[323] which Andersen and Freedman[324] have termed an ahistorical "fantasy," stemming

---

[315] See e.g. Barton 1980; Fritz 1987.

[316] Mays 1969: 23; Wolff 1977: 135-39; Geyer 1986: 131; Fritz 1987: 27.

[317] Marti questioned the originality of the oracle against the Philistine cities. However, his view on the subject has remained without influence. See Wolff 1977: 144 and n. 50.

[318] 1989: 355-56.

[319] Andersen and Freedman reject the claim that the fact that the oracles against Tyre, Edom, and Judah do not include all of the five elements identified in the oracles against Aram, Philistia, Ammon, and Moab must be proof of their secondary addition to the series. In their opinion, the arguments can be used in support of the opposite claim, namely that the allegedly secondary oracles must have been integral to the original composition, since anyone adding passages secondarily would have been careful to cast them in the exact form of the originals.

[320] Wolff 1977: 149; Andersen and Freedman 1989: 141-44.

[321] Fritz 1987: 38.

[322] Geyer 1986: 140.

[323] Barton 1980: 35; Geyer 1986: 142; King 1988: 49; Andersen and Freedman 1989: 354-57.

[324] 1989: 256.

from the same visionary source of inspiration as Amos's visions in chapters 7-9.

The oracle against the Philistines serves as a case in point.

Even assuming that Amos 1:6-8 stems from c. 760 B.C.E., it is impossible to glean much information of a factual-historical nature from this oracle. After a formulaic announcement of irrevocable judgment against Gaza,[325] the charge of exiling a complete population group and selling them into slavery to Edom is mentioned. Although this charge may rest upon a historical matrix which was known to Amos's audience, either a specific raid on a town or an ongoing fiscal policy among the Philistines, the capture and enslavement of captives not being unknown in the ancient Near East,[326] neither the identity of the captives nor the specificity of the charge were of import to Amos, who was concerned with a punishable breach of a universal code of morality,[327] or with violations of ancient covenant treaties with the united monarchy.[328] Muntingh[329] does, however, perspicaciously observe that, as a major outlet for trade between Egypt, Arabia, and Canaan and the north, Gaza could very well have been an important marketplace for the international slave trade.

The oracle continues with the extension of punishment to three additional Philistine cities, ending with the ultimate pronouncement of doom, that not even a remnant shall remain of the Philistines. They will be destroyed down to the last survivor.

Among the cities of the traditional Philistine pentapolis, the absence of Gath from this list is striking. A number of theories have been proposed to explain this, some of which have been listed conveniently by Mays:[330]

1. The oracle may date to after the destruction of Gath by Sargon II in 712 B.C.E.[331]
2. Gath may have belonged to Judah at the time (see especially 2 Chr 26:6).
3. Gath may have been a vassal of Ashdod.

---

[325] Gaza is mentioned first among the Philistine cities in Jer 47. It was also the objective of Tiglath-pileser III's campaign against Philistia in 734 B.C.E. Taken together, these references to Gaza may be an indication of the preeminence of Gaza, at least economically, among the Philistine cities. See also Wolff 1977: 157; Andersen and Freedman 1989: 258.

[326] See e.g. Wolff 1977: 157-58; Barton 1980: 20; Deut 21:10-14; 2 Sam 12:31; CH 280-281.

[327] Wolff 1977: 157-58; Andersen and Freedman 1989: 258.

[328] Thus F. M. Cross in a personal communication.

[329] 1964-65: 135.

[330] 1969: 33.

[331] See Tadmor (1958: 83 and n. 242) and Rainey (1975: 73*-74*) about Sargon's capture of Gath.

4. Gath may have been removed from Philistine hands by Hazael's raid in the previous century (2 Kgs 12:18).

Another line of reasoning has been pursued by Katzenstein[332] who, following a venerable tradition, assumed that the "remnant of the Philistines" (v 8) must be a reference to the survivors of an alleged destruction of Gath. In view, however, of the likelihood that this phrase is actually a reference to the total annihilation of the Philistines, it appears unlikely in this case that Gath is the referent.

Any resolution of these questions must remain tentative.

Ashdod (?) Witnesses Samaria's Evil: Amos 3:9

(9) Announce in the strongholds of Ashdod[333] and in the strongholds of the land[334] of Egypt, say: "Gather on the mountains[335] of Samaria and see the great tumult in it and the oppression[336] in its midst."

---

[332] 1973: 135, 197.

[333] Thus the MT, Targ, and Vulg. G εν ασσυριοις "in Assyria." The disagreement between the MT באשדוד and the retroverted G באשור will be discussed below.

[334] The suggestion has been made to delete this word (ארץ) with G (see Elliger in *BHS*). However, the word does appear in the admittedly oftentimes derivative G^{LC}, and the poetic structure of the first two phrases in the verse would appear to require its inclusion both on metrical and on structural grounds:

| השמיעו על-ארמנות באשדוד | a b c |
| ועל-ארמנות בארץ מצרים | b C' |

This bicolon exhibits parallelism and with the inclusion of בארץ achieves both an even stress count (3/3) and a fairly even syllable count (10/9). Wolff (1977: 189) has conjectured that the G translation of ארמנות as χωραις "places," which is often employed to translate Hebrew ארץ, caused G to leave out translating ארץ in order to avoid redundancy. Andersen and Freedman (1989: 405-06) simply draw attention to G's somewhat loose translation of Amos and point out that χωραι can be employed to translate either אדמות or ארצות, the former of which is orthographically similar to the MT ארמנות.

[335] Thus the MT in the plural. In G the more common singular form is found, το ορος, which can be retroverted into Hebrew as הר. The expression הר שומרון "Mount Samaria" also appears in Amos 4:1; 6:1. A decision for one of the variants depends on one's understanding of the invitation to the nations to observe the sins of Israel, whether they are to surround and look down on Samaria (from the "hills"), or whether they are to observe the situation from inside the city itself ("hill").

[336] Although עשוקים is here translated as an abstract noun "oppression" in parallelism with מהומת "tumult" (on which see GKC para. 124 e), the word can also be translated as the noun "oppressed" (Wolff 1977: 190).

It is questionable whether this passage deals with Ashdod, and, even if it does, there would be little to glean from the passage other than another indication that Philistia was lurking somewhere in Amos's consciousness.

The evidence of G points to a parallelism of Assyria and Egypt, a pairing which would make much more sense than the pairing of Ashdod and Egypt. As Andersen and Freedman[337] have indicated, Egypt and Assyria were a frequent pair among the eighth century prophets. However, because this would be the only mention of Assyria in Amos, Wolff[338] has argued that Assyria was not yet on Amos's political horizon. In addition, Wolff felt that the pairing of Ashdod and Egypt, as the more difficult reading, would not have arisen as a secondary reading.[339]

As to Wolff's first argument, in the light of Shalmaneser III's and Adad-nirari III's campaigns to the west, including the one of 796 B.C.E., in which the latter received tribute from many of the states of Canaan, it is not unreasonable to assume that Amos was familiar with Assyria. However, more important to this argument, is the question of the aim of Amos in listing Egypt and another country. No argument stronger than Mays's contention[340] that Egypt and Ashdod were paragons of "violence and injustice" has been put forward. How much more this would apply to the dreaded Assyrian war machine. In fact, what Amos's aim in mentioning Egypt and Assyria was was to list the names of the nations at the extremes of the fertile crescent. The nations in between had been the objects of his indictments in chapters 1-2.

As to Wolff's second argument, Andersen and Freedman[341] are probably correct in referring to the pairing of Ashdod and Egypt as a "too difficult" reading. The orthographic similarity of the two words probably occasioned a scribe to misread. Thus it is most likely that Ashdod was not originally mentioned in this verse.

---

[337] 1989: 404, 406.

[338] 1977: 190, 192-93.

[339] See also Mays (1969: 62), who surmised that the G version arose on account of the translator's feeling that Ashdod was inappropriate paired with Egypt.

[340] 1969: 63.

[341] 1989: 404.

Gath Compared with Zion[342] and Samaria: Amos 6:2

(2) Cross over to Calneh and see, then go from there to Great Hamath, then go down[343] to Philistine Gath. Are (you) better than these kingdoms? Is their area larger than your area?

An interpretation of this verse is very difficult.[344] There have been two major lines of reasoning in the secondary literature. First is to assume that v 2 represents a quote of the arrogant ruling classes of Samaria and, possibly, Jerusalem.[345] Second is to attribute the quote to the prophet, at least in the context of the oracle in vv 1-6/7 as it has been transmitted. There is also heated discussion about whether v 2 was integral to the original oracle, a later updating of the oracle by Amos,[346] or by a member of his prophetic school.[347]

Is this verse a simple comparison of cities arbitrarily chosen because they were roughly equivalent in size, or wealth, or power? Or does this oracle list these cities in unison because of a common shared fate?

If the verse is to be understood as referring to the previous destruction of the three cities in question, then it cannot be dated before 738 B.C.E., when Hamath and Kullani (Calneh = Calno in Isa 10:9) were taken by Tiglath-pileser III. Gath, however, although captured by Uzziah in the second quarter of the eighth century, would not have fallen under Assyrian influence until Tiglath-pileser's campaigns of 734-732. This has led Wolff[348] to date v 2 to the period between 738 and 733. Andersen and Freedman,[349] on the other hand, felt that the thrust of the verse is a comparison of the power and wealth of the three cities, all of which would be subjected to the same fate in the

---

[342] On the problems of reading "Zion" with the MT in Amos 6:1, see Wolff 1977: 269-70.

[343] G adds εκειθεν "from there," which is equivalent to Hebrew משם. Although it would fit the context, it may be a dittography from the previous phrase in G.

[344] That G also had difficulty understanding and interpreting this verse is made evident by G's translation of כלנה "Calneh" as παντες "all" (deriving the form from Hebrew כל/kol "all"), and of הטובים "better" as τας κρατιστας "the best/strongest/mightiest," which reflects an understanding of הטובים as an adjective modifying גת-פלשתים "Philistine Gath."

[345] I.e. Zion, about which see n. XXX above; Mays 1969: 115; Wolff 1977: 271.

[346] Andersen and Freedman 1989: 559.

[347] Wolff 1977: 275.

[348] 1977: 274.

[349] 1989: 558-59.

years to come. In their view, Amos composed this oracle with a prescient political sense, drawing on his knowledge of the presumed line of Assyrian march. What they have emphasized, however, is that this verse cannot be employed in reconstructing a history of Gath.[350]

Philistine Exodus: Amos 9:7

(7) "Are you not like the Cushites for me?" says YHWH, "Did I not bring Israel up out of Egypt, and the Philistines from Caphtor,[351] and Aram from Qir[352] ?"

This verse is of extreme importance for the scholar of Israel's religion, containing as it does a breathtaking rhetorical question which denies the uniqueness of the Exodus.[353] However, its importance for the historian is considerably less. Of interest in this regard is primarily the ancient Israelites' ethnic understanding of the origins of the Philistines and the Arameans.[354] Thus the text contributes to an understanding of Israel's ethnic world-view. However, in the context of political history it contributes little.

Philistine Soothsayers: Isa 2:5-6

(5) [355] House of Jacob, come and let us walk in YHWH's light! (6) For you have ignored[356] your people, House of Jacob;[357] for they are filled

---

[350] Andersen and Freedman 1989: 560-61.

[351] In place of "Caphtor" the G reads καππαδοκιας "Cappadocia."

[352] Thus MT מקיר. G εκ βοθρου "from the pit," reading Hebrew ממקור/מקור. This may have been occasioned by the common orthographic confusion betweem *waw* and *yod*, although an attempt to interpret the obscure מקיר may also have played a role.

[353] See e.g. Mays 1969: 157-59; Wolff 1977: 344-49; Andersen and Freedman 1989: 867-85.

[354] On the question of Philistine origins, see Dothan 1982a: 21-23; Brug 1985: 8-15, 201-05.

[355] G begins the verse with the prosaic και νυν "and now."

[356] Hebrew נטשתה. Watts (1985: 30, 32) has suggested retroverting the G ανηκε γαρ τον λαον αυτου into Hebrew as כי נטה את העמו, which he then translates as "For it applies to his people." Unfortunately,

with ... from the east[358] and soothsayers[359] like the Philistines; and with the children of foreigners they clap (their hands?).[360]

V 6 is a verse which bristles with difficulties. It is, however, just one of the verses in Isa 2, a chapter which is considered one of the most difficult in the Isaianic corpus.[361] Other than the problems of understanding the individual words and their relationship to each other as outlined above, the context of the verse and its general interpretation have remained a source of conflict.

Leaving aside Watts's idiosyncratic interpretation of the whole book of Isaiah as a work redacted in the fifth century B.C.E. as a drama in twelve acts,[362] it has been most common to divide chapter 2 between vv 5 and 6,[363]

---

the syntax of the retroverted phrase, with the definite article prefixed to a noun with a pronominal suffix, causes more difficulty than it resolves.

[357] Thus MT. G τον οικον του ισραηλ "the house of Israel."

[358] It has long been felt that there is either a word missing in this phrase or that the original wording has been corrupted. Proposals for restoring the phrase have included inserting the word קסמים/qōsĕmîm "sorcerers" before מקדם "from the east" (Kaiser 1983: 55 n. 1, where it is written incorrectly with a *nun* at the end; Hayes and Irvine 1987: 85), reading either that word or מעקדים "magicians" in place of מקדם (Thomas in *BHS*), or "extrapolating" from the retroverted G ארצם "their country" or Targ ארעכון "your (pl.) country" and inserting ארמים "Arameans" before מקדם (Roberts 1985: 300-01; see also Buchanan [1912: 58] who reconstructs ארצו "his country" on the basis of G). In translating מקדם, G employs the phrase το απ' αρχης "from the beginning."

[359] Although Bergsträsser (1918: para. 20 e) declared עננים/'ōnĕnîm a mistake for the Polel participle מעננים/mĕ'ōnĕnîm, *HALAT* (881b) has cited the form as correctly derived on the basis of GKC para. 52 s, in which the preformative *mem* of the Pu'al participle can be dropped in nominal forms.

[360] This final phrase of v 6 has also caused great consternation among biblical critics. Starting from G's και τεκνα πολλα αλλοφυλα εγενηθη "and many foreign children were born to them," this phrase has resisted satisfactory interpretation. Although the words "children of foreigners/foreign children" (A. B. Ehrlich's [1912: 11] "poetic" *Dinge fremden Ursprungs*) can be readily understood, their relationship to the verb ישפיקו is unclear. The root שפק has been related to its homonym ספק (see BDB 706b). However, there are two possible semantic fields into which this opens. The first would be to understand the verb as derived from the meaning of striking or clapping one's hands. The second would be to derive it from the meaning of abounding, such as Ehrlich (1912: 11) does. The more common solution is the first and would entail the emendation of ובילדי "and with the children" to ובידי "and into the hands" (see e.g. BDB 706b; JB), unless one assumes that the sense of hands is included in the verb. But what would that gesture imply? Roberts (1985: 301) concluded that that would indicate Israel and its allies "making derisive gestures toward Jerusalem," while Hayes and Irvine (1987: 86) concluded that it would indicate the making of agreements between Israel and its allies (see also Buchanan's [1912: 49] "strikes bargains with (?)" and Watts's [1985: 30] "do business with"). A third solution would be to follow the Targumic ובנימוסי "according to the customs of," as does the NJV/NJPS.

[361] See e.g. Buchanan (1912: 48) quoting Duhm; Hayes and Irvine 1987: 83. Referring to the unit Isa 2:5-22, Duhm (1914: 17) claimed: *"Dies Stück ist das schlechtest erhaltene des ganzen Buches."*

[362] See Watts 1985: esp. xlix-liv.

and to view it as an accusation of God for abandoning his people.[364] However, as Buchanan[365] rightly noted, v 6 forms an improbable beginning to a poetic composition. Although he recognized the similarity in language between vv 5 and 6, Buchanan[366] went on to reject their primary relationship, assuming that v 5 was a later and derivative "homiletic reflection" of v 6. Roberts[367] has recently taken this observation to its logical conclusion and most persuasively argued for the primary relationship between vv 5 and 6, highlighting the chiasm achieved by the dual occurrence of the vocative "House of Jacob," the subject of the verb נטשתה, in these verses. In this he is following a translation and interpretative tradition that reaches back to the Targum, through various medieval Jewish commentators, to A. B. Ehrlich[368] and the modern NJPS/NJV translation of the Bible.

The reference to Philistine soothsayers, however, is puzzling. Although oracular recourse to Philistine deities was not unknown in ancient Israel, 2 Kgs 1 being a case in point, nowhere else is this type of activity presented as a unique characteristic of the Philistines.

Following Cazelles,[369] Roberts[370] has argued that the core of Isa 2 is to be dated to the period of the Syro-Ephraimite war. In the latter's opinion, most of the traces of editorial activity in reworking earlier Isaianic prophecies for later audiences can be attributed to Isaiah, who had a career spanning close to half a century, rather than to his successors. With his dating of the prophecy to the mid-730's B.C.E., Roberts has sought a parallel to this passage in Isa 9:11, in both of which passages, bound together by the use of מקדם "from the east," he has found references to the Philistines and the Arameans. Basing himself then on his dating of the passage and on the seemingly cultic reference in v 6b, Roberts[371] has speculated that the Syro-Ephraimite

---

[363] Buchanan 1912: 48; Kaiser 1983: 56; Hayes and Irvine 1987: 82-83, 85; RSV; JB; see also Roberts's (1985: 290-91) review of the history of theories of composition of chapter 2.

[364] Thus making God the subject of נטשתה; see Buchanan 1912: 49-50; Kaiser 1983: 59; Hayes and Irvine 1987: 84; RSV; JB.

[365] 1912: 49.

[366] 1912: 48.

[367] 1985: 293-94, 298-99.

[368] 1912: 10.

[369] 1980: 412-13.

[370] 1985: 292-93.

[371] 1985: 301, 304-05.

coalition was not only military in nature, but included "at least an accomodation to the gods of the Arameans and the Philistines."[372] Unfortunately, this theory rests on too many unproven assumptions, such as the date of chapter 2, the involvement of the Philistines in an Aramean-led coalition, and the thrust of the seriously defective v 6, to enable it to be employed in the reconstruction of the history of the period.

Philistia and Aram Oppress Israel: Isa 9:11--Eng 9:12

(11) Aram from the front and the Philistines[373] from the back[374] have devoured Israel with an open mouth;[375] in spite of this his anger has not receded, and his arm remains extended.

The critical question with this short snippet of a longer series of oracles[376] is whether it reflects a historical set of circumstances or whether the usage of Aram and Philistia is meant figuratively.

If the text of Isaiah is referring to a historical moment, then one must find a period when both Aram and Philistia were enemies of Israel. Since Aram, Ashkelon, and Israel were united in opposition to Tiglath-pileser III until the fall of Damascus, one must search for a date before 734 B.C.E. Depending on one's dating of the Syro-Ephraimite coalition against Judah, whether before or after the initial appearance of the Assyrians in 734, time must be left previous to this date for a period of common action by Aram and Israel.[377]

---

[372] Roberts 1985: 305.

[373] Thus the MT. G ελληνας "Greeks." Aquilla, Symmachus and Theodotian follow the MT and read τους φυλιστιειμ.

[374] "from the front ... from the back": Hebrew מקדם ... מאחור. These words can also be translated as "from the east ... from the west."

[375] : "with an open mouth": Hebrew בכל-פה. A. B. Ehrlich (1912: 38) suggested emending this phrase to בכל-פאה "on every side." His suggestion has not found wider acceptance

[376] As is so often the case when dealing with prophetic texts, the relationship of the various literary sub-units to each other and to their contextual situation is a matter of much speculation. Buchanan (1912: 182) delimited the unit to which v 11 belongs as including vv 7-11. Kaiser (1983: 22), on the other hand, extended the unit until Isa 10:4 (thus also Irvine 1990: 235-50), to give just two examples.

[377] Buchanan (1912: 184) and Thompson (1982: 18) both dated the passage to the time before the Syro-Ephraimite war. Hayes and Irvine (1987: 186-87; See also Irvine 1990: 239-40) conjectured that while Aram took Transjordan and Galilee from Israel, Aram may have joined the Philistines in seizing control of the Sharon Plain. They thus assume the originality of the reference to Rezin in v 10, a reference which

Whether the Philistines were hostile or friendly to Israel in the period before the Syro-Ephraimite war cannot be determined. On the basis of 2 Chr 28:18, the Philistines seem to have been acting in opposition to Judah's interests only. Yet the inclusion of Gimzo in the territory ostensibly seized from Judah would possibly indicate some Philistine interest in what had, at least once, been Israel's territory.

The image of Aram and the Philistines devouring Israel front and back could also be understood metaphorically. These two traditional enemies of Israel served to define the limits of the petty powers with which Israel often found itself in conflict, quite possibly the external equivalent of the internal "from Dan to Beersheba." For the first few centuries of Israelite existence as a nation, in other words from the turn of the first millennium B.C.E. until the time of Tiglath-pileser, the traditional powers of Egypt and Mesopotamia exercised but little influence on the life of the states of Canaan. Thence arose the more immediate concern with Aram and Philistia as threats to Israel. It may thus be best to conclude with Buchanan[378] that Aram and Philistia are employed figuratively in this verse to represent Israel's enemies, although the reference as such is most readily understandable in the light of a period when Israel and Aram were in conflict.

---

is questioned by many (e.g. Kaiser 1983: 221; NJPS/NJV; RSV; see also G). Attempts to find a historical referent for this verse have included Kaiser's (1983: 222) suggestion that in this verse may be a reference to Saul's Philistine wars.

[378] 1912: 184.

APPENDIX B

ASSYRIAN SOURCES

For the latter part of the period of time that is the scope of this study, namely the first quarter of the first millennium B.C.E., the richest source of contemporaneous ancient documentation bearing on the history of the Philistines is to be found in the cuneiform literature of Assyria. As the interest of the Assyrian empire turned westward, it was inevitable that the region of Philistia would become enmeshed in the net of Assyrian imperialism.

Adad-nirari III

The first possible mention of Philistia *per se* occurs before any mention of individual Philistine cities in two texts from the reign of Adad-nirari III.[1]

---

[1] Upon reading *ANET*, one would assume that the first mention of a Philistine site in Assyrian cuneiform dates to the reign of Shalmaneser III. According to A. L. Oppenheim, Band III of Shalmaneser's Balawat Gates is a depiction of "Phoenicia, Tyre, Sidon, Gaza," the last-mentioned presumably being the Philistine city (*ANET* 281). That "Gaza" is not meant to refer to another city by the same name is indicated by the index to the volume which knows of only one city by this name (*ANET* 513). However, there are a number of difficulties with such an ascription. First, the city which is being conquered by Shalmaneser's forces in the third band, and which Oppenheim understood as Gaza, is named Ḫazazu in the cuneiform. Ḫazazu was a well known city in northern Syria, which belonged at that time to the land of Patina, originally known as Ḫattina in the scholarly literature (Hawkins 1972-75a and b; see also Tadmor 1975: 37). It is to be kept distinct from Ḫazati/Ḫazzutu, which was the cuneiform name of Philistine Gaza (for Ḫazat and references, see Parpola 1970: 159; for Ḫazazu, see 1970: 160). Second, there is no evidence that Shalmaneser ever campaigned as far south as southern Palestine (about which, see Chapter Three above). Third, Ḫazazu is mentioned again in the Kurkh Monolith Inscription as one of the cities of Patina which Shalmaneser conquered in his campaign of 858 B.C.E. (Ḫa-za-zu *KB* 1.160, 161 col. i line 11; text: III R pls. 7-8; edition: *KB* 1.150-175; translations: *ARAB* 1 paras, 594-611; *TGI* 49-50 [col. ii 90-102]; *ANET* 277-79 [cols. i 29 - ii 13, 78-102]; *TUAT* 1/4 360-62 [col. ii 86-102]). Indeed, in this case, Oppenheim transcribed it as such (*ANET* 278). Thus, the first mention of Philistia in Assyrian sources cannot be dated as early as the time of Shalmaneser III in the mid ninth century B.C.E. Other that the one reference in *ANET*, all other secondary sources viewed by the author follow the reading of Ḫazazu adopted here. See e.g. L. W. King 1915: 12, 23, pls. xiii-xviii; *ARAB* 1 paras. 613-14.

Nimrud Slab Inscription

Text: I R pl. 35 #1. Editions: Tadmor 1973: 148-50 (s.v. the Calah slab); *KB* 1: 190-93. Translations: *ARAB* 1 paras. 738-41; *ANET* 281-82 (lines 1-21); *DOTT* 51 (lines 1-22); *TGI* 53-54 (lines 11-16); *TUAT* 1/4 367-68 (lines 11-21). See also: Schramm 1973: 115-116.

The Nimrud slab inscription of Adad-nirari III was found in 1854 by Loftus in his excavation of the site of ancient Calah. The original was lost, and publication was possible only from paper squeezes by Norris in the first volume of Rawlinson's *Cuneiform Inscriptions of Western Asia* (= I R pl. 35 #1). The lost slab represented the top half of a large monumental inscription of the type known variously as "display" or "summary inscriptions" in English, and as "*Übersichts-*" or "*Prunkinschriften*" in German.[2] Tadmor has defined the following elements as typical of the genre: "(a) a prologue, consisting of invocation to the gods and the king's titulature; (b) a geographically arranged summary of events; (c) the main section explaining the circumstances leading to the composition of the inscription, introduced by the formula *ina ūmēšūma* = 'at that time'; (d) an epilogue with maledictions."[3] The Nimrud slab inscription contains Tadmor's elements "a" (lines 1-14) and "b" (lines 15-25). This scheme can be further subdivided as follows: a) lines 1-5a list Adad-nirari's titulature, followed by a list of states which he supposedly brought into Assyrian vassalage (lines 5b-14a); b) lines 14b (just one word)-21 deal with his campaigns to the west, whose specific

---

[2] M. Weippert (1992: 43-46) has argued that the Nimrud slab inscription was a "*Bauinschrift*," although he also classifies it among the category of "*Prunkinschriften*." For a discussion of the terminology involved, see Tadmor 1973: 141 and nn. 2-4. It appears that E. Schrader, who originally identified the genre, first suggested the term "*Übersichtsinschrift*," which he later changed to what has become the more accepted term, "*Prunkinschrift*." Olmstead translated the latter term into English as "Display Inscription." Tadmor has more recently been advocating a translation into English of Schrader's original term as "Summary Inscription." See also Grayson 1980: 152 and n. 60, who finds the term "display" "inaccurate." We will be following Tadmor's terminology. The "summary inscription" distinguishes itself from the "annal" in its condensation and telescoping of the chronologically arranged events (mainly royal victories) of the latter into more general geographical catagories, or according to political importance. See also Olmstead 1916: 4-6, in which Olmstead warns about the "inferior value" of the genre relative to the annal in historical reconstruction; Tadmor 1967b: 7; Eph'al 1982: 22. Summary inscriptions are to be found not only on commemorative stelae and slabs, which had limited space and "displayed" the great deeds of the ruler setting them up, but also buried in foundations.

[3] Tadmor 1973: 141. Grayson (1980: 153-54), for whom summary inscriptions are a sub-group of the general category of commemorative inscriptions (along with annals), divides the genre into two groups: inscriptions with and those without mention of military conquests. Grayson identifies sub-groups of each group, each with a basic form and "additional optional elements."

objective was the conquest of the Aramean state of Damascus (KUR ša-ANŠE-šú[4]), which dominated Syria and Palestine in the latter half of the ninth century B.C.E.,[5] while the final section of the inscription (lines 22-25) begins an account of Adad-nirari's relations with southern Mesopotamia, i.e. Babylon.

The section of the Nimrud slab inscription of interest here is the second part of the prologue, i.e. lines 5b-14a, in which are listed the states subservient to Adad-nirari.[6] Lines 5b-11a list the territories to the east (šá na-paḫ ᵈUTU-ši). Lines 11b-14a list the subservient territories in Syria and Palestine, "from the Euphrates" (TA UGU ⁱᵈA.RAT) to the Mediterranean ("the great sea of the setting sun" [= west], a-di UGU tam-tim GAL-ti šá SILIM-mu ᵈUTU-ši). This expanse of the western fertile crescent included

---

[4] = māt ša-imērišu, the "Eseltreiberland" of TUAT 1/4 (passim), was the name of the Aramean kingdom of Damascus as distinct from the capital city of Damascus, which was called (ᵃˡ)Dimašqa/i in the cuneiform (Parpola 1970: 103-04; Cazelles 1969: 115 n. 11; for a brief discussion of ša imērišu and relevant literature, see Cross 1972: 40 n. 16; an extended discussion is to be found in Pitard 1987: 14-17). Albeit, the distinction between city and country was not always rigidly kept (Page 1968: 144). This was the state known in the Hebrew Bible as Aram-Damascus ('ăram dammeśeq 2 Sam 8:5, 6; 'ăram darmeśeq 1 Chr 18:5, 6).

[5] See B. Mazar 1962: 114; Millard and Tadmor 1973: 64.

[6] Although Adad-nirari referred to himself as the conquerer (kāšid) of all of the states listed, it appears unlikely that he campaigned farther south than Aram. This can be deduced from the fact that, of the three major inscriptions of Adad-nirari (the Nimrud slab; the Saba'a inscription [about which see below]; and the Tell al-Rimah inscription [editio princeps: Page 1968: 139-53, pls. xxxix-xli; editions: Donner 1970: 50- 51 {lines 1-12}; Tadmor 1973: 141-144 {lines 4-12}; M. Weippert 1992: 60-62 {lines 13-21}; translation: TUAT 1/4: 368 {lines 4-12}; see also Schramm 1973: 113-15]), the former two concur in assigning priority to the conquest of Aram-Damascus, while the latter emphasizes the collection of tribute from its king. This king is called Mari' in the cuneiform of all three inscriptions. This term is thought to be either a transcription of the Aramaic title of the king "my lord" into Akkadian, akin to the transcription of the Egyptian royal title into Hebrew as "pharaoh" (TUAT 1/4: 368 n. 15b; ANET 281b n. 2; Cody 1970: 372; Soggin 1970: 366), or, following a suggestion of Albright's, an abbreviation of an original personal name *Mari-Hadad (Albright 1942b: 28 n. 16; Cross 1972: 37, 41 n. 22, 42 [who views the name as a hypocoristicon, representing the personal name as opposed to the throne name of the ruler]; Millard and Tadmor 1973: 63 n. 22 [who follow the above, yet refer to the name as an "enigma"]). Mari' has been variously identified with Ben-Hadad II (Albright 1942b: 28 n. 16), Ben- Hadad III (Tadmor 1969b: 135-36 [albeit, in this early article Tadmor viewed māri' as a title]; Millard and Tadmor 1973: 63 n. 22; Shea 1978: 110 [who also considered Hazael as a possible identification, which is the possibility he preferred in 1985a: 10]), or Ben-Hadad IV (Cross 1972: 42). More recently Pitard (1987: 165-66) has supported the identification of Mari' with Ben-Hadad (Bir-Hadad) III, while leaving open the possibility that the name represents either an Akkadian scribal misunderstanding or an alternate name of the ruler. The inscriptions do not mention campaigns farther south, only the collection of tribute (biltu) madattu. For a discussion of the type of tribute and its significance, see Chapter Four.

Hatti and all of Amurru, Tyre and Sidon,[7] Israel, Edom, and Philistia (KUR Pa-la-as-tú).[8]

> *(4) ša ina tukulti Aššur bēlīšu ittallakūma[9] malkī ša kibrat erbetti (5) ušeknišu[10] ana šēpīšu kāšid ištu māt[11] Siluna (6) ša napāh šamši māt Namri[12] māt Ellipi māt Harhar māt Araziaš (7) māt Mesu māt Madai šadû Gizilbunda[13] ana sihirtīšu (8) māt Munna māt Parsua māt Allabria māt Abdadana (9) māt Na'iri ana pāṭ gimrīša māt Andiu ša ašaršu rūqu (10) BAD.HU[14] šadû ana pāṭ gimrīšu adi muhhi tâmtim rabīti (11) ša napāh šamši ištu muhhi Puratti māt Hatti māt Amurri ana sihirtīša (12) māt Ṣurru[15] māt Ṣidunu māt Humri[16] māt Udumu māt Palastu (13) adi muhhi tâmtim rabīti ša šulmu šamši ana šēpīya (14) ušekniš biltu madattu elīšunu ukīn ...*

---

[7] Tadmor (1973: 149) maintains that Tyre and Sidon (*Ṣurru-Ṣidunnu*) are to be considered as one entity, i.e. Phoenicia.

[8] *Palastu* stands for the region of Philistine settlement, and not for Palestine (see Tadmor 1973: 149; *TUAT* 1/4: 367; *TGI* 54 n. 3; against *ANET*'s [281] "Palestine" and Wiseman's "S. Phoenicia" [1964: 119]).

[9] = DU.DU-ku-ma: In the published text of Tadmor's transliteration of this inscription (1973: 148), the KU sign is missing from this word.

[10] = ú-šék(!)-ni-šú: The ŠÉK– sign is written in a peculiar manner with an extra vertical wedge bisecting the final three horizontals, forming a sign which appears to consist of KIN + ÁŠ.

[11] = KUR(!) : written as MU. This is obviously a scribal error (see Tadmor 1973: 148).

[12] = ZALÁG– : Following Tadmor (1973: 149) and Schramm (1969: 126-27), I read "Namri" rather than "Saban" (*ARAB* 1 262, albeit with a question mark; *ANET* 281) or "Ṣab" ("*Hochländer*" in *KB* 1: 190-91).

[13] KUR gi-zil-bu-un-da : Tadmor's suggestion (1973: 149) to transcribe KUR as *šadû* on the basis of the masculine singular suffix of *sihirtīšu* appears convincing. The variation in lines 9 and 10 between the feminine suffix following the name of a country (*māt Na'iri ana pāṭ gimrīša*) and the masculine suffix preceded by *šadû* (*šadû ana pāṭ gimrīšu*) adds weight to this suggestion. However, the phrase *māt Andiu ša ašaršu rūqu* at the end of line 9 would appear to damage this line of argumentation. Although Tadmor allows for exceptions to the rule governing this, perhaps the phrase should be transcribed as *šadû Andiu*?

[14] BAD.HU : This word remains enigmatic. Both L. Abel (mid-bak in *KB* 1: 190) and Oppenheim (pit-hu in *ANET* 281b n. 2) understood the word as the first element in a construct relationship with *šadû* (KUR-ú). However, as Tadmor has pointed out (1973: 149), if this were the case one would expect to see the genitive form *šadî* in place of *šadû*. Comparison with other constructs in this text would support this line of reasoning: *napāh šamši* (lines 6, 11) and *šulmu šamši* (line 13). Thus Tadmor's suggestion to read <KUR> BAD-hu "Mount BAD-hu" deserves serious attention, in spite of the fact that such a geographical location is otherwise unknown. KUR-ú would in this case be the subject of the following phrase.

[15] = KUR(!) ṣur-ru : The KUR sign, which is written correctly with one diagonal wedge over two diagonals, has here been inverted to two diagonals over one.

[16] = KUR hu-um-ri-i : Tadmor (1973: 149) corrects this geographical name to KUR <É> hu-um-ri-i ("'the Land of Bit-Humri' -- not 'Omriland'") on the basis of parallel constructions.

(4) Who goes forth under the protection of Ashur, his lord, and causes rulers from the four corners of the earth (5) to bow down at his feet. The conqueror from Siluna (6) of the rising sun (east), Namri, Ellipi, Harhar, Araziash, (7) Mesu, Media, Mount Gizilbunda in its entirety, (8) Munna, Parsua, Allabria, Abdadana, (9) Na'iri to its farthermost extent, Andiu, which lies far away, (10) BAD.ḪU, the mountain to its farthest extent, as far as the great sea (11) of the rising sun; from the Euphrates, Hatti, Amurru in its entirety, (12) Tyre, Sidon, Israel, Edom, Philistia, (13) as far as the great sea of the setting sun (Mediterranean) I caused (them) to bow down (14) at my feet. (The payment of) tax and tribute I imposed upon them.

Saba'a Stela

Editio princeps: Unger 1916. Editions: Tadmor 1973: 144-48; Donner 1970: 52-53 (lines 11b-22). Translations: *ARAB* 1 paras. 732-37; *ANET* 282 (lines 11-20); *DOTT* 51-52 (lines 11-20); *TUAT* 1/4 369 (lines 11-20). See also: Schramm 1973: 111-113.

The Saba'a stele was discovered in 1905 in the desert southwest of the Sinjar Hills. The extreme weathering of the surface of the stone has made the reading and interpretation of the inscription difficult.[17] However, as of the time of its original publication, it was thought to recount *inter alia* a campaign by Adad-nirari against Philistia. According to Unger[18] lines 11-13 were to be read in the following manner:

"11) ... ina šatti V^{kám} ina kussi šárru-ti rabiš
12) [ú-š]i-bu-ma^{19} mâta ad-ki ummân-at ^{mâtu}Aššur [rapš]âte^{meš} ana
^{mâtu}Pa(Rasur)^{20} - la-aš-[tú]

---

[17] Unger 1916: 7.

[18] 1916: 8-11, see also 16-17.

[19] This phrase, from *ina šatti* to *ušibūma*, has been taken, as of Unger's original publication, to refer to Adad-nirari's taking the throne in the fifth year of his reign after spending his minority under a five year regency by Semiramis/Sammuramat (Unger 1916: 16-20; *ARAB* 1 paras. 730, 732; Page 1968: 147 and n. 26; von Soden 1954: 90; see also the translations in *ANET* 282 and *DOTT* 51, and the historical reconstructions of Labat 1967: 40 and of Hallo in Hallo and Simpson 1971: 128). Recently, however, this interpretation of the phrase has come under attack. Advances in the study of Akkadian grammar and a correction to Unger's copy of the inscription (1916 pl. 2) have led to a new interpretation of the phrase. First, following a suggestion of B. Meissner, both Donner (1970: 52 n. 9, 55-56) and Tadmor (1969a: 48 n. 15; 1973: 146 n. 22) restore a ŠA sign in line 11 between KAM and *ina*. Then, following the adverbial

13) [a-na alâ]ku lu aḳ-bi ...
11) ... Als ich mich im 5. Jahre auf den Thron meiner Majestät erhaben
12) [set]zte, bot ich das Land auf, den [zahlrei]chen Heeren Assyriens nach
dem   Lande   Palas[tu] (Philisterland)
13) [zu zieh]en befahl ich, ..."

This reference to Philistia would be of paramount importance, since a) it
would indicate direct Assyrian intervention in the affairs of southern Palestine
at an early date, and b) it would provide a firm date in Philistine history. This
reading of Philistia is one which had, until recently, been widely accepted
among scholars.[21]

However in 1969, Cazelles[22] and Tadmor,[23] working independently,
began casting doubt on the accuracy of the reading. Cazelles tentatively
proposed a reading of *Ḫatti* in place of *Palastu*, in anticipation of a future
collation of the text. Tadmor found three major problems with the accepted
reading: 1) the expected Assyrian transcription of Peleshet should have been
Palastu, as it is in the Nimrud slab (see above), rather than Palaštu (Assyrian
/s/ = West Semitic /š/); 2) there is a lack of any other evidence that Adad-
nirari ever ventured farther south than Damascus; and 3) Palastu never
referred to Palestine in the modern sense of the word. Added to this was the
evidence of the Tell al-Rimah inscription which in a parallel passage reads
DIŠ KUR ḫat-te DU-ka lu aq-bi (*ana māt Ḫatte alāka lū aqbi*) "I gave the
command to march against Hatti" (line 4). Thus Tadmor advocated reading
the passage in the Saba'a stele as *māt Ḫat-te x[y]*, or even as *māt Ḫat-te*
⸢*rabīte*⸣. The publication of an additional fragment of a stele from Sheikh
Hammad (BM 1311224) lends additional support to this theory.[24] In line 3, it
offers another parallel passage (a-na KUR ḫat-t[i]). Finally, a collation from a
latex squeeze and a photograph by J. D. Hawkins has set the reading of the

---

use of *ša* in temporal clauses as outlined in *GAG* para. 165d, they translate the phrase as "in the fifth year
since I magnificently took my seat on the royal throne" (Tadmor 1973: 146). See also Poebel 1943: 82;
TUAT 1/4: 369.

[20] Unger (1916: 14) attributed the erasure to a doubling of the PA sign.

[21] *ARAB* 1 para. 734 (Palashtu = Palestine); *ANET* 282 (Palestine); *DOTT* 51; Parpola 1970: 272;
Donner 1973: 52-53 (who, presumably recognizing the difficulty of the Assyrian transcription of West
Semitic *plšt* as *Palaštu*, transliterated the word in question as "ᴷᵁᴿPa-{pa}-la-ás-[tú]").

[22] 1969: 115 n. 10.

[23] 1969: 46-48; see also 1973 146 n. 23.

[24] Millard and Tadmor 1973: 57-60, pl. xxix.

Saba'a stele as DIŠ KUR ḫat-te-e.[25] And that is indeed the reading that is generally followed today.[26]

Thus we are left with only one reference to Philistia during the reign of Adad-nirari III: the reference to tribute on the Nimrud slab inscription.

Tiglath-pileser III

It was during the reign of Tiglath-pileser III (745-727 B.C.E.) that the Assyrians first campaigned in south-western Palestine. The era of Tiglath-pileser thus ushered in a new period in the history of the region. However, it was not only for our limited geographical scope that Tiglath-pileser indicated a break with the past. Tiglath-pileser was the founder and driving force behind the Assyrian Imperium.[27] He charted the course of subsequent historical development in the ancient Near East. As of his time, Syria and Palestine were subject to continual domination by empires which had an ever widening claim to universal sovereignty.

The frustrations of dealing with the texts of Tiglath-Pileser have been legion. First is the fragmentary state of the texts themselves.[28] Second has been the deficient quality of the one edition of Tiglath-pileser's texts which has been available for the past century. The latter situation has been remedied by the recent and long-awaited publication of Tadmor's *The Inscriptions of Tiglath-pileser III*.[29]

---

[25] Tadmor 1973: 145.

[26] Cf. Borger in *TUAT* 1/4: 369, who accepts Tadmor's first reading in italics.

[27] For a discussion of the historical significance of Tiglath-pileser III, see Chapter Four above. See also Anspacher 1912: 9, 18 and *passim*; Bright 1981: 270-271; Donner 1986: 297-299; 1977: 418-420; Labat 1967: 55-58; Roux 1964: 253-257; von Soden, 1954: 91-93.

[28] General discussions concerning the texts of Tiglath-pileser, the condition of their transmission, and the state of scholarly work on the texts can be found in Anspacher 1912: 1-9 (the scholarly discussion is obviously somewhat outdated, although it is very thorough in its treatment up to the early part of this century); Tadmor 1967b *passim*; M. Weippert 1973: 26-28; Wiseman 1956: 117-118.

[29] = Tadmor 1994. The deficiencies of Rost's 1893 edition are discussed below. Although his *magnum opus* was only published in 1994, Tadmor conscientiously shared his findings throughout the long years of his research with the scholarly community, as his many articles and the frequent references in the literature to his work-in-progress attest (cf. M. Weippert 1973: 27; Eph'al 1982: 23 and n. 60; Tadmor and Cogan 1979: 491 n. 1; the latter two studies even cited texts according to Tadmor's unpublished edition).

Most of both the extant and the non-extant texts of Tiglath-Pileser III were found during the course of Layard's excavations at Nimrud, ancient Calah, during the years 1845-1847 and 1849-1851.[30] Early in his first season of excavation, Layard discovered a structure that he named the South-West Palace. In it, he discovered a number of limestone slabs inscribed on one side with both reliefs and inscriptions. Some of the slabs were found on the floor, some of them were found against the walls with the unworked portion facing out, and some of the completed slabs had had their edges trimmed, damaging the reliefs or inscriptions on them. Layard correctly surmised that the valuable limestone slabs must have been brought from another location for secondary use in this palace. When he discovered the Central Palace, this assumption was confirmed. There he found about a hundred slabs, all of which had been removed from their original positions, prior to their shipment to a new location.[31] Ultimately, it was established that the South-West Palace was erected by Esarhaddon, whose plundering of his predecessors' palaces, most importantly the Central Palace of Tiglath-pileser III,[32] for limestone on which to record his own mighty deeds was stopped only by his own untimely death in 669 B.C.E.[33] Of the many inscriptions of Tiglath-pileser found by Layard, many have survived only in drawings or in paper squeezes. The squeezes in particular have suffered a sad fate. They were rapidly digested in the bowels of the British Museum and are no longer to be found.[34] There can thus be no recourse to the original text in many of the inscriptions of Tiglath-pileser. Rassam and Loftus in the 1850's turned up little additional inscriptional material at Calah. G. Smith found the *"Throntafelinschrift"* K 3751 in 1873.

---

[30] Layard, one of the great pioneers of the "heroic age of Assyriology" (Tadmor 1967b: 172), was an expert popularizer of his adventures, archaeological and otherwise. See Layard 1849 and 1854; also Lloyd 1980: 87-94, 99-129, 148-150; and Waterfield 1968: 115-224. For a succint account of the discovery of the texts of Tiglath-pileser III, see Tadmor 1994: 10-16.

[31] Layard (1849: 2. 19-20) based his assumption on the observation that the slabs had once been held in place by brackets, on the disruption of pictures in the middle, and on the fact that Assyrian reliefs were carved only upon final placement of the blank limestone slabs.

[32] For descriptions of the Central Palace see Barnett and Falkner 1962: 1-7; Reade 1968: 69-73, pl. xviii. See also Tiglath-pileser's own description of his palace in the Nimrud Tablet (K 3751 = II R pl. 67 = Rost pl. xxxvii; translation of lines 67-86 in *ARAB* 1 para. 804).

[33] Although the loss of great parts of the historical inscriptions of Tiglath-pileser leaves major gaps in our understanding of the history of the period (albeit, it has provided the lack of certainty needed for the healthy pursuit of a number of academic careers), Olmstead (1923: 203) took a calm view of the situation: "The actual loss may be easily exaggerated, for the missing portions would have added more names of cities plundered and tribes subdued, but the remainder would have consisted of the same formulas with which we have become so wearisomely familiar. There has been certainly no loss to literature."

[34] See Tadmor 1967b; 1994: 15.

Mallowan's excavations in the early 1950's turned up a last few inscriptions in clay. The excavations of Meuszynski in the 1970's uncovered three inscribed slabs. The latter have yet to be published.[35] The overall situation is one of the existence of a number of fragmentary inscriptions, on both stone and clay, of both the annal and summary inscription types.

For almost exactly one century there existed just one attempt at a critical edition of Tiglath-pileser's inscriptions, Rost's *Die Keilschrifttexte Tiglat-Pilesers III. nach den Papierabklatschen und Originalen des Britischen Museums*.[36] However, it is deficient from quite a number of methodological standpoints.[37] Rather than following Schrader's 1880 work in isolating various series of Tiglath-pileser's annals, Rost presented an eclectic text numbered by consecutive lines, indicating neither the source of certain readings nor the gaps in the text.[38] He restored and changed the text at will, with no indication of his "improvements" to the text. In addition, there are quite a number of instances in which his copies of the various texts and his transcriptions are at variance.

As mentioned above, Tadmor has recently published a comprehensive study of all inscriptional materials from the reign of Tiglath-pileser. Following the studies of Schrader (who distinguished between annalistic sources and summary inscriptions and attempted to divide the annal fragments into parallel series) and consulting the previously neglected original pencil drawings of Layard, G. Smith, Rawlinson, and Boutcher, Tadmor has classified the inscriptions by annal series and summary inscription number.[39] Since it was known from preliminary publication,[40] Tadmor's system of numbering had become the standard even before its official publication and will be employed in the following discussion.

---

[35] See Tadmor 1994: 16, 37.

[36] = Rost 1893.

[37] See the discussion in Tadmor 1994: 18-20.

[38] In this, Rost was following in the methodological footsteps of Winckler, who used this approach in his edition of the annals of Sargon II six years before Rost (Tadmor 1967b: 7-8; 1994: 19).

[39] For Schrader's contribution, see Tadmor 1967b: 7. On the importance of Layard's pencil "MS A", see Tadmor 1967b: 8-10; 1994: 20-22. Tadmor's division of the annals into series and the years they cover are presented in 1967b: 12-19; and 1994: 28-37. For a reclassification of Layard 66 from annal series "E" to a display or summary inscription see Eph'al 1982: 32, 33 n. 90; Tadmor 1994: 25 n. 64, 198-199. On the difficulties of the classification of the texts, see Tadmor 1994: 22-25.

[40] Especially useful in this regard is Eph'al 1982: 21-36.

Annal Fragments

ITP *Annal 18* = *Lay 29b* = *Rost xviiib*

Text: *ITP* pls. XV, XXIII; Lay 29b; Rost xviiib. Edition: Rost lines 229-40, pp. 38-41; Tadmor 1994: 80-83. Translations: *ARAB* 1 para. 779 (following Rost, Luckenbill's divisions between paragraphs do not necessarily follow breaks between annal fragments); *ANET* 283b; *TUAT* 1/4 372-73; Irvine 1990: 32.[41] See also Eph'al 1982: 24-25; Schramm 1973: 130-31; Tadmor 1994: 32.

This slab forms a part of Tadmor's Series C$_1$, from which only Layard's drawings survive.[42] The events of which it tells have been dated to 733 B.C.E.,[43] although an ascription to the early part of the following year cannot be ruled out.[44] This slab is extremely fragmentary, so historical reconstruction becomes most difficult.

The first seven lines of the fragment (Rost 229-34) tell of Tiglath-pileser's victories against members of the Syro-Ephraimite league. The na-ge-e šá KUR É [...] "provinces of the land of the House [of ...]" (line 230)[45] may be a reference to the 16 na-ge-e šá KUR šá-ANŠE.NÍTA-šú "provinces of Aram-Damascus" that are mentioned in line 209 (Rost xxii = Lay 72b + 73a = *ITP* Annal 23). However, since lines 231-34 list the number of prisoners from cities captured in the Galilee, it may be wiser to restore the phrase to na-ge-e šá KUR É-[ḫu-um-ri-a/i] "provinces of the land of the House of Omri" (= Israel).[46] We would then be able to piece together the geographical progression of events in this campaign, north to south, from the isolation of Rezin in Damascus and the disloyalty of Samsi queen of the Arabs (Rost xxii

---

[41] On the following pages Irvine presents an interpretation of the historical significance of the fragment. His translation of the text, however, must be used with caution, since his annotations to the text do not inspire much confidence in his Akkadian abilities (see e.g. p. 32 n.29).

[42] Tadmor 1967b: 12-13. Other slabs in the series include Lay 71a + 71b + 72a; Lay 45b$_2$; III R pl. 9 #1; Lay 45b$_1$. This series, inscribed across monumental reliefs, consisted of 16 to 20 line slabs. It is partially paralleled by Series C$_2$, and, despite methodological difficulties, Tadmor feels that the two series may in fact have formed one. In his later edition (Tadmor 1994), Tadmor has not distinguished between subseries. Thus there are only three Series: A, B, and C. See Tadmor 1994: 29 fig. 3.

[43] Schramm 1973: 130; Tadmor 1964: 267, 1967b: 13, 19.

[44] See Eph'al 1982: 26-27.

[45] Eph'al (1982: 24) mentions the "districts of the land of *Bīt* ^{m} ..." However, according to my reading of Layard's and Rost's published drawings of the passage, there is no *Personenkeil* after the É sign, nor can one be clearly read in Layard's MS A (published in Tadmor 1994: pl. XV). See Tadmor 1994: 80-81 regarding the possible restorations of the phrase.

[46] See III R pl. 10 #2 = Rost *"Kleinere Inschriften* I" pls. xxv + xxvi = *ITP* Summ. 4 lines 6, 15.

= Lay 72b + 73a = *ITP* Annal 23), through the truncating of Israelite territory and the failed revolt of Mitinti in the tablet under discussion.

Line 235 begins an account of the revolt of Mitinti of Ashkelon against Tiglath-pileser. Presumably Mitinti had entered into a vassal relationship with Tiglath-pileser as a consequence of Tiglath-pileser's campaign to Philistia in 734. At any rate, Mitinti saw fit to ally himself with Rezin of Damascus in attempting to throw off the Assyrian yoke. As a consequence of the isolation of Rezin in Damascus,[47] Mitinti, whatever his ultimate fate, was replaced on the throne by Rukibtu, who was able to spare his city through immediate subjugation to Assyria. The last three lines of the tablet are particularly difficult to interpret. Line 238 would appear to record Rukibtu's approach to Tiglath-pileser, including the presentation of a "gift" of which only the amount, 500, is preserved. Line 239 would then record the entry either of Rukibtu into Ashkelon as the newly installed ruler, or of Tiglath-pileser (into the same city?) as the new overlord. Whether the fifteen cities mentioned at the end of the line belong to this pericope or with another one concerned with Idibi'ilu cannot be determined. As Eph'al has indicated, it is unlikely that Ashkelon would have been forced to cede territory to Idibi'ilu, since they did not share a common border, and the city-state of Gaza lay between them.[48]

This annal text will be treated in conjunction with the following fragment.

ITP *Annal 24 = Lay 72b + 73a "line endings" = Rost xviiia*

Text and editition: Tadmor 1994: 80-83, pl. XXIII. See also pp. 220-221.

Until the publication of Tadmor's edition of *The Inscriptions of Tiglath-pileser III* this fragment had never had an official and independent treatment. In his drawings of 72b + 73a, Layard erroneously attached this fragment to the end of the lines. The tablet was drawn as a separate entity in Rost's edition. However, the contents of the tablet, which seem to form a parallel to *ITP* 18 = Lay 29b = Rost xviiib, were not accorded separate treatment in his

---

[47] This information is very important for a dating of the events. Assuming that Rost xxii = Lay 72b + 73a = *ITP* Annal 23 presents a passage almost immediately preceding *ITP* Annal 18 = Lay 29b = Rost xviiib enables us to reconstruct Tiglath-pileser's strategy in isolating and besieging his most powerful opponent, Rezin, in his capital (733 B.C.E.), then dealing with Rezin's rebellious allies, the Arabs, Israel and Ashkelon, before returning to deliver the coup-de-grace to Rezin (732 B.C.E.) that is lacking in the Assyrian annals, but is recorded in the Hebrew Bible (2 Kgs 16:9).

[48] Eph'al 1982: 24-25 and n. 65. Against Alt 1953: 2. 237 n. 5; 3. 420 n. 1.

eclectic edition of the annals. This fragment has obviously been used in all standard reconstructions of lines 229-37 of the annals (the literature would therefore be the same as for the previous tablet), yet I have found that line 15 of this fragment, which would fall between lines 236 and 237 of Rost's version of the annals, has not been consistently reflected in the literature.[49]

Annal Fragments -- Transliteration and Restoration

Text I = *ITP* Annal 18 = Lay 29b = Rost xviiib
Text II = *ITP* Annal 24 = Lay 72b + 73a "line endings" = Rost xviiia
Text III = eclectic transcription & restoration according to Rost's numeration

I line   8) [   ] as-qa-lu-na-a-a AŠ a-di-[   ]
II line   12) ᵐmi-ti-in-ti KUR a[s-   ]
III line 235) ᵐ*Mitinti māt Asqalunāya ina adê̂ya iḫṭima*[50]]

II   13) it-ti-ia it-ta-[   ]
III 235-36) *ittīya itta*[*balkat*   ]

I   9) [   ]-ḫi-a-ni e-mur-ma AŠ mi-qit [   ]
II   14) [   ] e-mur-ma ù ip-l[aḫ[51]   ]
III 236) [... *dabdê* ᵐ*Ra*]*ḫiani*[52] *ēmurma ina miqit* [*ṭēmi*[53] ...]/ *u ip*[*laḫ libbāšu*[54] ...]

---

[49] On this last point, see Eph'al 1982: 25; Schramm 1973: 130-131; Tadmor 1967b: 18.

[50] A number of the restorations in this and other passages in the inscriptions of Tiglath-pileser III base themselves on the work of G. Smith (1876: 253-87) and Rost (1893) and have become standard in the literature. Where this is the case, there will be no further note.

[51] The correct reading of the last three signs was only made possible by the publication of Layard's MS A. Annal 24 thus preserves a variant text compared with Annal 18.

[52] Following Landsberger (1948: 66-67 n. 169), this name is read with a ḪI sign and an A sign rather than as a ṢUN (= ḪI + A) sign. Although it was once felt that *Rasunni* was a possible reading of the text, based on the MT *Rĕṣîn* (< רצין 2 Kgs 15:37; 16:5, 6, 9; Isa 7:1, 4, 8; 8:6, 9:10) and on the G Ρα(α)σσων etc., the value ṢUN for ḪI + A has been discarded. ṢUN still appears in Labat's alphabetic list of sign values (1976: 269), although it has disappeared as a possibility from the body of his text (1976: 189, sign # 404), where the only value given for ḪI + A is ḪÁ (see also von Soden and Röllig 1967: 47; Borger 1986: 160). The name Rezin is most probably derived from an original Aramaic *Raḏyan* (see M. Weippert 1973: 46 and n. 83; Pitard 1987: 181-82).

[53] There have been essentially two restorations for this phrase. The first is championed by Luckenbill (*ARAB* 1 para. 779) and *CAD* (M/2 105a). They would read that Mitinti died *ina miqit išati* "in a conflagration," a phrase derived, at least in *CAD*, from the annals of Ashurbanipal col. iv line 51. The second interpretation is favored by scholars such as von Soden (*AHW* 657b). He would restore the phrase

II 15) ḫa-at-ti ra-ma-ni-[ ]
III [236/7]) ḫatti rāmānī[šu imqussu⁵⁵ (< imqut + šu) ...]

I 10) [ ] AŠ GIŠ.GU.ZA-šú ú-šib a-na [ ]
II 16) ᵐru-ú-kib-tu DUMU [ ]
III 237) ᵐRukibtu mār [lā mammāna⁵⁶] ina ᵍⁱˢkussêšu ūsib⁵⁷ ana [⁵⁸]

I 11) [ ] i-dul-ma ú-ṣa-la-ni 5 ME [ ]
III 238) [...] idūlma uṣallâni 500 [...]

I 12) [ ]-ma a-na URU-šu TU-ub 15 URU [...]
III 239) [...]-ma ana ālīšu ērub⁵⁹ 15 āl[āni ...]

---

to ina miqit ṭēmi "in Verzweiflung." This would appear to be the restoration most accepted in the literature (see ANET 283b; TUAT 1/4 373; Rost 1893: 39; Tadmor 1964: 268), although the exact nuance of the term and its historical implications are open to question. See Chapter Three for an extended discussion.

⁵⁴ On the restoration of this idiom, see Tadmor 1994: 82-83.

⁵⁵ This restoration bases itself on the idiom found in AHW 336b and CAD H 150b and M/1 248b, in which additional instances from Assyrian royal inscriptions can be found. Borger (1957: 116) cites this passage as the first occurence of this idiom.

⁵⁶ The inconvenient break in the text where Rukibtu's patrimony should be has almost universally been restored by assuming that Rukibtu was Mitinti's son. The two possible restorations in this case would be either mār[šu] (G. Smith 1876: 284; TUAT 1/4 373) or mār [ᵐMitinti] (Rost 1893: 38; ARAB 1 para. 779; ANET 283b; Tadmor 1964: 268). Tadmor (1994: 83) has recently raised the possibility that "one may also restore 'the son [of his (i.e. Mitinti's) brother]'." For reasons detailed above, I prefer to restore the text on the basis of the well attested idiom implying occupation of the throne by someone not (directly?) in line for it. The phrase mār lā mammāna appears in two summary inscriptions of Tiglath-pileser III: in ND 4301 + 4305 = ITP Summ. 9 line 28 (Wiseman 1956: 122, 124, 126, 129) and in K 3751 = II R 67 = ITP Summ. 7 line 15'. For additional attestations of the idiom, see AHW 601a and CAD M/1 200b.

⁵⁷ Luckenbill (ARAB 1 para. 779) translated this word as "I set," presumably emending the text from the G ūsib to the Š ušēšib on the basis of K 3751 = I R 67 rev. line 15. In this he was followed by Tadmor (1964: 268), who translated ūsib as "hôšabtí/ הושבתי." In his later edition, Tadmor (1994: 83) translated the word as written, namely "sat." There is no need to assume scribal error in this instance. In the event of a coup d'etat, it would make sense for the usurper to "set himself" on the throne.

⁵⁸ Tadmor (1994: 82-83) restores the word šarrūti at this point and translates the phrase "as [king."

⁵⁹ As Eph'al (1982: 24 n. 64) has rightly pointed out, TU-ub can be read as either the first or the third person preterite form of the verb erēbu. In his discussion Eph'al makes the choice of transcription one between ērub as the first person and īrub as the third. Although Eph'al's choice between forms is technically and grammatically correct, since the language of the Neo-Assyrian royal inscriptions is Standard Babylonian, it is always possible that an Assyrianism could have crept into the text, in which case the form ērub would have been employed for both persons (see GAG para. 97c, paradigm 17). The standard translation is being followed in assuming that it was Tiglath-pileser III who entered a city (presumably Ashkelon), while leaving open the possibility that someone else, perhaps Rukibtu, is the

I   13) [   ]-di-bi-'i-i-lu KUR a-ru-bu [   ]
III 240) [... ᵐ*I*]*dibi 'ilu mātArubu* [...]

235) Mitinti the Ashkelonite [broke my] treaty [and] against me
236) he revolted ... he saw [the defeat] of Rezin and in desper[ation] ... he
      feared for his life ...
237) Rukibtu, son of [a nobody], seized his throne. To ...
238) ... he wandered about and implored me. 500 ...
239) ... and I/he entered into his city. 15 cities ...
240) ... Idibi'ilu of Arabia ...

Summary Inscriptions

ITP *Summ. 4 = III R 10 #2 = Rost xxv + xxvi*

Text: III R pl. 10 #2; Rost pls. xxv + xxvi; *ITP* pls. XLIX-LI. Editions: Rost 78-83 "*Kleinere Inschriften* 1;" *KB* 2: 30-33 (lines 6-19; according to *KB* following G. Smith's system of numeration in III R 10 #2: lines 17-30); Spieckermann 1982: 325-27 (lines 8-14); Tadmor 1994: 136-43. Translations: *ANET* 283b-84a (lines 1-34); *ARAB* 1 paras. 815-19 (albeit, Luckenbill referred to the text as a "fragmentary annals text"); *DOTT* 55 (lines 1-19); *TGI* 58-59 (lines 1-19); *TUAT* 1/4 373-74 (lines 1-34); Vogt 1964: 352 (lines 1-19); Irvine 1990: 62-64.. See also: Borger and Tadmor 1982: 244-45; Eph'al 1982: 27-28; Schramm 1973: 132.

This is a 38 line inscription engraved on a stone slab. It was found during the course of Layard's excavations of Nimrud. The original was presumably left at the site. The text was first published by G. Smith, working from paper squeezes, in III R pl. 10 #2. Although the published version does not indicate it, Tadmor's reexamination of G. Smith's notebooks has shown that Smith pieced together at least five squeeze fragments in preparing his published copy.[60] On the basis of the arrangement of the events which the inscription relates, Rost[61] correctly identified it as a "*Prunkinschrift*," an identification which has been rendered certain on the basis of the parallels in ND 400 and ND 4301+ discussed below. Presumably the inscription of which this is a

---

subject of the verb (see Rost 1893: 41; *ANET* 283b; *ARAB* 1 para. 779; *TUAT* 1/4 373; and Tadmor 1964: 286; 1994: 83 for the former translation; G. Smith 1876: 284 for the latter).

[60] Tadmor 1967b: 14 n. 51.

[61] 1893: iii.

fragment was originally much longer and did not only relate happenings in the west.

The contents of the inscription can be outlined as follows:[62]

lines 1-5a	conquests in Syria
lines 5b-8a	conquests along the Phoenician coast and Damascus
lines 8b-15a	Hanunu of Gaza
lines 15b-19a	Israel and the change of king from Pekah to Hoshea
lines 19b-26	Samsi, queen of the Arabs
lines 27-33	tribute from various nomadic tribes
lines 34-35	appointment of Idibi'ilu over the border of Egypt
lines 36-38	fragmentary and unclear[63]

8) ... ^{m}Hanunu $^{\bar{a}l}$Hazzatāya (9) [ša lapān ^{giš}]kakkīya ipparši[dūma^{64} ana māt] Muṣri innabtu ^{al}Hazzutu^{65} (10) [akšud^{66} ...] bušâšu ilāni[šu ...^{67} ṣalam ilāni rabûti] bēlīya^{68} u ṣalam^{69} šarrūtīya (11) [ša ḫurāṣi ēpuš i]na qereb e[kalli ša ^{al}Hazzuti ... an]a ilāni mātīšunu amnūma (12) [biltu madattu^{70}] ukīnšunū[ti ... is]ḫupšūma^{71} kī<ma> iṣṣūri (13)

---

[62] Following Eph'al 1982: 28; and Tadmor 1994: 137. The latter also includes a possible dating scheme for the individual events.

[63] Tadmor (1994: 137) speculates that the reference here may be to the making of a stele.

[64] On the occurrence of the subjective, in contrast to the indicative in parallel passages, see Tadmor 1994: 139.

[65] On the occurrence of Hazzutu in place of the more common Hazziti, see Tadmor 1994: 139.

[66] Most translators restore the missing verb at the beginning of line 10 as akšud "I captured." For the Akkadian see Spieckermann 1982: 325. Tadmor (1994: 138-139) has also suggested ērub "I entered" as a possibility. If the mention of Hanunu in line 8 is to be taken as the subject of the sentence rather than as an anacoluthon, a possibility which suggests itself on the basis of the syntax of the putative parallel in ND 400 line 14, then a restoration as umaššir "he abandoned" cannot be ruled out. It should be noted that a number of the restorations in this passage base themselves on parallels in ND 400 and ND 4301+. Where this is the case, there will be no further note. Please refer to the comparison of the texts below.

[67] Tadmor (1994: 138-139) has suggested restoring the break with either ašlul "I despoiled" or ēkim "I seized."

[68] = EN(!).MES(!)-ia: Although the drawings of these partially preserved signs do not substantiate these readings, the parallel in ND 400 line 16 does.

[69] = ALAM(!): Written as NÁ. This is obviously a scribal error for the ALAM sign, the second part of which is identical to the NÁ sign.

[70] Most translations suggest this restoration. The Akkadian bases itself on the common idiom. See, e.g., CAD M/1 13-14. For an additional suggestion, see Tadmor 1994: 140.

[... i]pparšidma[72] [...] ana ašrīšu utīršūma (14) [ᵃˡḪazzutu[73] a]na bīt-[kārī[74] ša māt Aššur amnu ḫurāṣu] kaspu lubulti birme kitê (15) [...[75]] rabûti ᵍⁱˢ [... am]ḫur ...

8) ... (As for) Hanunu of Gaza, (9) [who had fled before my wea]pons and escap[ed to] Egypt, Gaza (10) [I captured ...] his property, [his] gods [... an image of the great gods], my masters, and an image of my kingship (11) [of gold I had made. I]n the midst of the pa[lace of Gaza I set up[76], a]s the gods of their land I reckoned and (12) [the payment of tax and tribute] I imposed on the[m ... o]verwhelmed him,[77] and like a bird (13) [... he] fled [...] to his place I returned him, and (14) [Gaza I reckoned as an Assyrian custom] house. [Gold], silver, garments with multicolored trim, linen, (15) [...] great [...] I received.

ITP *Summ. 7 = K 3751 = II R 67 = Rost xxxv-xxxviii*

Text: II R pl. 67; Rost pls. xxxv - xxxviii; *ITP* pls. LIV-LV. Editions: Rost 54-77 "*Throntafelinschrift*;" *KB* 2: 8-25; M. Weippert 1973: 52 (only transliteration of lines 7'-12'); Tadmor 1994: 154-175. Translations: *ARAB* 1 paras. 787-804; *ANET* 282 (lines 56-63, 66 = lines 6'-13', 16'); *DOTT* 55-56 (lines 6'-16'); *TUAT* 1/4 374-75 (lines 3'-16') Irvine 1990: 40-41 (lines 7'-13'). See also: Eph'al 1982: 28-29; Na'aman 1979: 69; Olmstead 1916: 33-34; Schramm 1973: 133-35.

---

[71] = is]-ḫup(!)-šu(!)-ma: Following the standard restoration. The sign read as ḪUP as drawn may represent the right half of the ḪUP sign. The ŠU sign is missing one of its horizontals, thus resembling the NA sign in this text.

[72] = i]p-par-šid(!)-ma: The ŠID sign has been copied as the Ú sign. A true ŠID sign would have a long horizontal wedge on the bottom and would lack the two short horizontal tails on the middle of the right side of the sign. Tadmor (1994: 140) has proposed reading the text as written. Hence, he reads the Ú sign as ŠAM and the word as *ipparšamma* (< *ipparšidma*).

[73] Although some (e.g. Borger in *TUAT* 1/4 373, 376) would hesitate before restoring the name of the city designated a custom house by Tiglath-pileser III, a reading of "Gaza" would appear to fit the context, especially if one accepts Spieckermann's reading of ND 4301+ line 16' (Spieckermann 1982: 327).

[74] On the institution of the *bīt-kāri*, which in Gaza was most likely an Assyrian commercial institution associated with the port, which collected duties and whose profits went directly into Assyrian hands, see Lewy 1956: 35-51 (including a discussion of *kāru* as an element in town names); Wiseman 1956: 129; Tadmor 1975: 38; Elat 1978: 26; Na'aman 1979a: 83-84.

[75] Tadmor (1994: 140) has restored the word *sīsê* "horses" in this break.

[76] Spieckermann (1982: 326) has suggested restoring *ulziz*. This is not, however, reflected in the above transcription.

[77] Oppenheim in *ANET* (283b-84a) viewed Menahem of Israel as the object of the verb. However, the parallels in ND 400 and ND 4301+ indicate that Hanunu is still the subject of the passage.

Although this clay tablet bears a number from the Kuyunjik collection of the British Museum, it was found at Nimrud. Indeed, amplifying suggestions made by Wiseman[78] and Tadmor,[79] Na'aman[80] has suggested that K 3751 = II R 67 is a long-distance join of ND 400. However, since the possiblity exists that there were multiple copies of the same text, Tadmor[81] decided to treat the texts separately. The tablet, inscribed on both sides, represents the top half or less of an original draft for a display inscription summarizing the first seventeen years of Tiglath-pileser's rule. It thus comes from near the end of that monarch's reign. Tadmor has classified the text as a detailed display inscription, more extensive in language than the normal summary inscription such as ND 4301+.[82]

Although Olmstead[83] has viewed as "unfortunate" the fact that a good part of the tablet is taken up with an extended introduction and conclusion, what is left of the historical section indicates that the tablet followed the standard geographical sequence from southeast (Babylon on the obverse) in an arc around to southwest (Syria and Palestine on the reverse). In lines 7' to 13' is a list of tributaries from the west. On the basis of partially parallel lists and historical deduction, this list has been viewed as a conglomerate, drawing on lists of tributaries from the years 738 (lines 7'-9') and 734 B.C.E. (lines 10'-12').[84] The tributaries of 734 include Mitinti of Ashkelon and Hanunu of Gaza. The section ends in lines 12' to 13' with a standardized list of tribute received by Tiglath-pileser III from the west, which is of little use in the specific reconstruction of Philistine history.

$10')$ [^{m}Ma]tanbi'il ^{al}[85] Armadāya ^{m}Sanipu ^{al}Bīt-Ammanāya ^{m}Salamanu ^{māt}Ma'abāya ^{m}[...] $(11')$ [^{m}Mi]tinti ^{māt}Asqalunāya ^{m}Iauḫazi ^{māt}Iaudāya

---

[78] 1951: 21 and n. 2.

[79] 1972: 223 n. 6.

[80] 1979: 69 and n. 4.

[81] 1994: 156.

[82] Tadmor 1972: 223; 1994: 154.

[83] 1916: 33.

[84] Thus M. Weippert 1973: 52-53; and Eph'al 1982: 29 n. 76. See, however, Irvine (1990: 40-44), who dates the list of tributaries as a whole to 734/33 B.C.E.

[85] The URU sign is written without the first horizontal wedge.

^{m}*Qaušmalaka* ^{māt}*Udumāya* ^{m}*Muše-x*^{86} *[...] (12') [*^{m}*Ḥa]nunu* ^{āl}*Ḥazatāya*
...

10') [Ma]tanbi'il^{87} of Arvad, Sanipu of the House of Ammon, Salamanu of Moab, ... (11') [Mi]tinti of Ashkelon, Jehoahaz (= Ahaz) of Judah, Qaushmalaka of Edom, Mushe-x of ... (12') [Ha]nunu of Gaza ...

ITP *Summ. 8 = ND 400 (BM 131982)*

Editio princeps: Wiseman 1951: 21-24, pl. xi. Editions: Spieckermann 1982: 325-27 (lines 14-18); Tadmor 1972: 223-28 (lines 20-27). Translations: Alt 1953: 2. 152, 155, 157 (lines 1-19); Tadmor 1964: 264-66 (lines 1-27); 1994: 176-79, pl. LVI; *TUAT* 1/4 375-76 (lines 2-27); Vogt 1964: 349 (lines 2-19); Irvine 1990: 44-46 (lines 1-27). See also: Eph'al 1982: 29-30; Schramm 1973: 137.

Almost an even century after the discovery of III R pl. 10 #2, the clay fragment ND 400 was uncovered in 1950 in the fill of the "Governor's Palace" during the renewed excavations at Nimrud. According to Wiseman,^{88} who was responsible for the prompt publication of this fragment, only about one third of each line is preserved. As with II R 67 and ND 4301+, it is reasonable to assume that this clay tablet was a draft for an inscription on stone. Although Wiseman ^{89} and Vogt^{90} have referred to this tablet as an annal fragment, it is probably best to conclude with Tadmor^{91} that this tablet, along with its long distance join II R pl. 67,^{92} is an extended summary inscription.^{93}

---

^{86} Tadmor (1966: 89 and n. 13) had proposed reading the partially preserved sign at the end of this name as either ḪU or PAK, possibly the king of either Ekron or Ashdod. However, after a collation by W. G. Lambert, Tadmor (1994: 170) now reads *Mu-us*(!)-x.

^{87} M. Weippert (1973: 53) has questioned whether he should more correctly belong to the tributaries of 738, in spite of his lack of mention in parallel texts. Since the kings of Ashkelon and Gaza are mentioned in this list, it has been proposed that the names of the kings of Ashdod and Ekron may have originally belonged to this text. See Tadmor 1994: 170.

^{88} 1951: 21.

^{89} 1951: 21.

^{90} 1964: 349.

^{91} 1964: 223.

^{92} Na'aman 1979a: 69 and n. 4.

^{93} See also the classification in Schramm 1973: 137; Eph'al 1982: 29.

The events of which the tablet tells can be outlined in the following manner:[94]

line 1   unreadable

lines 2-13   These lines are very difficult to interpret due to the lack of preserved names. Lines 2-4 tell of the capture of an island city, possibly Tyre.[95] In line 5 the submission (?) of an unnamed king is related, followed in lines 6-7 by a listing of his tribute. The handing over of Kashpuna into the hands of Tiglath-pileser's representative, the governor of Simirra, is related in lines 8-9. Lines 10-13 tell of a major battle and its consequences (obviously favorable to the Assyrians). Due to the southerly geographical progression of this text, the location of the battle should be sought in southern Phoenicia, Syria, or in Israel.[96]

lines 14-18a Hanunu of Gaza

lines 18b-19 The setting up of a stele in Nahal-Musur, and the receipt of tribute from there(?), return to Assyria.

A dividing line follows, after which the tablet continues:

lines 20-21   submission of an unnamed ruler[97]

lines 22-23   submission of Siruatti the Meunite

lines 24-27   Samsi queen of the Arabs

14) ... ^{m}Han]unu ^{al}Hazzatāya lapan kakkī<ya> dannūti iplaḫma a[na māt Muṣri innabit ...] (15) [...^{98} x bilat ḫ]urāṣi 800 bilat kaspi nišī adi maršītīšunu aššassu mārīšu [mārātīšu ...] (16) [...^{99}] ṣalam ilānī rabûti bēliya ṣalam šarrūtiya ša ḫurāṣi [ēpuš ina qereb ekalli ša ^{al}Hazzuti ...] (17) [... biltu madattu^{100} elīšu]nu ukīn^{101} u šū ultu māt Muṣri kīma^{102} iṣṣū[ri ...] (18) [... Aš]šur amnu ...

---

[94] Following Eph'al 1982: 30; and Tadmor 1994: 156-157.

[95] Irvine (1990: 46-49) argues that the island city was Arvad, rather than Tyre.

[96] Tadmor (1994: 156) describes lines 1-9 as concerning a campaign against a city in Phoenicia, while he distinguishes lines 10-13 and ascribes them to a punitive measure against either Tyre or Israel.

[97] Tadmor (1994: 156) conjectures that this might be a reference to the submission of the king of Egypt.

[98] Tadmor (1994: 176) has suggested restoring the name of Gaza and either *akšud* "I captured" or *ērub* "I entered."

[99] Tadmor (1994: 176-177) restores the break as *bušâšu ilānī^{meš}-šú ašlul/ēkim* "his property (and) his gods I despoiled/seized."

[100] See the translation of Tadmor (1964: 264; *not* represented in 1994: 178-179); *contra* Borger (*TUAT* 1/4: 376) and Spieckermann (1982: 326). We have already encountered the phrase *biltu madattu elīšunu*

14) ... Han]unu of Gaza feared my mighty weapons and [fled to Egypt[103] ... (15) ... x talents of g]old, 800 talents of silver, people with their possessions, his wife, his sons, [his daughters ... (16) ...[104]] an image of the great gods, my lords, an image of my kingship of gold [I made, in the midst of the palace of Gaza I set up ... (17) ... the payment of tax and tribute upon th]em I imposed. And as for him, out of Egypt like a bir[d] [... (18) ... of As]syria I reckoned.[105]

ITP *Summ. 9 = ND 4301 + 4305 + 5422 (+ 5419 + K 2649)*[106]

Text: Wiseman 1956: 117-29, pls. xxii, xxiii (ND 4301 + 4305); Wiseman 1964: 119-21, pl. xxvi (ND 5419 + 5422); Rost pl. xxiv-c (K 2649). Edition: Tadmor 1994: 180-191. Partial editions: Tadmor 1962: 116-17 (lines 1'-4'); Spieckermann 1982: 325-27 (lines 13'-16'). Translations: *TGI* 57-58 (lines 1'-16'); *TUAT* 1/4 376-78 (lines 1'-25'); Vogt 1964: 350-51 (lines 1'-16'); Irvine 1990: 56-58 (lines 1'-31'). See also: Borger and Tadmor 1982: 245-46; Eph'al 1982: 31-32; Schramm 1973: 135-36.

The various fragments that make up this tablet were found and pieced together over a number of years. However, the fragments which interest us in the context of this study, namely ND 4301 + 4305, were found in 1955 during the course of excavations at Nimrud and were promptly published by Wiseman in 1956. Once again we are dealing with a summary inscription written on clay, presumably as a draft for one to be inscribed on stone. The different pericopes, separated from one another by dividing lines, are

---

ukīn in the Nimrud Slab Inscription of Adad-nirari III, line 14. For a slightly different and longer restoration of the break in lines 16-17, see Tadmor 1994: 176-179.

[101] The KIN sign is written (copied?) with the first horizontal wedge bisecting the first vertical, rather than beneath it.

[102] The GIM sign is written (copied?) with one diagonal wedge in the inside of the sign rather than two.

[103] Tadmor (1964: 264; 1994: 176-177) has suggested restoring "I captured Gaza" after the mention of Hanunu's flight to Egypt (see III R pl. 10 #2 lines 9-10).

[104] Both Borger (*TUAT* 1/4: 376) and Tadmor (1964: 264) would restore the phrase "I plundered his property and his gods" in the break at the beginning of the line. See also Spieckermann 1982: 326.

[105] Both Borger (*TUAT* 1/4: 376) and Spieckermann (1982: 327) link this phrase with the establishment of a *bīt kāri* at Gaza (see III R pl. 10 #2 line 14). Tadmor (1964: 264) on the other hand saw here a reference to the Assyrian policy of forced transfer of population to Gaza ("I reckoned [them as As]syrians"). In his later work, Tadmor (1994: 178-179) has accepted the former suggestion.

[106] On the relationship of these tablets with each other, see Tadmor 1994: 180, 193. Although he acknowledges a possible relationship, he treats ND 5419 (Summ. 12) and K 2649 (Summ. 10) separately from the rest. DT 3 [Summ. 11] has also been brought into the discussion.

arranged according to a geographical progression, with no thought given to chronological sequence.[107]

The surviving portion of the obverse of ND 4301 + 4305 deals with Tiglath-pileser's campaigns to the north of Assyria. The reverse, on the other hand, lists his conquests to the west, in Syria and Palestine. These latter activities may be outlined as follows:[108]

lines 1'-2'   Hatarikka in northern Syria.

lines 3'-4'   Incorporation of Aram into Assyria.

lines 5'-8'   Defeat and tribute of Hiram of Tyre.

lines 9'-11' Although no name has survived from this section, it is reasonable to assume that it referred to the defeat of Israel, the deposition of Pekah, and the tribute of Hoshea at Sarrabanu.[109]

line 12'   The taking of booty from an unnamed location. Wiseman[110] has speculated that this represents Ahaz's tribute; Vogt[111] felt that it may have referred to Philistine tribute; while Eph'al[112] has sought here a reference to booty from the region of Nahal Musur. Tadmor[113] has suggested that the reference may be to the tribute of Ashkelon.

lines 13'-16' Hanunu and the subjugation of Gaza.

lines 17'-22' Subjugation of Samsi, queen of the Arabs.

lines 23'-25' The obeisance and tribute from a ruler who had not previously been subject to Assyria. Wiseman[114] has conjectured that this represents an embassy from Egypt,[115] or perhaps from Cilicia or other part of Asia Minor.

---

[107] See Vogt 1964: 351 and Wiseman 1956: 118-19.

[108] Following Eph'al 1982: 31-32; and Tadmor 1994: 181.

[109] See Wiseman 1956: 124, 126 [in which he correctly restores the name of Hoshea in line 10', yet refers to the section as pertaining to Judah on p. 119]; Borger and Tadmor 1982: 245-46; Eph'al 1982: 31-32.

[110] 1956: 121.

[111] 1964: 351.

[112] 1982: 31 n. 86.

[113] 1994: 181, 189.

[114] 1956: 122.

[115] Thus also Tadmor 1994: 181.

line 26'   A summary of tribute of which only the amounts of gold and silver received are preserved. Eph'al[116] has speculated that the large amount of tribute listed here may represent the total from either Palestine or the western reaches of the Assyrian empire. Tadmor,[117] however, has restored a reference to Tyre and its king, Metanna, in this line.

lines 27'-29' The deposition of Uassurme of Tabal for failure to render tribute to Assyria, and his replacement by Hulli, the "son of a nobody."

lines 30'-31' Fragmentary and unclear.[118]

13') [...] innabit ^{al}Ḫazzu[tu ...]
14') [...] ēpuš ina qereb ekalli ša ^{al}Ḫa[zzuti ...]
15') [...] iṣṣūri ultu māt Muṣri [...]
16') [...]-x[119] ana bīt-kāri ša māt Aššur^{ki} [...]

13') ... he fled. Gaza ...
14') ... I made. In the midst of the palace of Gaza ...
15') ... [like] a bird from Egypt ...
16') ... x into an Assyrian custom house ...

Hanunu of Gaza: Comparison of Texts[120]

I =   III R pl. 10 #2 = *ITP* Summ. 8
II =   ND 400 = *ITP* Summ. 4
III = ND 4301+ = *ITP* Summ. 9

I)   (8) ^{m}Ḫanunu ^{al}Ḫazzatāya (9) [ša lapān ^{giš}]kakkīya ipparši[dūma
II)   (14) ^{m}Ḫan]unu ^{al}Ḫazzatāya lapān ^{giš}kakkī dannūti iplaḫma

---

[116] 1982: 32.

[117] 1994: 191.

[118] Tadmor (1994: 181) speculates that the reference may be to "some distant Arabian tribes."

[119] Wiseman (1956: 126) read this sign as ŠU. Spieckermann (1982: 327), however, has suggested reading Ḫa-az-z]u!-tu!, which would fit the context very nicely, but is not indicated by Wiseman's drawing (pl. xxiii).

[120] Compare Tadmor 1994: 222-225.

III)   *[*   *]*

I)   *ana māt] Muṣri innabtu* ^{āl}*Ḫazzutu [*   *]*
II)   *a[na*   *]*
III) *(13') [...] innabit* ^{āl}*Ḫazzu[tu ...*   *]*

I)   *[*   *]*
II)   *(15) [... bilat ḫ]urāṣi 800 bilat kaspi nisī adi maršītīšunu*
III) *[*   *]*

I)   *[*   *(10)*   *] bušâšu ilānīšu [*   *]*
II)   *aššassu mārīšu[*   *]*
III) *[*   *]*

I)   *[*   *] bēlīya u ṣalam šarrūtīya [*   *]*
II)   *(16) ṣalam ilānī rabûti bēlīya ṣalam šarrūtīya ša ḫurāṣi*
III) *[*   *]*

I)   *(11) [*   *i]na qereb e[kalli ... an]a ilānī mātīšunu amnūma*
II)   *[*   *]*
III) *(14) [...] ēpuš ina qereb ekalli ša* ^{āl}*Ḫa[zzuti ...*   *]*

I)   *(12) [...] ukīnšun[ūti ... is]ḫupšūma kī iṣṣūri*
II)   *(17) [...]nu ukīn u šū ultu māt Muṣri kīma iṣṣū[ri ...*   *]*
III) *(15) [*   *...*   *] iṣṣūri ultu māt Muṣri [...*   *]*

I)   *(13) [... i]pparšidm[a ...] ana ašrīšu utīršūma*
II)   *[*   *]*
III) *[*   *]*

I)   *[...*   *(14)*   *...*   *a]na bīt [...*   *]*
II)   *(18) [*   *...*   *Aš]šur amnu ...*
III) *(16) [...*   *]tu(?) ana bīt-kāri ša māt Aššur^{ki} [...*   *]*

I)   *[... ḫurāṣu] kaspu lubulti birme kitû (15) [...] rabûti*
II)   *...*
III) *[*   *]*

I)   ^{giš}*[... am]ḫur ...*
II)   *...*
III) *[*   *]*

Miscellaneous Texts

Nimrud Letter 12 = ND 2715

Editio princeps: Saggs 1955: 127-30, pl. xxx. See also Postgate 1974: 131 no. 1.2 (lines 10-18, 21-22).

This letter is one of a number found during the excavations of Nimrud, ancient Calah, during 1952. It is one of two definitely written by an Assyrian official named Qurdi-Ashur-lamur to the king[121] concerning the administration of Tyre and Sidon. Saggs[122] has dated ND 2715 to the time between Tiglath-pileser III's first and second series of western campaigns, in other words to between the years 738/7 and 735/4 B.C.E., a time after the organization of the Syrian provinces, and before the conquest of Philistia. He based this conclusion on the presence of Assyrian officials in Phoenicia, and on the apparently hostile intentions toward Philistia expressed through the prohibition of trade in lumber mentioned in ND 2715 lines 26-27.[123] With the exception of Oded,[124] who dated the letter to the time after the conquest of Kashpuna and its annexation to the province of Simirra, events which he dated to 734, Saggs's dating does not appear to have occasioned debate.

In ND 2715 Qurdi-Ashur-lamur reports on recent disturbances in the area of Tyre, Sidon, and Kashpuna,[125] and on his handling of the situations. The first incident of which he tells concerns Phoenician resentment of Assyrian control of their trade in timber. As a representative of the Assyrian commercial interest in Phoenician trade, Qurdi-Ashur-lamur attempted to impress upon the Phoenicians a new manner of preparing their felled trees for trade, namely by working them in the cities and not on the mountains, thus affording the Assyrian tax collectors the opportunity of watching over the

---

[121] The other being Nimrud Letter 13 = ND 2686.

[122] 1955: 150.

[123] Saggs (1955: 150 n. 1) has suggested that the prohibition of the export of timber to both Egypt and Philistia expressed in these lines could also indicate that Tiglath-pileser III contemplated future military action against Egypt.

[124] 1974: 48.

[125] Kashpuna was a city on or near the Mediterranean coast, which became an Assyrian administrative center under Tiglath-pileser. About Kashpuna and its original misreading as Rashpuna in the annals of Tiglath-pileser see Tadmor 1985.

trade. Under no circumstances would Qurdi-Ashur-lamur allow the indigenous population to sell their wood to either the Egyptians or the Philistines (lines 26-27). The overall contents of the letter can be outlined as follows:

lines 1-2   introductory rubric
lines 2-29   Phoenician revolt against Assyrian tax collectors; Qurdi-Ashur-lamur lays down the law
lines 30-43a concerning the fortification of Kashpuna
lines 43b-49 the settling of Iasubaeans in Kashpuna

(1) ana šarri bēlīya (2) aradka ᵐQurdī-Aššur-lāmur (3) issu muḫḫi ᵃˡŞurāya ša šarru iqbûni ... (21) urkīte issaparūni¹²⁶ ᵃᵐᵉˡmākisu (22) ittaşu ina ᵃˡŞidunni ussēribū (23) kī annê aqtibaššunu (24) nuk işē¹²⁷ šēridāni (25) dullākunu ina libbi epešā (26) ana ᵐᵃᵗMuşurāya ana (27) ᵐᵃᵗPalastāya lā taddanā¹²⁸ (28) ūlā mā¹²⁹ lā urammakunu (29) ana šadê lā tēlīā¹³⁰ ...

---

¹²⁶ = i-sa-par-u-ni: This word has been parsed following *CAD* M/1 130b as a G Perfect from the verb *šapāru* (< *ištaparuni*). Saggs (1955: 127, 129) transliterated the word as i-sa-tú-u-ni and derived it from a putative verb *šetu* [sic] "to escape, to flee." Thus Saggs (1955: 128) translated lines 21-23 as "Afterwards (when the people) had fled (and) the tax-collector had come out (and) I had sent him back into Sidon, I spoke to them in this manner." *CAD* M/1 130b translated lines 21-22 as "later they sent word to me and brought the tax collector into Sidon." In a similar vein Postgate (1974:131) translated lines 21-22 as "Afterwards they sent to me, and they brought the tax-collector (back) into Sidon."

¹²⁷ Written as PA.MEŠ instead of the expected GIŠ.MEŠ, it also appears in lines 9 and 10 of this letter. The frequency of its occurrence has led Saggs (1955: 129) to speculate that this does not represent a sloppy scribe, but rather may indeed be meant to be read PA. MEŠ. In support of this he cites Thompson, who has assigned the meaning of a top of a tree to PA.

¹²⁸ = ta-da-na: Saggs (1955: 129) has commented on the defective spelling of this word. However defective spellings seem to be a characteristic of the scribe of this letter. See, e.g., in the passage under discussion: *issaparūni* (< i-sa-par-u-ni in line 21), *ittaşu* (< i-ta-şu in line 22), *ussēribū* (< ú-se-ri-bu in line 22), *urammakunu* (< ú-ra-ma-ku-nu in line 28).

¹²⁹ = ma(!)-a: According to Saggs's drawing, the MA sign looks like an ÁŠ sign, with the horizontal lines cutting through the vertical wedge to the right. This is the same "problem" as reading what look likes a PA sign in lines 9, 10, and 24 as GIŠ.

¹³⁰ This verb is here translated as a negative imperative "do not go up!" This accords with the interpretation of the passage, emphasizing and reiterating that the Phoenician foresters are not to work the wood in the mountains, but in the city, under the watchful eye of the Assyrian tax collector. Saggs (1955: 128), however, has translated line 29 as dependent on the *ūla* of line 28 "Otherwise I will not free you (and) you shall not go up to the mountain."

(1) To the king, my lord, (2) (thus) your servant, Qurdi-Ashur-lamur: (3) Concerning the Tyrians, about whom the king said to me: ... (21[131]) Afterwards they sent to me (saying that) the tax collector, (22) who had left, they had brought into Sidon. (23) Thus I spoke to them: (24) "Have the wood brought down here. (25) Do your work in the center (of the city). (26-27) Do not give/sell (it) to the Egyptians (nor) to the Philistines, (28) or else I will not release you. Do not go up into the mountains!" ...

Relief Depicting the Capture of Gezer

Barnett and Falkner 1962: 24, 40-41, pl. lxii. See also Lance 1967: 42-44; Tadmor 1994: 210-211, and fig. 11 (p. 247).

During the course of Layard's excavations at Nimrud, he found a number of inscribed slabs, the originals of which he did not save. He did however attempt to draw them in order to record their contents for posterity. One such slab known only from Layard's drawing was taken from wall a of the South-West Palace of Tiglath-pileser III and depicted the Assyrian storming of a city. From the inscription in the upper right corner, we can deduce that the depicted city was most probably the well-known city of Gezer, which lies in the Judean foothills near the Shephelah (map reference 14251407).[132]

The inscription records the name of the stormed city as $^{\bar{a}l}Gazru$. As for the relief on the slab, it is a well crafted picture, the scene being divided naturally into halves as well as into quadrants. The left half of the picture is devoted to the Assyrians attacking Gazru, the latter of which takes up the right side of the relief. The upper half of the relief is equally balanced, with three Assyrian attackers in the upper left quadrant facing three defenders in the upper right quadrant. Taking up the lower left quadrant is an Assyrian siege engine with two battering rams loosening bricks from the city wall. The lower right quadrant is devoted to the city fortifications. Turning again to the upper left quadrant, above the siege engine an Assyrian warrior with crested helmet, small round shield, and spear in hand strides mightily across the plane dividing the Assyrian and the Gazrite halves of the picture. Behind him are

---

[131] The interpretation of this and the following line is quite difficult. This is due to both the scribe's tendency to write words defectively, and to the uncertainty concerning subject and person.

[132] For a review of literature regarding the identification of Gazru with Gezer see Reich and Brandl 1985: 41.

two additional Assyrian soldiers. One is shooting with his bow and arrow, while the second grasps a sword in one hand and a man-sized shield behind which the two of them are sheltered in the other. The three defenders atop the walls are all unarmed and ungirded. The leftmost stretches out his hands imploringly before the crested Assyrian warrior. The defender in the middle, standing as is the one to the right of him astride a tower, lifts his hands above his head in surrender. The rightmost defender crosses his arms in a gesture of submission.

The importance of this relief lies not in its depiction of the inhabitants of Gezer -- Barnett and Falkner[133] see nothing distinctive in either their tunics or long hair and beards. Rather the importance of the picture lies in its addition to our knowledge about the western campaigns of Tiglath-pileser. If Gazru is Gezer, as is almost universally assumed, then this relief is our only source for the capture of the city by Tiglath-pileser III, since it is not mentioned in the fragmentary annals. The depicted battle must have occurred during the years 734-732 B.C.E., during the only period during which Tiglath-pileser campaigned in southern Palestine. The importance of this incident for this study lies in the probable inclusion of Gezer at this time in Philistine territory. This must be deduced from 2 Chr 28:18, in which the Philistines had encroached upon Judahite territory in the Shephelah and the Negeb, capturing the towns of Beth-Shemesh, Aijalon, Gederoth, Soco, Timnah, and Gimzo, before the coming of Tiglath-pileser to Palestine. Evidence has been uncovered of a massive destruction at Gezer which can probably be dated to the time of Tiglath-pileser's campaigns.[134]

Eponym Canon C^b 1 = K 51

Text: II R pl. 52. Edition: Ungnad 1938: 428-31; Millard 1994: 44-45, 59, pl. 12 (re: campaigns of 734-732 B.C.E.).

The Assyrian method of recording the passage of time consisted of the naming of each year after a high official, the so-called eponym or *līmu*. A number of eponym series exhibiting differing characteristics has been identified.[135] Those of the C^b series contain the name of the official, his city

---

[133] 1962: 40-41.

[134] Gezer I: 33 n. 3; Gezer II: 73; Gezer III: 15-18; Dever 1985: 226.

[135] See Ungnad 1938: 413-14; Millard 1994: 1-21.

of origin, and, of crucial importance for the study of Assyrian chronology, a
historical notation.[136] This provides a chronological framework into which
episodes from both annals and summary inscriptions can then be fit. Although
the names of the eponyms are missing from the lines which relate to the years
734-732 B.C.E., these can be restored on the basis of Eponym Canon C^a 1 (K
4329 = II R pl. 68 #1 = III R pl. 1).[137] The following lines from the Eponym
Canon provide the framework for Tiglath-pileser's activity in the Levant
during the years 734-732 B.C.E.

40) *[ina līme ^{m}Bēl-dan] ša ^{al}Kalḫa ana māt Pilista*[138]
41) *[ina līme ^{m}Aššur-danninanni] ša ^{al}Mazamua ana māt Dimašqa*
42) *[ina līme ^{m}Nabû-bēl-uṣur] ša ^{al}Si'me ana māt Dimašqa*

40) In the eponymate of Bel-dan of Calah, to/against Philistia (734 B.C.E.).
41) In the eponymate of Ashur-danninanni of Mazamua, to/against Damascus
(733   B.C.E.).
42) In the eponymate of Nabu-Bel-usur of Sime, to/against Damascus (732
B.C.E.).

---

[136] In Millard's (1994: 4-5) terminology these are the "Class B Eponym Chronicles," which he
distinguishes from the "Class A Eponym Lists."

[137] See Ungnad 1938: 416-28. This is Millard's "A1", to which he adds the evidence from "A7" (=
Ungnad C^c). See Millard 1994: 17-18, 44-45

[138] A horizontal line follows this entry in the cuneiform text. Since it appears to have no function at this
point (generally to divide the various reigns from each other), it has been termed a scribal error. See
Millard 1994: 12-13, 19.

BIBLIOGRAPHY[*]

Abel, F.-M.
    1938   *Géographie de la Palestine*. Two volumes. Paris: Gabalda.
ABD   *Anchor Bible Dictionary*, ed. D. N. Freedman. New York-London-Toronto-Sydney-Auckland: Doubleday, 1992.
Aharoni, Y.
    1958   The Negeb of Judah. *Israel Exploration Journal* 8: 26-38.
    1974   *Carta's Atlas of the Bible*. Second edition. Hebrew. Jerusalem: Carta.
    1979   *The Land of the Bible: A Historical Geography*. Second edition. Philadelphia: Westminster.
Ahituv, S.
    1971a Obed-Edom. *Encyclopaedia Biblica* (Hebrew) 6: 15.
    1971b Philistia, Philistines. *Encyclopaedia Biblica* (Hebrew) 6: 484-500.
    1979   *The Egyptian Topographical Lists Relating to the History of Palestine in the Biblical Period*. Hebrew. Hebrew University Dissertation.
    1984   *Canaanite Toponyms in Ancient Egyptian Documents*. Jerusalem: Magnes.
AHW   W. von Soden, *Akkadisches Handwörterbuch*. Three volumes. Wiesbaden: Harrassowitz. 1965-81.
Albright, W. F.
    1920-21 | A Colony of Cretan Mercenaries on the Coast of the Negeb. *Journal of the Palestine Oriental Society* 1: 187-94.
    1942a King Joiachin in Exile. *Biblical Archaeologist* 5: 49-55.
    1942b A Votive Stele Erected by Ben-Hadad I of Damascus to the God Melcarth. *Bulletin of the American Schools of Oriental Research* 87: 23-29.
    1955   The Son of Tabeel (Isaiah 7:6). *Bulletin of the American Schools of Oriental Research* 140: 34-35.
    1968   *Yahweh and the Gods of Canaan: A Historical Analysis of Two Contrasting Faiths*. London: University of London. Reprinted Winona Lake, IN: Eisenbrauns.
    1975   Syria, the Philistines, and Phoenicia. Pp. 507-36 in: *Cambridge Ancient History* Vol. 2, Part 2. Third edition. Eds. I. E. S. Edwards, C. J. Gadd, N. G. L. Hammond, E. Sollberger. Cambridge: Cambridge University Press.
Alt, A.
    1936   Zu II Samuel 8 1. *Zeitschrift für die alttestamentliche Wissenschaft* 54: 149-52.
    1945   Neue assyrische Nachrichten über Palästina und Syrien. *Zeitschrift des deutschen Palästina-Vereins* 67: 128-159 (pp. 128-146 = 1953: 2.226-241).

---

[*] Non-bibliographic abbreviations follow the standards of the *Journal of Biblical Literature*.

1952 Ein Gesandter aus Philistäa in Aegypten. *Bibliotheca Orientalis* 9: 163-64.

1953 *Kleine Schriften zur Geschichte des Volkes Israel.* Three volumes (Vol. 3 published in 1959). Munich: Beck.

1968 *Essays on Old Testament History and Religion.* Trans. R. A. Wilson from the German 1953, 1959, 1964. Garden City, NY: Doubleday (Anchor).

el-Amin, M.

1953 Die Reliefs mit Beischriften von Sargon II. in Dur-Sharrukin. *Sumer* 9: 35-59.

Andersen, F. I., and Freedman, D. N.

1989 *Amos: A New Translation with Introduction and Commentary.* Anchor Bible 24A. New York-London-Toronto-Sydney-Auckland: Doubleday.

ANET J. B. Pritchard, ed., *Ancient Near Eastern Texts Relating to the Old Testament.* Third edition with supplement. Princeton, NJ: Princeton University, 1969.

Anspacher, A. S.

1912 *Tiglath Pileser III.* New York: Columbia, reprinted New York: AMS, 1966.

ARAB D. D. Luckenbill, *Ancient Records of Assyria and Babylonia.* Two volumes. Chicago: University of Chicago, 1926.

Ashdod I M. Dothan and D. N. Freedman, *Ashdod I: The First Season of Excavations, 1962* in: *'Atiqot* (English series) 7 (1967).

Ashdod II/III M. Dothan, D. N. Freedman, et al., *Ashdod II/III: The Second and Third Seasons of Excavation, 1963, 1965, Soundings in 1967* in: *'Atiqot* (English series) 9-10 (1971).

Ashdod IV Moshe Dothan and Yosef Porath, *Ashdod IV: Excavation of Area M, The Fortifications of the Lower City* in: *'Atiqot* (English series) 15 (1982).

Avi-Yonah, M., and Eph'al, Y.

1975 Ashkelon. *Encyclopedia of Archaeological Excavations in the Holy Land* 1: 121-30.

Baillet, M., Milik, J. T., and de Vaux, R.

1962 *Les 'petites grottes' de Qumrân.* Discoveries in the Judean Desert 3. Oxford: Clarendon.

Bakir, A. el-Mohsen

1952 *Slavery in Pharaonic Egypt.* Supplément aux annales du service des antiquités de l'Égypte 18. Cairo: Institut Français d'archéologie orientale.

Barnett, R. D.

1975 The Sea Peoples. *Cambridge Ancient History*[3] *II/2*: 359-78.

1990 Six Fingers and Toes: Polydactylism in the Ancient World. *Biblical Archaeology Review* 16/3: 46-51.

Barnett, R. D., and Falkner, M.

1962 *The Sculptures of Assur-nasir-apli II (883-859 B.C.), Tiglath-pileser III (745-727 B.C.), Esarhaddon (681-669 B.C.) from the Central and South-West Palaces at Nimrud.* London: British Museum.

Barré, M. L.

1992 Treaties in the ANE. *ABD* 6: 653-56.

Barrois, G. A.
    1962   Rephaim, Valley of. *Interpreter's Dictionary of the Bible* 2: 35-36.
Barton, J.
    1980   *Amos's Oracles against the Nations: A study of Amos 1.3-2.5.* Society for
            Old Testament Study Monograph Series 6. Cambridge: Cambridge
            University.
Beck, B. L.
    1980   *The International Roles of the Philistines During the Biblical Period.*
            Southern Baptist Theological Seminary Ph.D. Dissertation.
Begrich, J.
    1929   Der Syrisch-Ephraimitische Krieg und seine weltpolitischen
            Zusammenhänge. *Zeitschrift der deutschen morgenländischen Gesellschaft*
            83: 213-37.
Ben-Zvi, E.
    1990   Tracing Prophetic Literature in the Book of Kings: The Case of II Kings
            15,37. *Zeitschrift für die alttestamentliche Wissenschaft* 102: 100-05.
Bergsträsser, G.
    1918   *Hebräische Grammatik, I. Teil: Einleitung, Schrift- und Lautlehre.*
            Leipzig: J. C. Hinrichs. Reprinted Hildesheim: Georg Olms, 1962.
    1929   *Hebräische Grammatik, II. Teil: Verbum.* Leipzig: J. C. Hinrichs.
            Reprinted Hildesheim: Georg Olms, 1962.
Beyer, G.
    1931   Das Festungsystem Rehabeams. *Zeitschrift des deutschen Palästina-
            Vereins* 54: 113-34
BHK   *Biblia Hebraica*, ed. R. Kittel. Third Edition. Stuttgart: Württembergische
            Bibelanstalt, 1937.
BHS   *Biblia Hebraica Stuttgartensia*, eds. K. Elliger and W. Rudolph. Stuttgart:
            Deutsche Bibelstiftung, 1967/77.
Bickert, R
    1987   König Ahas und der Prophet Jesaja: Ein Beitrag zum Problem des syrisch-
            ephraimitischen Krieges. *Zeitschrift für die alttestamentliche Wissenschaft*
            99: 361-84.
Bietak, M.
    1993   The Sea Peoples and the End of the Egyptian Administration in Canaan.
            Pp. 292-306 in: *Biblical Archaeology Today, 1990: Proceedings of the
            Second International Congress on Biblical Archaeology, Jerusalem, June-
            July 1990*, eds. A. Biran and J. Aviram. Jerusalem: Israel Exploration
            Society & The Israel Academy of Sciences and Humanities.
Boecker, H. J.
    1976   *Recht und Gesetz im Alten Testament und im Alten Orient.* Neukirchener
            Studienbücher 10. Neukirchen-Vluyn: Neukirchener.
Boessneck, J. -- see Ziegler, R.
Boling, R. G., and Wright, G. E.
    1982   *Joshua.* Anchor Bible 6. Garden City, NY: Doubleday.

Borger, R.
1979   *Babylonisch-assyrische Lesestücke.* Second edition. Analecta orientalia 54. Rome: Pontifical Biblical Institute.
1986   *Assyrisch-babylonische Zeichenliste.* Third edition. Alter Orient und Altes Testament 33/33A. Neukirchen-Vluyn: Neukirchner.

Borger, R., and Tadmor, H.
1982   Zwei Beiträge zur alttestamentlichen Wissenschaft aufgrund der Inschriften Tiglatpilesers III. *Zeitschrift für die alttestamentliche Wissenschaft* 94: 244-51.

Bork, F.
1939-41 | Philistäische Namen und Vokabeln. *Archiv für Orientforschung* 13: 226-30

Brandl, B. -- see Reich, R.

Breasted, J. H.
1906   *Ancient Records of Egypt IV.* Chicago: University of Chicago.

Bright, J.
1976   The Organization and Administration of the Israelite Empire. Pp. 193-208 in: *Magnalia Dei: The Mighty Acts of God.* Wright Festschrift. Eds. F. M. Cross, W. E. Lemke, P. D. Miller, Jr. Garden City, NY: Doubleday.
1981   *A History of Israel.* Third edition. Philadelphia: Westminster.

Brinkman, J.
1968   *A Political History of Post-Kassite Babylon.* Analecta Orientalia 43. Rome: Pontifical Biblical Institute.
1984   *Prelude to Empire: Babylonian Society and Politics, 747-626 B.C.* Occasional Publications of the Babylonian Fund 7. Philadelphia: University Museum.

Broshi, M.
1977   Judeideh, Tell. *Encyclopedia of Archaeological Excavations in the Holy Land* 3: 694-96.

Broshi, M., and Finkelstein, I.
1992   The Population of Palestine in Iron Age II. *Bulletin of the American Schools of Oriental Research* 287: 47-60.

Brug, J. F.
1985   *A Literary and Archaeological Study of the Philistines.* BAR International Series 265. Oxford: BAR.

Buchanan, G. B.
1912   *A Critical and Exegetical Commentary on the Book of Isaiah. Volume I. Introduction and Commentary on I - XXVII.* International Critical Commentary. New York: Charles Scribner's Sons.

Budde, K.
1930   Jesaja und Ahaz. *Zeitschrift der deutschen morgenländischen Gesellschaft* 84: 125-38.

Bunimovitz, S.
1990   Problems in the "Ethnic" Identification of the Philistine Material Culture. *Tel Aviv* 17: 210-22.

Burney, C. F.
  1903   *Notes on the Hebrew Text of the Books of Kings.* Reprinted New York:
          Ktav, 1970.
CAD   *The Assyrian Dictionary of the Oriental Institute of the University of
          Chicago.* Chicago: Oriental Institute and Glückstadt: J. J. Augustin. 1956-.
Cardellini, I.
  1981   *Die biblischen "Sklaven"-Gesetze im Lichte des keilschriftlichen
          Sklavenrechts: Ein Beitrag zur Tradition, Überlieferung und Redaktion
          der alttestamentlichen Rechtstexte.* Bonner biblische Beiträge 55.
          Königstein-Bonn: Peter Hanstein.
Cazelles, H.
  1969   Une nouvelle stèle d'Adad-nirari d'Assyrie et Joas d'Israel. *Comptes
          rendus de l'Academie des inscriptions et belles-lettres* 1969: 106-117.
  1978   Problèmes de la Guerre Syro-Ephraimite. *Eretz Israel* 14: 70*-78*.
  1980   Qui aurait visé, à l'origine, Isaïe II 2-5? *Vetus Testamentum* 30: 409-20.
Cifola, B.
  1988   Ramses III and the Sea Peoples: A Structural Analysis of the Medinet
          Habu Inscriptions. *Orientalia NS* 57: 275-306.
Cody, A.
  1970   A New Inscription from Tell al-Rimah and King Jehoash of Israel.
          Catholic Biblical Quarterly 32: 325-40.
Cogan, M. -- see also Tadmor, H.
  1974   *Imperialism and Religion: Assyria, Judah and Israel in the Eighth and
          Seventh Centuries B.C.E.* Society of Biblical Literature Monograph Series.
          Missoula, MT: Scholars Press.
Cogan, M., and Tadmor, H.
  1988   *II Kings.* Anchor Bible 11. Garden City, NY: Doubleday.
Cohn, R. L. -- see Dothan, T.
Conroy, C.
  1978   *Absalom! Absalom!: Narrative and Language in 2 Sam 13-20.* Analecta
          Biblica 81. Rome: Pontifical Institute.
Corney, R. W.
  1962a   Achish. *Interpreter's Dictionary of the Bible* 1: 27a.
  1962b   Obed-Edom. *Interpreter's Dictionary of the Bible* 3: 579-80.
Cross, F. M.
  1972   The Stele Dedicated to Melcarth by Ben-Hadad of Damascus. *Bulletin of
          the American Schools of Oriental Research* 205: 36-42.
  1973   *Canaanite Myth and Hebrew Epic: Essays in the History of Religion of
          Israel.* Cambridge, MA-London: Harvard University.
Cross, F. M., and Freedman, D. N.
  1952   *Early Hebrew Orthography: A Study of the Epigraphic Evidence.*
          American Oriental Series 36. New Haven: American Oriental Society.
Cross, F. M., and Wright, G. E.
  1956   The Boundary and Province Lists of the Kingdom of Judah. *Journal of
          Biblical Literature* 75: 202-26.

Curtis, E. L., and Madsen, A. A.
    1910   *A Critical and Exegetical Commentary on the Books of Chronicles.*
            International Critical Commentary. Edinburgh: T. & T. Clark.
Dahood, M.
    1967   Hebrew-Ugaritic Lexicography V. *Biblica* 48: 421-38.
Dalley, S.
    1985   Foreign Chariotry and Cavalry in the Armies of Tiglath-Pileser III and
            Sargon II. *Iraq* 47: 31-48.
David, M.
    1949   *Een nieuw-ontdekte babylonische Wet uit de Tijd vóór Hammurabi.*
            Leiden: Brill.
De Meulenaere, H.
    1967   Die Dritte Zwischenzeit und das Äthiopische Reich. Pp. 220-55 in: *Die
            Altorientalischen Reiche III*, eds. E. Cassin, J. Bottero, and J. Vercoutter.
            Fischer Weltgeschichte 4. Frankfurt: Fischer Taschenbuch Verlag.
Delcor, M.
    1966   Philistins. *Dictionnaire de la Bible, Supplement* 7: 1233-88.
    1978   Les Cherethim et les Crétois. *Vetus Testamentum* 28: 409-22.
Dever, W. G.
    1967   Excavations at Gezer. *Biblical Archaeologist* 30: 47-62.
    1982   Monumental Architecture in Ancient Israel in the Period of the United
            Monarchy. Pp. 269-306 in: *Studies in the Period of David and Solomon
            and Other Essays*, ed. T. Ishida. Winona Lake, IN: Eisenbrauns.
    1985   Solomonic and Assyrian Period 'Palaces' at Gezer. *Israel Exploration
            Journal* 35: 217-30.
    1990a   Of Myths and Methods. *Bulletin of the American Schools of Oriental
            Research* 277/278: 121-30.
    1990b   *Recent Archaeological Discoveries and Biblical Research.* Seattle and
            London: University of Washington.
    1992   The Chronology of Syria-Palestine in the Second Millennium B.C.E.: A
            Review of Current Issues. *Bulletin of the American Schools of Oriental
            Research* 288: 1-25.
    1995   Orienting the Study of Trade in Near Eastern Archaeology. Pp. 111-119 in:
            *Recent Excavations in Israel: A View to the West. Reports on Kabri, Nami,
            Miqne-Ekron, Dor, and Ashkelon*, ed. Seymour Gitin. AIA Colloquia and
            Conference Papers, No. 1. Dubuque: Kendall/Hunt Publishing Co.
DeVries, S. J.
    1985   *1 Kings.* Word Biblical Commentary 12. Waco, TX: Word Books.
Dillard, R. B.
    1987   *2 Chronicles.* Word Biblical Commentary 15. Waco, TX: Word Books.
Doermann, R. W.
    1987   Archaeology and Biblical Interpretation: Tell el-Hesi. Pp. 129-46 in:
            *Archaeology and Biblical Interpretation: Essays in Memory of D. Glenn
            Rose*, eds. L. G. Perdue, L. E. Toombs, and G. L. Johnson. Atlanta: John
            Knox.

Donner, H.
 1970   Adadnirari III. und die Vasallen des Westens. Pp. 49-59 in: *Archäologie
         und altes Testament.* Festschrift Galling. Eds. A. Kuschke and E. Kutsch.
         Tübingen: Mohr.
 1977   The Separate States of Israel and Judah. Pp. 381-434 in: *Israelite and
         Judean History.* Eds. J. H. Hayes and J. M. Miller. Philadelphia:
         Westminster.
 1982   Israel und Tyrus im Zeitalter Davids und Salomos: Zur gegenseitigen
         Abhängigkeit von Innen- und Aussenpolitik. *Journal of Northwest Semitic
         Languages* 10: 43-52.
 1986   *Geschichte des Volkes Israel und seiner Nachbarn in Grundzüge* 2. Altes
         Testament Deutsch Ergänzungsreihe 4/2. Göttingen: Vandenhoeck &
         Ruprecht.
Donner, H., and Röllig, W.
 1969-73 | *Kanaanäische und Aramäische Inscriften.* Three volumes. Wiesbaden:
         Otto Harrasowitz.
Dothan, M. -- see also Dothan, T.
 1967   Ashdod: A City of the Philistine Pentapolis. *Archaeology* 20: 178-86.
 1970   The Musicians of Ashdod. *Archaeology* 23: 301-11.
 1971   Ashdod of the Philistines. Pp. 17-27 in: *New Directions in Biblical
         Archaeology*, eds. D. N. Freedman and J. C. Greenfield. Garden City, NY:
         Doubleday.
 1975   Ashdod. *Encyclopedia of Archaeological Excavations in the Holy Land* 1:
         103-19.
 1977   Mor, Tel. *Encyclopedia of Archaeological Excavations in the Holy Land*
         3: 889-90.
 1989   Archaeological Evidence for Movements of the Early 'Sea Peoples' in
         Canaan. Pp. 59-70 in: *Recent Excavations in Israel: Studies in Iron Age
         Archaeology*, eds. S. Gitin and W. G. Dever. Annual of the American
         Schools of Oriental Research 49. Winona Lake, IN: Eisenbrauns.
 1993   Ethnicity and Archaeology: Some Observations on the Sea Peoples at
         Ashdod. Pp. 53-55 in: *Biblical Archaeology Today, 1990: Proceedings of
         the Second International Congress on Biblical Archaeology, Jerusalem,
         June-July 1990*, eds. A. Biran and J. Aviram. Jerusalem: Israel Exploration
         Society & The Israel Academy of Sciences and Humanities.
 1993a Ashdod. *NEAEHL* 1: 93-102.
Dothan, M., and Porath, Y.
 1982   Ashdod IV: Excavation of Area M, The Fortifications of the Lower City.
         'Atiqot (English Series) 15.
Dothan, T. -- See also Gitin, S.; Gunneweg, J.
 1971   Philistines: Material Culture. *Encyclopaedia Biblica* (Hebrew) 6: 500-08.
 1982a *The Philistines and Their Material Culture.* Jerusalem: Israel Exploration
         Society.
 1982b What We Know About the Philistines. *Biblical Archaeology Review* 8/4:
         20-44.

1987   The Rise and Fall of Ekron of the Philistines: Recent Excavations at an
        Urban Border Site; Part I: The Late Bronze and Early Iron Ages. *Biblical
        Archaeologist* 50: 200-06.
1989   The Arrival of the Sea Peoples: Cultural Diversity in Iron Age Canaan. Pp.
        1-14 in: *Recent Excavations in Israel: Studies in Iron Age Archaeology*,
        eds. S. Gitin and W. G. Dever. Annual of the American Schools of
        Oriental Research 49. Winona Lake, IN: Eisenbrauns.
1992   Philistines: Archaeology. *ABD* 5: 328-33.
1995   Tel Miqne-Ekron: The Aegean Affinities of the Sea Peoples' (Philistines')
        Settlement in Iron Age I. Pp. 41-59 in: *Recent Excavations in Israel: A
        View to the West. Reports on Kabri, Nami, Miqne-Ekron, Dor, and
        Ashkelon*, ed. Seymour Gitin. AIA Colloquia and Conference Papers, No.
        1. Dubuque: Kendall/Hunt Publishing Co.

Dothan, T., and Cohn, R. L.
1994   The Philistine as Other: Biblical Rhetoric and Archaeological Reality. Pp.
        61-73 in: *The Other in Jewish Thought and History: Constructions of
        Jewish Culture and Identity*, eds. L. J. Silberstein and R. L. Cohn. New
        York-London: New York University.

Dothan, T., and Dothan, M.
1992   *People of the Sea: The Search for the Philistines*. New York: Macmillan.

Dothan, T., and Gitin, S.
1993   Miqne, Tel (Ekron). *NEAEHL* 3: .

DOTT   D. W. Thomas, ed., *Documents from Old Testament Times*. New York-
        Evanston: Harper & Row.

Driver, G. R.
1958   Geographical Problems. *Eretz Israel* 5: 16*-20*.

Driver, G. R., and Miles, J. C.
1952   *The Babylonian Laws*. Two volumes. Oxford: Clarendon.

Driver, S. R.
1892   *A Treatise on the Use of the Tenses in Hebrew*. Third edition. Oxford:
        Clarendon.
1912   *Notes on the Hebrew Text and the Topography of the Books of Samuel*.
        Second edition. Oxford: Clarendon. Reprinted Winona Lake, IN: Alpha
        Publications, 1984.

Duhm, B.
1914   *Das Buch Jesaia*. Göttinger Handkommentar zum Alten Testament.
        Third edition. Göttingen: Vandenhoeck & Ruprecht.

Edel, E.
1984   Die Sikeloi in den ägyptischen Seevölkertexten und in Keilschrifturkunden.
        Biblische Notizen 23: 7-8.

Ehrlich, A. B.
1900   *Mikrâ ki-Pheschutô*. Vol. 2. Reprinted New York: Ktav, 1969.
1901   *Mikrâ ki-Pheschutô*. Vol. 3. Reprinted New York: Ktav, 1969.
1910   *Randglossen zur Hebräischen Bibel*. Vol. 3. Leipzig: J. C. Hinrichs.
1912   *Randglossen zur Hebräischen Bibel*. Vol. 5. Leipzig: J. C. Hinrichs.

Ehrlich, C. S.
1991 Coalition Politics in Eighth Century B.C.E. Palestine: The Philistines and the Syro-Ephraimite War. *Zeitschrift des deutschen Palästina-Vereins* 107: 48-58.
1994 Sklavenauslieferung in der Bibel und im alten Orient. *Trumah* 4: 111-18.
Eissfeldt, O.
1936 *Philister und Phoenizier.* Das Alte Orient 34. Leipzig.
1943 Israelische-philistäische Grenzverschiebungen von David bis auf die Assyrerzeit. *Zeitschrift des deutschen Palästina-Vereins* 66: 115-128.
1967 Syrien und Palästina vom Ausgang des 11. bis zum Ausgang des 6. Jahrhunderts v. Chr. Vom Aufkommen des Königtums in Israel bis zum Ende des jüdischen Exils. Pp. 135-203 in: *Die Altorientalischen Reiche III*, eds. E. Cassin, J. Bottero, and J. Vercoutter. Fischer Weltgeschichte 4. Frankfurt/Main: Fischer Taschenbuch Verlag.
Elat, M.
1975a The Campaigns of Shalmaneser III against Aram and Israel. *Israel Exploration Journal* 25: 25-35.
1975b The Political Status of the Kingdom of Judah within the Assyrian Empire in the 7th Century B.C.E. Pp. 61-70 in: *Investigations at Lachish: The Sanctuary and the Residency.* Lachish V. Ed. Y. Aharoni. Tel Aviv: Gateway.
1977 *Economic Relations in the Lands of the Bible c. 1000-539 B.C.* Hebrew. Jerusalem: Bialik & Israel Exploration Society.
1978 The Economic Relations of the Neo-Assyrian Empire with Egypt. *Journal of the American Oriental Society* 98: 20-34.
Elliger, K.
1935 Die dreissig Helden Davids. *Palästina Jahrbuch* 31: 29-75.
Eph'al, I.
1982 *The Ancient Arabs.* Jerusalem: Magnes.
Falkner, M. -- see Barnett, R. D.
Fensham, F. C.
1967 A possible explanation of the name Baal-Zebub of Ekron. *Zeitschrift für die alttestamentliche Wissenschaft* 79: 361-64.
Finkelstein, I. -- see also Broshi, M.
1990 On Archaeological Methods and Historical Considerations: Iron Age II Gezer and Samaria. *Bulletin of the American Schools of Oriental Research* 277/278: 109-19.
Fitzmyer, J. A.
1967 *The Aramaic Inscriptions of Sefire.* Biblica et orientalia 19. Rome: Pontifical Biblical Institute.
Fokkelman, J. P.
1981 *Narrative Art and Poetry in the Books of Samuel. Volume I: King David (II Sam. 9-20 & I Kings 1-2).* Studia Semitica Neerlandica 20. Assen, The Netherlands: Van Gorcum.

Forrer, E.
    1919   *Die Provinzeinteilung des Assyrischen Reiches (Teil 1)*. Berlin: Friedrich-
            Wilhelms Universität.
Foster, B. R.
    1993   *Before the Muses: An Anthology of Akkadian Literature. Volume II:
            Mature, Late*. Bathesda, MD: CDL Press.
Freedman, D. N. -- see Andersen, F. I., and Cross, F. M.
Friedrich, J.
    1959   *Die hethitischen Gesetze. Transkription, Übersetzung, sprachliche
            Erläuterungen und vollständiges Wörterverzeichnis*. Leiden: Brill.
Fritz, V.
    1981   The 'List of Rehoboam's Fortresses' in 2 Chr 11:5-12 -- A Document from
            the time of Josiah. *Eretz Israel* 15: 46*-53*.
    1987   Die Fremdvölkersprüche des Amos. *Vetus Testamentum* 37: 26-38.
Funk, R. W.
    1975   Beth-Zur. *Encyclopedia of Archaeological Excavations in the Holy Land*
            1: 263-67.
GAG   W. von Soden. *Grundriss der akkadischen Grammatik*. Analecta orientalia
            33, 47. Rome: Pontifical Biblical Institute. 1969.
Galling, K.
    1968   *Textbuch zur Geschichte Israels*. Second edition. Tübingen: Mohr. [=
            TGI].
    1970   Review of Kathleen M. Kenyon, *Archäologie im Heiligen Land* (Trans.
            from English; Neukirchen: Neukirchener, 1967). *Zeitschrift für die
            alttestamentliche Wissenschaft* 86: 91-92.
Garbini, G.
    1986   Philistine Seals. Pp. 443-49 in: *The Archaeology of Jordan and Other
            Studies*, eds. L. Geraty and L. Herr. Berrien Springs, MI: Andrews
            University.
    1988   *History and Ideology in Ancient Israel*. London: Crossroad.
Gardiner, A.
    1961   *Egypt of the Pharaohs*. London-Oxford-New York: Oxford University.
Garelli, P.
    1991   The Achievement of Tiglath-pileser III: Novelty or Continuity? Pp. 46-51
            in: M. Cogan and I. Eph'al, eds., *Ah, Assyria...: Studies in Assyrian
            History and Ancient Near Eastern Historiography Presented to Hayim
            Tadmor*. Jerusalem: Magnes.
Garfinkel, Y.
    1988   2 Chr 11:5-10 Fortified Cities List and the lmlk Stamps--Reply to Nadav
            Na'aman. *Bulletin of the American Schools of Oriental Research* 271: 69-
            73.
Garsiel, M.
    1975   *The Kingdom of David: Studies in History and Inquiries in
            Historiography*. Hebrew. Tel Aviv: Don Publishing House and the Israel
            Society for Biblical Research.

Geyer, J. B.
    1986   Mythology and Culture in the Oracles Against the Nations. *Vetus Testamentum* 36: 129-45.

Gezer I W. G. Dever, H. D. Lance, and G. E. Wright, *Gezer I: Preliminary Report of the 1964-66 Seasons.* Annual of the Hebrew Union College Biblical and Archaeological School in Jerusalem. Jerusalem, Keter. 1970.

Gezer II W. G. Dever, ed., H. D. Lance, R. G. Bullard, D. P. Cole, and J. D. Seger, *Gezer II: Report of the 1967-70 Seasons in Fields I and II.* Annual of the Hebrew Union College/Nelson Glueck School of Biblical Archaeology. Jerusalem: Keter. 1974.

Gezer III S. Gitin, *Gezer III: A Ceramic Typology of the Late Iron II, Persian and Hellenistic Periods at Tell Gezer.* Annual of the Nelson Glueck School of Biblical Archaeology III. Jerusalem: H.U.C. Press. 1990.

Gichon, M.
    1964   The System of Fortifications in the Kingdom of Judah. Pp. 410-25 in: *The Military History of the Land of Israel in Biblical Times*, ed. J. Liver. Hebrew. Jerusalem: "Maarachoth" Israel Defence Forces.

Gitin, S. -- see also Dothan, T.; Gunneweg, J.
    1987   Urban Growth and Decline at Ekron in the Iron II Period. *Biblical Archaeologist* 50: 206-22 (= Gitin and T. Dothan 1987: 206-22).

    1989   Tel Miqne-Ekron: A Type-Site for the Inner Coastal Plain in the Iron Age II Period. Pp. 23-58 in: *Recent Excavations in Israel: Studies in Iron Age Archaeology*, eds. S. Gitin and W. G. Dever. Annual of the American Schools of Oriental Research 49. Winona Lake, IN: Eisenbrauns.

    1989a Incense Altars from Ekron, Israel and Judah: Context and Typology. *Eretz Israel* 20: 52*-67*.

    1990   Ekron of the Philistines, Part II: Olive Oil Suppliers to the World," *Biblical Archaeology Review* 16/2: 32-42, 59.

    1993   Seventh Century B.C.E. Cultic Elements at Ekron. Pp. 248-59 in: *Biblical Archaeology Today, 1990: Proceedings of the Second International Congress on Biblical Archaeology, Jerusalem, June-July 1990*, eds. A. Biran and J. Aviram. Jerusalem: Israel Exploration Society & The Israel Academy of Sciences and Humanities.

    1995   Tel Miqne-Ekron in the 7th Century B.C.E.: The Impact of Economic Innovation and Foreign Cultural Influences on a Neo-Assyrian Vassal City-State. Pp. 61-79 in: *Recent Excavations in Israel: A View to the West. Reports on Kabri, Nami, Miqne-Ekron, Dor, and Ashkelon*, ed. S. Gitin. AIA Colloquia and Conference Papers, No. 1; Dubuque: Kendall/Hunt Publishing Co.

Gitin, S., and Dotan, T.
    1987   The Rise and Fall of Ekron of the Philistines: Recent Excavations at an Urban Border Site. *Biblical Archaeologist* 50: 197-222.

Giveon, R.
    1972   An Egyptian Official in Gezer?. *Israel Exploration Journal* 22: 143-44.

GKC   W. Gesenius, E. Kautsch, and A. E. Cowley, *Gesenius' Hebrew Grammar*. Oxford: Clarendon, 1910.

Goetze, A.
     1956   *The Laws of Eshnunna*. Annual of the American Schools of Oriental Research 31. New Haven: Department of Antiquities of the Government of Iraq and the American Schools of Oriental Research.

Good, E. M.
     1966   Hosea 5:8-6:6: An Alternative to Alt. *Journal of Biblical Literature* 85: 273-86.

Gordon, C. H.
     1956   The Role of the Philistines. *Antiquity* 30: 22-26.
     1965   *Ugaritic Textbook*. Rome: Pontifical Biblical Institute.

Gray, J.
     1970   *I & II Kings*. Second edition. Old Testament Library. Philadelphia: Westminster.

Grayson, A. K.
     1980   Assyria and Babylonia. *Orientalia* 49: 140-94.
              Assyrian Royal Inscriptions. London.
     1981   Assyrian Royal Inscriptions: Literary Characteristics. Pp. 35-47 in: *Assyrian Royal Inscriptions: New Horizons in Literary, Ideological, and Historical Analysis*, ed. F. M. Fales. Oriens Antiqui Collectio 17. Rome: Istituto per l'Oriente.
     1992   Mesopotamia, History of (Babylonia). *ABD* 4: 755-77.

Green, A. R.
     1978   Solomon and Siamun: A Synchronism Between Early Dynastic Israel and the Twenty-First Dynasty of Egypt. *Journal of Biblical Literature* 97: 353-67.

Greenberg, M.
     1976   Some Postulates of Biblical Criminal Law. Pp. 18-37 in: *The Jewish Expression*, ed. J. Goldin. New Haven-London: Yale University.
     1986   More Reflections on Biblical Criminal Law. *Scripta Hierosolymitana* 31: 1-17

Greenfield, J. C.
     1962   Philistines. *Interpreter's Dictionary of the Bible* 3: 791-95.
     1962a   Cherethites and Pelethites. *Interpreter's Dictionary of the Bible* 1: 557.
     1972   Philistines. *Encyclopedia Judaica* 13: 399-404.
     1976   Philistines. *Interpreter's Dictionary of the Bible, Supplement* 666-67.

Groom, N.
     1981   *Frankincense and Myrrh: A Study of the Arabian Incense Trade*. Arab Background Series. London-New York: Longman and Beirut: Librairie du Liban.

Grønbaek, J. H.
     1971   *Die Geschichte vom Aufstieg Davids (1. Sam. 15-2. Sam. 5): Tradition und Komposition*. Acta Theologica Danica 10. Copenhagen: Prostant Apud Munksgaard.

Gunn, D. M.
  1982 *The Story of King David: Genre and Interpretation.* JSOT Supplement
       Series 6. Sheffield: JSOT Press.
Gunneweg, J., Perlman, I., Dothan, T., and Gitin, S.
  1986 On the Origin of Pottery from Tel Miqne-Ekron. *Bulletin of the American
       Schools of Oriental Research* 264: 3-16.
Haase, R.
  1968 *Die Fragmente der hethitischen Gesetze. Transkribiert und nach
       Paragraphen geordnet.* Wiesbaden: Otto Harrassowitz.
HALAT   W. Baumgartner and others, *Hebräisches und aramäisches Lexikon zum
       Alten Testament.* Leiden: Brill, 1967-.
Hallo, W. W.
  1964 From Qarqar to Carchemish: Assyria and Israel in the Light of New
       Discoveries. *Biblical Archaeologist Reader* 2: 152-88 = *Biblical
       Archaeologist* 23 (1960) 33-61.
Hallo, W. W., and Simpson, W. K.
  1971 *The Ancient Near East: A History.* New York-Chicago-San Francisco-
       Atlanta: Harcourt Brace Jovanovich.
Hamborg, G. R.
  1981 Reasons for Judgement in the Oracles Against the Nations of the Prophet
       Isaiah. *Vetus Testamentum* 31: 145-159.
Har-El, M.
  1977 The Valley of the Craftsmen (Ge' Haharašim). *PEQ* 109: 75-86..
Hatch, E., and Redpath, H. A.
  1897 *A Concordance to the Septuagint.* Three volumes (Third published 1906).
       Oxford: Clarendon. Reprinted Grand Rapids, MI: Baker House, 1987.
Hauer, C. E.
  1970 Jerusalem, the Stronghold and Rephaim. *Catholic Biblical Quarterly* 32:
       571-78.
Hawkins, J. D.
  1972-75a | Hattin. *Reallexikon der Assyriologie* 4: 160-62.
  1972-75b | Hazazu. *Reallexikon der Assyriologie* 4: 240.
Hayes, J. H. -- see also Miller, J. M.
  1968 The Usage of Oracles Against Foreign Nations in Ancient Israel. *Journal
       of Biblical Literature* 87: 81-92.
Hayes, J. H., and Hooker, P. K.
  1988 *A New Chronology for the Kings of Israel and Judah and Its Implications
       for Biblical History and Literature.* Atlanta: John Knox.
Hayes, J. H., and Irvine, S. A.
  1987 *Isaiah, the Eighth Century Prophet: His Times and His Preaching.*
       Nashville: Abingdon.
Herrmann, S.
  1981 *A History of Israel in Old Testament Times.* Second revised edition. Trans.
       John Bowden from German, 1973, 1980. Philadelphia: Fortress.

1989   The So-Called "Fortress System of Rehoboam," 2 Chr 11:5-12: Theoretical Considerations. *Eretz Israel* 20: 72*-78*.

Hertzberg, H. W.
1964   *I & II Samuel*. Trans. J. S. Bowden from German, 1960. Old Testament Library. Philadelphia: Westminster.

Hesse, B.
1986   Animal Use at Tel Miqne-Ekron in the Bronze Age and Iron Age. *Bulletin of the American Schools of Oriental Research* 264: 17-27.

Hobbs, T. R.
1985   *2 Kings*. Word Biblical Commentary 13. Waco, TX: Word Books.

Hoffmann, Y.
1977   *The Prophecies Against Foreign Nations in the Bible*. Hebrew. Tel-Aviv: Hakibbutz Hammeuchad.

Holladay, J. S., Jr.
1990   Red Slip, Burnish, and the Solomonic Gateway at Gezer. *Bulletin of the American Schools of Oriental Research* 277/278: 23-70.

Honeyman, A. M.
1948   The Evidence for Regnal Names Among the Hebrews. *Journal of Biblical Literature* 67: 13-25.

Hooker, P. K. -- see Hayes, J. H.
Houwink ten Cate, P. H. J.
1992   Hittite History. *ABD* 3: 219-25.

Hübner, U.
1989   Schweine, Schweineknochen und ein Speiseverbot im alten Israel. *Vetus Testamentum* 39: 225-36.

Irvine, S. A. -- see also Hayes, J. H.
1990   *Isaiah, Ahaz, and the Syro-Ephraimitic Crisis*. Society of Biblical Literature Dissertation Series 123. Atlanta: Scholars Press.

I - V R   Sigla for texts from Rawlinson 1861-1909.
ITP   Siglum for texts cited according to Tadmor 1994.

Japhet, S.
1993   *I & II Chronicles: A Commentary*. Old Testament Library. Louisville: Westminster/John Knox.

Jastrow, M.
1950   *A Dictionary of the Targumim, the Talmud Babli and Yerushalmi, and the Midrashic Literature*. New York, Pardes.

Jepsen, A.
1970   Ein neuer Fixpunkt für die Chronologie der israelitischen Könige? *Vetus Testamentum* 20: 359-61.

Johnson, B. L., and Stager, L. E.
1995   Ashkelon: Wine Emporium of the Holy Land. Pp. 95-109 in: *Recent Excavations in Israel: A View to the West. Reports on Kabri, Nami, Miqne-Ekron, Dor, and Ashkelon*, ed. S. Gitin. AIA Colloquia and Conference Papers, No. 1. Dubuque: Kendall/Hunt Publishing Co.

Jones, G. H.
    1984   *1 and 2 Kings.* Two volumes. New Century Bible. Grand Rapids, MI:
              Eerdmans.

Kaiser, O.
    1974   *Isaiah 13-39.* Trans. R. A. Wilson from German, 1973. Old Testament
              Library. Philadelphia: Westminster.
    1983   *Isaiah 1-12.* Second edition. Trans. J. Bowden from German, 1981. Old
              Testament Library. Philadelphia: Westminster.

Kalimi, I.
    1995   *Zur Geschichtsschreibung des Chronisten: Literarisch-historiographische*
              Abweichungen der Chronik von ihren Paralleltexten in den Samuel- und
              Königsbüchern. Beihefte zur Zeitschrift für die alttestamentliche
              Wissenschaft 226. Berlin-New York: Walter de Gruyter.

Kallai, Z.
    1960   *The Northern Boundaries of Judah.* Hebrew. Jerusalem: Magnes, 1960.

Kaplan, J.
    1975   Ashdod-Yam. *Encyclopedia of Archaeological Excavations in the Holy*
              Land 1: 119-20.

Kassis, H.
    1965   Gath and the Structure of the 'Philistine' Society. *Journal of Biblical*
              Literature 84: 259-71.

Katzenstein, H. J.
    1973   *The History of Tyre.* Jerusalem: Schocken.
    1983   Before Pharaoh Conquered Gaza (Jeremiah XLVII 1). *Vetus Testamentum*
              33: 249-51.
    1992   Philistines: History. *Anchor Bible Dictionary* 5: 326-28.

KB   *Keilinschrifliche Bibliothek.* = Schrader 1889-96.

Keel, O.
    1994   Philistine 'Anchor' Seals. *Israel Exploration Journal* 44: 21-35.

Kelm, G. L.
    1984-85 | Timnah -- a City of Conflict Within the Traditional Buffer Zone of the
              Shephelah. *Bulletin of the Anglo-Israel Archaeology Society* 54-61.

Kelm, G. L., and Mazar, A.
    1982   Three Seasons of Excavations at Tel Batash - Biblical Timnah. *Bulletin of*
              the American Schools of Oriental Research 248: 1-36.
    1984   Timnah: A Biblical City in the Sorek Valley. *Archaeology* 37/3: 58-59, 78-
              79.
    1989   Excavating in Samson Country: Philistines and Israelites at Tel Batash.
              Biblical Archaeology Review 15/1: 36-49.
    1995   *Timnah: A Biblical City in the Sorek Valley.* Winona Lake, IN:
              Eisenbrauns.

Kempinski, A.
    1981   Baal-Perazim and the Conflicting Schools of Thought Regarding the
              Settlement. Hebrew. *Qadmoniot* 14: 63-64.

Kenyon, K. M.
    1971   *Royal Cities of the Old Testament*. New York: Schocken.
    1974   *Digging Up Jerusalem*. New York-Washington: Praeger.
King, L. W.
    1915   *Bronze Reliefs from the Gates of Shalmaneser, King of Assyria B.C. 860-
           825*. London: British Museum.
King, P. J.
    1988   *Amos, Hosea, Micah -- An Archaeological Commentary*. Philadephia:
           Westminster.
    1989   The Eighth, Greatest of Centuries. *Journal of Biblical Literature* 108: 3-
           15.
Kitchen, K. A.
    1973   The Philistines. Pp. 53-78 in: Peoples of Old Testament Times, ed. D. J.
           Wiseman. Oxford: Clarendon.
    1986   *The Third Intermediate Period in Egypt (1100-650 B.C.)*. Second edition
           with supplement. Aris & Phillips.
Klíma, J., Petschow, H., Cardascia, G., and Korošec, V.
    1957-71 | Gesetze. *Reallexikon der Assyriologie* 3: 243-97.
Klostermann, A.
    1887   *Die Bücher Samuelis und der Könige*. Nördlingen: C. H. Beck.
Kramer, S. N.
    1983   The Ur-Nammu Law Code: Who Was Its Author? *Orientalia* 52: 453-56.
Labat, R.
    1967   Assyrien und seine Nachbarländer (Babylonien, Elam, Iran) von 1000 bis
           617 v. Chr./ Das neubabylonische Reich bis 539 v. Chr. Pp. 9-111 in: *Die
           altorientalischen Reiche III*, eds. E. Cassin, J. Bottero, and J. Vercoutter.
           Fischer Weltgeschichte 4. Frankfurt/Main: Fischer Taschenbuch Verlag.
Lamprichs, R.
    1995   *Die Westexpansion des neuassyrischen Reiches: Eine Strukturanalyse*.
           Alter Orient und Altes Testament 239. Kevelaer: Butzon & Bercker/
           Neukirchen-Vluyn: Neukirchener.
Lance, H. D.
    1967   Gezer in the Land and in History. *Biblical Archaeologist* 30: 34-47.
    1976   Solomon, Siamun, and the Double Ax. Pp. 209-23 in: *Magnalia Dei: The
           Mighty Acts of God*. Wright Festschrift. Eds. F. M. Cross, W. E. Lemke,
           P. D. Miller, Jr. Garden City, NY: Doubleday.
Landsberger, B.
    1948   *Sam'al*. Ankara: Türkische Historische Gesellschaft.
de Langhe, R.
    1939   Les Textes de Ras Shamra-Ugarit et leurs apports a l'Histoire des Origines
           israelites. *Ephemerides Theologicae Lovaniensis* 16: 245-327.
Lay   Siglum for texts from Layard 1851.
Layard, A. H.
    1849   *Nineveh and Its Remains*. 2 volumes. Second edition. London: John
           Murray.

1851   *Inscriptions in the Cuneiform Character from Assyrian Monuments*.
        London: Harrison & Son.
1854   *Discoveries Among the Ruins of Nineveh and Babylon*. Second abridged
        edition. New York: A. S. Barnes, the original was published by G. P.
        Putnam in 1853.

Lemaire, A.
1993   Joas de Samarie, Barhadad de Damas, Zakkur de Hamat. La Syrie-
        Palestine vers 800 av. J.-C. *Eretz Israel* 24: 148*-157*.

Lemke, W. E.
1965   The Synoptic Problem in the Chronicler's History. *Harvard Theological
        Review* 58: 349-63.

Levine, L. D.
1972   Menahem and Tiglath-pileser: A New Synchronism. *Bulletin of the
        American Schools of Oriental Research* 206: 40-42.

Lewy, J.
1956   On Some Institutions of the Old Assyrian Empire. *Hebrew Union College
        Annual* 27: 1-79.

L'Heureux, C.
1976   The *yᵉlîdê hārāpāʾ* -- A Cultic Association of Warriors. Pp. 83-85 in:
        Essays in Honor of George Ernest Wright, eds. E. F. Campbell and R. G.
        Boling. Missoula, MT: Scholars Press (= *Bulletin of the American Schools
        of Oriental Research* 220/221, 1975-76).

Lipinski, E.
1971   Note de Topographie Historique: Baʿli-Ra'ši et Ra'šu Qudšu. *Revue
        Biblique* 78: 84-92.

Lloyd, S.
1980   *Foundations in the Dust*. Revised edition. London-New York: Thames and
        Hudson.

London, G.
1989   A Comparison of Two Contemporaneous Lifestyles of the Late Second
        Millennium B.C. *Bulletin of the American Schools of Oriental Research*
        273: 37-55

Luckenbill, D. D.
1924   *The Annals of Sennacherib*. Oriental Institute Publications 2. Chicago:
        University of Chicago.
1926   *Ancient Records of Assyria and Babylonia*. 2 volumes. Chicago:
        University of Chicago. [= ARAB].

Macalister, R. A. S.
1914   *The Philistines: Their History and Civilization*. The Schweich Lectures,
        1911. London: Oxford University.

McCarter, P. K., Jr.
1980   *I Samuel*. Anchor Bible 8. Garden City, NY: Doubleday.
1984   *II Samuel*. Anchor Bible 9. Garden City, NY: Doubleday.
1986   The Historical David. *Interpretation* 40: 117-29.

McCarthy, D. J.
    1978   *Treaty and Covenant.* Revised edition. Analecta Biblica 21a. Rome:
            Pontifical Biblical Institute.
Machinist, P.
    1983   Assyria and its Image in the First Isaiah. *Journal of the American Oriental
            Society* 103: 719-737.
Madsen, A. A. -- see Curtis, E. L.
Maisler, B. -- see Mazar, B.
Malamat, A.
    1962   Mari and the Bible: Some Patterns of Tribal Organization and Institutions.
            Journal of the American Oriental Society 82: 143-50.
    1963   Aspects of the Foreign Policies of David and Solomon. *Journal of Near
            Eastern Studies* 22: 1-17.
    1964   The Kingdom of David and Solomon in Its Contact with Egypt and Aram
            Naharaim. *Biblical Archaeologist Reader* 2: 89-98.
    1982   A Political Look at the Kingdom of David and Solomon and Its Relation
            with Egypt. Pp. 189-204 in: *Studies in the Period of David and Solomon
            and Other Essays*, ed. T. Ishida. Winona Lake, IN: Eisenbrauns.
    1983   *Das davidische und salomonische Königreich und seine Beziehungen zu
            Ägypten und Syrien. Zur Entstehung eines Grossreichs.* Österreichische
            Akademie der Wissenschaften, Philosophisch-historische Klasse,
            Sitzungsberichte, 407. Band. Vienna: Österreichische Akademie der
            Wissenschaften.
    1989   *Mari and the Early Israelite Experience: The Schweich Lectures of the
            British Academy 1984.* Oxford: Oxford University Press.
Marcus, D.
    1977   Sharruludari, Son of Rukibtu, Their Former King: A Detail of Phoenician
            Chronology. *Journal of the Ancient Near Eastern Society of Columbia
            University* 9: 27-30.
Martin, W. J.
    1936   *Tribut und Tributleistungen bei den Assyrern.* Studia Orientalia viii/1.
            Helsinki: Societas Orientalis Fennica.
Mays, J. L.
    1969   *Amos.* Old Testament Library. Philadelphia: Westminster.
Mazar, A. -- see also Kelm, G. L.
    1980   *Excavations at Tell Qasile, Part One, The Philistine Sanctuary:
            Architecture and Cult Objects.* Qedem 12. Jerusalem: Institute of
            Archaeology at the Hebrew University.
    1985   Between Judah and Philistia: Timnah (Tel Batash) in the Iron Age II. *Eretz
            Israel* 18: 300-24, pls. 60-65. Hebrew, English summary pp. 75*-76*.
    1985a *Excavations at Tell Qasile, Part Two, The Philistine Sanctuary: Various
            Finds, the Pottery, Conclusions, Appendixes.* Qedem 20. Jerusalem:
            Institute of Archaeology at the Hebrew University.

1990   *Archaeology of the Land of the Bible, 10,000 - 586 B.C.E.* Anchor Bible
        Reference Library. New York-London-Toronto-Sydney-Auckland:
        Doubleday.

1992   The Iron Age I. Pp. 258-301 in: *The Archaeology of Ancient Israel*, ed. A.
        Ben-Tor. Trans. from Hebrew by Rafi Greenberg; New Haven-London:
        Yale University.

1992a   Temples of the Middle and Late Bronze Ages and the Iron Age. Pp. 161-
        187 in: *The Architecture of Ancient Israel From the Prehistoric to the
        Persian Periods*, eds. A. Kempinski and R. Reich. Jerusalem: Israel
        Exploration Society.

1993   Qasile, Tell: Excavations in Area C. *NEAEHL* 4: 1207-08.

1994   The Northern Shephelah in the Iron Age: Some Issues in Biblical History
        and Archaeology. Pp. 247-267 in: *Scripture and Other Artifacts: Essays
        on the Bible and Archaeology in Honor of Philip J. King*, eds. Michael D.
        Coogan, J. Cheryl Exum, and Lawrence E. Stager. Louisville, KY:
        Westminster/John Knox.

Mazar (Maisler), B.

1947/8 A New Assyrian - Israelite Synchronism? *Tarbiz* 19: 123-24. Hebrew.

1953   The Campaign of Sennacherib to the Land of Judah *Eretz Israel* 2: 170-75.
        Hebrew.

1954   Gath and Gittaim. *Israel Exploration Journal* 4: 227-35.

1956   The Campaign of Pharaoh Shishak to Palestine. Pp. 57-66 in: *Congress
        Volume: Strassbourg, 1956.* Published 1957. *Vetus Testamentum
        Supplements* 4. Leiden: Brill.

1957   The Tobiads. *Israel Exploration Journal* 7: 137-45, 229-38.

1960   The Cities of the Territory of Dan. *Israel Exploration Journal* 10: 65-77.

1962   The Aramean Empire and its Relations with Israel. *Biblical Archaeologist*
        35: 98-120 (= B. Mazar 1986: 151-72).

1963   David's Reign in Hebron and the Conquest of Jerusalem. Pp. 235-44 in: *In
        the Time of Harvest: Essays in Honor of Abba Hillel Silver*, ed. D. J.
        Silver. London-New York: Macmillan.

1964   *The Philistines and the Rise of Israel and Tyre.* Proceedings of the Israel
        Academy of Sciences and Humanities I/7 (= B. Mazar 1986: 63-82).

1979   The Era of David and Solomon. Pp. 76-99, 326 in: *The Age of the
        Monarchies: Political History*, ed. A. Malamat. World History of the
        Jewish People, First Series, Volume 4-I. Jerusalem: Massada.

1986   *The Early Biblical Period: Historical Studies*, eds. S. Ahituv and B. A.
        Levine. Jerusalem: Israel Exploration Society.

1992   *Biblical Israel: State and People.* Shmuel Ahituv, ed. Jerusaelm: Magnes.

Mendelsohn, I.

1949   *Slavery in the Ancient Near East.* New York: Oxford University.

1955   On Slavery at Alalakh. *Israel Exploration Journal* 5: 65-72.

Milik, J. T. -- see Baillet, M.

Millard, A. (R.)
> 1994   *The Eponyms of the Assyrian Empire 910-612 BC.* State Archives of
>   Assyria Studies 2. Helsinki: Neo-Assyrian Text Corpus Project.

Millard, A. R., and Tadmor, H.
> 1973   Adad-nirari III in Syria: Another Stele Fragment and the Dates of his
>   Campaigns. *Iraq* 35: 57-64, pl. xxix.

Miller, J. M.
> 1987   Rehoboam's Cities of Defense and the Levitical City Lists. Pp. 273-86 in:
>   *Archaeology and Biblical Interpretation: Essays in Memory of D. Glenn
>   Rose*, eds. L. G. Perdue, L. E. Toombs, and G. L. Johnson. Atlanta: John
>   Knox.

Miller, J. M., and Hayes, J. H.
> 1986   *A History of Ancient Israel and Judah.* Philadelphia: Westminster.

Miller, P. D., and Roberts, J. J. M.
> 1977   *The Hand of the Lord: A Reassessment of the "Ark Narrative" of 1
>   Samuel.* Baltimore-London: Johns Hopkins University.

Milsom, D.
> 1986   The Design of the Royal Gates at Megiddo, Hazor, and Gezer. *Zeitschrift
>   des deutschen Palästina-Vereins* 102: 87-92.

Mitchell, T. L.
> 1967   Philistia. Pp. 405-28 in: *Archeology and Old Testament Study*, ed. D. W.
>   Thomas. Oxford: Clarendon.

Mittmann, S.
> 1983   Die "Handschelle" der Philister (2Sam 8,1). Pp. 327-41 in: *Fontes atque
>   pontes: Eine Festgabe für Hellmut Brunner*, ed. M. Görg. Ägypten und
>   Altes Testament 5. Wiesbaden: Otto Harrassowitz.

Montet, P.
> 1941   *Le drame d'Avaris: Essai sur la pénétration des Semites en Egypte.* Paris:
>   Paul Geuthner.
> 1959   *L'Egypte et la Bible.* Cahiers d'Archéologie Biblique 11. Neuchatel,
>   Switzerland: Editions Delachaux & Niestle.

Montgomery, J. A., and Gehman, H. S.
> 1951   *A Critical and Exegetical Commentary on the Book of Kings.* International
>   Critical Commentary. Edinburgh: T. & T. Clark.

Moran, W. L.
> 1992   *The Amarna Letters.* Baltimore-London: Johns Hopkins University.

Muntingh, L. M.
> 1964-65 | Political and International Relations of Israel's Neighbouring Peoples
>   According to the Oracles of Amos. *Ou-Testamenties Werkgemeenskap in
>   Suid-Afrika* 7/8: 134-42.

Myers, J. M.
> 1965a   *I Chronicles.* Anchor Bible 12. Garden City, NY: Doubleday.
> 1965b   *II Chronicles.* Anchor Bible 13. Garden City, NY: Doubleday.

Na'aman, N.
    1974   Sennacherib's 'Letter to God' on his Campaign to Judah. *Bulletin of the American Schools of Oriental Research* 214: 26-28.
    1979a   The Brook of Egypt and Assyrian Policy on the Border of Egypt. *Tel Aviv* 6: 68-90.
    1979b   Sennacherib's Campaign to Judah and the Date of the LMLK Stamps. *Vetus Testamentum* 29: 61-86.
    1986   Historical and Chronological Notes on the Kingdoms of Israel and Judah in the Eighth Century B.C. *Vetus Testamentum* 36: 71-92.
    1986a   *Borders and Districts in Biblical Historiography: Seven Studies in Biblical Geographical Lists.* Jerusalem Biblical Studies 4. Jerusalem: Simor.
    1986b   Hezekiah's Fortified Cities and the LMLK Stamps. *Bulletin of the American Schools of Oriental Research* 261: 5-21.
    1988   The Date of 2 Chronicles 11:5-10--A Reply to Y. Garfinkel. *Bulletin of the American Schools of Oriental Research* 271: 74-77.
    1991   Forced Participation in Alliances in the Course of the Assyrian Campaigns to the West. Pp. 80-98 in: *Ah, Assyria...: Studies in Assyrian History and Ancient Near Eastern Historiography Presented to Hayim Tadmor*, eds. M. Cogan and I. Eph'al. Jerusalem: Magnes.
    1995   Rezin of Damascus and the Land of Gilead. *Zeitschrift des deutschen Palästina-Vereins* 111: 105-17.
Naveh, J.
    1958   Khirbet al-Muqanna' -- Ekron: An Archaeological Survey. *Israel Exploration Journal* 8: 87-100, 165-70.
    1970   The Scripts in Palestine and Transjordan in the Iron Age. Pp. 277-83 in: *Near Eastern Archaeology in the Twentieth Century*, Glueck Festschrift, ed. J. A. Sanders. Garden City, New York: Doubleday.
    1982   *Early History of the Alphabet.* Jerusalem: Magnes.
    1985   Writing and Scripts in Seventh-Century B.C.E. Philistia: The Evidence from Tell Jemmeh. *Israel Exploration Journal* 35: 8-21.
NEAEHL   *New Encyclopedia of Archaeological Excavations in the Holy Land*, ed. E. Stern. New York: Simon and Schuster. 1993.
Niemann, H. M.
    1985   *Die Daniten: Studien zur Geschichte eines altisraelitischen Stammes.* Forschungen zur Religion und Literatur des Alten und Neuen Testaments 135; Göttingen: Vandenhoeck & Ruprecht.
Noort, E.
    1993   Seevölker, materielle Kultur und Pantheon: Bemerkungen zur Benutzung archäologischer Daten - ein kritischer Bericht. Pp. 363-89 in: *Religionsgeschichtliche Beziehungen zwischen Kleinasien, Nordsyrien und dem Alten Testament*, eds. B. Janowski, K. Koch, and G. Wilhelm. Orbis biblicus et orientalis 129. Freiburg, CH: Universitätsverlag & Göttingen: Vandenhoeck & Ruprecht.
    1994   *Die Seevölker in Palästina.* Palaestina Antiqua 8. Kampen: Kok Pharos.

Noth, M.
　　1938　Die Wege der Pharaonenheere in Palästina und Syrien: IV. Die
　　　　　Schoschenkliste. *Zeitschrift des deutschen Palästina-Vereins* 61: 277-304.
　　1960　*The History of Israel*. Second edition. Trans. by P. R. Ackroyd from
　　　　　German. New York: Harper & Brothers.
Nougayrol, J.
　　1956　*Le palais royal d'Ugarit IV: Textes accadiens des archives sud*. Mission
　　　　　de Ras Shamra 9. Paris.
Oded, B.
　　1972　The Historical Background of the Syro-Ephraimite War Reconsidered.
　　　　　Catholic Biblical Quarterly 34: 153-65.
　　1974　The Phoenician Cities and the Assyrian Empire in the Time of Tiglath-
　　　　　Pileser III. *Zeitschrift des deutschen Palästina-Vereins* 90: 38-49.
　　1979　Neighbors on the West. Pp. 222-46 in: *The Age of the Monarchies:
　　　　　Political History*, ed. A. Malamat. The World History of the Jewish
　　　　　People, First Series, Vol. 4-I. Jerusalem: Masada.
Olmstead, A. T. E.
　　1916　*Assyrian Historiography: A Source Study*. Univ. of Missouri Studies,
　　　　　Social Science Series Vol. III No. 1. Columbia, MO: Univ. of Missouri.
　　1923　*History of Assyria*. New York: Charles Scribner's.
Olyan, S.
　　1988　*Asherah and the Cult of Yahweh in Israel*. Society of Biblical Literature
　　　　　Monograph Series 34. Atlanta: Scholars Press.
Oren, E. D.
　　1982　Ziklag: A Biblical City on the Edge of the Negev. *Biblical Archaeologist*
　　　　　45: 155-66.
Otto, E.
　　1953　*Ägypten: Der Weg des Pharaonenreiches*. Stuttgart: Kohlhammer.
Otto, Eckart
　　1989　*Rechtsgeschichte der Redaktionen im Kodex Ešnunna und im
　　　　　"Bundesbuch": Eine redaktionsgeschichtliche und rechtsvergleichende
　　　　　Studie zu altbabylonischen und altisraelitischen Rechtsüberlieferungen*.
　　　　　Orbis biblicus et orientalis 85. Freiburg, CH: Universitätsverlag &
　　　　　Göttingen: Vandenhoeck & Ruprecht.
Otzen, B.
　　1977-78 | Israel Under the Assyrians. *Annual of the Swedish Theological Institute*
　　　　　11: 96-110.
Ovadiah, A.
　　1976　Gaza. *Encyclopedia of Archaeological Excavations in the Holy Land* 2:
　　　　　408-17.
Page, S.
　　1968　A Stela of Adad-Nirari III and Nergal-Eres from Tell al Rimah. *Iraq*
　　　　　30: 139-53, pls. xxxix-xli.

von Pákozdy, L. M.
  1956   'Elḥånån -- der frühere Name Davids? *Zeitschrift für die
         alttestamentliche Wissenschaft* 68: 257-59.
Parker, B.
  1961   Administrative Tablets from the North-West Palace, Nimrud. *Iraq* 23: 15-
         67, pls. ix-xxx.
Parpola, S.
  1970   *Neo-Assyrian Toponyms.* Alter Orient und Altes Testament 6. Kevelaer
         and Neukirchen-Vluyn: Butzon & Bercker and Neukirchener.
  1987   *The Correspondence of Sargon II, Part I: Letters from Assyria and the
         West.* State Archives of Assyria 1. Helsinki: Helsinki University.
Parpola, S., and Watanabe, K.
  1988   *Neo-Assyrian Treaties and Loyalty Oaths.* State Archives of Assyria 2.
         Helsinki: Helsinki University.
Pečírková, J.
  1987   The Administrative Methods of Assyrian Imperialism. *Archiv Orientální*
         55: 162-75.
Peckham, B.
  1976   Israel and Phoenicia. Pp. 224-48 in: *Magnalia Dei: The Mighty Acts of
         God*, Wright Festschrift, eds. F. M. Cross, W. E. Lemke, P. D. Miller, Jr.
         Garden City, NY: Doubleday.
Perlman, I. -- see Gunneweg, J.
Pfeiffer, R. H.
  1948   *Introduction to the Old Testament.* Revised edition. New York: Harper &
         Brothers.
Pisano, S., S. J.
  1984   *Additions or Omissions in the Books of Samuel: The Significant Pluses
         and Minuses in the Massoretic, LXX and Qumran Texts.* Orbis biblicus et
         orientalis 57. Freiburg, CH: Universitätsverlag; Göttingen: Vandenhoeck &
         Ruprecht.
Pitard, W. T.
  1987   *Ancient Damascus: A Historical Study of the Syrian City-State from
         Earliest Times until its Fall to the Assyrians in 732 B.C.E.* Winona Lake,
         IN: Eisenbrauns.
Poebel, A.
  1943   The Assyrian King List from Khorsabad - Concluded. *Journal of Near
         Eastern Studies* 2: 56-90.
Porten, B.
  1981   The Identity of King Adon. *Biblical Archaeologist* 44: 36-52.
Postgate, J. N.
  1974   *Taxation and Conscription in the Assyrian Empire.* Studia Pohl: Series
         Maior 3; Rome: Biblical Institute.
Pritchard, J. B., ed.
  1969   *Ancient Near Eastern Texts Relating to the Old Testament.* Third edition
         with supplement. Princeton, NJ: Princeton University. [= *ANET*].

1987   *The Harper Atlas of the Bible*. New York: Harper & Row.

Raban, A., and Stieglitz, R. R.
    1991   The Sea Peoples and Their Contributions to Civilization. *Biblical Archaeology Review* 17/6: .

von Rad, G.
    1933   Das Reich Israel und die Philister. *Palästina Jahrbuch* 29: 30-42.

Rainey, A. F.
    1975   The Identification of Philistine Gath: A Problem in Source Analysis for Historical Geography. *Eretz Israel* 12: 63*-76*.
    1982   Toponymic Problems (cont.). *Tel Aviv* 9: 130-36.

Rawlinson, H. C., ed.
    1861-1909 | *The Cuneiform Inscriptions of Western Asia*. Five volumes. London. [= I - V R].

Reade, J. E.
    1968   The Palace of Tiglath-pileser III. *Iraq* 30: 69-73, pl. xviii.
    1976   Sargon's Campaigns of 720, 716, and 715 B.C.: Evidence from the Scultures. *Journal of Near Eastern Studies* 35: 95-104.

Redford, D. B.
    1973   Studies in Relations Between Palestine and Egypt During the First Millennium B.C.: II. The Twenty-second Dynasty. *Journal of the American Oriental Society* 93: 3-17.
    1992   *Egypt, Canaan, and Israel in Ancient Times*. Princeton: Princeton University Press.

Reich, R., and Brandl, B.
    1985   Gezer under Assyrian Rule. *Palestine Exploration Quarterly* 117: 41-54.

Renger, J.
    1972   Flucht als soziales Problem in der altbabylonischen Gesellschaft. Pp. 167-82 in: *Gesellschaftsklassen im Alten Zweistromland und in den angrenzenden Gebieten -- XVIII. Rencontre assyriologique internationale, München, 29. Juni bis 3. Juli 1970*, ed. D. O. Edzard. Bayerische Akademie der Wissenschaften, Philosophisch-historische Klasse, Abhandlungen - Neue Folge Heft 75. München: Bayerische Akademie der Wissenschaften (C. H. Beck).

Reventlow, H. Graf
    1993   *Die Propheten Haggai, Sacharja und Malechi*. Ninth edition. Das Alte Testament Deutsch 25/2. Göttingen: Vandenhoeck & Ruprecht.

Rinaldi, G.
    1963   Quelques remarques sur la politique d'Azarias (Ozias) de Juda en Philistie (2 Chron. 26, 6ss.). *Vetus Testamentum Supplements* 9 (*Congress Volume Bonn*): 225-35.

Roberts, J. J. M. -- see also Miller, P. D.
    1985   Isaiah 2 and the Prophet's Message to the North. *Jewish Quarterly Review* 75: 290-308.

Rofé, A.
  1973   Baal, the Prophet and the Angel (II Kings 1): A Study in the History of
         Literature and Religion. *Beer-Sheva* 1: 222-31. Hebrew.
Rohl, D. M.
  1995   Review of W. L. Moran, *The Amarna Letters* (Baltimore-London: Johns
         Hopkins University, 1992). *PEQ* 127: 78-79.
Röllig, W. -- see Donner, H., and von Soden, W.
Rost, P.
  1893   *Die Keilschrifttexte Tiglat-Pilesers III. nach den Papierabklatschen und
         Originalen des Britischen Museums.* Two volumes. Leipzig: Pfeiffer.
Roux, G.
  1964   *Ancient Iraq.* Cleveland-New York: World.
Saggs, H. W. F.
  1955   The Nimrud Letters, 1952 - Part II. *Iraq* 17: 126-54, pls. xxx-xxxv.
  1963   Assyrian Warfare in the Sargonid Period. *Iraq* 25: 145-54.
  1984   *The Might That Was Assyria.* Sidgwick & Jackson Great Civilization
         Series. London: Sidgwick & Jackson.
Sass, B.
  1983   The Revadim Seal and its Archaic Phoenician Inscription. *Anatolian
         Studies* 33: 169-75.
Schrader, E.
  1880   *Zur Kritik der Inschriften Tiglath-pileser's II, des Asarhaddon und des
         Asurbanipal.* Abhandlungen der Königlichen Akademie der Wissenschaften
         zu Berlin. Berlin.
  1889-96 | *Keilinschrifliche Bibliothek.* Four volumes. Berlin: H. Reuther (& O.
         Reichard). [= KB].
  1903   *Die Keilinschriften und das Alte Testament.* Third edition. Eds. H.
         Zimmern and H. Winckler. Berlin: Reuther & Reichard.
Schramm, W.
  1969   Das Land ZAB der assyrischen Königsinschriften. *Orientalia* 38: 126-27.
  1973   *Einleitung in die assyrischen Königsinschriften, zweiter Teil, 934-722 v.
         Chr.* Handbuch der Orientalistik, erste Abteilung, Ergänzungsband Fünf,
         erster Abschnitt. Leiden-Köln: Brill.
Schult, H.
  1965   Ein inschriftlicher Beleg für "Plethi"? *Zeitschrift des deutschen Palästina-
         Vereins* 81: 74-79.
Schunck, K.-D.
  1983   Davids "Schlupfwinkel" in Juda. *Vetus Testamentum* 33: 110-13.
Schütte, W.
  1987   Eine originale Stimme aus dem syrisch-ephraimitischen Krieg. Zu Hos 5,8-
         6,6. *Zeitschrift für die alttestamentliche Wissenschaft* 99: 406-08.
Seger, J. D.
  1992   Gath. *ABD* 2: 908-09.

Segal, H. H.
    1965-66 | The Composition of the Books of Samuel. *Jewish Quarterly Review* 56:
        32-50
Seger, J. D.
    1984   The Location of Biblical Ziklag. *Biblical Archaeologist* 47: 47-53.
Shaw, C. S.
    1987   Micah 1:10-16 Reconsidered. *Journal of Biblical Literature* 106:223-29.
Shea, W. H.
    1978   Adad-Nirari III and Jehoash of Israel. *Journal of Cuneiform Studies*
        30:101-13.
Shenkel, J. D.
    1968   *Chronology and Recensional Development in the Greek Text of Kings.*
        Harvard Semitic Monographs 1. Cambridge, MA: Harvard University.
Singer, I.
    1985   The Beginning of Philistine Settlement in Canaan and the Northern
        Boundary of Philistia. *Tel Aviv* 12: 109-14.
    1988   Merneptah's Campaign to Canaan and the Egyptian Occupation of the
        Southern Coastal Plain of Palestine in the Ramesside Period. *Bulletin of the
        American Schools of Oriental Research* 269: 1-10.
Smith, G.
    1876   *Assyrian Discoveries.* Third edition. New York: Scribner, Armstrong &
        Co.
Smith, H. P.
    1899   *A Critical and Exegetical Commentary on the Books of Samuel.*
        International Critical Commentary. Edinburgh: T. & T. Clark.
von Soden, W.
    1954   *Herrscher im alten Orient.* Verständliche Wissenschaft 54. Berlin-
        Göttingen-Heidelberg: Springer.
    1963   Die Assyrer und der Krieg. *Iraq* 25: 131-44.
    1965-81 | *Akkadisches Handwörterbuch* Three volumes. Wiesbaden:
        Harrassowitz. [= *AHW*].
    1969   *Grundriss der akkadischen Grammatik.* Analecta orientalia 33, 47. Rome:
        Pontifical Biblical Institute. [= *GAG*].
von Soden, W., and Röllig, W.
    1967   *Das Akkadische Syllabar.* Second edition. Analecta orientalia 42. Rome:
        Pontifical Biblical Institute.
Soggin, J. A.
    1970   Ein ausserbiblisches Zeugnis für die Chronologie des J°hô'āš/Jô'āš, König
        von Israel. *Vetus Testamentum* 20: 366-68.
    1984   *A History of Ancient Israel: From the Beginnings to the Bar Kochba
        Revolt, A.D. 135.* Trans. J. Bowden from Italian, 1984. Old Testament
        Library. Philadelphia: Westminster.
Spieckermann, H.
    1982   *Juda unter Assur in der Sargonidenzeit.* Göttingen: Vandenhoeck &
        Ruprecht.

Stager, L. E. -- see also Johnson, B. L.
    1991   When Canaanites and Philistines Ruled Ashkelon. *Biblical Archaeology Review* 17/2: 24-43.
    1991a *Ashkelon Discovered: From Canaanites and Philistines to Romans and Moslems.* Washington, D.C.: Biblical Archaeology Society.
    1993   Ashkelon. *NEAEHL* 1: 103-12.
Steele, F. R.
    1948   *The Code of Lipit-Ishtar.* Philadelphia: University of Pennsylvania.
Steindorff, G.
    1939   The Statuette of an Egyptian Commissioner in Syria. *Journal of Egyptian Archaeology* 25: 30-33, pl. vii.
Stern, E.
    1993   The Renewal of Trade in the Eastern Mediterranean in Iron Age I. Pp. 325-34 in: *Biblical Archaeology Today, 1990: Proceedings of the Second International Congress on Biblical Archaeology, Jerusalem, June-July 1990,* eds. A. Biran and J. Aviram. Jerusalem: Israel Exploration Society & The Israel Academy of Sciences and Humanities.
    1994   *Dor: Ruler of the Seas.* Jerusalem: Israel Exploration Society.
    1995   Tel Dor: A Phoenician-Israelite Trading Center. Pp. 81-93 in: *Recent Excavations in Israel: A View to the West. Reports on Kabri, Nami, Miqne-Ekron, Dor, and Ashkelon,* ed. S. Gitin. AIA Colloquia and Conference Papers, No. 1; Dubuque: Kendall/Hunt Publishing Co.
Stieglitz, R. R. -- see Raban, A.
Stone, B. J.
    1995   The Philistines and Acculturation: Culture Change and Ethnic Continuity in the Iron Age. *Bulletin of the American Schools of Oriental Research* 298: 7-35.
Swete, H. B.
    1914   *An Introduction to the Old Testament in Greek.* Cambridge: Cambridge University. Reprinted: Peabody, MA: Hendrickson, 1989.
Tadmor, H. -- see also Millard, A. R.; Borger, R.; Cogan, M.
    1958   The Campaigns of Sargon II of Assur: A Chronological-Historical Study. *Journal of Cuneiform Studies* 12: 22-40, 77-100.
    1961a Azriyau of Yaudi. *Scripta Hierosolymitana* 8: 232-71.
    1961b Que and Musri. *Israel Exploration Journal* 11: 143-50.
    1962   The Southern Border of Aram. *Israel Exploration Journal* 12: 114-22.
    1964   The Assyrian Campaigns to Philistia. Pp. 261-85 in: *The Military History of the Land of Israel in Biblical Times,* ed. J. Liver. Hebrew. Jerusalem: "Maarachoth" Israel Defense Forces.
    1966   Philistia Under Assyrian Rule. *Biblical Archaeologist* 29: 86-102.
    1967a Fragments of a Stele of Sargon II from the Excavations of Ashdod. *Eretz Israel* 8: 241-45, pl. 41. Hebrew. English summary p. 75*.
    1967b *Introductory Remarks to a New Edition of the Annals of Tiglath-Pileser III.* Proceedings of the Israel Academy of Sciences and Humanities II/9.

1969a A Note on the Saba'a Stele of Adad-nirari III. *Israel Exploration Journal*
       19: 46-48.
1969b The Stele of Adad-Nirari III from Tell el-Rimah. *Qadmoniot* 2: 135-36.
       Hebrew.
1972   The Me'unites in the Book of Chronicles in the Light of an Assyrian
       Document. Pp. 222-30 in: *Bible and Jewish History: Studies in Bible and
       Jewish History Dedicated to the Memory of Jacob Liver*, ed. B.
       Uffenheimer. Hebrew. Tel-Aviv: University of Tel-Aviv. English summary
       p. xxiii.
1973   The Historical Inscriptions of Adad-nirari III. *Iraq* 35: 141-50.
1975   Assyria and the West: The Ninth Century and Its Aftermath. Pp. 36-48 in:
       *Unity and Diversity: Essays in the History, Literature, and Religion of the
       Ancient Near East*, eds. H. Goedicke and J. J. M. Roberts. Baltimore-
       London: Johns Hopkins University.
1981   History and Ideology in the Assyrian Royal Inscriptions. Pp. 13-33 in:
       *Assyrian Royal Inscriptions: New Horizons in Literary, Ideological, and
       Historical Analysis*, ed. F. M. Fales. Oriens Antiqui Collectio 17. Rome:
       Istituto per l'Oriente.
1982   Traditional Institutions and the Monarchy: Social and Political Tensions in
       the Time of David and Solomon. Pp. 239-57 in: *Studies in the Period of
       David and Solomon and Other Essays*, ed. T. Ishida. Winona Lake, IN:
       Eisenbrauns.
1982a Treaty and Oath in the Ancient Near East: A Historian's Approach. Pp.
       127-52 in: *Humanizing America's Iconic Book: Society of Biblical
       Literature Centennial Addresses, 1980*, eds. G. M. Tucker and D. A.
       Knight. Society of Biblical Literature Biblical Scholarship in North
       America 6. Chico, CA: Scholars Press.
1985   "Rashpuna" - A Case of Epigraphic Error. *Eretz Israel* 18: 180-82.
       Hebrew. English summary p. 71*.
1994   *The Inscriptions of Tiglath-Pileser III, King of Assyria*. Jerusalem: The
       Israel Academy of Sciences and Humanities. [= ITP].
Tadmor, H., and Cogan, M.
1979   Ahaz and Tiglath-Pileser in the Book of Kings: Historiographic
       Considerations. *Biblica* 60: 491-508.
TGI   K. Galling, ed., *Textbuch zur Geschichte Israels*. Second edition.
       Tübingen: Mohr.
Thiele, E. R.
1965   *The Mysterious Numbers of the Hebrew Kings*. Second edition. Grand
       Rapids, MI: Eerdmans.
Thomas, D. W., ed.
1961   *Documents from Old Testament Times*. New York-Evanston: Harper &
       Row. [= *DOTT*].
Thompson, M. E. W.
1982   *Situation and Theology: Old Testament Interpretations of the Syro-
       Ephraimite War*. Sheffield: Almond Press.

Tidwell, N. L.
    1979   The Philistine Incursions into the Valley of Rephaim (2 Sam. v 17 ff.).
             Vetus Testamentum Supplements 30: 190-212.

Timm, S.
    1980   Die territoriale Ausdehnung des Staates Israel zur Zeit der Omriden.
             Zeitschrift des deutschen Palästina-Vereins 96: 20-40.

Tolkowsky, S.
    1920-21 | Metheg Ha-Ammah. *Journal of the Palestine Oriental Society* 1: 195-
             201.

Tov, E.
    1981   *The Text-Critical Use of the Septuagint in Biblical Research.* Jerusalem
             Biblical Studies 3. Jerusalem: Simor.
    1992   *Textual Criticism of the Hebrew Bible.* Minneapolis: Fortress and Assen/
             Maastricht: Van Gorcum.

TUAT   O. Kaiser ed., *Texte aus der Umwelt des Alten Testaments.* Gütersloh:
             Gerd Mohn. 1982-.

Ulrich, E. C., Jr.
    1978   *The Qumran Text of Samuel and Josephus.* Harvard Semitic Monographs
             19. Chico, CA: Scholars Press.

Unger, E.
    1916   *Reliefstele Adadniraris III aus Saba'a und Semiramis.* Publikationen des
             kaiserlichen Ottomanischen Museums 2. Contantinople: Ahmed Ihsan.
    1970   *Babylon: Die Heilige Stadt nach Beschreibung der Babylonier.* Berlin: De
             Gruyter. Reprint of the 1931 edition with the addition of a preface by R.
             Borger.

Ungnad, E.
    1938   Eponymen. *Reallexikon der Assyriologie* 2: 412-57.

Ussishkin, D.
    1978   Excavations at Tel Lachish -- 1973-1977, Preliminary Report. *Tel Aviv* 5:
             1-97, pls. 1-32.
    1990   Notes on Megiddo, Gezer, Ashdod, and Tel Batash in the Tenth to Ninth
             Centuries B.C. *Bulletin of the American Schools of Oriental Research*
             277/278: 71-91.

Van Beek, G. W.
    1960   Frankincense and Myrrh. *Biblical Archaeologist* 23: 70-95 (= *Biblical
             Archaeologist Reader* 2: 99-126).

de Vaux, R. -- see also Baillet, M.
    1958   *Les Livres des Rois.* La Sainte Bible. Paris: Editions du Cerf.
    1965   *Ancient Israel: Social Institutions.* Trans. from the French, 1958. New
             York-Toronto: McGraw-Hill.

Vieweger, D.
    1994   Review of *Biblical Archaeology Today, 1990.* Jerusalem: Israel
             Exploration Society. 1993; and of *Biblical Archaeology Today, 1990,
             Supplement.* Jerusalem: Israel Exploration Society, 1993. *Theologische
             Literaturzeitung* 119: 770-77.

Vigouroux, F.
    1908   Philistins. *Dictionnaire de la Bible* 5: 286-300.
Virolleaud, C.
    1936   *La légende de Keret, roi des Sidoniens.* Mission de Ras Shamra 2. Paris:
            Paul Geuthner.
Vogt, E.
    1964   Die Texte Tiglat-Pilesers III. über die Eroberung Palästinas. *Biblica* 45:
            348-54.
Wagner, S.
    1984   knʿ. Cols. 216-24 in: *Theologisches Wörterbuch zum Alten Testament IV*,
            eds. G. J. Botterweck, H. Ringgren, and H.-J. Fabry. Stuttgart-Berlin-
            Köln-Mainz: W. Kohlhammer.
Wapnish, P.
    1993   Archaeozoology: The Integration of Faunal Data with Biblical
            Archaeology. Pp. 426-42 in: *Biblical Archaeology Today, 1990:
            Proceedings of the Second International Congress on Biblical
            Archaeology, Jerusalem, June-July 1990*, eds. A. Biran and J. Aviram.
            Jerusalem: Israel Exploration Society & The Israel Academy of Sciences
            and Humanities.
Watanabe, K. - see also Parpola, S.
    1987   *Die adê-Vereidigung anlässlich der Thronfolgeregelung Asarhaddons.*
            Baghdader Mitteilungen Beiheft 3. Berlin: Gebr. Mann Verlag.
Waterfield, G.
    1968   *Layard of Nineveh.* New York-Washington: Frederick A. Praeger.
Watts, J. D. W.
    1985   *Isaiah 1-33.* Word Biblical Commentary 24. Waco, TX: Word Books.
Weidner, E. F.
    1923   *Politische Dokumente aus Kleinasien. Die Staatsverträge in akkadischer
            Sprache aus dem Archiv von Boghazköi.* Boghazköi-Studien 9. Leipzig: J.
            C. Hinrichs.
Weippert, H.
    1988   *Palästina in vorhellenistischer Zeit* (Handbuch der Archäologie,
            Vorderasien II/1; München: C. H. Beck.
Weippert, M.
    1971   Review of Trude Dothan, *The Philistines and their Material Culture*
            (Hebrew; Jerusalem: Israel Exploration Society, 1967). *Göttingische
            Gelehrte Anzeigen* 223: .
    1973   Menahem von Israel und seine Zeitgenossen in einer Steleninschrift des
            assyrischen Königs Tiglathpileser III aus dem Iran. *Zeitschrift des
            deutschen Palästina-Vereins* 89: 26-53.
    1992   Die Feldzüge Adadnararis III. nach Syrien: Voraussetzungen, Verlauf,
            Folgen. *Zeitschrift des deutschen Palästina-Vereins* 108: 42-67.
Wellhausen, J.
    1871   *Der Text der Bücher Samuelis.* Göttingen: Vandenhoeck & Ruprecht.

Welten, P.
  1973   *Geschichte und Geschichtsdarstellung in den Chronikbüchern.*
          Wissenschaftliche Monographien zum Alten und Neuen Testament 42.
          Neukirchen-Vluyn: Neukirchner Verlag.
Wightman, G. J.
  1990   The Myth of Solomon. *Bulletin of the American Schools of Oriental
          Research* 277/278: 5-22.
Williamson, H. G. M.
  1982   *1 and 2 Chronicles.* New Century Bible. Grand Rapids, MI: Eerdmans;
          London: Marshall, Morgan & Scott.
Wiseman, D. J.
  1951   Two Historical Inscriptions from Nimrud. *Iraq* 13: 21-26, pls. xi-xii.
  1953   *The Alalakh Tablets.* Occasional Publications of the British Institute of
          Archaeology at Ankara 2. London: British Institute of Archaeology at
          Ankara.
  1956   A Fragmentary Inscription of Tiglath-pileser III from Nimrud. *Iraq* 18:
          117-29, pls xxii-xxiii.
  1964   Fragments of Historical Texts from Nimrud. *Iraq* 26: 118-24.
Wolff, H. W.
  1977   *Joel and Amos.* Hermeneia. Philadelphia: Fortress.
Wood, B. G.
  1991   The Philistines Enter Canaan: Were They Egyptian Lackeys or Invading
          Conquerers? *Biblical Archaeology Review* 17/6: 44-52, 89-92.
Würthwein, E.
  1977   *Das Erste Buch der Könige: Kapitel 1-16.* Altes Testament Deutsch 11/1.
          Göttingen: Vandenhoeck & Ruprecht.
  1984   *Die Bücher der Könige: 1. Kön. 17-2. Kön. 25.* Altes Testament Deutsch
          11/2. Göttingen: Vandenhoeck & Ruprecht.
Wright, G. E. -- see also Boling, R. G., Cross, F. M.
  1966   Fresh Evidence for the Philistine Story. *Biblical Archaeologist* 29: 70-86.
  1967   The Provinces of Solomon (I Kings 4:7-19). *Eretz Israel* 8: 58*-68*.
Yadin, Y.
  1955   Goliath's Javelin and the *měnôr 'ōrěgîm. Palestine Exploration Quarterly*
          87: 58-69.
  1968   And Dan, Why Did He Remain in Ships? *Australian Journal of Biblical
          Archaeology* 1: 9-23.
Yaron, R.
  1969   *The Laws of Eshnunna.* Jerusalem: Magnes.
Yeivin, S.
  1964   The Wars of David. Pp. 149-65 in: *The Military History of the Land of
          Israel in Biblical Times,* ed. J. Liver. Hebrew. Jerusalem: "Maarachoth"
          Israel Defense Forces.

Ziegler, R., and Boessneck, J.
   1990   Tierreste der Eisenzeit II. Pp. 133-58 in: *Kinneret: Ergebnisse der Ausgrabungen auf dem* Tell el-'Oreme *am See Gennesaret 1982-1985*, ed. V. Fritz. Abhandlungen des deutschen Palästina-Vereins 15. Wiesbaden: Otto Harrassowitz.

INDICES[*]

Personal and Divine Names

---

[*] References are to citations in the main body of the text, excluding source texts and their translations. Owing to a computer quirk discovered during the final printing process, isolated references may be off by a page.

Toponyms

Authors

Biblical Literature

Ancient Near Eastern Literature

STUDIES IN THE HISTORY AND CULTURE OF THE ANCIENT NEAR EAST

EDITED BY

B. HALPERN AND M.H.E. WEIPPERT

ISSN 0169-9024